CAPTAINS' LOGS SUPPLEMENTAL

THE UNAUTHORIZED GUIDE TO THE NEW TREK VOYAGES

Edward Gross and Mark A. Altman

LITTLE, BROWN AND COMPANY

A *Little, Brown* Book

First published in Great Britain in 1996
by Little, Brown and Company

Mark Altman dedicates this book to the memory of his late grandmother, Edna Schiff.

Edward Gross dedicates this book to his wife, Eileen, who encouraged the dream but never without the fantasy. Without her . . .

Special Thanks to: Our agent at the Linda Chester Agency, Laurie Fox; our new editor, Geoffrey Kloske; copyeditor Betsy Uhrig; the many people who agreed to be interviewed about *Star Trek* by us; and our former editor Mark Chimsky, the man with the plan who made it all possible.

The authors also extend their gratitude to journalists Kevin Stevens and Amanda Finch of *Universe* magazine. Of course, no acknowledgement would be complete without thanking the many creative and talented people on *Star Trek* without whose co-operation this book would not be possible.

A CIP catalogue record for this book is available from the British Library.

ISBN 0 316 88354 9

Little, Brown and Company (UK)
Brettenham House
Lancaster Place
London WC2E 7EN

••CONTENTS••

• • • •

INTRODUCTION

Welcome to *Captains' Logs Supplemental,* the latest volume in the *Captains' Logs* series from Little, Brown and Company.

In volume one, *Captains' Logs: The Unauthorized Complete Trek Voyages,* we provided complete episode guides to the original *Star Trek* series, the so-called lost years of the 1970s, the motion-picture series through *Star Trek: Generations* and all seven years of *Star Trek: The Next Generation.*

Now, as you find yourself wading through the facts and figures amassed in these pages, you will learn about *Deep Space Nine* and *Voyager* — the latest incarnations of *Star Trek* — and the people whose creative struggles have produced some of the most provocative science-fiction entertainment and television of our time. We hope those who already enjoy these series on a weekly basis will be able to think about them in a new light.

For those who haven't yet embraced the sagas of the space station on the edge of the final frontier and a starship on its lonely quest home, we hope equally fervently that they'll begin to reassess their feelings and perhaps reconsider shows that we think are among the best television has to offer.

As always, our thanks for picking up this book and our best wishes for you to live long and prosper.

Mark A. Altman

Edward Gross

June 1996

• • • •

CHAPTER ONE

Deep Space Nine: In the Beginning

In the wake of *Star Trek*'s thirtieth anniversary, it's difficult to fathom that this perennial staple of pop culture has been with us for over three decades. Since that first memorable five-year voyage of the starship *Enterprise* (cut down to three by NBC), *Star Trek* has lived long and prospered.

Star Trek's continued endurance and success have confounded many conventionally thinking TV pundits, who find it difficult to account for the franchise's ability to intrigue and enchant audiences with its tales of future cosmic pioneers who forge ahead despite sometimes overwhelming odds. They are the ones who probably find it even more unfathomable that the preoccupation of the show's fans continues even as the show itself evolves into new incarnations. Long after the original episodes were successfully syndicated on television, *Star Trek: The Next Generation* emerged as a worthy successor to the original, now referred to as "Classic *Trek.*"

Given the phenomenal worldwide success of *The Next Generation*, it was inevitable that yet another *Trek* series would be spawned. The difference, however, was that Gene Roddenberry, the "Great Bird of the Galaxy," the man whose vision had initially guided the first two versions of his creation, would not be along for the voyage. As plans moved forward for a third *Trek* series, Roddenberry fell ill and passed away.

Although Roddenberry's handson involvement in *Trek* had diminished over the years as his health suffered, knowing the Great Bird was on his perch, looking down, always comforted fans who trusted that *Star Trek* would never deviate too dramatically from the template laid out by its originator. With his passing, those same fans wondered if *Trek* would strike out in a new and less satisfying direction. After all, it had been Roddenberry who championed the notion that *Star Trek* was about a world in which humans had

finally overcome such contemporary problems as poverty, famine, avarice and most of the other seven deadly sins (lust, however, was still more than abundant in the twenty-third and twenty-fourth centuries — look no further than the quarters of James T. Kirk or William T. Riker for proof of this). However, with Roddenberry gone, it seemed inevitable that the writers who had long chafed under the Great Bird's stringent guidelines for what made *Trek Trek* would resort to the old tropes of drama that had served everyone from Shakespeare to Stephen King so well.

While *Trek* has continued to boldly go in subsequent years, often traveling roads not taken by its creator, it would be hard to accuse its stewards (producers Rick Berman, Michael Piller and, more recently, Jeri Taylor) of not respecting the will of Roddenberry. Which brings us to the most recent chapters in the saga, *Star Trek: Deep Space Nine* and its sister series, *Star Trek: Voyager*, the latest products of a franchise that has reportedly earned over $2 billion for Paramount Pictures — a studio that had to be cajoled kicking and screaming into reviving *Trek* only two decades ago, first for an aborted TV venture dubbed *Trek: Phase 2* and later as a successful series of feature films.

In 1987 Paramount engaged in the risky venture of introducing a new *Star Trek* series to television, *The Next Generation*. The show, coming in the aftermath of *Star Trek: Starfleet Academy* (a proposed motion picture that would have recast the original beloved characters in a story of their years at the Academy, which was shelved due to the wrath of outraged fans), could have been perceived as the height of blasphemy — not difficult to fathom considering the fact that for many *Star Trek* is more of a religious experience than simply a television show. However, *The Next Generation* was able to avoid being perceived as a simple effort to cash in on the success of the original *Star Trek* thanks to Roddenberry's involvement, which proved that *Star Trek* was more important as a concept than it was as a vehicle for the characters of Kirk, Spock, McCoy, et al.

Given *TNG*'s incredible success, it would be hard to refute that point. So when that series soared to new heights in the ratings and began attracting an

equally, if not even *more* fervent following than the original, it seemed inevitable that Paramount would consider the idea of a spin-off. After all, by 1991 the last chapter of the Classic *Trek* feature-film franchise had been written, and *The Next Generation* was winding its way into its latter seasons with impending contract negotiations jeopardizing the future of the show. There was also the desire by the studio to have characters from *The Next Generation* replace the aging original cast on the big screen.

However, in creating a sister series, co-creators Rick Berman and Michael Piller, veterans of *The Next Generation* and, in the case of Berman, Roddenberry's handpicked successor, realized that they would need to address the liabilities of a universe in which interpersonal conflict was anathema. As a result, *Deep Space Nine* is a place populated by races from across the galaxy, only some of them Starfleet officers. The world they inhabit is gritty and alien, unlike the sterile and nearly perfect utopia within the confines of a starship inhabited solely by Starfleet officers.

"It's an alien space station that doesn't work the way they want it to, and that in itself created a lot of conflict," says executive producer Rick Berman. "At the same time, our core characters are Starfleet officers: Sisko, O'Brien, the doctor [Bashir] and Dax in no way vary from *The Next Generation* in terms of the lack of conflict among themselves. That was a rule that we had to follow. We needed to create a series that wasn't a franchise based on people aboard a starship, because we knew there would be a couple of years of overlap between the two shows."

Herman Zimmerman, *Deep Space Nine*'s production designer, points out that in the wake of Roddenberry's death, the *Star Trek* universe has been interpreted by many creative individuals who have inherited Roddenberry's concepts over its nearly thirty-year existence.

"From my point of view, Gene Roddenberry created, without being maudlin, an eternal idealization of the future," says Zimmerman, who designed the original sets for *The Next Generation* as well as the fifth, sixth, and seventh features, *The Final Frontier*, the *Undiscov-*

• • • •

Rick Berman, Voyager's *Kate Mulgrew, Michael Piller and Jeri Taylor present a special award to astronaut Sally Ride (copyright © 1995 by Albert Ortega).*

ered Country and *Generations.* "The characters that he created came out of his imagination pretty much whole cloth. You could compare 'The Cage' to *Sign of Four,* which was written by Arthur Conan Doyle. Sherlock Holmes and Watson and Moriarty and La Strade and the Baker Street Irregulars have a charm and an identity that are immediately discernible from that very first novel. Seventy years later, a fellow named Nicholas Meyer can take the same characters and write a very believable Arthur Conan Doyle story, maybe even better, using all those same characters and ideas and call it *The Seven Percent Solution.*

"Gene Roddenberry created Kirk and Spock and McCoy, Uhura, Sulu, Chekov, Picard, Riker, Troi, etc., and when they were first introduced to the audience, just like those characters from Arthur Conan Doyle, they were whole. They haven't changed, [although] they may have grown," he continues. "They've been interpreted, and that's the beauty of Gene's vision, from his positive view of the future and his ability to mix and match personalities that play well together. I think any good director, writer, producer, can take

those criteria, those characters, that idea, that vision, and make it work. Within that we have the grittiness that Nicholas Meyer prefers, the Hyatt Regency approach that Gene liked in *The Next Generation* and we have the bizarre, darker alien version of the stories in *Deep Space Nine.* [Technical consultant and scenic artist supervisor] Mike Okuda and I philosophize once in a while, and he said something very poignant when we were probably halfway through the set construction of the first two-hour [*DS9* episode] and very heavily into doing all the details. He said [the show is] beginning to have a life of its own. *Star Trek* from the very beginning has had that snowball effect. It has evolved and it does have a life of its own, and we'll see it for many more years in the future."

In fact, it's hard to defend the *Star Trek* purists who would use the so-called darker *Trek* of *Deep Space Nine* as a justification to decry the new series as blaspheming Gene Roddenberry's vision. *DS9,* in a way, is more faithful to the original *Star Trek* premise than even *The Next Generation. Deep Space Nine* revives the interpersonal conflict and witty banter of the classic show's popular triumvirate of Kirk,

Spock and McCoy while retaining the elements of *TNG* that have made it one of the most successful series on television.

As anyone familiar with the production of *Star Trek: The Next Generation* would readily attest, it's Rick Berman who was the great bird behind its phenomenal success, aided and abetted by his coexecutive producer, Michael Piller, who began overseeing the writing staff of the show in its third year. Berman is the one who successfully moved the series through early production turmoil and turned it into a critical and ratings success. He is the man that Paramount has entrusted with its leading tent pole and studio franchise; he is the true heir to the Roddenberry universe.

Berman's complete autonomy over the *Star Trek* universe was ceded on *Deep Space Nine,* where he rules, albeit benevolently, in tandem with co-creator Michael Piller and, subsequently, executive producer Ira Steven Behr.

"We don't do anything without their approval," says Zimmerman. "They know where this series is going, and we make all sorts of elaborate proposals based on what we think from our imagination the scripts require. But in the final analysis it is their guiding hand that says yes or no to any given idea."

"I am a writer," says Piller, who became creative consultant to the series in its third season. "I live in a world of imagination, just ask my wife. I depend enormously on Rick's intuitions and his talents in production and I know Rick depends a great deal on Herman's. In all of the production and the editing and the look of the show, I am there as another voice, thinking, offering my best wisdom and counsel, but I depend a great deal on Mr. Berman for those things."

Piller and Berman's collaboration, which had an effect on determining the look of the show as well as the casting due to their different tastes, lies in stark contrast to what their relationship had been on *The Next Generation,* where Berman always had the final word. This was evidenced by their well-documented disagreement over the ending of the fifth-season *Next Generation* episode "The Perfect Mate" in which Berman overruled Piller's proposed ending for the episode in which Picard disrupts the wedding cere-

••••

mony between the beautiful empath Kamala and Par Lenor.

"The bottom line is that I worked for Rick on *The Next Generation* and I work *with* Rick on *Deep Space Nine*," says Piller. "Our working relationship is virtually identical except that when a decision of critical importance has to be made, we really reach a consensus. On *Deep Space Nine,* sometimes I win and sometimes he wins. . . . He always won on *The Next Generation.*"

"We rarely disagree on script points," adds Berman. "We spend a lot of time with writers making scripts work after first drafts come in, and he and I rarely disagree. I rarely disagree with him in terms of casting and in terms of production."

In examining the first few months of *Deep Space Nine*'s production, Piller was pleased with the course taken by the show. "It's been a blessed project," he said at the time. "We wrote a story; the studio loved it. I wrote a script, and everybody seemed to love it. We cast a group of actors that are delightful. Colm Meaney told Rick that he hasn't worked with a group of actors this fine since he was in the Abbey. I was able to hire Ira Behr, who was my key man to be able to execute this plan. We care a great deal about what we're doing, and the studio couldn't be more supportive. I'm the guy who's always sort of looking over his shoulder for the footsteps and I haven't heard them yet."

Although Deep Space Nine is a nonmoving station seemingly offering a finite number of story possibilities, Piller suggests that it's easier to come up with plot lines for the show than it was for *The Next Generation.*

"We can still get into a runabout and go anywhere we want," says Piller of the ship's ministarships, which take the crew through the wormhole into the Gamma Quadrant (later supplanted by the *Defiant,* a larger, more powerful ship drafted into service for the show's third season). "What we have here that we don't have on the *Enterprise* is a community that's beyond a life business. We have people at play on the Promenade and at Quark's [bar], and people who are not involved directly in the running of the Starfleet operation who are main characters on the show. That makes it easier."

The dilemma, admits Piller, is overcoming the fact that well over two hundred stories have been told in *Trek*'s previous incarnations. "The bottom line is that the kind of stories that worked on *The Next Generation* are the same kind that we want to tell on *Deep Space Nine,*" says Piller. "But we'll tell those stories illuminating different characters and different alien groups, but still explore the human condition and use the metaphors that work so well. It's the universe of science fiction and the universe of Gene Roddenberry. We cannot do stories on *Deep Space Nine* that wouldn't work on the other shows. The problems are the same. We can't repeat ourselves. We have to come up with fresh and original material, and it's very, very difficult."

After successfully working together on *The Next Generation* for a number of years, Berman and Piller had become intrigued with the idea of creating and producing their own show, which would not necessarily take place in the *Star Trek* universe.

"Michael had been working with me for two years and he and I had lunch together very often. We started talking about developing other television series," recalls Berman. "We talked about *Star Trek* spin-offs, and we talked about a lot of other shows as well. There were many, many series we discussed. The only one that was really a spin-off was *Deep Space Nine.* I went to Gene and mentioned we were thinking about a spin-off, and he said great and that we should talk about it sometime. Unfortunately, we never did because he was not well then and he got worse and worse."

Ironically, former Paramount studio chief Brandon Tartikoff summoned Berman to his office shortly thereafter to discuss creating a new show for the studio. "Brandon said, 'I would like you to create another television show for us,'" explains Berman. "He said he wanted a science-fiction show, and I said, 'You mean a *Star Trek* show?' and he said, 'No, I don't care if it's *Star Trek.* I want another science-fiction show I can say is being created by the guy who's been bringing you *Star Trek: The Next Generation* for the last five years.' I told Brandon that I had been working with Mike Piller on a number of ideas. It was one of those 'Oh, and by the way, I just happen to have one right here.' So Mike and I started talking again. At that point there was no question that the person I wanted to bring in to work on something like this was Michael, and it basically came down to two of the ideas we had been playing with."

Michael Piller explains that the studio was initially against doing another *Star Trek* series but was eventually won over by the premise for the proposed spin-off. Among the ideas Piller and Berman had toyed with was the original premise for *Deep Space Nine,* involving a space station on the outer fringes of Federation space, and one that was a science-fiction series set during medieval times on earth.

Says Piller, "We decided on *Deep Space Nine,* in a very fledgling stage, and we went to the studio guys and laid out a pretty general idea. They said go and work on it, and we spent a number of months coming up with the premise before the story was written with the earliest bible of the show: what the location would be, what the backstory would be and so on. The studio said go for it."

With the studio green-lighting production, Piller and Berman spent a lot of late nights together over take-out food from the Paramount commissary devising

Rick Berman and Michael Piller, creators of **Deep Space Nine** *(copyright © 1995 by Albert Ortega).*

• • • •

the final premise for the series, which, unlike the prior two *Star Trek* series, would not take place on a Federation starship. "Mike and I knew that if we were ever going to do another *Star Trek* show it would have to take place somewhere where adventure could come to us as opposed to us going to adventure. That's why we came up with the idea of a wormhole."

Berman is adamant that the decision to set the series on a space station was not cost related. (Though conventional logic suggests that a stationary locale would be a money saver over the adventures of a starship whose mandate was to explore brave new worlds.) "It had nothing to do with budget," he says. "*Deep Space* is more expensive than any show Paramount's ever done. You couldn't have two shows on the air with people on starships. We needed to come up with something new and put twenty-fourth-century people into a new environment. If you can't be in a vehicle that's taking you to where adventure is, then you have to put yourself somewhere where adventure comes to you. The idea of the wormhole titillated us and we added to that the whole Bajoran backstory, which Michael and I had created a year before."

The establishment of the Bajoran culture was done early in the fifth season of *The Next Generation* in an episode called "Ensign Ro," in which Piller and Berman introduced the character of Ro Laren, a Bajoran played by Michelle Forbes. Ro is a disgraced Starfleet officer and member of a race that has been forced from its home planet by the Cardassians, the newest malevolent *Trek* baddies (first seen in the fourth season's "The Wounded"), with whom the Federation has an uneasy truce.

"We must have had fifty meetings before we felt comfortable with what we had come up with," says Berman. "The premise of the show grew the way a child grows from something that is young and simple to something that is more complex. The premise has never made a major left or right turn. The characters and backstory have become more focused, as have the settings, the people and the interrelationships."

Ultimately, the most important aspect of the new series for the producers

was making it less constraining by allowing interpersonal conflict between the characters. "The problem with *Star Trek: The Next Generation* is Gene created a group of characters that he purposely chose not to allow conflict between," says Berman. "Starfleet officers cannot be in conflict, thus it's murderous to write these shows because there is no good drama without conflict, and the conflict has to come from outside the group."

In order to bring conflict to the twenty-fourth century without violating the perceived Roddenberry dictum, Berman and Piller agreed to introduce non-Starfleet personnel into the mix who aren't governed by the same set of constraints that Federation officers had been in the previous series.

"What we wanted to do was something that was somewhat paradoxical — bring conflict but not break away from Gene's rules," says Berman. "They still play paramount importance in what we're doing. We created an environment where Starfleet officers were in a location that they weren't happy about being in, and they were in a location where the people who lived there weren't all that happy about their being there. We also created a situation where we had people who were members of our core group who were not Starfleet: the security shapeshifter, Odo; the Bajoran major, Kira; the bartender, Quark. A group of our integral people are not Starfleet officers, and the ones that are Starfleet officers aren't crazy about where they are, so we have a lot of frustration and conflict."

In the beginning there was also an emphasis on Bajoran spirituality, which Piller argues did not go against the atheist, antireligious beliefs of Roddenberry. "I don't think it goes against Gene," he says. "If he were still with us — and he's still on our shoulders as we think about these conceptual issues — I don't think it would bother him one bit. What he felt very strongly about is that humans, and to some degree Federation members, had a humanist attitude. His humans do not overtly celebrate religious beliefs. What we have simply done in creating an environment that will bring conflict to our people, which we wanted desperately to do, is to put a group of people with a group of aliens that are different than we

are, who had a difference and a conflict with our humanist beliefs. Giving them strong spiritual mystical orbs and prophet worship forces our humanist people to deal with another alien race that is as different from us as the Klingons are. They're different in the spirituality of their existence. We're saying if there's a problem here, let's fix the problem, and they're saying the prophets have to be satisfied, and that causes conflict.

"Gene would be the first to tell you it doesn't matter what alien race you're talking about, how hideous they seem to be, there are no bad aliens. Each of them has a culture that must be defined, recognized and appreciated for what it is. We've simply created a new alien race with a new set of circumstances and haven't changed Gene's vision of what humanity is in the twenty-fourth century. We're simply showing how we are affected by that conflict with that alien race."

"I think Piller and Rick are both in a very good place," says writer-producer Ira Steven Behr, a veteran of *Star Trek: The Next Generation* who was lured back into the fold with the prospect of working on a harder-edged *Trek*. Behr has subsequently been promoted to coexecutive producer for the show's third season and executive producer during the fifth (Piller took a creative consultant credit on the show when he left to develop *Star Trek: Voyager* and the short-lived *Legend* series for the United Paramount Network). "With all the hassles of doing two shows [in the beginning] and mistakes and all the things that happen, we still got along, and it's been fun. I kept saying to Mike and Rick I don't want to go back and do *Star Trek* again. Good or bad, they kept saying, 'This is going to be a different show; we're really trying to keep it in the whole *Star Trek* ethos, but we're going to make this a different show.' And I'm thinking, this is easy to say, but once you've done something it's tough to suddenly shift gears and do this other thing and do them both at the same time. I was a bit skeptical, but then I read the pilot and I started to say, 'Hmm, this has some potential.'

"What I was figuring was if you're going to have two hours of *Star Trek* on a week, not counting all those repeats, they really have to be different than each other. People are getting their orgasm off watching *The Next Generation*. Once a week is enough for most people. We're asking them to come again, and in order to do that, you have to give them different stuff. I think that's what we're doing, and as I [originally sat] there and watched dailies, I kept saying to Rick and Michael that people were going to be surprised by this show."

Behr echoes the party line that the show isn't darker, simply different . . . perhaps reflected in its grittier mise-en-scène and tone. "This isn't an angst-ridden, existential show," he says. "I'm not trying to make it more than it is. It's still an hour of television; it's still an hour of *Star Trek* television. But there's definite conflict, and there are characters who are carrying all kinds of things around with them, and I'm not just talking about Sisko losing his wife, which is a nice television convention. There's people like Odo and Kira, who are intensely driven people with things they have to deal with. You end up watching a lot of scenes where people are not agreeing with each other. Plus the look of the show has a feeling that's a lot different in the lighting and the architecture than *The Next Generation*."

Like *The Next Generation*, *Deep Space Nine* is shot on three soundstages on the Paramount lot, occasionally venturing off the studio grounds for location

shooting. The station's operations center (ops), which boasts a science station, the Cardassian equivalent of the captain's ready room, a replicator, transporter pad and environmental controls, is located on Stage Four along with crew quarters, station corridors and the station's docking bay and launch pads. Adjacent to Stage Four is the home of the Promenade, which houses the station's holosuites and Quark's bar.

"It's a space station that's in a way smaller than the *Enterprise*," says Herman Zimmerman. "It occupies a larger volume of space, but the actual structure is mostly space and not interior volume. It has the sense of being more enclosed except for the Promenade, which is a larger stage. It's more like the interior of a submarine, a nice atomic submarine, mind you, but a submarine nonetheless."

For Berman, Zimmerman was a natural choice to design the new show's alien look. His close collaboration with the production designer and Piller has helped firmly entrench *Deep Space Nine* as the cutting edge of televised science fiction while also allowing Zimmerman creative freedom.

"Herman and I have been close for many years, even after he left *Next Generation*," says Berman. "I knew I wanted to bring Herman into this from the start, and the exterior of the station was something that we spent a lot of time on. There were dozens of designs, most of which I didn't like. Some of which Michael liked and I didn't, others I liked and Michael didn't. Finally, we came up with an idea that worked very nicely and constantly changed that. As far as the interior designs, we knew we wanted the Promenade and a big area that had all the shops and stores and a bar, and let Herman go about his magical way."

Once on board, Zimmerman immediately began working on concepts for the fledgling series — despite the fact that initially he had very little to work from since Berman and Piller were still refining their concepts as to what the show would be. "The first thing I had to do was find out what the scripts were going to be like, and there was some hesitation about that," says Zimmerman. "I spent quite a few weeks working without any script, just story ideas and what we thought the exte-

rior of the station would look like. The producers were so heavily involved with the tail end of the fifth season on *Next Generation* that I was pretty much left to my own devices. I probably have seven inches of single-spaced paper stacked with drawings that never came about: ideas that came and went as we got closer to an agreement on what the show should be about and what the station should look like and what sort of people we were going to put into this environment. Some of the ideas from the early days were useful, and quite a few of them were not. It was an interesting and creative time for me."

Unlike his early work on *The Next Generation*, for which Zimmerman updated the established sets of the original series and the feature films, *Deep Space Nine* was a blank slate that forced the designer to envision totally new *Trek* concepts. "First, we worked on what the exterior of the station would look like. Then we were very heavily into designing what the interior would look like, and we went through a number of ramifications. At first, Berman and Piller thought the station should be falling apart and in a very bad state of disrepair, showing the effects of time and neglect and so on. But as we started developing sketches for what that kind of a station would look like, none of us liked it. We were saying to ourselves, this is space, the final frontier, four hundred years in the future, and we should be as high tech and slick and believable in scientific terms as possible. We did a fairly sharp one-eighty and went to another concept."

It was decided that since the station was built by Bajoran slave labor for use by the Cardassians in strip-mining the planet Bajor of its precious mineral resources, a Cardassian influence would be incorporated into the design of the station. "The Cardassians as a race had been seen in *Next Generation*. Where they've been seen, their makeup and their costume had already been developed. [Costume designer] Bob Blackman's costumes showed a kind of a chest-plate armor that looked like a crustacean. Taking off from that very fundamental idea, we decided the Cardassians like structure and they'd like to see the structure on the outside instead of hiding it inside the walls. The station itself and all the exterior sets are designed so that you can see the support columns and beams and the skin of the station applied to the structure rather than the skin covering up the structure as you would in a Beverly Hills mansion."

Although Zimmerman's deconstructionist approach to the architecture of Deep Space Nine resulted in a very different look for *Trek,* he believes it is still true to the established streamlined look of that particular universe. "It's streamlined in a different way," he explains. "It's a design that is at the same time honest and a little bit awesome because of the size of the beams that support everything. The size of the windows, the shapes of the doorways and the way the doors operate are all very intimidating. They're not user friendly in the way that the *Next Generation* sets were user friendly, and that was intentional. The idea of the creators of the series was that our Starfleet people would never feel exactly at home; they would never be terribly comfortable and always aware it was an alien environment in which they were working."

On Stage Seventeen, in addition to Quark's three-story bar and the Promenade, are the holosuites, where inhabitants of the station can go to satiate their erotic desires, among other things. "They are like the holodecks of *Next Generation,* and we can program pretty much any kind of experience for any kind of location we want to," says Zimmerman. "But what we are doing on *Deep Space Nine* that we weren't able to do on *Next Generation* is we see the inside of the holodeck and see the machinery that runs it. When we did *Next Generation,* we were in a budget constraint that made us do a set that is a wireframe look; it's a grid of squares when the holodeck is not activated, and they just see a black void with yellow grids. In the Cardassian holodeck, when the lights go off, so to speak, you see the machinery that creates the imagery. It's a step forward for us and it's something we always wanted to do on *Next Generation* but were never able to achieve."

However, you don't need a holodeck to convince you that the illusions being created on Stage Seventeen are totally effective. "You can very much lose yourself in it," says actress Nana Visitor, who plays second-in-command Kira Nerys. "There's that slight edge of insanity — which I don't know if all actors have — where you cross over into the fantasy and you're there and this is really happening. It's very easy to do on *Deep Space Nine* on these sets."

The station's interior design is based on Zimmerman's exterior aesthetics, which exist as four enormous miniatures, the largest being six feet by six feet. "The exterior of the miniature of Deep Space Nine is composed of three concentric horizontal rings," details Zimmerman. "The outer ring is a docking ring, the middle ring is an environment and cargo ring and the center ring is the Promenade and the power core of the station. The operations center is on a pedestal that's attached to the center of the power core. The Cardassians like things in threes, according to our philosophy, so there are three concentric rings, and on the outside ring there are three vertical pylons that are docking pylons. The vertical pylons are also docking positions. At the very end of each of the pylons are weapon banks, phaser and photon torpedo locations, which are arranged mathematically in such a way [that] they make a very pleasing exterior shape seen from a distance. Any fan should be able to recognize the shape of Deep Space Nine the way they recognize the exterior shape of the *Enterprise.*"

The actual Deep Space Nine miniature used by visual effects supervisor

Rob Legato and his team for the show's optical effects was realized in a six-foot-diameter model. "The model is a wonderful amalgamation of everyone in the art department," says noted illustrator Ricardo Delgado, who worked on the first year of the series before leaving for more lucrative feature work. "The basic configuration was Herman's idea, and everyone extrapolated from that. [Designers] Nathan Crowley and Joe Hodges set the standard for Cardassian architecture, which is a wonderful mixture of pseudo-fascist and crustacean. The way we thought of it was that the Cardassians are really bad guys, so fascist architecture — real serious and dark — was called for. It's like looking at an insect. There's a shell on top of it, and if you pull off the outer shell, there's some really cool intestines on the inside of the insect, and that's where Mike [Okuda], Doug Drexler and Denise Okuda come in. They do some really wonderful graphics and bring those 'intestines' out and give them a really unique quality."

Although *Deep Space Nine* is set in the same universe as previous *Star Trek* series, the fact that the station's architecture is Cardassian rather than human influenced set up a challenge for the *Deep Space Nine* art department. "The two directions we had to go in is that we knew we were part of a time-honored history of design, and yet we knew that we were also establishing a new sense of direction," says Delgado. "The fact that we were both honoring Federation design and coming up with our own gave us a great deal of range to come up with designs. Coming up with a distinct look while retaining the aspect of *Star Trek* was the best part of the job."

Fortunately, due to Paramount's unprecedented success with *The Next Generation,* the studio was less restrictive in financing the start-up of *Deep Space Nine,* allowing Zimmerman and his team the luxury of creating a very exciting visual motif for the show. "We spent more money on *Deep Space Nine*'s pilot than we were allowed to spend on *Star Trek VI,*" says Zimmerman of the set construction budget. "The two-hour pilot was stunning and it's every bit as good in its way as the original pilot for the original series was back in 1966. 'The Cage' was a brilliant piece of science-fiction work — especially for when it was done. 'The Emissary' is equally as good."

Unlike *The Next Generation*, which was able to recycle many of the feature-film sets (in fact, the *Enterprise* bridge set on Stage Nine used as the battle bridge in *TNG's* pilot, "Encounter at Farpoint," was first built for the aborted mid-seventies *Trek* TV revival and, until it was struck after filming was completed on *Star Trek: Generations*, the oldest standing set on the Paramount lot), *Deep Space Nine* started with empty soundstages and a blank slate.

"With *The Next Generation* we started out with a lot of feature *Enterprise* leftovers," says Zimmerman. "We were able to resurrect the corridors, which were wonderful, and by rebuilding the sick bay we had lots of space to work with. Basically, on *Next Generation* the new sets were the bridge, the ops lounge, the crew's quarters and, at the end of the first season, Ten-Forward [*TNG's* bar set]. With *Deep Space Nine* we started out with a blank sheet of paper. We had three fairly large empty soundstages and we've filled them with some of the most bizarre scenery that I think the television audience has seen in a while."

In order to realize the alien Cardassian look of the station, Zimmerman constructed fiberglass molds that allow him to duplicate panels and features that he wouldn't normally be able to replicate on a limited budget. "We have created an architecture that will be seen to be unique," says Zimmerman. "We have made all these fantastic shapes in fiberglass and can repeat them fairly inexpensively having made the molds for them."

"I'm most proud of the interior of the station," says Delgado. "It was very important to me because when you sit down and think about it, you're setting a design standard for a show for the next five years and beyond. People around the world are going to see the model for Deep Space Nine — and I can say I helped design that model. I'm proud of that.

"I'm also proud of the operations center, ops," he adds. "That's a really cool bridge; I don't know how anyone can be disappointed walking onto that set. You're expecting the bridge of the *Enterprise,* and you don't get that at all. Boy, that thing is

big. The third thing is the Promenade. To my knowledge, that has to be the largest set ever constructed for television. Walking through and seeing all the shops, the bar, the versateller [ATM] is really enjoyable. A little bit of trivia: I was the one who came up with the sketch for the versateller on the Promenade — and they built the thing. It wasn't in the script, but I sketched it out, and the next thing you know it's lit, and a Ferengi bank is running it, and there's all kinds of logos on it, including a Romulan logo."

Keen-eyed visitors to the set will also notice the familiar U.N.C.L.E. logo from *The Man from U.N.C.L.E.,* an homage by technical consultant and scenic artist supervisor Mike Okuda, a longtime *Trek* fan whose professional association with *Trek* is now over a decade old. "Because Deep Space Nine is essentially a Cardassian facility, we had a lot of fun coming up with a new look, new technology, new architectural details, new control-panel layouts and new styles of readouts," says Okuda. "It was a great challenge. A lot of it is essentially trying to come up with familiar things but doing it in unfamiliar ways. For example, control panels, the format for buttons on the control panels. We have very specific styles for the movie Starfleet and very specific styles for the *Next Generation* Starfleet. Doug Drexler came up with some very bizarre styles of keyboards and button layouts that look functional but are very different from previous versions of *Star Trek.*

"Despite the fact that the *Enterprise* and Deep Space Nine were theoretically built by completely different cultures and are very different technologies, they're both made in the present day on planet Earth at a film studio using present-day technology," continues Okuda. "Hence, the technologies used to create both looks are very similar. It's only in the artistry, in the design and execution, that they become different.

"Cardassians have a lot more [console displays] that are based on radical design, outward-flowing displays. Theirs is a much more graphically oriented technology. They have relatively small amounts of text or symbology. Hopefully, the information comes from the design — as opposed to Starfleet, which has an enormous amount of text

and statistical tabular information in its readouts."

Walking on the vast sets of *Star Trek: Deep Space Nine,* it's easy to become lost in the reality of the show's fantasy world. With its minute attention to detail, expansive production design and 360-degree architecture, which surrounds you on all sides, *Deep Space Nine* can easily appear as real as any theater multiplex, shopping mall or office building one might frequent in the twentieth century.

It is the job of the production team of the show, along with the directors and actors, to capture that reality week after week so that viewers at home can find themselves as immersed in the *Star Trek* universe as those who work every day on its many sets. However, compared to *The Next Generation, Deep Space Nine* presents its own unique challenges and complications.

"It can be frustrating for a director because there is more prosthesis makeup, for instance," says supervising producer and part-time director David Livingston. "If one person isn't ready one time you just wait, and that's the director's time. The sets are more difficult to shoot than *The Next Generation* and they take longer to shoot because some of them are multilevel, the lighting is darker and moodier, and it's time consuming."

Another complication in the beginning was the fact that the crew was not as familiar with the *Deep Space* sets as the *Next Generation* production team had become with the *TNG* stages after six years. "That adds a 'burden' to the directors, because it takes away their time," says Livingston. "The first season everyone is still getting to know these sets: Walls that should be wild aren't wild yet. Some of the design elements that Herman built, as you know, are unbelievable sets. They are smaller, in general, than *The Next Generation,* which gives them a better look because you see more detail and people are forced together and there are weirder angles and stuff."

The differences from *Next Generation,* however, are what make *Deep Space Nine's* sets unique. Even those viewers who may not be taken with the show's story lines would find it difficult not to be awed by the show's production design. Says former *Deep Space Nine* di-

• • • •

11

rector of photography Marvin Rush, who joined the show after having worked on *TNG* (and subsequently left to take over the photography reins on *Voyager*), "I think the most significant thing is that the requirement was to make it look different. It was a conscious choice. Obviously, the fact that it's a meaner-spirited place is reflected in the architecture — it's got a lot of hard, angular edges. If you think of the Federation as being normal looking, Deep Space Nine has got a very different geometry to it, and the color scheme of the walls is much darker. The feeling of the set is more foreboding, which plays into the lighting style for me. One of the techniques I've used was to make sure the show had more contrast. If you compare them, the bridge of the *Enterprise* has a big soft white dome over it and it creates an office-building kind of feel to it, like any conventional interior today. When you see that, you pretty much have to light it that way because it drives the choices."

Rush's lighting scheme reflected the differences between the darkness of *Deep Space Nine* and the brighter, more pristine look of Starfleet in *The Next Generation*. "In this set, we use much darker and more sinister lighting," he says. "We use harder, less diffused light. There are more areas where light is lower and people can come in and out of the light. Overall, it's more contrasty. All these things create an additional sense of contrast and more tension. As we went along, the station became more familiar to our audience and also to our cast, so ops became a little less contrasty. In the pilot, it was broken down and wasn't working. Now ops is a little bit more elevated [in terms of lighting]. When there's jeopardy, you want more contrast to give a sense of danger."

Another aspect of the production design that distinguishes *DS9* from its sister series is the fact that most of its sets are smaller than those on either *The Next Generation* or *Voyager*. Although ops and the Promenade are vast, the corridors, quarters and ancillary sets, including the swing sets (areas used for sets that change every episode) used for planetscapes, are more compact. "Some of those directors use long lenses to compensate and give the illusion of depth," says Livingston. "[Director] David Carson is famous for his

use of long lenses. Other directors, like Corey Allen, use wide-angle lenses. It just depends on their particular bent. But the sets are smaller stylistically, and that's the way we're approaching the show.

"The fun part is to try and do something new. [Director] Cliff Bole came up to me after doing a *Next Generation*, telling me he was frustrated about what to do on the bridge, that there's nothing new. At some point, you just have to let that go and say, 'OK, we're just going to go in and shoot the bridge.' But *Deep Space Nine* offers all kinds of opportunities for directors to come in and apply their own style to shooting the sets."

For *The Next Generation*, Marvin Rush had devised plans for lighting the bridge. The ability to prelight the standing set resulted in a speedier shooting schedule. "On the bridge, we had Plan A and Plan B, which were routine lighting setups based on certain given situations: where the cast was going to be at, and where the camera was going to be placed," says Rush. "We have an open architecture on the *Enterprise* where the furniture is essentially fixed. The floor level is very large and very open and unobstructed, but ops on *Deep Space Nine* is anything but that. The potential for laying dolly track and placing the camera is much more constrained. A lot of the furniture pieces don't strike, and you can't move them; they're built in. We also have multiple levels, and whenever you have multilevels, the dolly track becomes a real problem. You either spend a lot of time building platforms or you simply use where you can put the camera and you don't try and do things that can't be easily done. For all those reasons, it's hard to have a 'Plan A/Plan B.' "

Another consideration in shooting the operations center on *Deep Space* is the fact that it serves the function of a variety of sets aboard the *Enterprise*. "This set functions as four sets," Rush continues. "It functions as the bridge, as engineering, as the transporter room, and the fourth set is observation. All those sets are tied into one set. It's a very busy set with lots of things visually going on."

In lighting ops, Rush was very conscious of creating a distinct look for the command center. One aspect of ops that is reflected in his design scheme is

that the room also functions as engineering, with large pulsating lighting pylons representing the station's power source. "One of the things we decided to do was push highlights on the show," says Rush. "There's a lot of blown-out practicals. In fact, the display system, what we call the engine, which is the lighted panel columns, is running right on the clip of overexposure, riding very, very hot. All those things tend to give a sense of greater contrast and greater energy to the set."

When it came time for Rick Berman to choose a costume designer for *Deep Space Nine*, he recruited Robert Blackman as one of the few *Next Generation* crew members to do double duty on both series. (Blackman has subsequently re-upped for duty as *Voyager*'s costume designer.)

"My favorite thing is we did twelve Cardassian suits for the pilot [of *DS9*] and then we got to use eleven of them on *Next Generation*," says Blackman of the synergy between *Star Trek* shows that helped maximize his production dollars in creating wardrobe for alien worlds. "There are aliens walking around on the Promenade that give the notion of this floating hotel, this United Nations in space. I find it wonderful. Unlike *Next Generation*, where it was primarily humanoids with a small smattering of aliens, on *Deep Space Nine* it is the converse, with a small smattering of humans constantly facing one kind of alien after another. We recycle some; we mix components that we have in stock."

"Aliens on *Deep Space Nine* is a way of life; it's expected," explains makeup supervisor Michael Westmore, another veteran of *The Next Generation* currently doing double duty on *Deep Space* and *Voyager*. "Aside from the simple fact that there are many more of them, the aliens of *Deep Space Nine* don't differ markedly in conception from those that appeared on *The Next Generation*. It's the same time period.

"Each show has its own individual new ones that will come into it, but as far as background creatures, we have, for example, the Bolian, the character who plays the barber on *The Next Generation*. You see that same race in the Promenade on *Deep Space*, so we know that there isn't just one of these things out there, that

• • • •

there is a race of these people. There's one in the [DS9] pilot. He's an officer in the opening sequences, and now we have a female one who has been seen in the Promenade walking around. We're able to tie that particular alien race up and weave it between both shows. I've done that with several others. There was another alien, a bald orange creature with a turkey throat and a spoon nose called a Rotciv, that I put together just to walk down the Promenade. It turned out to be so interesting that we put him in a little teeny bar on *Next Generation,* and now we have him back in the Promenade again."

A problem that some directors have encountered on the show is that the heavy use of prosthetics can prove constraining. "You can't get too close," says veteran *Star Trek* director Winrich Kolbe of filming prosthetics. "I like to sometimes go into really tight close-ups, but you have to shoot them a little bit wider. That's something that I run into on every show." As a rule, the Cardassians are also shot using long wide-angle lenses to achieve a certain look, partly necessitated by their complicated makeup. "We've had some problems with makeup and we've been using more diffusion than on any show I've ever done," says DP (director of photography) Marvin Rush. "We've had to back off a little bit on close-ups. You can't tell on some of the more bizarre aliens because they're so removed from what we know as human. It's very forgiving; on this show you never see pieces of rubber peeling up."

The area of Deep Space Nine where the widest variety of aliens is to be glimpsed at any given time is the Promenade, the large multilevel shopping mall–like area that has no real equivalent on the *Enterprise* or *Voyager.* "We had the occasional alien or Vulcan in Ten-Forward, but it's mainly been humans that we've had in there," says Westmore. "Over on *Deep Space Nine,* the space station is actually run by Bajorans, so we have a big mixture of Bajorans, and that means having to apply a nosepiece to all these people and having many more aliens."

Although many of the alien creatures are background characters, glimpsed only briefly and often from a distance as they quickly stroll past the camera in cor-

ridors or on the Promenade, Westmore has made it a point of pride to shun the practice of saving time and money by not putting as much detail into the makeup of the background characters as that of the principals. Despite his awareness that the attention he pays to making up the background aliens is missed by most viewers, Westmore takes satisfaction in the knowledge that there is a core of dedicated fans that takes note of even the smallest details of his work.

"Almost ninety-nine percent of the fan letters I get," Westmore points out, "are thanking me for the quality of the show, that you can watch the show and you don't see a Halloween mask. It's literally motion-picture quality. I think that's part of why I survived there for so long. I brought my motion-picture experience into it and I won't settle for any less than that."

As for humans aboard the station, it was Rick Berman who insisted on a new uniform for the *Deep Space Nine* personnel, rejecting budget-conscious overtures from producer David Livingston, who urged retaining the established Starfleet costumes to save money. (Ironically, when new uniforms for the film *Star Trek: Generations* proved untenable, reportedly because of noticeable panty lines, the producers resorted to using *DS9* uniforms to clothe the cast of the feature — throwing out a day's worth of

footage with the new costumes.) Responsible for achieving the new Starfleet look while remaining faithful to the established uniform design was Blackman, whose *Deep Space Nine* aesthetics went through a number of permutations before Berman and Piller settled on a final look for the new outfits.

"The thing that interests me is the reversal on *The Next Generation,*" says Blackman. "[TNG] Starfleet uniforms have a very dignified and ennobling kind of appearance with that vertical, perfectly done, military-esque kind of structure. In *Deep Space Nine,* we've taken it in another direction. It's very utilitarian. It's a cross between a NASA jumpsuit and a mechanic's jumpsuit."

Unlike the closely cropped, tight-fitting spandex of *TNG*'s early seasons and the equally closely cropped burgundy and yellow outfits after the uniforms' third-season refits, the *Deep Space Nine* uniforms are loose fitting and far less constraining. They do, however, hug the bosoms of the leads just as tightly as those on *The Next Generation* did, a *Star Trek* staple.

"They're very loose fitting and they have those T-shirts, and some people roll up their sleeves so they look like men at work," says Blackman. "I like that notion of a kind of looser and more accessible design. There's something about the dignity that was just wonderful in *The Next Generation,* but it's a little bit standoffish. There's a kind of propriety about it, and now we've got these guys who kind of open their jackets and their shirts and push their sleeves up and get down to it. It's a very hands-on existence. It's fascinating to me."

Looking back at *Deep Space Nine*'s continuing development, Herman Zimmerman comments, "I remember when we finished the pilot of *Next Generation* and Mr. Roddenberry said, 'People say you can't go home again, but we just proved that under the right conditions you can.' I remembered that, and that's when I thought it might be fun to do this without the encumbrance and necessary palette of design criteria that I had to stick to when we designed *The Next Generation,* and have a whole clean culture and design challenge to just start from scratch. It's been about the hardest thing I've ever done, and also the most fun."

• • • •

First-season director Paul Lynch concurs. "It's a much more interesting set. This has got so much more going for it. There are so many different things happening on this space station. On *Star Trek*, the rooms were basically the same each episode — the captain's quarters, the bridge, the meeting room, the medical bay. Here, because it's such a big space station, there's all sorts of things in it."

"The way the writing is going we're using more sets and smaller sets than I believe they did in stories on *Next Generation*," says Zimmerman. "We move around awfully fast for an hour show, and it goes very quickly. We started out with a larger number of standing sets to begin with, but there is no set as big as, for instance, Ten-Forward."

One of the most noticeable departures *Deep Space Nine* has made from established *Star Trek* production design is its use of multilevel sets on two of the three soundstages. While the operations center exists on several raised platforms, the Promenade and Quark's bar are built several stories up. While visually stunning, the setup creates unique problems for the directors and their craftspeople. "For a television series, the problems that we've created for the cinematographer are fairly difficult challenges," agrees Zimmerman. "These sets are built more in the nature of feature sets than the way a television series is generally set."

David Livingston, now a *Deep Space Nine* and *Voyager* director, notes that the use of multilevel sets was not because of space restrictions but to achieve a new look never before envisioned for the twenty-fourth century. "When we had our initial meetings, I pointed out that these sets were wonderful, but it would be difficult to shoot," says Livingston. "Ultimately, my recommendation was let's go for it, and the directors will just have to figure out how to do it. They cannot shoot the show the same way *The Next Generation* was shot. The bridge on *The Next Generation* is called 'the TWA waiting lounge,' and you can move the camera around with great fluidity and get from point A to point B easily. You can't do that in ops. The Promenade has a whole second story that you have to climb up to shoot on, but it looks great when you go up there. Quark's bar is certainly not Ten-

Forward. A lot of the sets are smaller and more cramped because that's the nature of the beast here. It does present opportunities and challenges for the director to pull it off in terms of the schedule, but I think it adds a visual dynamic that is in strong contrast to *The Next Generation*."

Director Paul Lynch agrees with Livingston. "The toughest thing always to shoot in *Star Trek* was the bridge because it was this big, sprawling space, and you had a lot of stuff happening at the back end and the front," he offers. "On *Deep Space Nine*, it's a lot easier in operations because things tend to be more gathered together, and you have more elements in the set, so it's more interesting. It gives you a bigger opportunity to do things visually than the control room of the starship. It's more fun and gives you more visual possibilities because there are limitations in *Star Trek* with just the sets themselves. Once you've shot the engine room, you've shot the engine room. And I shot it from just about every angle. Here you've got the main Promenade with everything from the bar that looks out into the corridors to the corridors that look into the security office. You have a great deal of visual choice, which is neat and more fun."

Among the techniques employed to shoot on the treacherous landscape of the *Deep Space Nine* sets is the utilization of camera cranes, which were infrequently used on *The Next Generation*. (There were exceptions, including Rob Bowman's second-season premiere, "The Child," as well as Livingston's show, "Power Play," in which O'Brien, Troi and Data are possessed by the spirits of three convicts stranded on an alien planet.) "We've used a device where you put the camera on the end of a crane and you put a remote-control head [called a hothead] onto the camera," says Livingston. "The camera operator sits in a chair and is tied by remote control and wired to the camera so the camera is just moving around by itself. That can be used for ops and on the Promenade. Its use is limited because of the production time it takes to do it. I think you will see a lot more swooping cameras on this show."

One problem many directors have encountered in shooting ops is the restricted camera movement created by

the multileveled set, which makes it difficult to dolly within the confined area.

"It was always a push because given the scope of the production that they do for any one episode, there was never really enough money, and you're always battling that," says Paul Lynch. "Strangely enough, even with the budgets they've got, they're so interested in perfection that it is very difficult to make the money stretch given the amount of time spent on makeup and special effects to get the quality show that Rick and Michael want. It's a difficult show in those circumstances, and the sets are much larger and more difficult to shoot than the sets on *The Next Generation*, which are much more simple."

What makes several of the sets additionally unique is the fact that they are fully enclosed, which means the soundstage walls are not visible and the set is constructed to encircle the stage completely. "The main challenge of three-hundred-sixty-degree sets [like that] is that everywhere you look, the director can point the camera," says Marvin Rush. "Most typical TV-show sets, even a lot of feature sets, end at the top of the walls. This is not a typical TV set. It has to be lit in such a way that when the director says I want to look here, here and here, you have a way of doing it. Obviously, the more set the director photographs in any given setup, the less room I have to light. That was a factor in building the sets, so they had internal built-in lighting to make it so that if the director asked me to do the impossible shot — the shot where you see everything — we could do it."

One way that Rick Berman and Michael Piller avoided costly delays in shooting was to hire only directors who had worked on *The Next Generation*. David Carson, who had helmed some of *Star Trek*'s most visually interesting shows, including "Yesterday's Enterprise," "The Next Phase" and "The Enemy," was picked to direct the pilot. "The whole idea of *Deep Space Nine* was different from *The Next Generation*," says Carson. "It's broken and alien and weird and peculiar, and *TNG* is none of those things. The sets were a little way along when I joined the project because they were so enormously complicated and cost so much money. I found I was able to make suggestions Rick and Herman liked, particularly with a view to the ease of shooting the sets."

"I like that depth," says director Winrich Kolbe of Quark's three-level bar. "That is one set I could shoot with a twenty-millimeter lens or a seventeen-millimeter lens and really get something big, and I think it needs to be shot that way. It is designed in such a way that there is not a blind spot in there unless you move all the way to the end and shoot the other way. But, generally speaking, it's a set that I think should be used, and I'm trying to use it. I'm not trying to restrict myself to just the lower echelon. If there's a scene that I can shoot with a long lens from below — shooting up and having people do their dialogue, or walk and talk, or whatever — I do so."

While Quark's bar is a brilliantly designed set that stretches upward to the roof of the soundstage, the extra time it takes to move equipment to and light the upper levels of the set sometimes precludes utilizing its more unique features. Says Kolbe, "What happens in episodic television is the director comes on the set and you begin to immediately zero in — if you know what you're doing — as to where can I put my camera? Where do I get maximum production value for mini-

mum amount of production time? That usually dictates where you want to go. There are certain areas you might love to put the camera, like in the bar, for instance. I would love to always put the camera up topside and shoot down, but that will take a lot of time. We did that in one shot and we actually made it on that particular day. We were lucky, I guess. Normally it's where can I get the camera in there? There are certain areas you can't put the camera in. So sometimes you say, 'God, it would be nice to have the camera in here, and if I get a Python or a Lauma crane, I could put the camera in there,' but that's usually the first thing that goes out of the budget. You have a choice of that actor and that Lauma crane, or that set and that Lauma crane, and usually you know pretty quickly what will stay and what will go."

Camera positions aren't the only changes that were made in the production of Deep Space Nine versus TNG. Other changes from the standard operating procedures included an increased reliance on computer-generated graphics for scientific and monitor displays. "When we started Next Generation, the producers were not sure they wanted to use video playback or computer-generated images because at that time the state of the art wasn't up to photographing twenty-four-frame film and thirty-frame video at the same time. Now we have a very reliable system for reducing video to twenty-four frames so it can be photographed," says Herman Zimmerman of the myriad monitors that can be found on every set, particularly the operations center, which is filled with display screens. "That's a big technical advantage that we've been able to achieve in five years. We have computer-generated graphics on video monitors and spent somewhere close to forty-five thousand dollars just on video monitors for the various sets. I think we have something like sixty-four video sets in the various places on the three stages."

It is somewhat ironic that Mike Okuda has spent so much of his time working with video monitor displays on Deep Space Nine in light of the fact that one of his major innovations when he began work on The Next Generation was in developing methods of creating moving readout images that could be accom-

plished without the more expensive video monitors. Okuda perfected the polar-motion gag, in which the illusion of motion is created in an image by rotating a piece of polarized material in front of a polarized illustration. It was by coming up with such clever solutions that Okuda developed a reputation for being able to achieve impressive visual-display effects without requiring the set to be equipped with expensive video monitors. In fact, the producers developed so much faith in him and his potential to do impressive things with Deep Space Nine that they sprang for the expense of installing actual video monitors all over the space station. Thus, by showing that he could get along without video monitors, Okuda was eventually given monitors to work with.

"The fact that in five years I'd generated probably hundreds of pieces of animation for The Next Generation for its postproduction readouts gave me the confidence," says Okuda, "and it gave the producers the confidence to say, 'OK, we can do this; it's not a big unknown, it's not a huge risk.' [As a result,] when you look at our sets, if you look at the operations center, the instrumentation is more alive."

Now that Okuda is responsible for the graphics on two major weekly science-fiction series (DS9 and Voyager), he has had to delegate much of the design work. "It has diminished my hands-on involvement with both shows," he says. "The studio asked me to take a more supervisory role with the graphics. Because I have two strong teams on both shows, I can just pop in to offer guidance and try not to make their lives too miserable."

In practical terms, this has meant that Okuda devotes most of his hands-on attention to designing the images that will appear on video monitors, leaving the design of the control panels to his assistants, Doug Drexler and Denise Okuda (who also happens to be his wife). Drexler designs the layouts of the control panels on a Macintosh. The layouts are then made into large-format lithographs that Denise "colorizes" by cutting out colored gels and gluing them to different sections of the lithographs.

One of the most impressive results of Denise's color work is the enormous simulated stained-glass window panel that stretches the entire height of

Quark's, Deep Space Nine's Ferengi bar. This piece presented Denise with a particular challenge because it was made from a relatively small lithograph that was enlarged many times. This meant that even a flaw the size of a human hair would be visible when the piece was blown up to full size. It was a tribute to Denise Okuda's skills with the gels that the final result, which serves as the visual centerpiece of the bar, displays no such defects.

Not surprisingly, Mike Okuda's day-to-day schedule doesn't leave him much time to catch his breath. "Generally we get a script approximately seven working days prior to the beginning of an episode," he details. "So we have seven days to design and prepare everything. On the seventh day, we start shooting. Doug and Denise will work with the set designers as well as our production designer to anticipate as much as possible what's going to happen. The challenge with all this, of course, is that the script is constantly evolving as the preparation goes on. They'll be adding sets; they'll be changing sets; the director will suddenly decide that he or she wants a particular kind of shot, so the set will change accordingly. Then, on the seventh day, we start shooting for seven to eight working days. During those seven to eight shooting days, we are prepping the following episode.

"Approximately two or three weeks later, I'll get a rough cut of an episode and I'll start working with the postproduction department to prepare animated graphics for burn-ins." These burn-ins are the animated screen displays that do not actually play on monitors during shooting but must be added as a postproduction visual effect.

Among those postproduction visual effects are the images projected on Deep Space Nine's massive central viewer in ops. Herman Zimmerman recalled Gene Roddenberry's insistence when *Star Trek: The Next Generation* was being assembled on creating a new viewscreen that would dominate the foreground of the bridge so the images projected on the monitor would dwarf the crew. This was used effectively in "Encounter at Farpoint," in which Captain Picard (Patrick Stewart) addresses a menacing Q (John de Lancie) towering above him on the huge screen. For *Deep Space Nine*, it was de-cided that an even more impressive viewscreen would be needed to improve upon *TNG*'s advances in much the way that *TNG*'s viewscreen had supplanted that of the original series (essentially the equivalent of today's big-screen televisions). For the operations center control screen, Zimmerman envisioned a huge monitor that never has an image on it unless it is called up by one of the operations officers.

"There are a lot of things [on *DS9*] that are new to *Star Trek* viewers that we hope they'll like. One of them is the viewscreen," says Zimmerman. "There isn't always a picture of the stars in space as there is on a starship, where you can't see the wall through it. There'll be some times when we will be seeing the image on the screen from behind the screen. When the viewer is turned off, we'll see the image disappear, and the camera will then move in on the people who have been watching it. It's an interesting, rather innovative photographic technique.

"The effect is done as a burn-in in postproduction. Unfortunately, because it's an optical, the viewscreen material can't be preproduced ahead of shooting because of the way the schedules are so compressed. We're able to cap the viewscreen instead of having it straight up and down, as if you were going to have a projection or a large television screen or a large backlit projection. We put a ring of neon around it, and that fuzzes the edge a little bit. We weren't sure if it was going to be an asset or a liability, but it turned out to be an asset. It gives the look of the image on the screen a slightly different edge, and that makes it more alien looking. A burn-in on the viewscreen is about the simplest thing to do. We shoot that footage during principal photography and it's inserted in postproduction. Although we do call it a blue screen, it's actually green because we're using blue neon surrounding the screen. We use a green saturated color, but you can key off of any saturated color."

"We spent three or four months building the Promenade," recalls Ricardo Delgado. "But it's not until you put smoke on the set, put people in front of the camera and aliens around it, that it comes to life. Then you believe that you're on a space station. You take it for granted that the whole thing exists. The whole show coming to life is the best part of it for me."

Another improvement over the familiar *Next Generation* technology is the use of a turbo-lift on the bridge, which actually can be seen descending and ascending as it transports officers to the heart of the station, the operations center. "The general consensus was we were competing with ourselves because *Next Generation* was a terribly successful show," says Zimmerman. "The idea of *Star Trek* is one that has captured the imagination of television audiences all over the world. We had to do something that was at least as interesting and hopefully more interesting. We were intent on making a dynamic place for the operations center. Unlike the bridge of a starship, the operations center doesn't go anywhere. It first orbits a planet and then it's moved near a wormhole.

"One of the things I've always wanted to do was have the turbo-lifts actually come into a room and leave a room, and we were able to do that [in ops]. We only had a certain amount of space under the stage that we could work with, so one of the criteria for raising a platform was to gain an extra few feet to operate these elevator mechanisms. We do see the actors come up out of the stage floor and we do see them disappear into the stage floor, and that's very effective. In other sets that isn't possible, so we just see the elevator doors open as we do in *The Next Generation*. But the Cardassians are a militaristic people and they prefer command from a high point, as any general would, so we made the commander's office at the upper level of the operations center. There are windows in the doors and windows on the sides of the doors and in the commander's office so he can be watching whatever is going on in the operations center. It's a combination of transporter room and engineering area that we would find in another level on the *Enterprise*. It also has a science area and a large conference room with a planning table."

Affecting the ambiance of all these creations is the unique color scheme Zimmerman devised for the series to differentiate it from previous *Trek*s. His overall production design bathed the sets in darker colors than had been seen on *TNG*, primarily grays and blacks with gold highlights. For its part, Mike Okuda's team also

used a separate and distinct range of colors for the control panels on Deep Space Nine. "We have a very specific color range that we use for Starfleet," says Okuda. "We have a separate and distinctly different color range for the Cardassians, as well as a third distinctly different color range for the *Star Trek* feature films. The features tend toward cool blues and greens. *The Next Generation* tended toward a pastel range of oranges, purples and mauves. The Cardassians' is an interesting color mix. Even though we're using very similar techniques to create a control panel [for both series], the fact that the designs are different, and that they're very distinctly different color ranges, will hopefully create a different look on film."

In addition to the improvement in the new series' production values over those of its progenitors, *Deep Space Nine* shows growth over its predecessors in other, less obvious ways as well. These include its more realistic depiction of women's roles in the future. Previously, *The Next Generation* had been criticized for its female roles' being too passive — and sometimes even sexist. (Who can forget the moment in "Q-pid" when the male crew members fenced their Nottingham

rivals while Troi and Dr. Crusher attempted to fend off their opponents by smashing flowerpots on their heads?)

Few would accuse the new show of such a failing. "Kira makes up for all of that," says Ira Behr grinning. "Ensign Ro made up for a lot of it on *The Next Generation*. Kira is a strong woman, and Dax must have a lot of nice conversations with herself. She's a little of everything. We have Keiko and [Miles] O'Brien arguing in the pilot about what her role is going to be because she didn't want to come to this station. I think the women are good."

In fact, it was the character of Ensign Ro that the producers had planned to bring on board *Deep Space Nine*. When actress Michelle Forbes passed on committing to the arduous shooting of a complex science-fiction series on a weekly basis, the writers created Major Kira Nerys, another Bajoran freedom fighter, who served a similar purpose for the producers and has become one of the most popular members of the *Deep Space* ensemble.

Notes Behr, "People might not realize this, but even Vash [Picard's love interest in *TNG*'s "Captain's Holiday," who returned in an episode of *Deep Space Nine*] was an attempt to bring in a ballsy woman who's not your typical *Star Trek* woman, a clear thinker both in terms of what she did in her own life and sex and the whole bit. There's a lot of talk now about being politically correct, and I think more times than not — given this is a show that's in a business that's extremely middle class and conservative, and given all those constraints — *Star Trek* is fairly politically correct, though that's not something I find really high up on the agenda."

Not surprisingly, the strong persona of Kira Nerys was an element about the series that immediately appealed to the actress who plays her, Nana Visitor. "All I went on was this script I was sent among all the other silly sitcoms and weirdo things of the season, and I saw this incredibly strong woman, great writing and emotionally connected scenes I felt I could play very well," says Visitor. "I auditioned, they liked what I did and that was it. Once they gave me the [show's] bible, they were very available to answer the questions — are we physically different

than humans? How humanoid are we? For all the questions I had, they had answers. *All* of them. I couldn't catch them on anything. That's all I really required — the backstory of who I am and what makes us tick. It's human relationships, and I think that's the strength of *Star Trek*. I think we're about human relationships, and if Kira changes and grows and learns to adapt and to understand, those are positive messages to be sending out. The fact that she's a strong female is something I don't think is a bad thing to have out there. I'm watching television now and I'm seeing a lot of women in very different kinds of roles, in positions of power, and not having to be the stereotypical female and the mom in the sitcom saying, 'Honey, get off the couch.' "

For Piller, offering a strong female protagonist was not an answer to criticism of *Next Generation*'s female roles, but a natural outgrowth of the *Trek* mythos. "I think we had very strong women on *Next Generation*," Piller says. "They were cast and created as caretaking roles. Their characters are caretakers by their jobs. Doctors and therapists are caretakers and they have a very mothering kind of role. The actors would have loved to have transcended that, but the fact is that you have to write the character you've been given by Mr. Roddenberry. As it evolved through the beginnings, you saw stronger and stronger women on *The Next Generation*. Ensign Ro is the best example of that I can think of. Tasha Yar was created for *Next Generation*, but it was a character that wasn't working and the actor wasn't happy. We went out of our way not to make the women on *Deep Space Nine* caretakers, although I think Dax is somewhat of a caretaker — but she is the science officer so she has a technical expertise to bring to it. There's no question that Kira was always going to be an action hero. I think we have gone out of the way to create women who are contemporary and really show us a full range of female experience."

Nana Visitor agrees. "Kira is a very powerful female and hopefully she will continue to be powerful in using what is available to her as a woman as opposed to an Arnold Schwarzenegger who wears a little bit of lipstick. She will be affirming for women in that sense, but along with that she's a Bajoran, and Bajoran females are very aggressive. She's physically trained and was trained as a terrorist. With those female affirming powers she has, she also has what we think of now as male assertive characteristics. She will get in physical fights. She's not afraid of confrontation. Interestingly, with the ancient Celts, the women fought right alongside of the men."

Visitor points to *Terminator 2* as reflecting the continuing evolution of women's action roles, which she feels Kira's persona is a part of. "Linda Hamilton was fighting for her child, which gives it a strong female impetus," she says. "I think that's the female connection there. There is a powerful reason for force being used and that's very true of my character. There's an emotionally strong bond with Bajor and the importance of the people and the culture and the spirituality being preserved. That's why she can find it in herself to do what she's done, and maybe that's the female connection."

In fact, Piller had even considered, in consultation with Berman, making the commander of the space station a woman — an ambition realized with the casting of Kate Mulgrew as Captain Janeway in their subsequent *Trek* series, *Voyager.* "We sat down, and one consideration was that a woman would be Sisko and the star of the show, and that too would have been an advancement for television," says Piller. "It's not that we didn't take it seriously; we just moved in a different direction because we couldn't put Ensign Ro as commander of the space station. We always figured her as the first officer, since she was an ensign."

Of course, as noted previously, Forbes balked at making the move to *Deep Space Nine,* forcing Piller and Berman to retool their pilot script, "Emissary," to accommodate a new Bajoran officer and second-in-command. "Michelle Forbes is a wonderful actress, and her character of Ensign Ro created the entire canvas for this new series," says Piller. "It had always been assumed that she would be one of the people spun off and moved over to the new series, [although] it wasn't part of the plan when she was created. So when we wrote [the DS9 pilot] we put it together, and it would have been fine. Then we showed it to Michelle, and she

said, 'It's a great script, but I really just don't want to commit to a long-term deal. I don't want to be in a series.' "

Paramount was reportedly locking its actors into seven-year commitments for the new series to avoid the costly renegotiations that had resulted when *The Next Generation* became a smash. Forbes was unwilling to put her feature career on hold. "She didn't really want to be in *Next Generation* the sixth year either," says Piller. "She had a feature she had just started and she wants to be a feature actress. She said she would be delighted to be a recurring character, but she didn't want to be a regular. We could not go into the new series that way. For a long time Rick and I talked about seeing if we could talk her into doing a year and we'll kill her at the end of the year — 'If we promise to kill you, will you do it?' But then we decided that we weren't going to have the audience make an emotional investment and then lose her at the end of the year, so we decided after giving her one last chance — on which she passed — to write her out."

Star Trek: The Next Generation's Michelle Forbes was written into a starring role on Deep Space Nine, *but she declined and was replaced by Nana Visitor (copyright © 1996 by Karen Witkowski).*

Fortunately, Forbes's departure from the series plans came as Piller was working on a rewrite of the show to strengthen its first act. Her departure meant changing the character of Ro to another Bajoran with a new and different backstory. This, he soon discovered, proved an advantage rather than a disadvantage for the new series. "I found there was a great deal more conflict in having the Bajoran not be Starfleet," says Piller. "Immediately you have different priorities and agendas, and the two people have a conflict with each other the moment they step onto the station. The [conflict] between Sisko and Ro would have been a much different one because ultimately she's Starfleet and has to do what the boss says. Kira can do things which are not appropriate Starfleet behavior. We created this character, and it was really a matter of rewriting two or three scenes that defined where she was from and a couple of speeches in other scenes which were mostly action-type scenes."

Once the character was on the page, it was up to Piller and Berman, with the help of casting director Junie Lowry-Johnson, to bring her to life. After all, Michelle Forbes, in only a handful of appearances, had become one of *The Next Generation's* most popular characters and would be a hard act to follow. "We went through a very long casting process and saw some very interesting actresses. Then Nana came in and just nailed it," says Piller. "Bang!"

Deep Space Nine's premiere boasted a hefty price tag — reportedly between $10 and $12 million — which made it one of the most expensive television pilots ever filmed, although many of the costs were amortized over the rest of the season. This includes the over $2 million spent on the show's sets. By comparison, the ambitious Universal space saga *Battlestar Galactica's* three-hour premier in 1978 cost $8 million and *Babylon 5's* in 1993 under $2 million.

Notes Berman, "When you create a premise pilot, which is what we did, you create a two-hour show where you have to set up an entire world and an entire group of characters and what brings them together. At the same time, you have to tell an entertaining and meaningful story. You have a big job cut out for you. Mike and I started creating the premise for this show, the backstories for the characters, the relationships they were going to have and what sort of story would unfold."

The advantage for Berman and Piller was the knowledge gained from their years of production experience on *TNG*, as well as the lessons learned from producing the first new *Star Trek* pilot, "Encounter at Farpoint." "What 'Farpoint' and five and a half years of *Star Trek* did was allow me to know what was possible and what wasn't," says Berman. "What our visual effects guys could give us and what they couldn't. What sets we could expect and what was pie in the sky."

Berman points out that as a result, the making of *Deep Space Nine* was considerably easier than when he and Gene Roddenberry first sat down to create *The Next Generation*. This experience also allowed him to avoid many of the ego clashes and production problems that had plagued the early start-up of that show. "Gene had to create a new television show from twenty-five years of mythology that had grown up over an old one, and he had to do it all whole cloth," says Berman of the challenge of reviving the *Star Trek* franchise for television. "In the case of *Deep Space Nine*, it was much easier for me than it was for Gene with *Next Generation* because *Deep Space Nine* was being produced primarily by people who had been on *Star Trek* for five years and understood what it's like to write a stylized twenty-fourth-century script. [They] know what words can be spoken and what words can't, and how to go about all of the things we do to create this television show as opposed to creating *MacGyver*.

"He also had a lot of people who felt they knew more about *Star Trek* than he did. He had to get pretty tough about it, and we had a group of writers that came in and didn't have the benefit of someone as strong as Mike Piller. People had no idea what *Star Trek: The Next Generation* was going to be about. Gene felt the obsessive necessity to put his own imprint on everything to get the show going, and I applaud him for that. By the time I was sort of in control of the series, in the second year, Gene had pretty much cemented his idea of what the show was going to be about, and it was my job to continue, to keep it going and not to formulate it, because he had done that."

Some have noted that the tone of "Emissary," the *Deep Space Nine* pilot, is far closer to that of the original series pilot, "The Cage," than "Encounter at Farpoint," with Sisko encountering a race of aliens who cannot understand linear existence so they force him to experience his best and worst memories. "I haven't seen 'The Cage' in years, but what brings to mind the memory of it is the imagination that takes you out of that locked cage — Gene's imagination," says Piller. "It takes you into green fields and the picnic and Susan Oliver and those wonderful moments. I would be lying if I did not say that image was with me when I wrote this script. I don't remember much about it. I don't remember the story, but I remember that friendly green pasture. I think it's definitely inspired by Roddenberry, and if people who have missed something in the new *Star Trek* feel that some funny bone or some nerve ending is being addressed in [*Deep Space Nine*], I know Rick and I will be delighted."

He points out that he was equally influenced by Roddenberry's "Farpoint" pilot. "There's a great deal about the structure [of "Emissary"] that's similar to 'Encounter at Farpoint,' " says Piller. "One of the tricks I learned from watching 'Farpoint' again was that they didn't introduce Riker and Geordi and Beverly until two or three acts in. I said to Rick when we were structuring this, 'Let's hold off the arrival of two of our regulars late enough that I can do something with the other characters.' My first suggestion was everyone was there and they're already at work, but it wasn't as effective."

Ironically, one of the strongest plot elements in "Encounter at Farpoint," the arrival of the menacing Q, was added by Roddenberry to pad out D. C. Fontana's script when he relented to studio demands that the opener clock in at two hours, as opposed to the ninety-minute premiere he had been lobbying for. "I think the Q thing did come out of a time requirement, but there isn't any question in my mind that the best thing in that show is the Q story," says Piller. "If it had been only that other story, it would have been a disappointment. The other thing that comes out of 'Farpoint' is a vision of Roddenberry's where we have Picard arguing for the future of mankind, representing the advo-

cate of humanity to this Q who puts humanity on trial. That's an extraordinary, philosophically ambitious idea, and it really helps to define why *Star Trek* is what it is. Without that, it would have been spaceships and monsters and special effects."

Despite Berman's quickly embracing his first draft of "Emissary," Piller admits to having been dissatisfied with his initial work on the teleplay. "Michael's never liked anything he's written," says Berman. "The story was forty pages long and extremely well defined when Michael sat down to write the teleplay. He wrote a first draft and then he and I spent about a month working on it. We discussed it, we made changes, draft after draft, and finally we got it to a point where we were pretty happy with it. But no one had seen it except the two of us. We had worked on it for a few weeks, and he became unhappy. We were looking for a direction and, as is typical of Michael, he was frustrated and felt that something wasn't working. He did a rewrite that was not a major rewrite at all, but it was a rewrite that brought into it the ideas that we had discussed all along that had to do with the Los Angeles riots, the idea of people rebuilding and of people living in an area that had been damaged and that had been violated. And the *spirit* that goes into the rebuilding of it. It was a good change but not a major change. More important than being a good change, it was a change that made Michael happy."

Incorporating a strong philosophical point of view into *Deep Space Nine* was essential to Piller, whose character Benjamin Sisko grapples with the alien creatures (actually threatened prophets) inside the Bajoran wormhole, to whom he tries to explain human linear existence. "The first day we sat down to meet about this, Rick said that somehow this story must have the philosophical ambition that the 'Encounter at Farpoint' script had and that *Star Trek* represents," recalls Piller. "Ultimately, what we created was this interaction and confrontation between alien and human that is not so different from 'Encounter at Farpoint,' but, of course, on a weekly basis we are exploring issues and philosophies through encounters with aliens. What we have in the pilot is aliens who have no under-

••••

standing of a linear existence. What does that mean for Sisko, who is trying to deal with the context of his own personal crisis as it comes out through this philosophical explanation of here's why you don't need to fear me? 'We are not a threat to you, and we're different, and differences can be good', he says, echoing the same theme — that humanity has overcome and we can coexist in the universe."

The theme of coexistence was amplified by Piller in his second draft when the Los Angeles riots magnified the problem of the divisiveness that exists in contemporary society. This gave him a new impetus for revising a teleplay he felt — as Berman has indicated — was too dull. "What happened was I had written the first draft of the script, which we had not sent to the studio yet, and Rick read it, and a lot of people liked it," details Piller. "But something was really bothering me, and I couldn't figure out what the devil it was. What it turned out to be was [that] the first hour wasn't good enough. Through the introduction to Sisko we saw things on the station, and it scared the hell out of me. When I looked at the second hour of [*TNG*'s] 'Unification,' which I'll always consider a character study of Spock, I realized it was also talky and nothing goes on. I was very unhappy with that. When I looked at this, I was really troubled because I was not falling in love with my own dialogue and my own characters and I was extremely critical. Rick will tell you that throughout this process he has said to me things like 'It must be terrible waking up every morning and being as negative as you are.' But I felt very strongly — and Rick will agree that I dragged him into this rewrite kicking and screaming — that the first hour was flat, that nothing happened and that it was basically dealing out the characters for everyone to see."

What Piller ultimately realized was that the characters existed without purpose in his original draft. But with the riots providing a metaphor for the rewrite, he was able to inject new life into the stalled script. "I said Sisko's not a hero," Piller notes. "Sisko's got to come in and have something to do and have a problem that he has to deal with as a hero. While our mystery is unfolding, which will ultimately blossom in the second hour, Sisko

must take this by the hand. In the first draft of the script, our guys essentially come to the Beverly Center [a Los Angeles shopping mall] and decide to stay. I said that's great, and the studio said we want to open with a shot of the Promenade and people gambling. So I wrote it that way and I realized it didn't work. Sadly, though, while I was going through this agonizing process, we had the riots in Los Angeles, and both Rick and I wanted to somehow say something in our show about humanity coexisting and coming together. And we want to build this into the alien interaction that we have in the second hour of the script."

Shortly thereafter, the high-tech *Deep Space Nine* had been transformed by Piller into a ruined and cannibalized wreck in space. In Piller's rewrite of the teleplay, he was clearly influenced by the devastation he was witnessing on television news reports about Los Angeles. "I had started thinking that it was not a dramatic situation for a man to come to the Beverly Center," says Piller. "It's not very dramatic for someone to go to their favorite mall and decide to stay. But for a man who goes to South Central Los Angeles and finds it in ruins and decides to stay, *that's* dramatic. In order to bring drama to the first hour, I argued with Rick that we should come to a space station that's in ru-

ins and that Sisko must begin the rebuilding process in the first hour in order to be driving the story."

Ironically, what developed out of Piller's new approach to the material was the relationship between Quark, the Ferengi barkeep, and Odo, the shape-shifting head of security, that many subsequent writers have embraced as the best character dynamic since the bickering between McCoy and Spock in the original *Star Trek*. "We had always had a shape-shifting gag for Odo in the end of act one and we had always had a Ferengi boy, Nog, that would become a friend of Sisko's son," says Piller. "In the rewrite, using all the elements that we had that were waiting to be thrown in, I put Nog at the scene of a crime and put him in trouble. I realized that when Sisko arrives at the scene where Odo is shape-shifting — where they meet at the end of act one — there is the situation where the Ferengi kid is going to jail for being an accomplice to a crime that has been committed. Sisko, who has come to this ruined Promenade, sees the Ferengi guys who used to run the bar and the gambling facilities ready to leave and decides he's going to use this to his advantage."

Sisko threatens to incarcerate Quark unless he stays aboard the station and helps in the rebuilding process as a "community leader." Despite being repulsed by the idea, Quark is reluctantly forced to stay at Sisko's behest. "In that scene where Odo is watching Sisko in action and Sisko is doing this number on Quark, I suddenly found myself writing these asides between Odo and Quark," says Piller smiling. "Quark is saying, 'What do you want me to stay for?' and Odo says, 'I'm a little mystified myself, Commander. The man is a gambler and a thief,' and Quark comes back and says, 'I am not a thief.' Odo says, 'Yes, you are. You're a thief,' and suddenly these guys are going at each other. I realized there's a magic there. There is a relationship there. These two guys have been archenemies that have been at each other's throats for the last several years — and they love it. They get off on this trying to one-up each other, and there's a love that comes within for one another between the good guy and the bad guy that we really explore in the first episode. That's the discovery of character and interaction Rick and I wanted to have. It's a conflict that's fun and restores to *Star Trek* something that hasn't really been in evidence since the original show."

Rene Auberjonois, who plays Odo, a veteran of the long-running sitcom *Benson*, notes that the chemistry between the cast, both as characters and actors, developed extremely quickly. "It always amazes me how quickly that happens," he says. "You can talk to actors about doing a film and you go on location for ten weeks and make lifelong friendships, and it happened here. Because of the nature of the world of *Deep Space Nine*, which is a space station, there's a sense of community. I have a relationship with Armin Shimerman, who plays Quark the Ferengi, which is very dear to me. It's sort of a love/hate relationship because our characters are the antithesis of one another. He is a con artist extraordinaire, and I am a man who just sees black and white. Something is either just or unjust. It's a very complex relationship, and although we're always bickering and I'm always after him, I think we've forged quite a friendship."

"The Ferengi have always seemed to be very broad and on the verge of slapstick," adds Shimerman. "On the other hand, that is how they've been established, so I must include that as well. I don't know what was in their heads about the comic values of myself, but what I think they found in the early episodes is the great comic potential between Odo and Quark. There's this sort of Mutt-and-Jeff relationship that both Rene and I savor a great deal."

Writer-producer Ira Behr shared Shimerman's enthusiasm for the developing relationship between Quark and Odo. "I think Michael and Rick realized that this is a learning process of finding out together who these people are and then, of course, you cast the goddamn thing and the actors make it who they are," he says. "Then you sit back and say, 'OK, maybe that's not what I had in mind exactly,' but it works, and so all the best laid plans of all these things go out the window the second the cameras roll. What I found interesting and fun about this show is not so much each individual character, but how the characters began to interact. Making Odo and Quark this kind of twosome is

just going to have juice for ages because Odo is this kind of repressed, haunted figure, and Rene's really playing the makeup to a certain extent in that he's a man alone, which you don't see a lot in the twenty-fourth century. And Quark is a Ferengi. He's not your typical cringing Ferengi; he's a Ferengi with a little edge to him. Their comic relationship, I find, is something that's a lot of fun."

But even with Piller's teleplay completed weeks before production began, shooting the pilot was an incredibly arduous affair. It was made more complicated by delays in casting and set construction, which made it arguably an even more difficult shoot than "Encounter at Farpoint" six years earlier. "I had anxieties and hesitations about even wanting to do ["Emissary"] because I knew what a struggle it was going to be," says producer-turned-director David Livingston, a veteran of the *Next Generation* two-hour opener, for which he served as unit production manager. "Fortunately, I didn't have to deal with the day-to-day minutia of a production manager and I could sort of sit back a little bit. Bob della Santina is the wonderful production manager I hired to do this job — just took care of everything for me. It was tough, and I told everyone it was going to be tough. It wasn't like just doing another episode or a double episode. It's doing a whole new thing again. It was a pilot, and we had all forgotten what that was like. It was very difficult because there are so many dynamics working: building all these new sets and a whole new cast and new wardrobe. Michael Westmore had to create a bunch of new makeups, including Odo's, which was very difficult. All of those dynamics made it very, very difficult."

Shooting the pilot was a considerable challenge for veteran *Trek* director David Carson, who later went on to helm the seventh *Trek* feature, *Generations*. "It was very interesting and wonderfully challenging because you've got a lot of people you mustn't let down," he says. "But it's a good challenge. Unlike a lot of shows, where you're sort of stabbing in the dark, here you had a lot of background. I think if they had decided to make major departures from the way everything had been, it may have been a different kettle of fish. Because the pro-

ducers made sure they were sticking very closely to Gene Roddenberry's mapped-down path, we were really continuing the inheritance, as it were. My job as director rather than as writer was to make it look better, be bigger, be more effective and communicate better than it had before.

"I think the story went a long way beyond where *Star Trek* normally goes," he elaborates. "The decision was made *not* to pander to new audiences but to play to the strengths of the *Star Trek* audience. As a result, the story didn't take any prisoners. If you're not on that wavelength, then I think there are a lot of people who may have been confused by it. But if you have the patience to sit with it, then I think it all becomes completely clear as to what's going on.

"We made tremendous efforts in the two-hour show to put a lot of production value on the screen, to make it seem not like a TV movie but a really big, thunderous movie that you would sit in the movie house and see — and to give it a feeling of scale and complexity in the way that we shot it and the way that I directed the actors. It gives the audience the feeling that they're not just watching some other TV sequel, but that they're watching a movie."

In order to realize that ambition, Carson became deeply involved with the casting process along with the series producers, which led to several major discoveries, including Siddig El Fadil, who now goes by the less tongue-twisting name of Alexander Siddig, who plays Dr. Julian Bashir.

"Rick discovered Siddig on a PBS show, *A Dangerous Man,* a prequel to *Lawrence of Arabia,* in which he played King Farouk and was very good," says Michael Piller. "We'd been looking for Sisko from here to eternity and we told our casting people in Europe to find this fellow. We brought him in and we looked at him and he just jumped off the screen. There wasn't another doctor candidate. He was just delightful. We had not met Avery [Brooks, who plays Sisko] at that point and we asked ourselves, could Siddig possibly be Sisko? And we found out he was twenty-five years old, and that was too young."

"I read in London with about

thirty people," recalls the actor. "I think they auditioned all over Europe. And then I did one for the big cheeses here. It was bizarre; one day I did the test in London and two days later they asked me to fly to Hollywood — where I had never been — and on the same day they gave me the job, which was great."

Adds Behr, "I think Siddig is going to go through the roof. He's good looking, fun and he's got energy. I think the key to the show is that people have a lot of energy."

Unfortunately, as the doctor on board Deep Space Nine, Siddig has found himself wrestling with the enduring dilemma of technobabble, the mystical *Trek* mumbo science that passes for scientific reality in depicting a twenty-fourth-century civilization. "They have a sadistic love of it," jokes Siddig. "But I actually quite enjoy it. It's the nearest thing to Shakespeare — stretching the mind to get your tongue around it and make sense of it. I actually quite enjoy trying to see if I can make something of it without making it sound flat. That's part of the lie of trying to make it sound like I'm actually a doctor or a science officer. Data on *The Next Generation* is an unbelievable robot because he does it flawlessly.

"They're an extraordinary bunch of people," Siddig says of his costars. "One of the wonderful things for me being a young guy is, because of the snobby British training I've had, that we're taught no one can act except for the British people. But in this cast everyone has certainly done more Shakespeare than I've ever had hot dinners. They've been there and seen it and have been doing television since they were born. They've got an enormous amount to teach me, and I'm quite happy being at the bottom and holding on to someone's tail. The dynamic, as a cast and as characters, is interesting because it's still developing. We play at games, we go out and have drinks, but I'm still working it out, and that's probably my character. I'm the one character who's sitting there watching everybody all the time instead of getting in there and getting my hands dirty."

David Carson proclaims, "What a wonderful actor he is, freshly minted from British drama school. A very wonderful candor and openness of feeling about

him. And for such a young actor, very experienced with the lens. Very good at turning his hand to all the tricks of the emotions the writers have asked of him so far."

Also cast early in the process was Rene Auberjonois as Odo, a gelatinous liquid in his natural shape who has learned that he is a changeling and a member of the Founders, a group of shape-shifters who have enslaved races across the Gamma Quadrant under their militant rule. "Odo, in terms of the kind of person he is and his incredible dignity and sense of justice, is very appealing to me," says Auberjonois. "He's sort of a curmudgeon and he's a very rigid man. He's uptight, but he's also got a wonderful deadpan kind of humor."

As a shape-shifter who morphs into numerous shapes and sizes every episode, Auberjonois is the focus of many of the series' state-of-the-art visual effects. Since the work is often done in postproduction, it requires a special discipline to imagine a world of creatures and illusions that doesn't exist until visual effects supervisor Rob Legato's fertile imagination incorporates them.

"It's the nature of being an actor," says Auberjonois. "For people who are not professional actors, the easiest thing to do is just to remember what it's like to play house. I remember as a kid there was a place in the attic where my brother and I used to go to pretend to be scientists. It's just this willing suspension of disbelief. There's something wonderful about Odo because I turn into all these different things. We shoot things where I just sort of stand there and I know that I've just turned back from being a rat and its magical for me to see that."

Portraying Odo is not Auberjonois's first foray into the *Star Trek* universe. At the request of close friend and director Nicholas Meyer, the actor played the nefarious Colonel West in a subplot that was cut from *Star Trek VI*'s theatrical release but restored for its subsequent video edition. In the latter, the colonel plots with Klingon conspirators and the Romulan ambassador Nanclus to prevent a peace treaty from being signed between the Klingons and the Federation. Ultimately, Colonel West is revealed as the man under the Klingon makeup attempt-

ing to assassinate the Federation president at the Khitomer Peace Conference.

"I wasn't in *Star Trek VI* because the character was cut out," says Auberjonois, who admits to often being cast as a villain. "I have not seen it. I did it because Nick Meyer is a personal friend and asked me to. I was in Scotland hiking with my wife and rushed back to get the makeup all done. I've played a lot of different kinds of parts and I usually play villains and I love them. I remember when my son was much younger and I was doing *Richard III* at the same time I was doing *Benson*; he asked, 'Why do you always play the bad guy?' I said it's because they're usually the best part to play."

However, Auberjonois's Odo is certainly a hero of this series, and he's thrilled to be probing the limits of the final frontier. "It's evolving, and there are certain things that I know about him that are clear from the scripts that we've done so far and the bible," says the actor. "The writers know a lot more about where it's going than I do. I like not knowing and opening the script each week and seeing a new facet of the character for me to consider. I like that challenge each week. It keeps it fresh for me, which is very important when you're doing a week-in and week-out schedule. When you're doing a series, the characters always develop to a degree, but I think in this kind of situation, more than a sitcom, where the characters really are cast, and you know what's going to happen, there's a certain wisdom revealed. Odo has an incredible intelligence in one episode and in another there's a weakness in his character that's revealed, a rigidity he has to work through, a human quality which is very interesting."

Director David Carson praises Nana Visitor, who plays Kira. "The cast and company are so lucky to have her. She's one of these rare chameleon kind of actors who is able to assimilate herself into a character and transform it into something you don't expect. She's also very beautiful and she obviously delights in playing this role. I was very pleased when she walked into the room [to audition] and I think that once she did, she was the only Kira we thought could play the role. Of course, we weren't going to

• • • •

Actor Bruce Boxleitner and Nana Visitor as hosts of the Sci-Fi Universe *Awards (copyright © 1996 by Albert Ortega).*

tell anybody that until we'd signed a deal with her."

Visitor confesses to not having been an avid *Star Trek* fan when she joined the series. "I watched *Star Trek* when it was in reruns," she says. "I think I know them all from cooking dinner in my brownstone in New York. I was a fan of the quality of the show, but I was not a Trekkie."

Ironically, Visitor didn't even realize *Deep Space Nine* was a *Star Trek* spin-off when she read for the role. "I didn't get it and I didn't understand that this was *Star Trek* when I auditioned," Visitor explains. "I did not understand what I was getting into. I didn't even know I was wearing a nose [prosthetic] until I talked to Rick Berman. He said, 'At least the prosthetic is one of the smallest we have,' and I said, 'What prosthetic?' and he said, 'It's nothing; it's just a small elephant nose that you wear.' And he had me going for five seconds. I had no idea. I just knew I wanted to play this woman very badly."

Deep Space Nine is a region of the universe Visitor hopes to be exploring for a long time. "*Star Trek* has got so much strength and age behind it, and it's cutting-edge television," she opines. "We're do-

ing things I've never done or seen on television, and there's this kind of care and the kind of scripts I've never seen. Once in a while I'll have someone I haven't heard from in a year say, 'Wow, I hear you're on *Deep Space Nine;* I'm such a Trekkie.' Then I'll say, 'Gee, this is new and different.' I feel that in those very faraway moments on the telephone, but in the day-to-day, it doesn't mean a thing except they have the power to allow us to do what we do, and they give us wonderful material to do it with."

Also cast early in the process was Armin Shimerman, a veteran of several *Next Generation* episodes, who plays Quark. Having pioneered the weaselly role of a Ferengi in the first-season *Next Generation* episode introducing the race, "The Last Outpost," Shimerman was a natural choice for the role. The costar of such series as *Brooklyn Bridge* and *Beauty and the Beast,* Shimerman has also appeared in the films *Blind Date, Like Father, Like Son, Eye for an Eye* and *Death Warrant.* The actor is quick to contrast Quark with previous Ferengi incarnations, which many dismissed as an inept attempt to find a new adversary for the Federation during the early evolution of *The Next Generation.* Shimerman attributed his casting to his previous outings as a Ferengi on the series and felt he could best personify the new Ferengi character they had created for *Deep Space Nine.*

"They remembered me from five years before as one of the first Ferengi," says Shimerman. "I think what Rick said to me was they remembered how strong a Ferengi I was because they wanted that for Quark. He also has to be able to play chess with Sisko. They wanted that quality. I did not have to audition as many times for a series regular as I would if they had not seen my work and [kept] me in mind. The first time I had a callback, and usually there are a number of actors sitting there, it was only me and Max Grodenchik. He's played a Ferengi before. At the final audition, it was just me. They gave me the impression after I was cast that they had indeed written the part with me in mind."

Fortunately for fans of the series, Grodenchik was drafted into service as Rom, Quark's bumbling brother, who has proved one of the series' most engaging recurring characters.

Shimerman admits to a degree of frustration about working under the huge prosthetic appliance that covers his face but laughs that unlike LeVar Burton (who played blind chief engineer Geordi LaForge on *TNG*), at least he can use his eyes. "I think every actor would prefer if all of his face was shown," says Shimerman. "I would be a fool to say otherwise, but I think the mask works really well, and the combination of the mask and whatever inflections I can give to my voice and my eyes comes across quite well.

"It means working a little harder and being a little bit bigger. I'm used to playing roles where it's very low-key and underplayed. I've been trying to teach myself to do that for years. Now I'm being asked to overplay a little. It's just a new challenge."

David Carson reflects, "Armin and I worked together on another science-fiction show called *Alien Nation.* He's terrific. Like Rene, he took to the mask completely and is developing the character wonderfully well. Unlike some of the Ferengi characters there have been, Quark is not quite so silly. He has a much more malevolent presence, which I think is very good because it adds to the drama."

With most of the cast in place, the impending commencement of principal photography on August 18, 1991, made the rest of the casting search a race against the clock. It was imperative that Sisko and Dax be cast before photography began on the pilot. "It's an ugly business and it's interminable and it's exhausting," says Rick Berman. "We have a wonderful casting director [Junie Lowry-Johnson, C.S.A.], and we just began the process. I think that Rene Auberjonois is a remarkable actor; I think Nana is remarkable; and my favorite on *Star Trek* since the beginning has been Colm Meaney. I adore Colm's work."

Colm Meaney had served aboard the *Enterprise* since its first encounter at Farpoint, although most fans won't remember it since he was a nameless face on the battle bridge in that episode. After that, through sheer charisma, the actor elevated himself from an anonymous transporter chief to the only married recurring character on *The Next Generation.* Now he is a costar aboard Deep

• • • •

Space Nine. "I was in New York for a year with *Breaking the Code,* and that was the year of the writer's strike. *Star Trek* didn't get going again until September or October," recalls Meaney of his return to *The Next Generation* after having shot the pilot. "When I came back, they brought me on as Chief O'Brien. For the first five or six shows that I did, he just kept cropping up and I was 'Transporter Chief.' Then a script arrived, and suddenly he had a name."

Meaney has kept busy on the silver screen as well as the small screen, starring for Alan Parker in *The Commitments* as a reverent fan of Elvis (a role he returned to for Parker's *The Snapper*), playing a malevolent terrorist in *Under Siege* and a fighting Irishman in Ron Howard's *Far and Away.* During other treks away from the *Enterprise,* the actor has also appeared as the captain of an ill-fated 747 in *Die Hard 2,* a cop in *Dick Tracy* and as Dennis Quaid's brother in Alan Parker's *Come See the Paradise.* Unlike Michelle Forbes, Meaney agreed when approached by Berman and Piller to become a regular on *Deep Space Nine.*

"We knew we wanted to do something with O'Brien, whom we brought over to the show," says Ira Behr. "Colm is a really fine actor and he had limited chances on *The Next Generation.* [Now] he's a lead, and we're trying to find different and new things to do with him."

For Meaney, O'Brien has sort of become the everyman of *Star Trek.* "O'Brien is somebody who is more human," he says. "He obviously likes his job, but he also has other aspects to his personality. He doesn't have the element of being a fearless superhuman. There are situations they get into which, because of their Starfleet training, they react to as if it's normal, with steely nerves and all that, but I think O'Brien doesn't like that stuff too much."

Noting that he had worked with Meaney on *The Next Generation,* Carson says, "I think it's an interesting choice to have him come over from *Next Generation.* He wasn't particularly prominent over there, and to suddenly reveal him is a good way of linking the two series together without doing it heavy-handedly. I think that's a really good choice."

Although most of the cast was lined up before production began, late casting of the roles of Benjamin and Jake Sisko, as well as that of Dax, weeks into production on the pilot made it an extremely difficult shoot for the department heads.

"With Colm Meaney and Siddig and Rene and Nana Visitor and Armin, we had a core of five remarkable actors," says Berman of preparing to begin shooting the pilot. "It finally came down to our star and the role of Dax, which were the two killers."

The search for Commander Sisko ended only days before production began, reportedly prompting Avery Brooks to pronounce, "This is the role of my career." Prior to *DS9,* Brooks, in addition to touring in a play about the life of Paul Robeson, was best known as Hawk from ABC's *Spenser: For Hire* and the short-lived spin-off, *A Man Called Hawk.*

"Patrick Stewart had [left] a very big pair of shoes to fill, and we needed to find someone who was different but had the same stature and the same strength and power," says Rick Berman. "It was a very, very long search. We brought people from Belgium, we brought people from England, we saw German actors, English actors, we saw a lot of American actors, black actors, white actors, Hispanic actors, and we finally chose Avery Brooks, who was undoubtedly the best. But it was a very, very long process."

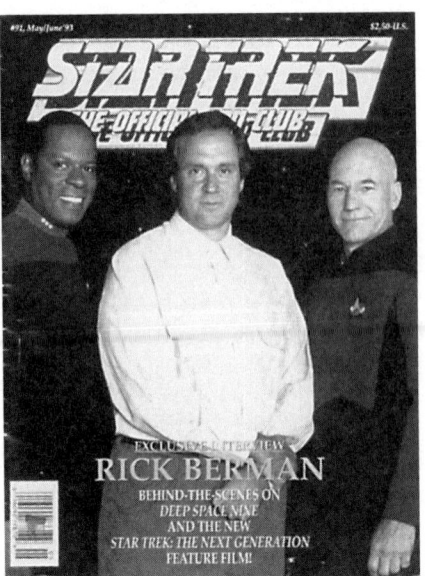

On the set of the pilot, attempting to order a cup of coffee from the operations center's replicator, Brooks, sporting a full head of hair and considerably subdued compared to the in-your-face attitude he had displayed as Hawk, was almost unrecognizable. However, once he opened his mouth it was immediately clear that the producers of *Deep Space Nine* had found a fitting successor to William Shatner and Patrick Stewart as the next lead of a *Star Trek* series. Brooks conveys not only the power and strength of a Starfleet commander but also the emotional depth and complexity that have endeared both previous captains to two generations of television viewers.

Unlike Stewart and Shatner, who were not well known when they were cast, Brooks had created a very recognizable persona during his three years playing Hawk. Executive producer Rick Berman didn't feel his lack of anonymity was a liability in casting him for the role of Sisko. "He played the second role on a show, and it did not last a long time," says Berman. "There are actors I tend to stay away from because I feel they have overly familiar faces. But to me a good actor is somebody you don't think about how familiar they are. If they're right, they're right."

Early rumors, denied by Michael Piller, had Richard Dean Anderson of *MacGyver* pegged as a front-runner for the role of Sisko. (Anderson was later cast as the lead of Piller's *Legend.*) Also in contention was *Alien Nation*'s Gary Graham, but it was eventually Brooks who was chosen days before the beginning of principal photography on the pilot for the highly coveted role.

For Brooks, *Deep Space Nine*'s approach to addressing contemporary issues, reflected in the fact that he portrays a single parent, is a refreshing change from the mundane fare offered on network television. This, he feels, illustrates the show's topicality in addressing nineties concerns within the framework of future society. "We're dealing with a single parent and single parenting," says Brooks. "In the last twenty years there's a very different notion in our society and, indeed, our world about what that means, so of course in an allegorical way this show is very nineties. We're on the verge of the twenty-first century, and then it will be very 'teens.' Teens in the twenty-first century."

Says Carson, "I think that Avery Brooks is a phenomenal actor. I've rarely come across an actor with a combination of his technical skill in front of the camera and an amazing strength of performing with the lens. He's a real joy to work with. And he's extraordinarily deft and constantly interesting, and I think the character gives him much more ability to have these differences in his psychological makeup than Picard, who's a much more straightforward character who you can probably predict will react a certain way in different situations. It's very difficult to do that with Sisko, and Avery plays with delight those opportunities."

Over the years, Brooks has modified his portrayal of Sisko, both physically and in his performance. For the middle of the third season, the actor shaved off his closely cropped hair and grew a fashionable nineties goatee. Playing the character with a harder edge, Brooks showed the once-reluctant hero embracing his role as Emissary and commander of Deep Space Nine and earning a promotion to captain, garnering new respect among many fans who had found his performance monotone and laconic. But in year four, his performance became riveting.

The final piece of the *Deep Space Nine* equation was the casting of Dax, the station's science officer. Writing the pilot, Piller and Berman were ultimately drawn to the race of the Trill, who exist as a joined species. The Trill were first examined in *The Next Generation*'s "The Host," in which a Trill ambassador who is having an affair with Dr. Crusher is discovered to be a parasite that exists within the body of a humanoid host.

"Originally, we had the science officer in a wheelchair, since she came from a planet with different gravity," says Piller. "Eventually Ro befriended her and found her a gravity-free environment on the station where she could fly around. Out of her office, she would be in a wheelchair, which was necessary for her to move around." (A character like this was finally realized in the second season's "Melora," but at the time the pilot was going to be shot, production requirements made her untenable as a series regular.)

Says Piller, "We looked at a variety of other alien species and, of them, the Trill seemed the most interesting." The Trill of *Deep Space Nine* now exists within the body of a twenty-eight-year-old female, but it knew Sisko in its previous body, that of an old man, creating a fascinating relationship between Dax and Sisko that has been mined for both dramatic and comedic gold over several seasons.

The search for the woman who could portray the Trill was the most arduous casting task of all, and when the producers finally decided on the beautiful and dynamic Terry Farrell *(Hellraiser III)* they were already weeks into production on the pilot. "I was stressed to death," admits Farrell of being the last actor to join the cast. "They did all my stuff in one week, and I had the flu and my period and was shooting sixteen-hour days and I had a big lump on my forehead that we reshot for two days."

"The most difficult role to cast is always a beautiful girl," says Berman. "Beautiful women are few and far between, and to find one who can act and who doesn't want to bypass television to go into the movies is very difficult since there are very few of them. Fortunately, we finally found Terry."

Of the casting process, Farrell adds, "It's so overwhelming. It's so incredible getting *Star Trek* anyway because it's such a legend. When I first got it, it was like a roller-coaster ride that I couldn't get off of, and you don't know what's going to happen."

Berman admits that part of the difficulty of casting the role was the problems they had in explaining the part to those auditioning. "It was very difficult to say you're a beautiful woman and a four-hundred-year-old androgynous character at the same time."

Recalls Piller, "We were already in production when we cast Terry, and part of the reason that it's so difficult to cast is because it's a character that's a little harder to define. I could write a book about Trills now, but what does that mean in the day-to-day existence of these people? How do we make it different from Terry Farrell? How do you make it something alien and yet accessible? It's a very interesting mix of qualities that I think the studio wanted. Rick and I felt that we wanted a woman

who was very attractive and yet a superior actress. We saw a lot of very talented young women, but they just didn't get it. Some would change their voices to make it sound like a man's voice coming out of a woman. It was hard. The casting people will tell you that the roles of people twenty-five to thirty-five [years old], attractive and brainy, are the hardest roles to cast in television. It's hard to find the next Meryl Streep. It's hard to find the next Glenn Close."

Fortunately, Farrell, who had recently finished work on Anthony Hickox's *Hellraiser III*, was called in by Junie Lowry-Johnson to audition. "Terry came in the last day or two of casting for this show, and we had her back a couple of times," says Piller. "We had two or three others that we were very interested in, but the truth is Terry was the only actress who came in to read where Rick and I looked at each other and agreed that she had hit the scenes that she was reading. We had finally got to the place where we had to cast somebody. Terry did not have the experience of some of the others, and we knew, and she knows, that there was a great challenge of acting and performance ahead of her. So far it's amazing to watch her because you can see a much stronger performance. She's starting to grow more and find this role."

Farrell agrees and says the key to her audition was playing the role with an amused detachment as opposed to attempting to personify a woman with a "short, fat snake inside."

"I think she has fun with people," says Farrell of Dax. "In the scene I had to audition in, I said I used to be an old man, and Avery expects to see him in that context. He had never seen me before as a woman, so how else do you play that other than to have fun with somebody? It would be fun if you dressed up in makeup and the other person doesn't know you're fooling them and they're trying to believe you're who they say you are, but you don't look anything like you did last week. Just having fun with it was the key for me."

Preparation Farrell didn't make for the role was boning up on her science. "In biology I did very well, I got straight A's, but this is different," says Farrell. "I'm not the doctor! You just open the writer's guide, and I call and ask Michael Piller,

• • • •

who's really nice if you have a question about the technical jargon. Sometimes they write a question mark where the 'tech' should be, and you wonder what's going to be the word there. Cough it up! I know they're going to freak me out, and then I end up getting something like 'The ionic L-band emission patterns don't match.' I'm supposed to know this by heart? Tech with a question mark? I'm getting more used to it now. That's what really upset me during the pilot because I didn't even know where to start. What am I talking about? I'd try to relate it to a car, and it wasn't working."

But when everyone had breathed a sigh of relief over casting the role, Paramount executives issued one of their few ultimatums after reviewing the first few days of dailies involving the character. The distinguishing marks on Farrell's forehead, denoting her as a Trill (as actor Franc Luz had worn as Odan in "The Host"), had to go. After the protracted search for a beautiful actress who could also act, the studio didn't want her to be defaced by ugly prosthetics. "There are different Klingons, and now there are different Trills," jokes Farrell. "Maybe I'm from the north of Trill and the other guy was from the south."

With the ensemble finally in place, principal photography on "Emissary" continued with rewrites coming in from Piller at the same time that some of the sets were still being completed. However, the biggest obstacle to the fledgling series had been overcome.

Herman Zimmerman suggests that this *Star Trek* ensemble is more faithful to Roddenberry's original hopes for *Star Trek* before the casting of William Shatner and Leonard Nimoy turned the show into a star vehicle. "If you want to go back to Mr. Roddenberry's original ideas, he wanted to create an ensemble cast and he did, but because of the really strong ability of Bill Shatner and Leonard Nimoy and the romance the audience had with those characters and the relationships between them and Dr. McCoy, it became more of a star cast than an ensemble cast. "In *Next Generation,* Gene achieved what he was really striving for in the first place. He has the strength of Picard in Patrick Stewart, but he has a very level, compe-

tent cast all the way through. I think he was more pleased than he was the first time around."

Avery Brooks admits to an early affinity for the material. "I'm new to it," says Brooks. "Of course, I was familiar with it because I grew up watching television, but I am definitely a fan now."

Former producer David Livingston maintains that while *DS9* carries forward the progressive traditions of color-blind casting established in the original *Star Trek* — which put black, Asian and Russian characters in lead roles — there was no intent to be politically correct in casting a black actor as the lead and other minorities in important supporting roles. "We got the best actors for the parts," he says. "*Star Trek* is about the fact that it doesn't matter what you look like or what your skin color is or if you have weird bumps on your head or stuff hanging out of your ears or weird-colored hair or a misshapen body. It doesn't matter in the twenty-fourth century. People don't deal with that anymore. First of all, you're exposed to so many bizarre, different kinds of people, who has time for prejudice? It's silly; it's an outmoded kind of thinking, and that's a credit to Gene and to Rick and Michael to continue that point of view. One of the key characters on this show is a Ferengi, and of all the creatures we've had, they're probably the most unappealing types. Yet now they're part of it."

"The only role that was ethnically locked was we wanted Sisko and his son to be the same race," says Berman. "We read people, black and white, for every role. In the case of Cirroc [Lofton], who plays Sisko's son, he is half Ethiopian on his mother's side; and Siddig is half Sudanese, so we have two actors who, on one side, are from Northeast Africa, which is very interesting."

Michael Piller agrees. "We were definitely looking for the best actors for the roles. And if the best actor for the role had been Asian, you would have had an Asian commander. We were faced right from the beginning with the challenge of making this show unique and different and step beyond *The Next Generation.* The last thing we wanted was to be accused of simply doing another *Star Trek*

and exploiting the formula. Rick and I had a very high ambition to contribute to television, to not just put another quality hour on the air but to try and advance television in our own way. We're very inspired by Gene, and Gene advanced television. We can't hope to do that in the same manner that he did because he was there first, in the pioneer days.

"The ground has been broken," he continues, "but I think so much of television rests on its laurels or looks backward or tries to find what works, what's safe. There has never been an hour dramatic series that has had a black lead that was successful. The old boys' network in the television community would tell you that it's a huge risk to put a black man in the lead because it will turn off a certain segment of your audience. Rick and I felt right from the beginning that we wanted the opportunity to consider a black lead for this show. We were delighted and impressed when the people at Paramount allowed us to have a full range of auditions to consider all races and all people. When it got down to it, we were delighted that Avery Brooks turned out to be the best actor we could find. We knew the pundits would tell us it was a risk, but if there was any franchise on television that could support this risk it would be *Star Trek,* and we felt we might be doing a little something for television."

• • • •

••••

Deep Space Nine: Season One

"*Star Trek,* by definition, is hokey," says Rick Berman. "We have costumes which are obviously science-fiction costumes and makeup, but it's very important to me that makeup and prosthetics don't look like masks from a really classy Halloween store. I don't want creatures to look like monsters. I don't want people dressed like 1950s sci-fi spacemen. People flying around in space suits and in starships going at speeds faster than light and speaking perfect English and nicely breathing the same air and walking around with the same gravity is preposterous, but it's a world we've all come to accept and use for a variety of metaphorical and entertaining reasons. Because the premise is somewhat outlandish, it is essential that the specific elements within it be grounded in very believable reality."

Defining the *Trek* philosophy further, Berman offers, "Our characters have to deal with each other in a very believable and realistic way. The hokiest elements for me are almost more so in story and script than anywhere else. The one major input I put into the scripts tends to be after they have been beat out and written and have to deal with dialogue and plot points. They deal with keeping the dialogue believable, logical, not melodramatic, not contrived, and keeping the stories clear. And keeping it from being swords and sorcery — which is a phrase Gene loved to use — and staying away from hokey and corny melodrama."

Following the *Deep Space Nine* premiere, the first year consisted of eighteen one-hour episodes, with shooting continuing through May of 1991. Once the pilot script was completed, Piller, along with his team of writer-producers, Ira Steven Behr and Peter Allan Fields (who had worked for a season on *The Next Generation* as well as classic television shows such as *The Man from U.N.C.L.E.*), began trading off rewrites of material purchased from freelancers.

"I think you can always take chances in the first season on a show like this," says Behr. "It's not like you're going to have six episodes and get canceled. You have chances to do things first year and chances in the fifth and sixth season, when you've done everything and you can say make it a Western or put them all naked in the holodeck. Those are the times to really have fun. The second and the third seasons, when suddenly you've made it, things tend to get a little bit stodgier on most television shows.

"As with everything in television, it's gearing your mind in a certain direction," he adds of writing for *Deep Space Nine.* "Writing is discipline; that's what everybody says. The difference between people who can write and people who can't, besides talent, comes down to discipline, which evokes a lot of other things as well. You have to realize the parameters of what you're doing. We sit around and come up with great thoughts and possibilities that cannot and will not be done. We have a good budget for this show, the highest budget on television. Nonetheless, we still don't do action all that well or a lot. We have some space battles, but the most action I've ever seen on *Star Trek* was [*TNG's*] 'The Best of Both Worlds,' which had shooting and running down corridors. So you're forced to do more cerebral and thoughtful and less intense television, which I guess kind of fits into the Gene Roddenberry world, which isn't people slapping each other in the face and drive-by shootings in space."

During the production meetings, Behr explains, is when he feels the impact of production realities limiting his ability to realize the story he hopes to put on screen. "You get cranky over the course of a season," he says. "Everything will kind of wear you down a bit, and we'll have those wonderful production meetings and hear those dreaded words, 'You haven't met pattern, and this show is above pattern and you've got to get rid of a scene.'" (The pattern budget is an average budget determined at the beginning of the season that allocates a certain amount to each department — ranging from visual effects to makeup and production design. While the individual budgets will change from episode to episode, it is imperative that it all balance out at the end of the season and not exceed the amount allocated by Paramount for the entire year.)

"The guest cast on *Deep Space Nine* is a lot different than that of *The Next Generation,*" Behr continues. "It's a space station. There are more speaking roles to show more people inhabit this environment. Unfortunately, the more speaking roles you have, the higher the budget is for guest cast, and you've got to make it up someplace else — the sets or opticals, and stuff like that. As I wrote my first script, one of the things I thought as I was going over it was dare he speak? Dare they speak? Well, dare I take out this optical so this person might be able to speak? It sounds fun and sometimes it is fun and it's creative, but by the twelfth show it's like, how many more weeks till the end of the season? It doesn't matter how you feel about the show and it's not about whether you love or hate your job. It's just survival."

Behr notes with some irony that while the original *Star Trek* is lauded for its allegorical exploration of then-contemporary sociopolitical concerns, the perception of the show has been altered by the passing of time. The same, he feels, will happen with *Deep Space Nine.* "I like the shows," he says. "I like to be proud of the shows. What I find with the old series is what you think you're saying, twenty years later turns out not to be what you were saying at all. The political winds change, and since we have to deal with things on such a fundamental, banal level, even when it comes to the quality shows, it's not really examining the human condition in a really deep way. I think none of us will know until they tell us what we did fifty years from now. We're trying to do an hour of television a week that we can be proud of and is entertaining and that can be thoughtful in some ways and, ultimately, leave enough behind us that could be sold at conventions. People will want to take the memos and the handwritten little notes we've sent each other and study them for hours and figure out what we meant. And if they find out what we meant, they should call me and tell me because half the time I don't know what I mean."

"[*Star Trek's* relevance is] one of the reasons for its longevity," echoes Alexander Siddig. "But also it's important that it's not pretentious. The stable of writers they've gotten try and get something

••••

underneath, but how many people actually connect *Deep Space Nine* with the problems of Eastern Europe at the moment? The writers try to do that, and sometimes it's not that subtle. For instance, there's a whole episode about how to deal with death or children or education. They're worthy scripts, but it's dangerous to get pretentious about it."

Anyone ever involved with *Star Trek: The Next Generation* or *Voyager* will tell you the hardest part of making the series has been finding writers who can craft stories that work within the parameters of the universe established by Gene Roddenberry. *Deep Space Nine* takes place in the same universe, but, thanks to the inclusion of non-Starfleet personnel as regulars, there's more leeway for conflict between the characters. As anyone who writes for *Star Trek* would attest, it's a godsend for those creating their adventures.

"We're always desperately looking for writers," says Rick Berman. "[For] *Deep Space Nine*, we went back in to get Ira Behr and Peter Fields over from *Next Generation*, and it came down to who was going to make up the remainder of our writing staff. In terms of both shows the rule is that we don't hire anybody, no matter who they are and what kind of reputation they have, unless they have written an episode successfully for us."

That particular rule grew out of the fact that many competent writers had been brought aboard *The Next Generation* before cutting their teeth on a twenty-fourth-century tale, often resulting in a short-lived tenure and an early departure.

"I've done television for eleven years, and there is no show more difficult that I've ever been involved with than *Star Trek*, on a number of levels," says Behr. "It's just difficult because you're not just trying to tell a story that could work or not work; you're trying to tell a story that works within very special, limited parameters. The only thing I can compare an episode of *Star Trek* to is another episode of *Star Trek*. The rules are so clear and it's such a unique kind of thing that in the third season of *The Next Generation* I would come up with ideas that I would think would be really good and work that other people would say you can't do. And I'd go, we can't do this, we can't do that, but we should do this and now it's maybe

not. All I know is now when I think of things, I think, how does it fit into the thirty years of *Star Trek* that came before it? I think that helps me from falling into the really, really big traps that it's easy to fall into, that you're going to reinvent the show. Every writer who's ever had an ax to grind, and there are definitely axes to grind, has complained about that. Having been through that fire, that ordeal, I'm not quite at that same place. I'm not saying we need more violence or we need more action or whatever it is, or we need to tackle something really, really controversial, because on the other side lies madness. The other way to go is, ultimately, you leave because it's just too difficult."

"In *Deep Space Nine*, these people don't know each other that well. Some are Starfleet, some are Federation, and the majority on the station is not," says Peter Fields. "It's the *Casablanca* analogy, a place with strangers coming in and out and all sorts of things going on. Our people are getting to know each other as well as the station, and anything that can go wrong will go wrong. If you think that makes it easier to write, it doesn't." Fields contributed to the *TNG* year-four euthanasia allegory, "Half a Life." A veteran of such series as *Hellinger's Law* (with Michael Piller), *The Man from U.N.C.L.E.* and *The Six Million Dollar Man*, he joined the writing staff of *Deep Space Nine* following the completion of *TNG*'s fifth season.

Behr admits he had first been approached by coexecutive producer Maurice Hurley during *The Next Generation*'s second season, when he was working at Paramount on the NBC series *The Bronx Zoo*, but rebuffed overtures to join the series when he went out to lunch with Hurley. "He told me what it would entail to work on the show, and I said 'Goodbye, thank you'," says Behr. "It was just very different than I was used to on series television."

Before discovering the *Star Trek* universe, Behr had worked on the short-lived ABC series *Once a Hero* and the MGM syndicated series *Fame*, which was, ironically, one of his first brushes with televised science fiction. "I did three years on *Fame*, which was a lot of fun and was also in syndication. We had no one looking over our shoulder," says Behr. "We got to do some wonderfully bizarre things on

the show, and the only time they gave us any trouble was the last show I was going to write after I knew we were canceled. It was going to be *Road Warrior* meets *Fame*. It was a show that takes place in the future, and you could only sing for the state. It was a fascist society, and we were going to have motorcycles going through the school and have Iggy Pop as the guest star. It was great, and I was in the midst of writing the episode when somehow MGM read somewhere that we planned to burn down the sets, which was a lie. We were going to trash them a bit, but it wasn't the last episode. We had one more after that, and they stopped me from writing it."

Behr was eventually persuaded by Michael Piller to join the writing staff during *The Next Generation*'s still tumultuous third season. He left at the end of his first year after penning "Captain's Holiday" and "The Vengeance Factor" and contributing to numerous other rewrites. "When I had left *Next Generation*, they offered me a two-year deal for the fourth and fifth season which, after going back and forth on, I decided not to take," recalls Behr. "I spent the last two years in feature development. I had three films in development, including one at Warner Brothers, but Michael [Piller] always kept the door open for me, and we'd go to a ball game every year or something like that. I got a call from Michael about doing 'Q-pid,' and he wanted to know if I wanted to do it. I came in, we met, went off, wrote it, stopped by one day to watch them film. It was written and filmed while I was waiting to do a rewrite on *Hicock & Cody* for Joel Silver. The whole process was begun and done while I'm waiting for notes, so it shows you the difference between the two mediums. The writing is fun. I would tell anyone that writing a feature is a helluva lot more fun than writing television. It's just much fuller and richer in certain ways, except for the writing. Television is a lot more fun as a whole because you're with people. You're breaking stories in a room, you're watching dailies every day, the set is there."

Shortly thereafter, Piller once again approached Behr about being involved with a spin-off series. "Michael had talked to me a long time ago about doing a sequel or a spin-off to *Star Trek*," says Behr. "He said, 'I don't know where you're going to be, but we'd love to get you involved with it.' I said, 'I'll think about it.' I found it interesting, and they kept talking about stuff like 'darker' and 'grittier' and 'more character conflict,' and I said OK, and he said, 'We're going to do this thing, do you want to get into it?' "

Ultimately, Behr admits, the final decision about whether to come on board involved monetary considerations, an important arbiter for any full-time writer. "I met with Rick and Michael and basically, though this does not sound like something people would be interested to read, it basically came down to money, career," says Behr. "I had three movies in feature development, but it just doesn't pay the money that I could get doing this. It was partially financial and it partially gave me a chance to step back and let these things happen and get in on the ground floor of something that's going to take on a life of its own and be very huge. There's something fun about that."

Although Behr acknowledges that years of doing *Star Trek* helped the writers avoid a plethora of traps, he believes there are roads not taken that *Deep Space Nine* will need to explore on its own — without having learned the lessons taught by previous *Trek*s. "Rick will say a million times the experience of doing *The Next Generation* is obviously coming in handy," says Behr. "We're in a better position than we were with 'Farpoint,' which was from scratch. But at the same time, it's a television show, and the farther we get away from *TNG* the more we will fall into our own traps and see things that don't quite work. We'll make mistakes, and it sort of gives you an opportunity to make choices, bad and good, and we'll make them both. The thing I learned is it doesn't matter if it's good or bad, it's whether it's good or bad in *Star Trek* terminology."

Behr hypothesizes that a lot of *Deep Space Nine*'s depth may be lost on viewers who resort to superficial analysis without looking at the deeper subtexts and drama inherent in the show. "I think the arguments are still based on who do you like better," admits Behr, "Picard or Kirk or Sisko? What do you think? Does that set look better than Ten-Forward? Odo or Data? Dax or Spock? That's the level of this. [The level of discussion is] not fundamentally much different. It's just different enough to exist as itself."

Like many of the writers who have toiled on the final frontier, Behr was not a hard-core *Star Trek* fan when he joined *TNG*. "The thing that I found about *Next Generation* is that [the writers] all really loved *Star Trek*," he says. "I think that gives a core of solidarity that kind of helps the show because it's one of those shows that really works best when people give a damn about the whole mythos of *Star Trek*. I watched the first three seasons of *Star Trek* when it came out back in the sixties and I was a fan. My older sister and I watched it every week, but when the show went off the air I never was a Trekkie, never cared much about it. I enjoyed the series when it was on the air from sixty-six to sixty-nine, but I would have been just as happy if Jeffrey Hunter had played the lead. I liked him a lot too. I never watched *Next Generation* except once or twice before I came on staff."

Early in the series' development it had been difficult to generate story ideas since outside writers hadn't been exposed to the series yet. As Behr tells it, they certainly tried anyway. "It's not like the *Next Generation* people even waited to see the show," says Behr. "I would like to take everyone out who has tried to write a story, written a story, got hired to write a story and got cut off on a story and buy them dinner. It's like, into the valley of death rode the six hundred. These people took a wing and a prayer, some of them went off before we cast the show, while the sets were being built, and all they had to read was this pilot with all these new characters and a new environment that none of them knew. It's tough to hit a home run under those circumstances as a writer. I would not like to have tried it. So it all winds up falling on our shoulders, and basically Michael was running back and forth between both shows."

For Behr, the adulation that millions of fanatical followers feel for *Trek* is difficult to fathom. "I think we all have fears that no matter what we do, *Star Trek* will overshadow it," says Behr. "It's something best not to dwell on, which is why I feel the level of it is too bizarre. There's a lot of good things out there in the creative arts, great books that have been written — superb books, interesting movies, interest-ing plays. People should be sitting around talking about *The Sound and the Fury* and going to conventions to try and figure out how someone can write that book or *Waiting for Godot*. That to me is popular entertainment, as popular as anything that deserves a level of recognition. [*Star Trek*] gets that kind of recognition because, basically, life is full of jokes, and we don't know and don't understand what goes on.

Behr is wary of those who would read too much significance into the meaning of the show, pointing out that even the series' postulated utopian ethos is inherently dystopian. "To get there you have to believe in a utopian view, and I believe in a more dystopian view only because I know what I believe in is what I see," says Behr. "I think *Deep Space Nine* is an optimistic show and is predicated on the thought that human beings are basically going to rise above the situation we currently find ourselves in. The flaw in the thinking is it doesn't explain how we ever got there, and that's too big an issue to ever discuss. Whenever McFarland, [the publisher that] does all those weird movie and television books, does a book about what *Star Trek* actually means and the deep philosophy of *Star Trek*, they'll figure out whether we were ultimately a utopian or dystopian show."

As the writers continue to ply their trade, they discover more about the world of *Deep Space Nine.* Even as viewers become more familiar with the new *Trek* universe, the writers continue to learn more about their creation as well. "That's the adventure of the series," says Peter Fields. "When I switched over to *Deep Space Nine,* it was at the countdown, and it was an adventurous ride."

While there was some erosion in *DS9*'s ratings after its record-shattering premiere, in its first year, *Deep Space Nine* drew consistently strong ratings in the syndicated one-hour drama category, eventually settling in just a few ratings points behind its sister series, *The Next Generation* — itself a ratings juggernaut whose numbers continued to improve throughout the course of its seven seasons.

"I was very pleased with the way the first season went in a lot of respects," says Rick Berman. "First seasons of television shows tend to be potentially very chaotic. The first season of *Next Generation* certainly was. The first season of *Deep Space Nine* was very peaceful in terms of the actors, the crew, the writers and the budgets. As far as the episodes, there are things about them that I loved and things about them I didn't love. That's the way it is. If we were completely satisfied with what we did, we wouldn't be doing what we do. We're always looking to make things better. What I was most pleased with is the fact that the concept worked and we managed to create twenty stories that I think all hang pretty well on the armature that we'd built, the backstory and the characters."

Ironically, although the show was rife with logistical problems during its launch, its start-up was devoid of longlasting strife. "I think basically what we had was money from Paramount, the support of Paramount, and we've been left alone by Paramount," states Ira Behr, who in the first season served as supervising producer. "We we trying to create episodes for the series without even having a pilot shot, which was very difficult. This was a show that was treated with kid gloves and given every chance in the world to make good. We were able to reshoot scenes in the pilot that didn't work, money was given, we could tinker with the sets when we didn't like the way

they looked. Being part of the *Star Trek* phenomenon has really helped because this wasn't a show where the studio saw a possible thirteen episodes with a pickup for a season, and then maybe it'll get two or three years. They saw this as continuing the franchise, so the start-up was not difficult on that level."

"I thought it was going to be much tougher," admits Alexander Siddig. "The last thing I was doing was working in Israel on the West Bank on the Gaza Strip with fake Israeli soldiers and real Muslim Palestinians around. That was tough and very hard work. There were grueling sandstorms every day — so compared to that, this has been fine. I've been lucky."

Unlike "Encounter at Farpoint," where the studio was dubious of the fledgling *Next Generation*'s potential, fearing that audiences would not embrace a new cast of characters and actors, *Deep Space Nine* has had the benefit of *The Next Generation*'s groundbreaking success, proving that a sequel series could become a greater ratings and, arguably, aesthetic triumph than the show that spawned it.

"I'm very proud of it," says Michael Piller of *Deep Space Nine*'s freshman year in space. "It's a really good television show. It might not be the cup of tea for everyone, and maybe it turns off some *Next Generation* fans because it has a little rougher edge around it, but I had a wonderful time doing it."

Before *Deep Space Nine*'s premiere, there was some concern that the premise of the show would prove too constraining. Many have attributed *Star Trek*'s long-term success to the *Enterprise* itself, pointing out that the ship has been the true star of the show. Berman and Piller, however, have proven that one does not need a starship to continue charting the *Star Trek* universe. Says Berman, "It's very frustrating sometimes not having the *Enterprise* to be able to take you to warp six and places unknown, but I think, considering what we have constructed and the situation with Bajor and the space station, the writing staff and the actors and everyone involved became more acclimated to it, and it has continued to get better. If you go back to look at some of the episodes of the first season of *The Next Generation,* you'll see actors who weren't all that familiar with their characters, and charac-

ters who weren't familiar with their relationships with other characters. These things grow."

"Good drama is good drama," points out Fields. "The thing that scared me at first was when they told me it's about a space station next to a wormhole. First, I didn't know what a wormhole was. Secondly, the *Enterprise*'s mission was to boldly go where no one has gone before, and from what Michael told me about *DS9*, we were going to boldly sit where no one had sat before. I didn't really get a laugh when I said it because I was serious."

Fields points out that he sees *Star Trek* less as a science-fiction show than a period piece, simply set in the future instead of the past. "One of the things that detracts from *Deep Space Nine* in the eyes of some snobs is that you see people in alien masks and garb that we conceived for twenty-fourth-century people and it looks like a costume parody to them," he says. "That sometimes does an injustice to the very real drama of things. There have been shows that had they been done in a suit and tie, assuming they could have been, would have been Emmy winners. If it's about people and emotions, which includes aliens, then you've got drama. It doesn't mean melodrama — and it can include comedic moments. What Gene Roddenberry wanted to do was to create a twenty-fourth century we could all work toward and look forward to, and I think he's done that. I don't think it matters whether you're writing it about guys in tight pants in Sherwood Forest or the Death Star somewhere. It's just good drama."

The key to creating *Deep Space Nine*'s "good drama" has been devising compelling characters, which included casting talented actors who took the show's premise seriously. It's an evolution that has continued throughout the years. "You create characters and you continue to give words to those characters, but the actors you hire bring an element to those characters," says Rick Berman. "The element that they bring week after week causes you to write slightly differently, and slowly, over the course of several years, the characters start developing in a much fuller and richer way. The actors start to get to know the characters better and they

••••

get to know what their relationships with the other characters are. The writers see this and feel it, and it's a real collective effort on our part and the part of the actors in bringing these characters to life, making them more complex and giving them new layers. I've been delighted to see that that's happened in a very positive sense with every one of our characters on the show."

"We were a midseason show that started gearing up about a decade before we had to start shooting," comments Behr about the considerable amount of prep time the series was given by the studio both on a creative and production level. "We had that luxury, and I think that helped. A number of characters changed. I think Bashir changed, Dax changed, Sisko changed, Odo changed, in terms of what Michael and I had basically talked about in the very, very beginning. We finally had to say, this is going to be a little different than we anticipated, how do we make it work?"

Even in the earliest stages, both Berman and Piller believed that *Deep Space Nine*'s advantage over *The Next Generation* was its ability to allow for interpersonal conflict. This feeling is echoed by first-year staff writer and former *Next Generation* intern Evan Somers. "In order to develop that kind of conflict over time and for it to end up not seeming contrived, they had to come up with high-concept material to create conflict between characters and guest stars on *The Next Generation*. It's very high concept, science-fiction oriented and very clever. We didn't need to try that hard on *Deep Space Nine* because we had conflict built in. We had a station that, if not monitored carefully, can shake apart at the seams, and we had controlled conflict even among our senior officers. It's more a matter of controlling potential conflict rather than seeking it out.

"I think the diplomatic/military chain of command aboard the *Enterprise* is more formalized," he continues. "We've got Quark, who is a merchant with questionable morals. We've got Odo, who adheres to no man's laws, just the purity in truth of seeking justice in the face of others trying to buy him out and compromise his values. He doesn't represent Bajor or the Federation but a higher set of

values. We've also got Sisko, who seems rather isolated there on the station, which is different from *Next Generation* — which is the Federation on wheels. There's no one on the *Enterprise* that isn't a Starfleet officer, so they all have the same goals and are willing to cooperate to the same ends."

Not everyone agrees that the *Next Generation* formula was any more constricting. Says Fields, "I know that's the popular belief. I don't feel that way at all. I felt it was as easy or as difficult to write a dramatic scene on the *Enterprise* as it is on Deep Space Nine. If you get two guys in a compartment of a vessel, whether it's Ten-Forward or on the Promenade, you have two people facing each other with a dilemma, a problem. It doesn't matter whether you're in space or in Disneyland or your mother's kitchen, it's either good or it's not."

By combining character development with action/adventure, *Deep Space Nine* quickly latched on to a formula that helped distinguish its first season, which was personally satisfying for those who worked on it. "It was a better ride for me than I had any right or reason to expect it would be," says Fields. "You get into a formula sometimes, the obligatory scenes. We haven't found that on this show. Every script is not fun, because some of them are too hard to be fun, but looking back at them is fun. There's been great diversity, and we've had a chance to explore the characters as much as I thought we could and find facets of them that I really think portend great interest for the future."

In assessing the first season, Michael Piller believes that the eighteen episodes can be divided into three distinct groups of shows, initially driven by the desire to define the characters. "The first eight to ten shows were specifically designed to elaborate and expose the audience to each one of the characters," he says. "If you went through them show by show, you could see one was an Odo show, another a Dax show, an O'Brien show, etcetera. We wanted to really define those characters in a way *Next Generation* never did the first two seasons. We wanted those characters known to the audience right off the bat. We couldn't do it all in the pilot. We did Sisko in the pilot,

we did some Kira in the pilot and then each one after that exposed more of the characters.

"The next group of shows," Piller elaborates, "is trying to show two things: how the ensemble will work together and how far the series can stretch its wings. Then you have a third part of the season, which is paying the cost for the first two thirds. The shows at the end of the season were not bad shows by any means but were designed specifically to pay back some of the bills that we owed."

"The character things are always the best to write," notes Ira Behr. "The character stories to me are always intriguing. It's tough to find character stuff in 'If Wishes Were Horses' or 'Move Along Home.' It doesn't mean they're not good shows, but in terms of the writing, that's probably why I don't like 'The Passenger' — it's not really that character oriented. I don't have that visceral hold on it."

"Zooming through the starscape is fine, but it doesn't mean anything," agrees Fields. "I've been lucky in that I'm not very good at the technical stuff, and the shows that I was able to do were basically either one-on-one shows or internal. A lot of *Star Trek* fans don't like that kind of thing and it's their prerogative, but I do that better than I would do a technical story."

Joining the writing staff first season was Robert Hewitt Wolfe, who pitched to *Deep Space Nine* after selling the *Next Generation* episode "A Fistful of Datas" and had made a major spec-script sale of a science-fiction feature screenplay. Later in the year, former *TNG* intern Evan Somers came aboard as a staff writer at the urging of Ira Behr after doing a rewrite of "Battle Lines."

"It was originally supposed to be just Robert [Wolfe] in my pitch meeting," says Somers. "Ira was supposed to run off to some meeting, but at the last minute, he said, 'Well, it's Evan, the trainee; we owe him this.' He had somebody waiting, [but] he held him in abeyance and took my pitch. I got very close, and there was one dissenting voice. I understood why he didn't think it would work and I left feeling there was a chance, maybe I would come back to pitch. I asked Ira if he could steer me in a more precise direction, and he loaded me down with the most recent final drafts of all the episodes he had. He said they wanted more character-driven than plot-driven material, and that I tended toward the plot-driven. The next week, he calls me up and offers me a rewrite job on 'Battle Lines.' Apparently he had really gone out on a limb for me. They had hired a writer to work on it and were disappointed with his initial drafts. It was coming up on the Christmas holiday, and the staff of three was tied up with other rewrites. Ira went on a limb and told Michael I could do a good job on it. I'm sure inside he was praying I could. They told me they were extremely happy with it, and I got a call a few days later from Michael, and he said they were going to make me an offer to come on staff."

The first one-hour episode of the season to go before the cameras was "A Man Alone," a murder mystery in which Odo is accused of killing an old enemy. Work on the episode began a week after shooting on "Emissary" was completed on September 29, 1992. Under the directorial reins of Paul Lynch, "A Man Alone" represented a completely different type of storytelling than the pilot. "It was a very soft episode and a soft character show with some serious conflicts in it," says Michael Piller. "I wrote it to be as simple and straightforward as we could do. I was thinking we had used all the effects and gags at our command in the pilot and now let's do a very simple character show and see how it plays. I also wanted to explore the idea of looking at *Deep Space Nine* as [Steven] Bochco looked at *Hill Street Blues* and that station — although I wasn't interested in doing continuing stories. I wanted to show that within the building structure of DS9, there were lots of different things happening at once with different stories that are crossing paths. I wanted to do an A-B-C story and see if we could keep them all going at one time, interacting and intersecting. That was the goal, and from a script point of view, I thought it worked quite well. On film, it flattened out a little bit. We were just right out of the pilot and were still freshmanlike people in that episode."

The story structure Piller refers to had been a cornerstone of *The Next Generation* in its fifth and sixth seasons, often combining a ship-in-peril story, an A story, with a B story involving some sort of char-

acter dilemma. The stories often proved untenable and melded uncomfortably, sometimes having nothing to do with each other. In writing his script for "A Man Alone," Piller knew that he wanted the stories to be intrinsically as well as thematically linked.

Ira Behr doesn't feel that the show's murder-mystery story line fell too early in the season for the then-infant series. "We talked about that because we are aware of these things," he says. "We felt that what was nice about being the third *Star Trek* series is that there is no such thing as early in the season, to a certain extent. You could just as easily say that 'Move Along Home' was a third-season show and that you don't make your characters seem that potentially foolish the first year, but this is *Star Trek*. You want to believe your audience has a certain amount of sophistication, that they'll accept what you give them. It makes sense to do a murder mystery with a character that happens to be a figure of justice and law. You want to get him involved with a murder, and what better way to show his feelings about his job?"

Although on *The Next Generation* "bottle shows" set exclusively on board the *Enterprise* became synonyms for "money saver," Michael Piller realized starting with the station-bound "A Man Alone" that even episodes set entirely aboard the space station didn't necessarily translate into budget savings on *Deep*

Space Nine. "I thought 'A Man Alone,' which was the simplest bottle show I could create, would be $100,000 under pattern, but it was $200,000 *over* pattern. The space station also has more aliens, more costumes, more extras than we anticipated, and they weren't budgeted for, so we were going over $60,000 over budget on every episode just right off the bat; on makeups and costumes and hair, and it was a nightmare. The pilot created costs that bled over because we had to rebuild the sets from the pilot that had been destroyed by the Cardassians, and those costs got accrued to 'Man Alone.'"

Offers Rick Berman, "This show is harder to produce than *Next Generation* was budgetarily. You have to fill the place up with more people, costumes, and prosthetics and makeups. They end up being very expensive. It's an expensive show to shoot."

Although the first eight episodes took place largely on Deep Space Nine, the ambitious "Move Along Home," in which several members of the crew engage in a surreal interdimensional board game, was severely affected by budget woes. "I would have thought based on my *Next Generation* experience that at the midway point of the season I'd be in great shape," muses Piller. "I knew this episode was going to be hugely expensive, but I thought that I'd have money to burn because we had done so many shows on the space station."

In the episode, an alien race that is cheated by Quark transports the senior staff into an alternative reality where they must successfully complete a game simultaneously being played out in Quark's bar. "It was a killer," says David Livingston. "It came at a point in the season where we were over budget. We didn't know how we were going to do the show. We had to make substantial changes in it, and yet it was still a huge episode. David Carson pulled it off. He is a terrific director."

The episode featured a number of intricate alien domains, including that of the conclusion, in which Sisko, Kira and Dax are almost swallowed by a chasm when Quark elects to have his players take the dangerous path. Says Livingston, "The cave sequence at the end with the stunts was amazing. We spent a lot of time planning it along with laying

• • • •

the air bags that they fell onto. It just took a lot of time and a lot of thought. We had a lot of discussion about where the chasm would be and the logic of how one person that's injured couldn't get across and the other two could. We ended up putting on a matte shot to see the chasm, and it took a lot of careful planning."

By the end of the season, after several costly episodes, including "Move Along Home," "Vortex," "Battle Lines" and "The Storyteller," the producers needed to scale back their elaborate plans to bring the remaining episodes in line with the limitations of the year's pattern budget. " 'Duet' was conceived as a direct result of that very consideration," says Peter Fields of his story in which Kira confronts a Cardassian war criminal. It continues to be among the most highly regarded DS9 episodes ever produced. "It costs a lot to make this show and everybody does their best, but you run over, and in your first year you've already had the pilot and the studio says you've spent this wad of money on the pilot, now simmer down. Of course we had, but when you get to show seventeen or eighteen, you want your last show of the season to have some scope. On the next-to-last show of the season, they said, 'Pete, can you do us a favor? Can you please write a show that costs nothing?' I said, 'Of course, be glad to,' and then you leave the office because you've said yes to your boss and you die a thousand deaths."

Says Nana Visitor, " 'Duet' was a wonderful episode. It was kind of harrowing to have to deal with that subject matter every day, but the harder it is, the more rewarding it is. I think artistically that's always the case. When you have limitations set on you, that's when you have to start being creative. I think everyone had done that and amped up the creativity just a little bit."

"If you came to me at the beginning of the year and said [that] by the end of the first season [we were] going to be out of money to do big, sweeping shows, I would have said, 'Get me a gun; check, please,' " reflects Ira Behr. "But it forces you to look at the show on a different level. I'm really pleased with the mix we achieved. I felt the shows we did should be DS9 specific. To me, the episodes, good or bad, are probably shows you

wouldn't do on Next Generation. These are DS9 shows, and I think those are good shows to do."

In addition to budgetary constraints, Deep Space Nine wasn't spared the script crunches that have always typified the Star Trek development process. Midseason, after going two months without buying a pitch, Michael Piller was forced to resurrect material that he had purchased for previous seasons of The Next Generation, including "The Storyteller."

"It was a script that was written for Next Generation on spec by a writer named Kurt Michael Bensmiller, who wrote 'Time Squared,' " says Piller. "I had this script in my desk for three years and I bring it out every season and I say should we do this script this year? Everybody reads it and they say let's not do it. They just didn't like it. I needed some shows and I needed to put some things into development."

"I like 'The Storyteller' a lot because it gave us a chance to do Bashir and O'Brien, and that's the core of that show," explains Ira Behr, who has since gone on to explore their relationship in some of DS9's most engaging episodes. "It also gives a nice little feel for the Bajorans and shows that Bajor is indeed a very strange place. There are things happening in those little hamlets and villages that are certainly not your average Federation attitude toward life, religion and spirituality. What I wanted to do was a show that explored the fact that you have two guys working together and one, Bashir, wants to have a really close relationship, and the other one, O'Brien, is saying back off. This was a chance for them to get together. Colm's quite good. It's basically The Man Who Would Be King, and he's a wonderful person to make king."

Bashir and O'Brien were paired again in the second season's "Armageddon Game." Explains writer Morgan Gendel, "We worked out a story where you see some different shades and genuine heroism from Bashir. It's a man-on-the-lam story, and basically Bashir and O'Brien are on the lam together. It brings in a little element of nuclear disarmament, future style. Originally, it was going to be Dax and Bashir, and you would see a new relationship grow, but they felt they had

played that beat one too many times and there were some other directions they want to go with that.

"O'Brien and Bashir turned out wonderfully together because O'Brien is so closed up emotionally. He's the Sergeant Friday of Deep Space Nine, 'Just the facts, ma'am,' but such a terrific actor too. If you can play a situation where he has to go against that and needs the help of somebody else, or by circumstance feels the need to talk about something emotional, that's neat. Bashir has to go the other way. He's not the one you want to get stuck alone with — he's going to talk you to death — and yet he has to go the other way in this story and be the strong, silent type a little bit."

The changes in the characters' second-season arcs reflected the producers' realization that they were departing dramatically from the way they had initially envisioned them. "Bashir was originally going to be a much more conventional character than what he turned out to be," says Behr. "I know there's been some question about Bashir being a different type of Star Trek character and I think it's taken the audience some time to get in sync with that. I like the character a lot. Originally, he was conceived as just this kind of cocky, good-looking, somewhat arrogant young doctor. What he is now is obviously more than that, whether for good or bad depends on your tastes."

Bashir wasn't the only character to vary from his initial design. "Dax has obviously changed a little bit," says Behr. "She's gone away from the Trill as Mr. Spock. In a way, Terry Farrell is enabling us to make her a more interesting Trill. She has a much more interesting sex life than she was supposedly going to have, and by building the backstory on Curzon Dax in 'Dax' it opened up the whole issue that she is not your usual Trill. She's someone who you'd find at two o'clock in the morning partying with a bunch of Ferengi sitting at the bar when the bar is closed, drinking and gambling and just having a good time."

"I remember thinking about her as sort of a placid, Spock-like character with great wisdom and insight and a broad view," reflects Piller. "Sort of Grace Kelly on a good day. But as we did more with her we got the idea that this is basi-

• • • •

cally a character in turmoil, with all these experiences, entities and memories, heartbreaks, disappointments and violations of trusts, which makes her a very complex character who is really, in some ways, screwed up. What she appears to be is a very placid twenty-eight-year-old woman, but in fact she has a lot of angst that comes from six lifetimes of experience. I don't know how any of us might do with that experience. She's more and more complex as we go on."

One of the most important characteristics for the series was its commander, now captain, Benjamin Sisko, who had to have his own strong identity while remaining true to the spirit of leadership established in the two previous incarnations of *Star Trek.* "In the first season we didn't spend a great deal of time on Sisko after the pilot," says Piller. "I don't think there has ever been in the history of *Star Trek* a better developed character from the starting point as Sisko was in that pilot. I don't think you have ever known as much about any of the other characters on *Next Generation* or the original as you do about Sisko. We said a lot about him and we had not explored him in other ways. That might have been a mistake, but I wanted to see him as an officer and as a leader of an ensemble. I wanted that ensemble to work and the other people in the show to get their hour."

Says Morgan Gendel, "I think Sisko is a good character. He's a real rock. To me, he's like Mary Tyler Moore, who was the center of *The Mary Tyler Moore Show,* where you had all these other characters squirreling around her — but you couldn't do the show without her. To me, Sisko is the center of the hurricane."

"He's a different kind of commander than Picard and a different kind of commander than Kirk," says story editor Robert Wolfe. "He is more true to the military. I think he's a good role model and a strong guy in his own right."

Avery Brooks's casting affected the portrayal of Sisko dramatically, making him much more of an officer in the Kirk vein than that of Jean-Luc Picard. "Originally Sisko wasn't going to be quite the commander that he became," notes Ira Behr. "We thought he was going to be more easygoing. Surprisingly, some of the feedback that we've been getting from

people in the military is that Sisko is the closest thing to a true military commander that has yet been on *Star Trek,* more than Picard, more than Kirk. They feel his relationship with his people is much more like the way the true commander of a sub or a ship would behave, which is not so much that he's by the book, but there's a formal behavior to him and an attitude and a strength that I wasn't quite thinking of."

Sisko's strong, assertive leadership is countered by his warmth as a father. "In the scenes with Jake, which I think are very successful, you see a whole different side to him," says Behr. "You see he is very soft and gentle. I really like those scenes when they're together."

"I think the importance of the scenes between Sisko and his son cannot be underestimated," adds Michael Piller. "I think it's what defines him as a different kind of Starfleet hero; it makes us see how warm a character he is, and I think those moments are gold. We need to build as many of those into the episodes as we can. The two of them are very good together, and it's a very important relationship."

Sisko's relationship with Kira has also grown in importance over the years. It's a dynamic that epitomizes the differences between the Federation and Bajor, which also illustrates the common bond that exists between the two peoples. Says Behr, "We've explored the relationship between Sisko and Kira in little increments and see there is a true friendship growing there. He is aware of her as a human being and not just as a subordinate or as the Bajoran liaison or first officer. Sisko has a lot of levels both as an actor and as a character. It makes me feel comfortable about that whole seven-year cycle of shows because I think there's a lot that can be done with his character."

Nana Visitor is equally pleased with the response to her character. "It's beyond pleased," clarifies the actress. "It's so satisfying to me when I've gone to conventions and women have told me their four-year-old daughter — or son — pretends that they're Major Kira; that's very satisfying because they're identifying with her. The fact that it's a woman and she's in charge is not even an issue anymore."

Other characters that have changed include Rene Auberjonois's Odo,

who was patterned on the traditional law-enforcement icons of pop culture. "Odo was supposed to be Clint Eastwood," laughs Behr. "Instead, he has turned into the angriest, most neurotic, most vulnerable man in the galaxy — which I think is wonderful. It's a great character, and he's just given us a lot to write. It took at least half the first season for us to stop telling freelancers when they came in to think Clint Eastwood, because it's *not* Clint Eastwood. It's Clint Eastwood on a very bad day. It's Clint Eastwood who's remembering his mother used to beat him and that he had no love."

"Odo doesn't want to be a human being or a humanoid," muses Auberjonois, the talented stage and screen actor who personifies him. "He is forced to take the shape of a humanoid because it's the only way he can function in a society that he is almost trapped in."

"I find Odo fascinating because he is the odd man out again," says David Livingston. "He is like the Data character and yet he is unique from Data in that he has emotions, but they are emotions that he tries to hide. There have been a couple of times we have touched them. I think that makes him very compelling. Now that's on the serious side. The way Rene plays the character with such humor and charm and stature, I think, makes all that interesting."

"My ego is very comfortable with the fact that I think the audience likes the character," says Auberjonois. "They love the fact that he is a shape-shifter, and I do too. I love to watch it happen."

Working as part of a large ensemble has taken some getting used to, though, as Auberjonois has often found Odo uninvolved with the week's action. "There have been some shows where I've had maybe two or three lines and I stood in the wings," the actor points out. "In the pilot, Odo appeared as a very sort of grim, rigid, unbending character with very few real emotions. Now the writers have introduced aspects of his personality that I think have developed the character and evolved him and allowed him to go places emotionally each week that is a joy to play. The scripts that focused on my character the most are going to be the ones that an actor thinks are his favorite episodes, but even scripts in which I really

Star Trek *aliens unite: Ethan Phillips (Voyager's Neelix), Rene Auberjonois (Odo) and Armin Shimerman (Quark) (copyright © 1995 by Albert Ortega).*

was not at all featured, there is always *something.* They always manage to find a new aspect of the character that I get to investigate, and I'm just tickled. I couldn't be happier."

Auberjonois also spends a fair amount of time in the makeup chair, where a prosthetic is applied to give his face the quality of the formless shape-changer that can't quite become completely human. It's a process, and anonymity, he enjoys. "I have no problem with the appliance," says Auberjonois. "I taught mask work at Juilliard and I studied mask work. I have performed often in masks, and what Odo wears is essentially a mask. I find masks liberating rather than limiting because you can cut through a lot of crap about what your face does. It's sort of a cosmic joke, as I say to my wife, that I spent my life making funny faces and now I'm in a situation where my face is completely covered. You can tell it's me, but none of my skin is showing."

One of the few characters to remain true to the template set down in the series' original bible was Quark, although his popularity has proven surprising as Shimerman has made the groveling barkeep the first palatable Ferengi character.

"Quark has legitimized the Ferengi for the first time in the history of the series," says Ira Behr. "We're able to do things with the Ferengi now and we can look at the Ferengi just as we would look at the Klingons. The Ferengi have more to them than just the fact they are greedy little buggers in space. I think that comes from Armin's playing of the character and not making him a total buffoon."

"Some of the people who created these guys weren't necessarily high on the Ferengi to begin with either," recalls David Livingston. "I don't want to overpsychoanalyze this, but the Ferengi are us. They are the side of us we don't want to see, and maybe that's painful to some people. Maybe it's painful to the fans when they see themselves in it. Initially, they weren't funny. That's one reason why Armin is so popular, because he can make those human foibles humorous and palatable. We see how silly we are as people. You look at Quark and you want to take him in your arms and give him a hug. 'Why are you such a little shit?'"

Notes Shimerman, "In the Middle Ages, they used to have the seven deadly sins, and in the theater they had people who would impersonate each of those

sins, whether it was sloth or greed or pride. I think that the Ferengi are a number of those old seven deadly sins being stuck together. What they did in the medieval times is what they do on *Deep Space Nine,* which is that by pointing out humanity's shortcomings, its nastier sides and greedier sides, we will learn to see how ugly that is and perhaps we'll learn to eschew it in our own lives."

Offers director David Carson, "The thing about Armin's Ferengi is that he seems to have more facets than we've seen in the Ferengi. Not only is he cunning and all, but Armin has a power to him that makes him more dangerous and more threatening even though he's still a sort of nasty little Ferengi. He has a side that's very hard and tough and would make anybody think twice about attacking this guy. Sometimes the Ferengi are played without that toughness and played as these crafty, sly, we'll-do-anything-for-a-buck types, and Armin is that, but he also has this tough side, which means it's wrong for him to go over the top in that way — and he never has. His instincts have kept him well back from the edge."

Like Auberjonois, Shimerman quickly realized that when you work in a large ensemble, your character won't always be in the spotlight. "As the first season came to an end, I had less and less to do," he admits. "And it was a lesson for me. I was sort of spoiled in the middle part of the season because there was so much of Quark being used. In fact, there was a period of time when I was complaining that I was being used too much, because the makeup was causing me never to get my twelve-hour turnaround. I was getting no sleep whatsoever. But I sort of got used to that and spoiled by that. And toward the end of the first season, when I began to work maybe one day an episode, I had some problems with that. I like work; I have a great time working. It's a lot of fun. So they were taking my play toys away from me, and I was a little distraught, mixed up and unsettled at that. And as the episodes went by, I came to realize that I am part of the ensemble and I'm also not part of the Federation. *Star Trek* is intrinsically stories about the core group, which on *Deep Space Nine* is Sisko, Dax, Bashir and O'Brien. Major Kira is certainly part of that command group, and Odo is needed for his qualities as well. Quark is not part of that Federation team, and so it's harder and harder. I became a writer for a moment and saw how difficult it was to include me as much as I was before, and that was an education for me. I came to realize that there will be episodes where, like [*TNG*'s Lieutenant] Worf, I'm central, where I'm very important, but for the most part I should get used to the fact that I'm the second team; I'm not the first team. I'm important on the bench, but I'm not going to go in and play every game."

Says Peter Fields, "Armin Shimerman has got Quark down, and it's very difficult to make a likable character out of someone like that. This is not the dance-hall girl with a heart of gold; this is a Ferengi. It's not that everything has to be for profit. He's got feelings, but they're not the same values we have, and Armin has done a wonderful job of making a ludicrous, on the line of being cartoonish, character into a genuine vehicle for dramatic as well as fun stories."

Another character that has taken the writers by surprise is Rom, Quark's brother, played by Max Grodenchik, who was the other actor initially considered for the role of Quark. "We liked both actors who read for Quark and we felt we needed the stronger presence to deal with Sisko on a continuing basis," says Piller. "At the same time, Max is funny, and we decided when we made Nog a nephew as opposed to a son, we needed a brother to be a son to, and I think it's worked out very well."

Much to Shimerman's delight, Grodenchik has become a regular staple on the show. "When Max and I were auditioning for Quark, we both thought that if we didn't get Quark, Rom would be a good part to play, and it's worked out that way. Max is playing Rom and we're having a good time together, and in 'The Nagus' episode he had a chance to kill me and fulfill whatever fantasies he had," laughs Shimerman.

Max Grodenchik adds, "I got to know Armin a bit during the audition process. He had so much more history with the show. I'd be lying if I didn't say I was disappointed that I didn't get the role of Quark, but it made me feel better knowing that Armin landed the role. I thought it was fair and I also felt he was a

better foil for Sisko since I watched some of his old episodes and thought he could play strong emotions very well. When they asked me to do Rom, I was thrilled. I had no idea that it would turn into such a recurring role. I don't think things could have worked out better even if I had gotten Quark because I depend on Armin a lot. I ask him everything. Sometimes he even answers me."

"I love the relationship between Rom and Quark," says Behr. "Even though we play it for comedy, it's not easy being a brother; brothers can be very different people, and yet you're tied together in this somewhat of a love/hate relationship. We envisioned Rom as a straighter character. He was just a no-good Ferengi when he was originally conceived and now he's become a buffoon and also a figure who is a man with desires. He wants to have a piece of the pie; he would love to own Quark's, and we're going to be doing stuff with him and Nog. Nog obviously has a hard time dealing with Jake's relationship with Sisko, which is so much better than what he has with his father. That's the other relationship that took us most by surprise. We had no idea what we were going to do with Jake, but Jake and Nog make wonderful B stories. It gives you a chance to do some humor and it's another level you're not used to seeing on *Star Trek*. Before on *Star Trek*, kids were Wesley [Crusher]; they were still Starfleet. These kids are anything but Starfleet — they're kids."

Behr firmly established Rom, along with Jake and Nog's relationship, in "The Nagus," an episode in which Quark is offered the chance to divvy up shares in the wormhole, prompting his brother to plot an assassination attempt.

One issue that provided a source of disagreement on staff and in viewer circles early on was whether *Deep Space Nine*'s stationary venue was too claustrophobic, warranting further exploration of the Gamma Quadrant, the unexplored territory on the other side of the wormhole. "By the sixth or seventh episode, I wished we had done more at the beginning of the season that took us off the station," admits Michael Piller. "That is part of the shakedown cruise. We thought this would be a different kind of series, where you'd have such an interesting setting and cross section

of personalities and aliens that you would want to be doing more shows that explored the community of the space station, that it would provide enough color to support those stories. In a sense, we were looking at that to see if it was going to work, and I think it does, but we have learned that we must mix in more trips through the wormhole and more exploration of the Gamma Quadrant and more trips down to the Bajoran moons."

But Ira Behr is quick to point out that the station offers ripe opportunities for exploration within its own confines. "I hear people talk about that and I know Michael talks about that and I just don't agree." Behr attributes the criticism of the show's immobile nature to the fact that the station's diversity has failed to be exploited to its full potential. "I think people are a little bit disappointed because the station has not done everything that we wanted it to do," he says. "I think we can continue to explore the workings of the station. We tried it a little bit at the beginning of the [first] season, which is, what is day-to-day life on the station like — besides ships coming and going? That's something we've continued to explore as well. There is a lot of stuff to do, and as long as we go through the wormhole and have those kinds of adventures, I think it's fine that we're stationary."

A *Star Trek* tradition that *Deep Space Nine* didn't adhere to in ending the first season was that of the cliff-hanger. One story line originally considered was a crossover between *The Next Generation* and *Deep Space Nine* in which both crews faced a menacing intergalactic invasion force (an idea that served as the template for the second-season ender in which the Federation squares off for the first time against the Dominion, a new threat from the Gamma Quadrant). When that story line was vetoed by Rick Berman, Michael Piller instead wrote a story that "bookended" the season, addressing several residual themes raised in the pilot involving the prophets in the wormhole and Bajor. This gave the season a story arc that hadn't necessarily been planned.

"That was something Michael was insisting on, and it was clever of him to want to do that," says Ira Behr. "It's a good Kira story and it's a good Sisko story. I know people wanted to have the big cliff-hanger and I love cliff-hangers, but they do tend to be a gimmick, and unless you can find a gimmick that's going to work for you, why do it? We did not have a way to do it successfully because of the budget restraints. To say you have to have a cliff-hanger is ridiculous, and I thought this was an interesting, intelligent show that does a lot for the series."

"I don't want to make cliff-hangers a way of life on *Star Trek*," Piller explains. "I didn't feel coming off the excitement of the pilot and the newness of the series that we had to do a cliff-hanger. If we had a wonderful cliff-hanger that we wanted to do, I would have been behind it. We came up with one that had to do with the Cardassians' deciding they wanted DS9 back, and we looked at it and what it would cost to do it right. It would have required a lot of money. Being a responsible producer, I didn't feel we could do a cliff-hanger, which traditionally costs at least $100,000 more [because of their larger scope and action], and add it to the overage we already had on this season. We already had a conceptually interesting episode that could be a season ender that gave a completeness to the season. 'In the Hands of the Prophets' is not just another episode, it's a season-ending episode that reexamines the relationship between Bajor and the Federation and the relationship between Sisko and Kira, and gives us some thought-provoking drama."

Ultimately, whether you're a fan of the new series or not, Rick Berman and Michael Piller conclusively proved with *Deep Space Nine* that *Star Trek* has a long and interesting life ahead of it even after Gene Roddenberry's death, carrying on a tradition that began thirty years ago with *Star Trek*'s premiere, "The Cage." By all indications it will continue for at least another thirty years. "Rick and I had a vision that was the outgrowth of Gene Roddenberry's vision, and we have stayed very true to his ideals in this show," says Piller. "We expanded the universe and put on a successful television show, and not many people in this life get a chance to do that. It's been very rewarding and it ain't done yet, but it was an awfully good beginning."

• • • •

••••

CHAPTER THREE

Deep Space Nine: Season One Episode Guide

"Emissary"

"Past Prologue"

"A Man Alone"

"Babel"

"Captive Pursuit"

"Q-Less"

"Dax"

"The Passenger"

"Move Along Home"

"The Nagus"

"Vortex"

"Battle Lines"

"The Storyteller"

"Progress"

"If Wishes Were Horses"

"The Forsaken"

"Dramatis Personae"

"Duet"

"In the Hands of the Prophets"

Episodes #1&2
"Emissary"
Original Airdate: 1/4/93
Teleplay by Michael Piller
Story by Rick Berman and Michael Piller
Directed by David Carson
Guest Starring: Patrick Stewart (Captain Jean-Luc Picard/Locutus), Camille Saviola (Kai Opaka), Felicia M. Bell (Jennifer Sisko), Marc Alaimo (Gul Dukat)

Commander Benjamin Sisko is placed in command of the Deep Space Nine space station, located in orbit of the planet Bajor. DS9, as it's more commonly referred to, has recently been vacated by the Cardassians' occupying forces. Upon his arrival, Sisko finds that his new command team is only just being assembled and learns that the religious leader of Bajor, Kai Opaka, has the last in a series of orbs believed to have been confiscated by the Cardassians.

Investigating the orb, Sisko is plunged into the first known stable wormhole, wherein exist the alien prophets who fear humanity and cannot understand the nature of linear existence. While Sisko professes the basic goodness of humanity to the prophets, Major Kira Nerys and the rest of DS9 are placed in a battle situation with a Cardassian warship.

• • • •

The creation of the series' two-hour premiere was the single most difficult undertaking of *Deep Space Nine's* first year. The telefilm's budget is estimated at over $12 million, a staggering sum for the medium.

The pilot, which tells the story of Commander Benjamin Sisko's assignment to the station along with the introduction of its key personnel, began shooting on August 18, 1992, with principal photography completed on September 18.

Director David Carson says of the extensive preparation for the show, "I'm one of those people who believe preparation is an immensely important thing. You can save time and money by preparing properly and you can also examine everything from all the angles with all the possibilities that have to be thought about. You can then produce a product that is far superior to one that is shot from the hip, on the run, as it were. Although you may be very fortuitous when you shoot from the hip because it's very excit-

ing, and it does get the adrenaline going, I'm one of those people who tend to think that overall planning is one of the most important elements. If you have the time to plan properly and carefully put together a jigsaw that tells a story, you'll have a much more effective result in the end."

One frustrating element of the pilot for Carson was the late casting of many of the principals. "One of the great weaknesses we had because our casting was left till so late was we did not have enough time to rehearse. Normally that doesn't matter in television because you're not dealing with things that are rehearsable, but this project was so complicated in some of its philosophical content and so difficult, it would have benefited all of us greatly and helped in the gradation of the characters through the scenes."

Carson, who had helmed a number of pilots, was particularly enthralled with directing *Deep Space Nine's* two-hour premiere. "It was an extremely enjoyable experience," he offers. "We all had a great time doing it. I always thought that the film was rare, even in *Star Trek* terms, because of its philosophical content and the way it went about solving the emotional problems that it had in it. The show was very unique and very intelligent. Such a complicated and complex piece of work that was challenging on so many levels made for an extremely complex pattern for the audience to follow. You would think from time to time that it was like something out of European television in its content. Is America ready for this? As is often the case, television underestimates its audience — particularly the networks. I think the success of *DS9* goes another step to prove the audience is challenged and titillated by exciting and interesting and penetrating work."

Unlike the situation inherent in features, however, in television, the director's wishes are subordinate to those of the producers. "You are given your cut and you hand it over to the producers, and they do what they feel they want to do with it because after all, in episodic television you're a guest and you're not the prime mover of the project as you are, often, in a feature film. You come in and fulfill what needs to be done and return the product to the producers and the writers, who then shape it as they want to. Part of

the job is not to be pigheaded about the way you see it. It's all a matter of taste, and there's no real way of saying whose taste is right and whose taste is wrong, except that one believes that one's own taste always is right."

Carson's career began in England, where he started sweeping theater stages, eventually becoming artistic director of the Leeds Playhouse and Marlowe Theatre in Canterbury. Later he began writing musicals and plays in London and "putting them on and winning prizes in various places." Carson soon found himself working in British television, where he did rock videos and daytime soaps before he began doing films that include the critically acclaimed Jeremy Brecht *Sherlock Holmes* series, which aired on PBS in America.

One of the rare delights on the series during the pilot shoot was Carson's opportunity to shoot on location. "We did three days on location on the pilot," says DP Marvin Rush. "We shot on the beach at Leo Carillo, which has been used by thousands of productions. We did a nice job with it; it was a beautiful beach on a beautiful day with two very attractive people." Additional location shooting took place at Disney Ranch for the teaser's holodeck sequence and a picnic between Sisko and his wife re-created by the wormhole aliens. "Disney Ranch had a covered bridge that's very beautiful, and we shot the picnic sequence where Sisko and all the aliens are talking there," he adds. "We also went to a baseball field right below the Jet Propulsion Laboratory in La Crescenta. It was a fairly secluded, private place where we could make a late-thirties baseball training facility for the pilot."

Carson was pleased to have the opportunity to take the show off the lot for the pilot. "I think it's great to be able to do that on any show," he says. "It gives it great width and breadth — if the show calls for it, and this show did — and it was very cleverly woven into the strangeness of the story, which was very good. It was good that they were earth locations and as down to earth as baseball games and stuff like that. I enjoy working on stages also if one is able to use them imaginatively, where they don't look like stages. I think a stage can be as effective as a location,

• • • •

even though sometimes people who work on stages all the time yearn to do location work."

"I thought we had a very ambitious pilot," says Michael Piller, who wrote the teleplay based on a story he developed with Rick Berman. "I think the script that I wrote attempted to do things you don't ever see on television; that's really what you have to try to do if you want to be doing interesting, creative things. We took a lot of risks, and it was very ambitious, and when it was all done and on film and cut together, I thought it was going to be a disaster. Rick spent week after week in the editing room recutting, trimming, patching and fixing and, ultimately, at my insistence, reshooting major sequences. The postproduction people worked twenty-four hours a day for weeks to make those things look good. When I saw it on film for the first time, I was blown away and realized it finally worked."

Some of the reshooting involved several scenes with Avery Brooks. "We reshot Sisko's first scene with Kira," Piller recalls. "We didn't reshoot the Sisko/ Quark scene — although I wanted to. We also reshot part of the scene with Sisko and Jake in their quarters. They were all first-hour things, and the reason was I felt

that Sisko was very unlikable on first meeting and that if we did not make him more personable we would lose the audience. I felt it was terribly important that he be a competent, respect-worthy commander even though he was troubled when he came aboard. We asked Avery to go back in with Nana and reshoot a couple of things and make a few changes that softened him, which I think helped enormously."

Quite a bit of footage was trimmed from the show's final cut as well, most of it taking place aboard the *Saratoga,* Sisko's ill-fated starship, which was destroyed by the Borg.

"One of the things that appealed to me about the script was that it was very unusual to tell a story like this," says Carson. "Essentially, it's about a Starfleet officer who does not want to take over the command that he's told to take over. And he bitterly resents the officer that is ordering him to do this to such an extent that his resentment is literally murderous, because he believes that [this officer] was directly responsible for the death of his wife. That's a pretty strong story you have there. I think it was felt by the studio that we should tilt the balance back toward more affability; certain things were taken out of the script, like looking for other jobs.

"Michael's stage directions emphasized that Sisko was constantly unhappy, restless, disliking the Cardassian architecture and everything that went with it. He was appalled with what was going on there but nevertheless was there to do his job. But if you tell a story about a guy who's just there to do his job, he doesn't have that spark of get up and go, and let's solve the mystery that you associate with a *Star Trek* story. I think Michael and Rick were rightly very careful to keep the basic elements that have always been very common to *Star Trek* stories and characters. It's a fascinating process of trying to make sure the facets of the character that are presented immediately to the audience are rich and yet immediately accessible, and in that sense, I think there is good in both ways of doing it."

Says Rick Berman, putting a positive spin on the changes he had the clout to order, "The stuff that we reshot is very normal on a pilot. We probably did less than most two-hour pilots. It wasn't a

question of making [Sisko] more sympathetic, as far as I was concerned. I think Michael and I had very specific ideas about what we wanted, and the actors were just getting their feet wet."

"I was very happy to reshoot it," notes Carson of the scenes involving the commander. "I'm one of those people who shoot the first day and the second day and then want to do it all again because as you go along you learn more about the people you're working with and what you can do with them. The bits that we reshot showed more of a military man with a problem. When we confronted the script to start with in terms of performance, the basic premise of the script was, here is this man with his son coming to take over a space station where he doesn't want to be and an appointment which he resents. At that time, there were clear indications that he was being offered a job back at a university on Earth and he was sounding like he was going to take it. He would have done anything to get off the station. He also hated Picard for what he perceived he did to his wife. When you take those elements together and you set off to tell a story about a man who is basically your hero and leading DS9 into other worlds and galaxies for what you hope will be a long series, it's very difficult to find the balance in performance between angst and unhappiness and yet project a personality that your audience would want to let into their living room every time he comes on the screen. It's a very fine line to draw."

In total, over twenty minutes of footage were cut from the two-hour broadcast of "Emissary." "I miss it all," says Berman. "There's a wonderful scene where Sisko goes back down to Bajor to return the orb to Kai Opaka that we took out. Cutting is horrible, especially when it's something so close to you as the pilot was."

"When you shoot a lot of stuff and commit yourself to doing it, you do miss the bits and pieces that are inevitably lost when you have to get it down to time," agrees Carson. "I think there are sections of ['Emissary'] I would like to see back. When you try and bring it down to time, everybody loses something they like. In the end, you have to separate yourself from your own wishes and go with what's good for the project. There are details of storytelling I liked having in there. I always liked the balance of the teaser at a slightly longer length with some more details of exactly how Sisko finds everybody during the Borg attack and where they all are. As far as television is concerned, the special-effects people did such a wonderful job that its excitement was sustainable for longer."

Because of the conceptually challenging nature of the teleplay, the myriad script changes made the shooting more difficult. "I think one of the reasons is that you're dealing with complex subjects," Carson says. "It isn't like doing *Married . . . with Children*. You don't actually know what subject matter you're dealing with as you're going along. The number of checks and balances a script has to go through are very great. When I arrived to do [*TNG*'s] 'Yesterday's Enterprise,' it was nothing more than an outline to prepare with. It makes things very difficult when the scripts aren't ready. At the same time, I never think it's a good idea to have the scripts ready if they're not very good. I've always thought that it doesn't matter when the script arrives, provided that it's bloody good when it gets there. If you sort of settle for it six days in advance because you've got to make a schedule, and it isn't that good and you can do it on time and on budget, I don't think you're really winning the game."

"Every time I see the pilot, I start to cry," admits Terry Farrell. "I must have watched it at least six times. Sisko loves Jake and his wife so much — and everybody understands what it's like to live a little bit too much in your past and to live with the death of someone you love that much. How to figure out how to live without them is very scary."

"I think we were all happily surprised at the response," adds Rick Berman of the universal acclaim that greeted the series premiere. "I knew that we had created a show that had wonderful potential and, slowly but surely, I knew that it was coming together and was going to be wonderful. I expected it would be successful, but I didn't expect it would be as successful as it was and I was a little bit amazed. We were in *Time* and *Newsweek*. I think that both Michael and I are the kind of people who aren't all that

comfortable with praise. As a result, we just sort of brush it aside and plunge on, which is what we've been doing."

Says David Livingston, "We were just flabbergasted. When I went to the screening here on the lot, I hadn't seen it with all the music and effects and opticals and I was blown away by it. To know the audience responded the way they did was very gratifying. Rick's and Michael's vision, and then David Carson's execution and the wonderful cast we picked, all clicked."

Episode #3
"Past Prologue"
Original Airdate: 1/11/93
Written by Katharyn Powers
Directed by Winrich Kolbe
Guest Starring: Jeffrey Nordling (Tahna), Andrew Robinson (Garak), Barbara March (Lursa), Vaughn Armstrong (Gul Dunar), Richard Ryder (Bajoran Deputy), Susan Bay (Admiral), Gwynyth Walsh (B'Etor)

Kira is reunited with former Bajoran underground rebel Tahna, who comes to DS9 claiming that his days of violence are over. At the same time, Dr. Bashir

Andrew Robinson, who portrays the recurring character of Cardassian tailor Garak (copyright © 1996 by Albert Ortega).

meets with Cardassian tailor Garak, who is a rumored spy. Together they uncover a plot involving the Klingon sisters Lursa and B'Etor, who are delivering an explosive device to Tahna. The former resistance fighter, it turns out, plans on using the bomb to close up the wormhole and remove Bajor from the influence of both the Federation and the Cardassians.

••••

Writer Katharyn Powers, who also wrote *The Next Generation*'s "Code of Honor," recalls, "As filmed, the story was structurally very close to my original conception. One significant difference is that Tahna and Kira had once been lovers, but Michael Piller decided that that was too clichéd. Also, in my original story, Tahna planned to continue his terrorist activities, but he changed at the end after Kira convinced him that he should work for peace. Then he was assassinated by his own people. It would be like somebody from the IRA deciding that they were going to work for the British government and try and make peace between Ireland and Britain."

"We didn't want your typical Cardassian in there," says director Winrich Kolbe of the creation of one of *DS9*'s break-out characters, the Cardassian spy Garak. "Obviously it would have been hard to put a real Cardassian soldier in a clothing store. Perhaps it would have been terrific, who knows, but what we felt we had to deal with was somebody abnormal — at least as far as the Cardassians were concerned. It was one of those things where I wasn't quite sure whether Andy Robinson would be the right guy. I had a different idea as to what type of actor I wanted, but Andy Robinson was available and turned out to be terrific. What I wanted, which shows how far off I was, was Sydney Greenstreet. I have to admire an actor who has to come in at three in the morning and stay in that kind of makeup for the rest of the day and still be able to give a performance."

Comments Michael Piller, "One of the things about 'Past Prologue' that bothered me was that Bashir's performance was in a very broad range — and this was newness. I believe we have strange aliens, strange makeup, spaceships, explosions and wormholes and costumes that are crazy, so that the people

••••

within them have to be entirely credible. If those people get too big in their performances, then you go into opera, and it becomes space opera, foolish and unbelievable. Patrick Stewart really led the way with us in *Next Generation,* which is to underplay. When you think you're going to go big, you come down, and it has much more power and credibility. You *believe* there's a space station or a spaceship like *Enterprise.* The biggest problem with the early shows is that some of the performances were too big or too restrained. We had to find the even tone for the ensemble to work together. Our voices weren't quite right, and the performances were uneven. The first episode hurt the character of Bashir because he was so broad in those scenes with Andy Robinson that he looked like the greenest recruit in the history of the Starfleet, and that hurt him for two or three episodes. If we were shooting it today, his performance would be much more credible, and he wouldn't have the same reaction from the audience that he has now."

Klingon renegades Lursa and B'Etor, of course, were introduced in the *Next Generation* two-parter "Redemption," and were used as part of an attempt to tie *Deep Space Nine* into existing *Trek* continuity. The characters eventually perished in battle against the *Enterprise* in the feature film *Star Trek: Generations.*

"The creative synergy allows you incredible opportunities," remarks Piller. "It's interesting how we used them. Essentially, we had a story and, in the case of Lursa and B'Etor, we said, 'Hey, we've got a real kind of *Casablanca* spy story and we need someone to really be doing double dealings and bringing money and doing gun exchanges; why don't we use the Klingons — and use those characters that we love so much? It works out just fine to use those guys because then there's a connection and an identification. There's a backstory, there's a history, and all of these things make for a much richer series."

Says Ira Behr, "There's no doubt that people like [*TNG* characters like] Lwaxana [Troi] and Q and Vash and a bunch of others. They have a certain life to them as characters and an energy that certainly helped *The Next Generation* and helps us too. The characters that don't have to be Starfleet and don't have those

strings we have attached so often. A lot of times you have people performing those characters who take a lot of relish in doing them, so they're fun to have come back."

Piller doesn't feel that in exploiting *The Next Generation's* voluminous history *Deep Space Nine* has an unfair advantage, appealing to those already familiar with *Trek* lore. "You have to look at the shows themselves," he insists. "There's no question in my mind that conceptually, each of these shows would work because they're about the new characters. In 'Past Prologue,' there's a moral dilemma for Major Kira where she has to confront her loyalty to her past life and what her new life is going to be. It's really about her. It's illuminating our new characters. As I've always said, the guest stars are catalysts. There have been times when I have not been satisfied, more prior to my arrival, that the shows have been about the guest stars, but ultimately the shows that succeed are when the guest stars are serving as catalysts to illuminate our characters."

Episode #4
"A Man Alone"
Original Airdate: 1/18/93
Teleplay by Michael Piller
Story by Gerald Sanford and Michael Piller
Directed by Paul Lynch
Guest Starring: Rosalind Chao (Keiko O'Brien), Edward Laurance Albert (Zayra), Max Grodenchik (Rom), Peter Vogt (Bajoran Man #1), Aron Eisenberg (Nog), Stephen James Carver (Ibudan), Yom Klunts (Old Man/Ibudan)

Shortly after having a confrontation with Odo, a Bajoran (Ibudan) once arrested by the constable for murder turns up dead, and all eyes turn to Odo. While Odo attempts to overcome these suspicions and a tide of racism rising around him, Bashir discovers DNA samples in Ibudan's quarters that may reveal the identity of the true murderer.

At the same time, Keiko O'Brien attempts to launch a school for the children of DS9, and a friendship is forged between Jake Sisko and the Ferengi youth Nog.

••••

In explaining the original story premise that he pitched to the *DS9* staff, writer Gerald Sanford says, "I thought it might be an interesting show to have

someone accuse Odo of being a Nazi of the Cardassians who had murdered people. He's accused of this, although we find out later it's not true. So what I wanted to do was a story about what one's false accusations could lead to. Michael liked the idea, and we developed it. The more we talked about it, the more we came to a point where someone did accuse him of murder. Then we came up with the notion of using the holosuite where a client is killed and Odo is the only one who could have gotten in and gotten out. People blame him for it, and how does he get out of it? In my original version, the only one who believed Odo was innocent was Sisko, but even he starts to doubt him. He has to really go out on a limb, and finally there's so much evidence that goes against Odo that he too has to believe it. Even his own crew began to say, 'Hey, when you're caught up in the regime, you begin acting like the regime.' I really did want to say something, but it was totally changed around.

"When I first came on the show," Sanford elaborates, "they had sold it, but I was one of the first writers they hired, and they were trying to figure out how the show should develop. I came in with seven or eight ideas, and they liked three or four. Then they said, 'Gee, maybe we ought to do a sort of *Grand Hotel*–style episode and do a lot of vignettes all taking place around the station. I did one treatment the old way, using about two basic stories, and then Michael Piller said, 'Let's pick three more of these stories and make it really like *Grand Hotel,* a lot of things going on at once.' So I wrote the story up with about five of the vignettes and really never heard from them again."

Says Ira Behr, "I always thought the ending [of "A Man Alone"] was weak, with the *Mission: Impossible*–like taking off of the mask. There are things I find weak about some of these shows that have nothing to do with the writing. I felt that show was hurt by the pacing. Many of the shows at the beginning of the season lacked pacing. I liked what we tried to do with the character of Zayra, which is show a character that would be a problem for us to face on a semirecurring basis. That never really worked out. Plus we never brought him back either."

" 'A Man Alone' is a very soft

••••

episode and a soft character show with some serious conflicts in it, and it's a wonderful show that defines our characters in ways they weren't in the pilot," says Michael Piller. "It was felt it was too soft to be the first hour, so we decided that 'Past Prologue' would be more appropriate to follow the two-hour since it had a better action quotient and was a real opportunity for us to continue the themes that had been set up in the pilot and to see what happens when a terrorist comes on board. Oddly enough, I thought that in post the addition of music and effects lifted 'Man Alone,' where they didn't really help 'Past Prologue' much."

"It was the first chance to see Armin and Rene work together as a wonderful team and it was quite a compelling story," says director Paul Lynch. "It was the first show we shot, so they were a little more relaxed about schedule and as the show went on, they tightened up. It gave one a chance to explore what the *Deep Space Nine* series was about."

One of the biggest recurring problems for the show's craftsmen early on was Odo's unique makeup design. "The real trouble with Rene's makeup were some teething problems. What was on the air was pretty satisfactory, but it took a lot of time and effort and a moderate amount of grief to get there," recalls Marvin Rush. "The biggest problem was that it wasn't consistent from day to day. Some days it was more on the target than others. It was just a daunting task. It's not an easy appliance; you're asking for a smooth face. Rene is probably the most challenging one, and it has taken some extra time and care."

Episode #5
"Babel"
Original Airdate: 1/25/93
Teleplay by Michael McGreevey and Naren Shankar
Story by Sally Caves and Ira Steven Behr
Directed by Paul Lynch
Guest Starring: Jack Kehler (Jaheel), Matthew Faison (Surmak Ren), Ann Gillespie (Nurse Jabara), Geraldine Farrell (Balis Blin), Bo Zenga (Asoth), Richard Ryder (Bajoran Deputy), Frank Novak (Businessman), Kathleen Wirt (Aphasia Victim), Lee Brooks (Aphasia Victim), Todd Feder (Federation Male)

A Bajoran weapon designed to be utilized against the Cardassians when they occupied the space station is accidentally triggered. The result is a disease that sweeps through the station, rapidly infecting the crew and making them think and speak gibberish. Before it's too late, Kira must find the Bajoran scientist who helped develop the weapon eighteen years earlier and retrieve the cure.

••••

"We had this premise for over five years at *Next Generation,*" says Michael Piller. "It was written by the same person who wrote 'Hollow Pursuits' for us, and we had always been attracted to the idea that you could suddenly lose the ability to use language to communicate, and how people are able to communicate with each other. It was a new series, and you're desperate for stories so we gave it a whirl. We used the virus as a MacGuffin. It wasn't a great episode but had some wonderful moments in it."

"It was a rewrite I did after having written 'Quality of Life' for *Next Generation,*" says the show's former science adviser and *TNG* staff writer Naren Shankar. "It was a little rough, and I had trouble believing in it initially. In some ways it's kind of a cool idea, but what ultimately was never communicated was the sense of panic and helplessness which would accompany this sort of virus. You never saw people freaking out, which is what I think you would see a lot of if you suddenly thought nobody in the world could understand you. I know I would get upset. It just didn't come across, and you just walk through an empty station of quiet people instead of a rioting station of screaming people with flames coming out of things and people just going bananas. Obviously, from a production standpoint you can't do that, but it was unfortunate. It was a high-concept show, and you always run the risk that when you go to write it down there's not as much there as you think there might be. I liked the teaser and the ending, where we broke the ship away from the docking ring before it exploded."

"The inability to communicate was fun, but I don't think it went far enough," says Ira Behr. "It became 'Let's see who's going to get aphasia next,' and I thought that was a bit of a problem. Sisko's scenes with the kid were nice, and

the scenes with O'Brien were well done, although the pacing in the teaser was lethargic." As for the meaning of "Babel"'s aphasic babbling, "That's for the scholars," he offers, wryly noting that the actors were not allowed to improvise it on the set. "I don't think computers are powerful enough to pick out the secret messages that are in 'Babel.' We did not want the music of 'Babel' to be tampered with because when you do that on the set, there's a chance that by mistake you get some coherency in it, and we wanted it to lack even a hint of coherency — nor did we want anyone to tamper with the secret of the universe contained within that dialogue."

Episode #6
"Captive Pursuit"
Original Airdate: 2/1/93
Teleplay by Jill Sherman Donner and Michael Piller
Story by Jill Sherman Donner
Directed by Corey Allen
Guest Starring: Scott MacDonald (Tosk), Gerrit Graham (The Hunter), Kelly Curtis (Miss Sarda)

O'Brien uses a DS9 tractor beam to pull in a damaged vessel piloted by a reptilian alien who identifies himself only as Tosk. After an uneasy beginning, O'Brien and Tosk establish something of respect and friendship for each other. Things grow darker, however, when a group of armed aliens arrives on DS9 determined to capture Tosk.

Tosk, O'Brien and everyone else are surprised to note, accepts his fate easily, and the truth is soon revealed: Tosk and all of his people have been created specifically to be hunted as sport, and their role in society is considered an honorable one. Recognizing the reality of the situation, O'Brien pulls a few mechanical strings that allow the hunt to continue.

••••

"This was one of my favorite episodes of the season," says Michael Piller. "The real problem was to make it credible, and that's what I had to address in my rewrite. The relationship had to be strong enough that O'Brien would bond to this character enough to go against his Starfleet responsibilities."

Scott MacDonald, who played Tosk, returned on *The Next Generation* to

••••

Colm Meaney as Chief Miles O'Brien (copyright © 1995 by Albert Ortega).

play N'Vek in the sixth season's "Face of the Enemy," while Gerrit Graham materialized on board the starship *Voyager* as Q2 in the second-season *Voyager* episode "Death Wish."

" 'Captive Pursuit' was my favorite show of the first half dozen for all the obvious reasons," says Rick Berman. "Everything worked out well, and the character of Tosk was a creature who was immediately both fascinating and sympathetic. The relationship that developed between him and O'Brien was charming."

Comments Ira Behr, "It was a good show for O'Brien and it was a good show all the way down the line with the guy running around in the goddamned lizard suit. I immediately have that against it, but the whole point, from the very beginning, was we were in love with the idea of someone coming through the wormhole after this creature that they had basically bred for this hunt, and he lives at a level that we usually don't live on. We live on a much duller, plodding level of life experience. The fact that O'Brien gets involved with him I thought created a nice relationship. The whole episode was very well done."

Of all his designs so far for *Deep Space Nine,* makeup maestro Michael Westmore numbers Tosk among his personal favorites. "The scale system on his body is based on an alligator," he notes. "It's a scaly skin structure that's over all exposed skin. His sleeves are rolled up to his elbows, so his arms are scaly all the way up that high. We've got hands on him, a full head. I made a small set of dentures that go in his mouth, not to give him fangs but to break up his nice tooth line, and he's wearing contact lenses. It works really well, the way the rubber fits his face, around his head, and the way he twists his neck. He's able to put the stuff on and forget that he's in rubber. He's able to perform as if this were what he really looked like."

Ironically, the makeup was produced under a schedule so tight that it would seem to work against good results from any less talented makeup artist. "The first rubber was run on Wednesday," says Westmore, explaining the tight schedule within which he is often forced to work. "The second head that we were able to use came out on Thursday. I started to paint it Thursday night at six o'clock and finished painting it at nine. We were back in at five Friday morning, and the head was still wet. It was so fresh there was moisture inside the rubber head. We stuck it in the wig oven for a little bit just to dry it out. The rubber still wasn't fully dried out when we put it on the actor and he went on the set to work. That's the time frame that I am under. That's what I enjoy about the show — that we don't have tons of time. But the character turned out to be gorgeous."

Episode #7
"Q-Less"
Original Airdate: 2/8/93
Teleplay by Robert Hewitt Wolfe
Story by Hannah Louise Shearer
Directed by Paul Lynch
Guest Starring: John de Lancie (Q), Jennifer Hetrick (Vash), Van Epperson (Bajoran Clerk), Laura Cameron (Bajoran Woman), Tom McCleister (Kolos)

Vash, an archaeologist first introduced in the *Next Generation* episode "Captain's Holiday," is found in the Gamma Quadrant by a DS9 runabout.

Sisko is curious about how she got there, but Vash isn't talking, merely expressing her interest in having Quark auction off artifacts discovered on her adventure.

Shortly thereafter, though, Q appears, determined to convince Vash to rejoin him in their exploration of the cosmos. She refuses, and, partly in anger, Q takes it out on the DS9 crew, taunting Sisko in particular. While all of this is going on, the station begins to lose power. Everyone suspects Q is playing more of his games, but he insists that he's innocent while simultaneously refusing to help. Eventually it is discovered that one of Vash's artifacts is actually an alien creature that has been absorbing energy from the station.

••••

"It was a Vash episode to begin with," says Michael Piller. "We go in and find Vash and bring her back and we were struggling to find some focus for it. I said, 'If you're going to make it Vash, why not bring Q along?' because it's the natural way to get Q onto DS9. We wanted to do a Q show and yet we were very serious about doing it in a credible way. To have him come on and say, 'Look, is this the new show?' is silly. But this seemed to be a justifiable way. It gave us an opportunity to have Q play some games with some of the new characters and to see how Sisko would react. It was fun."

Staff writer Robert Wolfe wrote the teleplay based on an idea by Hannah Louise Shearer, another veteran of *The Next Generation*'s troubled first season. Her story didn't involve Q, but rather dealt with discovering an archaeologist in the Gamma Quadrant with an artifact that turned out to be an egg.

"They invited me in to pitch *DS9*, and I pitched a variety of things, none of which really went anywhere," admits Wolfe. "One of my ideas had some small parallels to the basic story they had for 'Q-Less,' and then they hired me to write that episode. There was already a story, but Q wasn't in it so I put Q into it and then wrote the teleplay. Q's a lot of fun to write in general. It was helpful in a way, because when I pitched the stories, they couldn't tell me who was playing the various parts. When I was just starting to write the episode, they were just beginning to shoot the pilot. I hadn't seen any-body, which was difficult, so it was kind of nice to have some familiar characters to work with and it was fun to explore the new characters through familiar faces."

Wolfe had pitched a Q story to *The Next Generation* that hadn't been bought in which Q turned Picard, Data and Troi into officers on a Romulan ship. "The reason it didn't go is the way I had them do it: there was no Romulan makeup involved; they weren't possessing the bodies. The visual gag was the same as *Quantum Leap*, where we would look at them and see them as themselves and maybe in a reverse shot we might see them as other people completely, but they didn't want to step on *Quantum Leap*'s toes."

Armin Shimerman joked that when veteran Trekker John de Lancie showed up on the sets, he projected the attitude that he was the star and the cast members were the guest stars. "It was interesting to watch the two of them together," he says of watching Avery Brooks's and de Lancie's characters' verbal jousts and literal fisticuffs in a Q-created bout of pugilism. "It was an interesting dynamic because Avery is the lead and so he has the responsibility and that recognition in himself. Yet John de Lancie came on the set with his own agenda, which is that he has played Q quite often and is very familiar with his end and thought of us sort of as the new kids. We were the regulars, he was the guest star, but he felt like he was the regular and we were the visitors."

"I love that Armin quote," says de Lancie. "I think that one of the things I had to be careful about is I couldn't be so chameleonlike as to be a different character just because I was on a different set. I had to carry on in the way that I know works for *Next Generation* and carry it into the new show so it would be seamless in a way. There would be kind of a bigness about Q that maybe permeates the tide pool."

In many ways, de Lancie seems to be the personification of Q, but that's a result of his success in making his transformation into the character seem so effortless. Says the actor, "I always say the words as written, but if there were twenty people who all had to come up to play the same scenes, there would be twenty different interpretations of it. Do I put myself into the character? Yes. Is the character me? Who knows? It's a melding, and that's the point of acting."

"It was only their seventh episode, so it was a little different than working on *Next Generation* in terms of working with new people," says actress Jennifer Hetrick, who returned to play Vash. "The environment was also very different in terms of the whole story line, where you have many more different aliens and characters. It was very colorful, and I kind of think of Quark's as the *Star Wars* cantina. The characters are also a lot of fun, and I liked working with John again and continuing the relationship between those two characters."

"She and I have worked a couple of times together other than *Star Trek*," says de Lancie, who last worked with Hetrick on ABC's *The Young Riders*. "We just spent a lot of time together trying to get our lines down, of which there were a lot. While it was a nice show, the urgency of my involvement and the kind of motivation behind it that I'm in love [with Vash]

Jennifer Hetrick, who guest starred in a first-season Deep Space Nine *episode reprising her* Star Trek: The Next Generation *role of Vash (copyright © 1996 by Albert Ortega).*

wasn't explored in a substantive way, which leaves you with a thin thing to play. As a result, the style, the quips and the panache with which things are done become very important."

Director Paul Lynch comments, "That's Q's modus operandi and that's why it was fun to do. They really did get down that fast-paced, fun stuff I like. There was a real push in order to do it in the time we had, because comedy takes time to make it work. If the timing doesn't work exactly, it doesn't work at all, and that takes take after take. We were always running against production conflicts because of that. To a degree, it's a little like *Moonlighting*, except that the reason *Moonlighting* sometimes took between twelve and eighteen days to do a one-hour episode was the amount of time it took to work out the timing in long sustained scenes, which is what you want. You want the scene to play without cuts, and that goes back to Howard Hawks, where you would just play a scene right through and let the camera watch it. That's what makes it funny. That takes a lot of time to rehearse, to stage and to shoot because if you're a beat off at any given point, you have to go back and do the whole thing over again. That was a hard show, but comedy, as they say, is always the toughest thing to do."

"John de Lancie said it was the funniest and best material he's had as Q," said Ira Behr. "I worked a lot on that episode. Michael likes to give challenges out to the staff and the challenge in 'Q-Less' was to write a scene that took place entirely in Vash's quarters: 'I want to take that as long as you can go. Make it as funny as you can and keep people coming in.' I think it worked extremely well. I still have the bruises on my forehead from banging my head against the wall from the tech part of it. The line 'Picard would have solved this technobabble' was a line we wrote with great glee because at that point we hated the goddamned technobabble. At the time, I thought it was going to swamp the episode, but then Rick and Michael started cutting it all back.

"At the beginning," he adds, "when we talked about doing this sort of stuff, we'd go slinking off saying that's a crutch. Is that going to be a good idea right off the bat to be thinking in those terms, like what can we do with Mrs. Troi or Lore, Data's brother? But after watching those early shows, you realize this show is so different from *Next Generation* in terms of its feel that we're not worried about that. We could even bring Picard back if we wanted, not that that's anything we're thinking about. It's a different show."

Episode #8
"Dax"
Original Airdate: 2/15/93
Teleplay by D. C. Fontana and Peter Allan Fields
Story by Peter Allan Fields
Directed by David Carson
Guest Starring: Gregory Itzin (Tandro), Anne Haney (Judge Renora), Richard Lineback (Selin Peers), Fionnula Flanagan (Enina)

Dax is charged with the murder of General Ardelon Tando — thirty years earlier. Sisko realizes that the charges are actually being leveled against Curzon Dax and not Jadzia (the current Trill host), and he refuses to allow her to be taken as a guilty criminal. What follows is an extradition hearing convened to determine if the host body of a Trill can be held responsible for the alleged crimes of the symbiont.

Jadzia, who has all of Curzon's memories, refuses to say much of anything regarding guilt or innocence, and it appears that she will be extradited, when the wife of General Tandro enters the proceedings, announcing that it would have been impossible for Curzon to have murdered her husband because Curzon was in bed with her at the time.

••••

Not only was "Dax" the first opportunity for the writers of the fledgling show to develop one of their most enigmatic characters, it was also an opportunity to do a smaller episode unlike the budget-busting shows that had preceded it.

Certainly, a moment that strains credulity is when Odo cons Quark into turning over the bar for the extradition hearing. It's hard to believe that a station the size of *Deep Space Nine* doesn't have a conference room. Counters Michael Piller, "We wanted to put it in the bar because it's an interesting set. We could have built a room for this to occur in, but

the truth is we had shown the space station destroyed in the pilot three weeks before, and there's no reason to believe there's a lot of usable space. Slowly, it's coming back on line; it was not a production requirement."

"There isn't a big conference room," says David Livingston. "Everything is used for commerce or it has cargo bays and stuff. The bar had chairs already and wasn't a clothing shop or some other mercantile place. We never discussed building [another room], and it looked OK. It saved us $50,000."

Says D. C. Fontana, a story editor on the original *Star Trek* as well as an early writer for *The Next Generation,* who wrote the first draft, "I participated very little. It was Peter Allan Fields's original story, and I did the teleplay and he rewrote me and we split the teleplay credit. The only thing I think that is interesting is that I am now the only writer who has written for four of the series. That's about all I think is interesting."

"It was a delightful time working together," says Piller of Fontana, whose agent had suggested her in response to queries sent out by Piller. "She had real trouble finding the Trill, as she would be the first to admit, and we had to really go back and put that into the script."

"I loved the scene with Avery," says Terry Farrell. "It was interesting working with him since neither of us talked to each other at all [off camera]. Normally we totally joke around and laugh, and I run around and chase him and try to stick my finger in his nose and pinch his butt, but it was really weird shooting 'Dax.' I wasn't talking to him, and he wasn't talking to me either. His character was angry and frustrated with my character. It's a rare moment when you do method acting on this show, and it's fun to pull out those techniques when you can. It makes it more interesting as an actor to do. It was the first time all of us found out that much about a Trill, including myself. I learned more about my character reading that episode than [from] anything else I had read."

After the enormity of the pilot, "Dax"'s intimate tone was quite a dramatic change for director David Carson. "I can do that too," he says laughing. "My background is in the theater, and I've

worked with actors in many different situations. Words, performance and character interpretation are things that I think very often can carry a story by themselves. If you have a good story and it's all set in one room and you have two or three or four good actors who can interpret that story well and make it fascinating, you don't need locations or huge sets or spaceships whizzing around. You can tell the story very simply on that basis. I was very pleased to do that; I thought it was a very successful show, marrying camera movement to performance and using the lighting to express the feelings of the piece. It worked very well as an intimate drama and in the courtroom scenes. I haven't done *L.A. Law* for nothing."

"A small episode, yet a very well-done one that stands up to anything that was done first season, to an extent," says Ira Behr. "It was one of Sisko's best shows [in the first season]. I think it showed him in a very good light. I liked the Odo stuff and I thought the ending when the wife comes back was touching. Being a Trill must be very difficult; it must be incredibly schizophrenic. I think it's good that we play a little of that instead of the initial Mr. Spock total control. I don't think Trills can be totally in control of their lifestyles. It's a very difficult thing to have seven lives, seven voices, seven memories in your head."

One of the continuing challenges of depicting the Trill for makeup artist Michael Westmore was the oft-changing look of the species. "The original Trills on *Next Generation* had a little forehead on and a little nosepiece," he says. "They decided to change that, so I do spotting on [Dax]. I have to personally do it by hand every day. It starts up at the top of her forehead, comes down around her hairline, in front of her ear, and down the sides of her neck. In the pilot, she's even lying on a table, bare to the top of her bustline — and I had to continue the spots down her body. It's a laborious job, but there seems to be no easy way to make a stencil up for that. It just has to be hand done every day."

Episode #9
"The Passenger"
Original Airdate: 2/22/93
Teleplay by Morgan Gendel, Robert Hewitt Wolfe and Michael Piller

••••

Story by Morgan Gendel
Directed by Paul Lynch
Guest Starring: Caitlin Brown (Kajada),
James Lashly (Lieutenant George
Primmin), Aron Eisenberg (Nog), James
Harper (Vantika)

While traveling in a runabout, Kira and Bashir pick up a distress signal from a disabled Kobliad ship. They beam over the pilot, a woman named Ty Kajada, and her passenger, a murderer named Rao Vantika. Vantika seemingly dies shortly after arriving on DS9, but he has actually managed to transfer his consciousness from his body to another, and continues to do so until he ends up in Bashir.

It is Vantika's goal to receive a large quantity of deuridium, a drug that is noted for prolonging the lives of his people. It is only through the ingenuity of Dax that the DS9 personnel are able to thwart his plan before he takes off in a waiting vessel.

••••

Freelance writer Morgan Gendel, who wrote *TNG*'s "The Inner Light" and "Starship Mine," was one of the first freelancers to contribute a script to *Deep Space Nine*. Gendel, a former NBC programming executive who has written for such shows as *Wiseguy, Hunter* and *Law & Order,* made good use of his experience writing cop shows for this story, which involved an escaped convict who may or may not have taken over the body of the police officer escorting him to prison.

"I thought the idea of a cop who's chasing himself was something you could only do in a science-fiction show," says Gendel. "When I first pitched it, they said they were looking to do a Hannibal Lecter–like character, and then the next pitch they would say, 'We want to make sure we're not doing that.' I pitched it to Ira and Peter, and they called me back and said, 'We want to talk about it with Michael [Piller],' and he was ready to say let's give it a whirl when Ira, rightfully, brought up the problems we were going to face.

"Ira's great. He's so straightforward and very direct to writers and to Michael, so you really get a sense of exactly where you stand. Ira was raising these fears about the episode — which I think turned out to be accurate, but I'm in there like a salesman and I don't want to walk away without the sale. I said, 'I hear what you're saying, Ira, but I think I can explore it and make it work out in story,' and I don't know if it was that enthusiasm or Michael felt sorry for me that day, but he said, 'OK, let's give a run at this,' and, of course, there were problems."

One of the most dramatic changes from Gendel's pitch in the final version of the story was the fact that it was Bashir who became possessed as opposed to the female cop, with whom Bashir was originally supposed to develop a romantic attachment. "In my first outline, the bad guy's essence was in the cop, and we captured her at the end of act four. What I did in act five was have this woman Bashir's fallen for trying to convince him to let her out of jail because he's planted a bomb on the station. Act five was all about 'What does Bashir do?' Does he trust his gut or his logic? His gut is telling him he's got to go, even at gunpoint, so that she can lead him to the bomb. That was the tension in act five, which leads up to where she changes back to Vantika and this whole run-and-jump thing."

In the episode, Quark becomes involved with the hijacking of a vital mineral shipment for which he never receives a comeuppance. "He is still the middleman," says Shimerman. "I say that in the

Alexander Siddig as Dr. Julian Bashir (copyright © 1995 by Albert Ortega).

episode, 'I'm just the middleman,' when they ask me if I'm going with them. He's just trying to make a buck. But it was a darker Quark, getting back to the Quark I think of in 'Emissary.' And that's good. Anytime that I get close to that I feel a little bit better. I feel more confident with that. Drama is always easier to play than comedy."

The implications of Quark's first truly illegal activity are never explored. While Shimerman enjoys his character's malevolent streak, he admits that sometimes it can go too far, which is a concern the writers are well aware of. "Quark has some bad friends," says staff writer Robert Wolfe. "He runs with a bad crowd. He's not the kind of guy who would kill anybody. He's not a cold-blooded murderer, but he's certainly not the greatest guy on the face of the earth. We use him for comedy, but Armin has done a good job of showing that dangerous streak in him."

"He is suckered in over his head by his own greed," says director Paul Lynch. "He doesn't really go looking for trouble, and if he had known what he was getting into he wouldn't have, but his own greed overruled him. It's a mystery and it owes a lot to the thriller conventions of Hitchcock, Murnau and De Palma."

"We had a very odd experience on the show," says Rick Berman. "Siddig made a choice of a voice to use that didn't work for us. It was too Bela Lugosi–like, and we replaced his entire part with him again, but we had him do it a different way. We didn't really know if it would work or not, but it was fine."

"I felt it was a very effective episode," says Michael Piller. "The guest cast gave great performances, and it gave Bashir a chance to do something unique and different. It's a very spooky mystery, and I liked all the misleads because just when you think you know what's going on, it turns out that you think maybe it's the security officer that's missing and then suddenly you get the final twist that it's Bashir. One of the things that's flawed in the episode is the scene on the ship where Bashir is grabbed by the throat. You sort of get the feeling that's something happening at that moment."

" 'The Passenger' was a show at the time I felt could have just as easily been [about *TNG*'s] Geordi," says Ira

••••

Behr, who believes the story lines should be series specific to *DS9* and not stories you could tell on *The Next Generation*. "There's nothing wrong with the episode; I just don't have much of a feeling for it. It could have just as easily taken place on the *Enterprise*."

Another aspect of the original concept that never made it to the final script was Gendel's idea for a song that Quark would sing while cleaning the bar. "I had him singing a whole little ditty, like a Hobbit," says Gendel. "I took a day to write this ditty about making money while he's serving people and shorting them on their drinks. I thought it was hysterical and also thought if I turned it in, they were going to laugh me out of the room. But Mike, if you're reading this and ever need a ditty, call me."

Episode #10
"Move Along Home"
Original Airdate: 3/15/93
Teleplay by Frederick Rappaport, Lisa Rich and Jeanne Carrigan-Fauci
Story by Michael Piller
Directed by David Carson
Guest Starring: Joel Brooks (Falow), James Lashly (Lieutenant George Primmin), Clara Bryant (Chandra)

When Quark cheats a delegation from the Gamma Quadrant, the aliens decide to extract revenge by forcing the Ferengi to participate in a game whose code phrase is "Move along home."

Unbeknownst to Quark, this particular game could turn out to be deadly for Sisko, Kira, Bashir and Dax when they literally become pawns who face one danger after another depending on how Quark plays the game. Gradually the group tries to work its way back to the station from the limbo it's trapped in, but Quark ultimately loses and seemingly sentences his comrades to death. Fortunately, though, as Falow, the leader of the delegation, notes, "It's only a game," and everyone is returned unharmed.

••••

"It's a flawed episode and perhaps the most expensive show next to the pilot," says Michael Piller. "It was a very neat concept. We wanted to do a contest on *Next Generation* and while we were having a discussion about the old *Prisoner* series on this show, the idea of making an episode with all these weird and strange things happening and 'How do I get out?' seemed very appealing. Finding ways of making that come to life in an affordable setting was not easy. It was a monster show, but the idea of Quark cheating an alien species and them taking it out on Quark by putting us through these hoops I thought was terrific. It was one of our strongest concepts, but I had some problems with the casting, and we couldn't afford to do extensive makeup or costumes. Essentially we ended up having these aliens who are strange and weird guys coming through the wormhole in leisure suits with odd hair and tattoos."

Offers Rick Berman, "It was a big show that had a tremendous amount of problems. It turned out much better than I thought it would. There were a lot of Lewis Carroll elements to the whole thing which were always a little bit on the verge of being hokey for me, but when all was said and done, I was pleasantly surprised."

British director David Carson jokes, "I think this was their way of punishing English people. It was very difficult because the scope of the show demanded a scale of building and sets which was certainly not in the budget, so therefore the corridors, which were pretty short, had to be expanded and doubled in length by clever use of backdrops and doors which were sometimes there and sometimes weren't. We shot in a very small space and tried to make it look as big as possible by using different perspectives.

"If you're dealing with a story where you have a maze, then the more amazing it can be, the better it is," he adds. "Certainly the first versions of the script were much more interesting and exciting. But in terms of television, we managed to make it interesting enough to have the idea that you're actually playing with people's lives. It's like Shakespeare's quotation from *King Lear* where he says, 'We are as like flies unto the gods. They kill us for their sport.' It's an interesting analogy."

"It had a lot of production problems and it went through so many changes," says Ira Behr. "It was another one of those wonderful 'we'll shoot this on location' shows that we ended up shooting in a corridor and had to try and make it look as interesting as possible. If

Terry Farrell (copyright © 1996 by Albert Ortega).

you asked me which would I rather sit down and watch, I'd rather see an episode of *The Prisoner*, which does not mean the show was totally successful. But I agree with Michael totally that we shot high. You have to keep shooting high. Sometimes you hit and sometimes you miss and sometimes you fall in between — and to me this kind of fell in between. Would I green-light that episode again? Absolutely."

One of Terry Farrell's biggest regrets was that her starring role in "Move Along Home" precluded her appearance in a *DS9/TNG* crossover taking place on a fifth-season *Next Generation* episode. "Birthright," in which the *Enterprise* visits the station, was rewritten to feature Dr. Bashir rather than Dax. Says Farrell, "I cried. I thought I should have fallen off the rock [in "Move Along Home"] so I could have gone over there [to *TNG*] instead of Sid disappearing, because when we were shooting 'Move Along Home' his character disappeared, and I was acting throughout the rest of it with Nana and Avery, and we got caught up together. I still have a couple of good scars on my knee from shooting that one."

Episode #11
"The Nagus"
Original Airdate: 3/22/93

••••

Teleplay by Ira Steven Behr
Story by David Livingston
Directed by David Livingston
Guest Starring: Max Grodenchik (Rom),
Aron Eisenberg (Nog), Tiny Ron (Maihardu), Lee Arenberg (Gral), Lou Wagner (Krax), Barry Gordon (Nava), Wallace Shawn (Zek)

An all-powerful Ferengi, the Royal Nagus Zek, arrives at Deep Space Nine to divvy up shares in the business opportunities awaiting them in the Gamma Quadrant. Before apparently dying, he bestows his crown upon an unsuspecting Quark, who then becomes the object of several assassination attempts — including one by his own brother. In the end, Zek turns out to be alive, merely testing his son to see if he is worthy of being Nagus. Despite the trickery, Zek is intrigued by Quark and promises to return.

••••

Zek, a recurring character on the series, is played by pint-sized playwright-actor Wallace Shawn, best known for his acting turns in *My Dinner with Andre*, *The Princess Bride* and, of course, in Woody Allen's *Manhattan* as Diane Keaton's irresistible ex.

"[Shawn] was brilliant," says David Livingston, who assumed the directorial reins of *DS9* for the first time for this episode. "It was Rick's idea to offer the part to Wally Shawn, and I complimented him at the end of the show. I said, 'You are a totally fearless actor. You went for it and didn't hold anything back.' When he did his first scene he didn't even know what a Ferengi was. I kept saying, 'More, more, bigger, bigger, let me tell you when it's too big.' I never told him to pull back. After he got the initial thing down, he sat on the stool at Quark's, which was the first scene we shot, and the moment he opened his mouth, the whole stage lit up and the cast was cracking up. The cast still quotes lines from the show with his inflection. Whenever someone makes a mistake on the set, we'll say, 'You failed miserably!' It was a comedy, and having him and Armin together was a treat for me."

"We had a great time," agrees Shimerman. "He was a hoot. I've always been a big fan of his. I think his first day he was a little discombobulated by all the makeup, but he got over that and at the end of the shoot he said he'd like to come back. At first he asked, 'How do I play this? What's a Ferengi?' and I gave him a little advice, but he didn't need it."

Says Livingston, "Armin was concerned that he might go over the top, and my comment to him was, 'You *can't* go over the top. These guys are Ferengis.' To have those two high-caliber people in these two roles wearing those big screwy makeups with the big ears and funny noses was a treat for me. It was a comedy, and I like comedy."

"We had, I think, seventeen Ferengi running around, and nobody knew who each other was," says Shimerman of "The Nagus." "It was a fun and different type of *Star Trek* episode, like the 'Tribbles' episode of the original. The death threat to Quark I don't think was all that serious. We were much more interested in getting laughs than getting anybody to sit on the edge of their seat."

"It was David Livingston's idea, and I steered him in the direction of *The Godfather,* and Ira executed as well as you possibly could," says Michael Piller of the show, which was originally entitled "Friend Like Me." "It's a very funny episode, and Wally Shawn is something you've never seen on *The Next Generation.* He's certainly a character that is the most different from anything you'd find on *The Next Generation.*"

Says Rick Berman, "We had a tape made of the episode for Ira Behr and David Livingston where we laid in *The Godfather* theme in the scene where Quark was made the Nagus and they come looking for favors from him. Neither David nor Ira realized we were joking. They thought we were doing it for real. I loved 'The Nagus' and thought that Ira did a wonderful job writing it."

Behr considers the episode a "character piece," not a comedy. "I know that sounds weird, but it was Quark suddenly being more than he was. He had a chance to be someone, and we examined what happens. I remember a friend of mine growing up who thought he was going to become a kid actor, someone had cast him as a part in a commercial, and within a week he became the biggest son of a bitch on the earth. He was basically saying, 'I'm going to be a star, fuck all of you,' and he meant it. His little head was turned, and I just thought it was interesting for Quark."

Episode #12
"Vortex"
Original Airdate: 4/19/93
Written by Sam Rolfe
Directed by Winrich Kolbe
Guest Starring: Cliff De Young (Croden), Randy Oglesby (Ah'Kel/Ro'Kel), Max Grodenchik (Rom), Kathleen Garrett (Vulcan Captain), Leslie Engelberg (Yareth), Gordon Clapp (Hadran)

After accidentally killing one of two Miradorn twins, an alien named Croden is placed under arrest by Odo. The surviving twin, Ah'Kel, vows vengeance, and then the government of Croden's homeworld, Rakhar, demands that he be brought there to stand trial. Croden, the government emphasizes, is a criminal.

Throughout his imprisonment on DS9, Croden tries to convince Odo that he knows of a colony of shape-shifters, and he reveals a small crystal medallion that comes from the colony. Odo isn't convinced, despite his desire to believe the story, and absolutely refuses to release Croden in exchange for the colony's location.

Odo is given the assignment of taking Croden back to Rakhar, but en route they are attacked by Ah'Kel's vessel. Croden leads them into a vortex to elude their pursuer and gives Odo coordinates for the planet that is supposedly inhabited by the changelings. Once there, however, Odo discovers only Croden's daughter, who is in cyber-sleep. As Croden explains it, he is a criminal at home because he spoke out against the government. As a result, they slaughtered most of his family. Only he and his daughter barely got away.

The three take off in the runabout, and Ah'Kel is tricked into using his weapons in an explosive area of the vortex, thus destroying himself. At the conclusion, Odo allows Croden and his daughter to beam over to a nearby Vulcan ship and safety. In return, he is given the crystal.

••••

"A very effective episode," says Michael Piller of "Vortex," written by the late Sam Rolfe, one of the creators of the classic *Have Gun, Will Travel.* "Sam Rolfe is a legendary writer, and I said, 'Sam, I want to do a Western in which Odo has to go through the wormhole taking back a prisoner and has a relationship with the prisoner that explores his backstory and the tensions of what it's like to be who he is.' He came up with a great story. I was mostly concerned that the sentimentality of the little girl on the planet was not going to play and that it was a little hokey. Frankly, I think it really did play and I found it quite touching. I was intrigued with the mystery, and the special effects they did in the vortex were sensational."

Says Ira Behr of the episode, "Where I was coming from was a movie called *Sleeping Dogs*, a New Zealand film with Sam Neill and Warren Oates that Roger Donaldson directed. It's about a man who's living a mundane kind of life and there's political turmoil and the next thing he knows he's a wanted terrorist — and he hasn't done anything. It's a wonderful little movie, and that's what we saw this guy as. Instead of being a criminal, he's a guy who woke up one day and doesn't know why, but he did something wrong on his planet and they're after him now and he has to kill some people to get away from there. I thought it was a good Odo show. I think we could say it was one of the shows where, for whatever reason, we needed pyrotechnics at this point in the season. The whole thing with the vortex put me to sleep; it became tech."

Of more concern to Armin Shimerman was Quark's involvement with a murder in "Vortex" for which there were no consequences. Recalls Shimerman, "I had this chat with Rick Berman and I asked him if we went over the line by having Quark participating in a really high crime. I thought that might be a little dangerous for the character and for the show because it means that he can get away with murder, which is not what I think the show is about. It also makes somewhat of a fool of Odo because it happens under his nose, and Sisko's for that matter, and lessens their characters as well."

Says David Livingston, "I thought the way [director Winrich] Kolbe shot the cave sequence where they go find the daughter was done very cleverly. That's a very small set. Kolbe made it look huge and cavernous, as though there were a lot

of different places and tunnels. He really filled it out. It was just a very imaginative use of staging and camera."

Winrich Kolbe, the German-born director affectionately dubbed "the Baron," comments of Odo, "It's intriguing because Odo is a person who's very distrustful, which makes the perfect sheriff. He pushes the envelope of what the police should be. The police should be trusting nobody, and Odo's philosophy of arrest first, ask questions later is an interesting aspect of his profession which obviously puts him into conflict with Sisko. We're talking about issues about society. We're talking about the death penalty, the Napoleonic code versus the Anglo-Saxon code. Are we guilty until proven innocent or innocent until proven guilty? That is something I find compelling.

"A critic might say, 'If you're doing this, it's basically propaganda for a certain philosophy' — which it probably is, although I'm not sure whether episodic television can seriously be accused of that one," he adds. "It's just too short, too superficial. Occasionally you hit a nerve, but most of the time these allegories are just pointing out something — but I would not say they are going to reform the world. Writers have been dealing with contemporary problems in terms of futuristic allegories for centuries. But it's got to be done intriguingly, in a new way. I feel that sometimes just to throw in an allegory because it's kind of pop-ish is not doing it any service. It just gets buried. But to deal with certain issues that we would have a problem dealing with on a present-day level is something that I support very, very strongly."

Episode #13
"Battle Lines"
Original Airdate: 4/26/93
Teleplay by Richard Danus and Evan Carlos Somers
Story by Hilary J. Bader
Directed by Paul Lynch
Guest Starring: Jonathan Banks (Shel-La), Camille Saviola (Kai Opaka), Paul Collins (Zlangco)

Sisko, Kira and Bashir take Kai Opaka on a trip through the wormhole and are forced to crash-land on an alien world, resulting in the death of the Kai. As

they attempt to communicate with DS9, the survivors encounter two warring factions engaged in an endless conflict as an alteration to their body chemistry has rendered them immortal — they can be wounded but can never die. This point is brought home when Kai Opaka revives and finds herself trapped on this planet as well.

Although Bashir theorizes a possible cure for these people, and Sisko is willing to bend the Prime Directive prescribing noninterference with alien cultures to allow him to use it, they are never given the opportunity: When a rescue runabout arrives, those at war make it clear that they're not ready to give up their battle just yet.

••••

" 'Battle Lines' is a good show," says Ira Behr. "We say good-bye to the Kai and we have some action. While it's not *The Wild Bunch*, it'll do. We have some vicious little fighting going on, hand to hand. People getting their throats cut and wounded and bleeding. It's an interesting show, and I like it."

"I think this is one of the best premises of the [first] season," says Michael Piller. "For all those people who have written in and said we want more alien violence and sex, this is the episode. [Former intern] Hilary Bader is another one of those people who just keeps coming up with one good fresh idea after another. This was a great idea about a planet where you can never die — it's a great premise for a science-fiction show, and we put Kai Opaka on there and she becomes a fundamental part of this tale. It's about rebirth and resurrection and spiritual, mystical things. One of the things I felt about [the] first season is that I'm finding people react very positively to the mystical component of the pilot of *Deep Space Nine*. I didn't do a lot more of them on *DS9* after we set it up on the pilot, but this is one of them. My feeling is we should be finding more of those kinds of things. I think they're more interesting than ships breaking down."

Says Rick Berman, "[Guest star] Jonathan Banks did a nice job, and there's some wonderful action in it. We deal with the death and rebirth of the Kai. I thought the concept of a punishment that is based on a microbe that allows these warring factions to never die was fascinating, as was the idea that you have to constantly be re-creating these battles and fighting one another. There was a lot of techno-babble in it that got very complex, but I thought by and large that it was quite nice."

"Battle Lines" was the rewrite that got intern Evan Somers hired on staff for the season. "I started working on 'Battle Lines' before the pilot aired and I saw the pilot and it confirmed some notions I had," he remarks. "I did a little rewriting, and it was an elucidating experience. We were forming a new show, and I was asked to come in and rewrite an episode that was an incredibly strong story that was dealing with characters I was fairly unfamiliar with."

Says David Livingston, "I worked with Jonathan Banks on *Otherworld* at Universal. That's where I knew him originally. I also knew his work with *Beverly Hills Cop* and then, of course, on *Wiseguy*. He is a very odd and unusual actor and he wears this wonderful makeup and did a terrific job. There are wonderful fight sequences with a lot of action. It's a very strong episode visually. The crew was exhausted after that episode, having to work on Stage Eighteen in the dirt and in those caves and cramped quarters. It's very trying."

Paul Lynch utilized Stage Eighteen for the episode's planetary exteriors and caves, often lit by flickering torches. "It was a wonderful set — a combination of standing sets and of adding pieces to the standing set," he says. "We had a wonderful spaceship that had crashed into it and the Kai is fabulous. She's a wonderful actress and, like a lot of these actors like Avery and Armin and Rene, she is a theater actress too. She gives a performance where part of it is the walking dead. She was such a marvelous person and human being that it was a joy to work with her."

Episode #14
"The Storyteller"
Original Airdate: 5/3/93
Teleplay by Kurt Michael Bensmiller and Ira Steven Behr
Story by Kurt Michael Bensmiller
Directed by David Livingston

Guest Starring: Kay E. Kuter (The Sirah), Lawrence Monoson (Hovath), Jim Jansen (Faren), Gina Philips (Varis), Aron Eisenberg (Nog), Jordan Lund (Woban), Amy Benedict (Woman)

While responding to a medical emergency in a small Bajoran village, O'Brien, who has accompanied Dr. Bashir, is pronounced by the dying storyteller, the sirah, to have been sent by the prophets. It has been the sirah's task to tell a tale to the villagers as the cloudlike demon Dal'Rok unleashes its fury, but when he collapses during an attack, he tells O'Brien how to fight off the manifestation, and O'Brien is successful. When the sirah dies, the villagers announce that O'Brien will take his place and they start to worship him as a god.

This places O'Brien's life in danger as he barely avoids an attack by Hovath, the former sirah's apprentice, who claims that he should have been the man's successor. Naturally, O'Brien is happy to give up the "throne" and he works with Hovath to help him send the Dal'Rok away and capture the respect of his people.

Alexander Siddig and Colm Meaney appearing at the Museum of Television and Radio.

••••

"It was very difficult to shoot, and we were way over budget on the opticals on that show because of the complexity of this thing that appears in the sky," says Rick Berman. "It was a little fanciful, but I like the science-fiction element involving a creature created by the collective imagination of this village as a way of bringing them closer together. The story's having to do with a little piece of one of the orbs that is held by the storyteller was a very interesting concept as well."

"One of the really big problems with this script, which is why it didn't appeal to anybody, is because it was not about any of our characters," says Michael Piller. "We were just watching the events occur by putting O'Brien in the middle, saying you have to solve it. What really appealed to me was the great theme that sometimes we create our own monsters so that we can defeat them and feel secure in our power. I was always in love with that theme, and finally we made it work. Ira did a lot of work on that script."

"We had thirty extras, wind, lighting, and it had a couple of major effects going on," says David Livingston of shooting on Stage Eighteen, the planetary swing set analogous to *The Next Generation*'s Planet Hell set. "They were really difficult working conditions. I had to use a bullhorn in order to communicate since I had lost my voice. It's physically very demanding on everybody to work on Stage Eighteen. The actors had to have big wind machines blowing in their faces, and it was very debilitating, but we got through it. It was fun, though. Screaming through a bullhorn is a real power trip."

Piller says of Livingston, "David's a wonderful director. I don't think we have a better director than David Livingston working on the series right now, because he lives in the *Star Trek* universe and understands it better than anyone else and has watched the work of directors, good and bad, as I have done as a writer reading the work of writers, good and bad, and has given himself a philosophy that has served him well. He's very talented, and I'm very impressed."

Frances Praksti *(Star Runners)* played one of the Bajoran women who was presented to O'Brien as a "gift" from

••••

the village. In an audition with seventy-five other women, she had to convincingly "give" herself to Livingston. "It took about an hour to do my nose, and once I had it on, it felt really comfortable," she recalls. "David Livingston was great; he didn't stop until he got exactly what he wanted. He didn't settle for good; it had to be perfect, and we must have done it about twenty-one times. I liked Colm and Siddig, who I felt bad for because he ate fifteen kiwis in that scene until we got it right. He said he'd never eat one again."

Siddig laughs about his close encounter with the kiwi of the worst kind. "That stuff burnt my mouth. I've satiated myself on fruit and I never had that sensation before. I don't know how many I had. They counted; it was somewhere in the region of the twenties within an hour. I had to put stuff on my lips because the citric acid went right through. I don't ever want to do that again. Next time, I'll be happy to do something mild, like a glass of milk."

Episode #15
"Progress"
Original Airdate: 5/9/93
Written by Peter Allan Fields
Directed by Les Landau
Guest Starring: Brian Keith (Mullibok), Aron Eisenberg (Nog), Nicholas Worth (Alien Captain), Michael Bofshever (Toran), Daniel Riordan (First Guard), Terrence Evans (Baltrim), Annie O'Donnell (Keena)

When a Bajoran farm on the moon of Jeraddo has to be evacuated so that a large-scale energy transfer tapping that moon's core can be executed, Kira and Dax travel there to make sure that everyone is gone. They find a stubborn farmer named Mullibok, who refuses to leave, even if his life is in danger. After some time passes, Dax returns to DS9, while Kira remains behind to try and convince the man of the threat.

As time goes on, Kira and Mullibok bond, with Kira even coming to the point where she considers abandoning her responsibilities so that the man can live out the rest of his life here. In the end, though — particularly after Sisko has beamed down and told her that she's no longer the underdog, that she represents something more to the people of Bajor — she realizes she must carry out her duty,

even if that means burning down Mullibok's home and taking the man against his will.

••••

"In the middle part of the year, we suddenly realized we had sort of lost Kira, which is immediately taken care of with this and several other episodes as the season goes on," says Michael Piller. "Brian Keith was the guest star, and I think it's very nice casting. I think it brings a certain reputation to your series when actors of quality choose to guest star on it. It's a very personal story and it's a story that's been oft told in contemporary times, and I think people relate to it. Our attempt was to show a softer side of Kira that would expand her character, and I think we do so in a marvelous way. It's really a two-man show, in a sense, but there's also a great scene between Kira and Sisko."

Adds Rick Berman, "I think it turned out real nice. The end is rather bittersweet. Brian Keith gave a performance that was very interesting and was in many ways better than I expected. It's a very poignant story in the relationship between Major Kira and this old man."

"I think it's a great show for Kira," offers Ira Behr. "We did fairly well with everyone, first season. We even gave Jake and Nog three B stories. I always wanted to do Milo Minderbinder from *Catch-22*, the guy who can acquire things, and we put these two kids together as the Milo Minderbinders of *Deep Space Nine* [in "Progress"], and it has some nice stuff in it."

Comments David Livingston, "It's an eminent-domain story and it's charming. Brian Keith was terrific. We couldn't give [director] Les [Landau] and [DP] Marvin Rush all the set we wanted to give them, so they had to come up with ways of shooting this set to make the exterior look believable. I think they did a great job."

The episode explored one of the most interesting conflicts yet established in the young series, that between Sisko of the Federation and Major Kira of Bajor. "Sometimes we have to work together with people with whom we occasionally disagree and have differences of opinion, yet despite that they are capable of fulfilling their job," says Winrich Kolbe. "In the pilot, I think Sisko said, 'I want you be-

cause you're Bajoran.' He could have had any one of a million Bajorans, somebody who would say, 'Yessir, whatever you want.' But he wanted somebody who comes from the background of Kira, who was in the underground against the Cardassians. A nationalist, so to speak. It intrigues me because I feel that, yes, we are changing, but we're not necessarily becoming more advanced. There's nationalism two thousand years from now and it will always be there because it's something genetically inside us. Like racism, which is something that's always coming out. We only seemingly live in a better society if we are able to combat it, but the moment we let our guard down, bingo, there's conflict. I like that in *DS9*, when it comes down to the Kira/Sisko conflict, it's politics. But it's the politics of Starfleet, of the larger unit which says, 'We want to expand our influence,' and the smaller unit, which is the planet Bajor, which says, 'Hey, it's all very nice, but you're taking over. We don't want you either.' Is she loyal to Starfleet? Is she loyal to Bajor? Can she be loyal to both of them? That's fun. I believe there will always be conflict, there will always be war. There will never be the point where we're all running around like we're on Valium. We have to handle it. We have to do something. There will never be a time when we say, 'Everything's been solved.' The moment that happens, it's time to buy a bouquet, go to the next cemetery and wait until it's your turn."

Shooting exterior planetscapes on stage has proven a difficult but rewarding challenge for the production team and Marvin Rush and his camera team. "There's two episodes where we went on a planet," says Rush. "I think 'Battle Lines' was good, but I have a feeling 'Progress' is better from the standpoint of a believable day exterior. My favorite episode of *TNG* was 'Inner Light,' which was an example of day exterior done on soundstage which was pretty successful. Day exterior on a soundstage is a really tough thing to do, however I like it. We did night exterior on stage for 'Darmok' on *Next Gen* fifth season. There's something really interesting when you're given the task to try and make day on stage look real. It isn't always successful, but it is a challenge, and I like a challenge so I hope they don't always take that away from me, because I really get a kick out of pulling it off."

The advantage to a location is the sweeping vistas it offers, acknowledges Rush. "You can't do vista on soundstage. You can try, but you can't really do it. Outside, you can have a mile of background. On a soundstage you can have at the most seventy-five, eighty feet; it's just impossible. You can simulate it, but you can't really do it. Even using all the tools, painted backings, forcing perspective using greens, smoke, and all the things you can do to make it seem more faraway, ultimately it's a soundstage, and you are constrained by that limit. 'Progress' would have been a different-looking show if we had gone on location. I'm not sure it would have looked better. The worst case would have been to see from stage the interiors looking out the windows to a painted backing and then to cut to a location that doesn't match. If you can make it somewhat believable on soundstage and you're consistent from cut to cut to cut, the suspension of disbelief will overcome some of that. If you have a mismatch, then your eye goes, 'That's bogus.'"

Episode #16
"If Wishes Were Horses"
Original Airdate: 5/17/93
Teleplay by Neil McCue Crawford,
William Crawford and Michael Piller
Story by Neil McCue Crawford and
William Crawford
Directed by Rob Legato
Guest Starring: Keone Young (Buck Bokai), Rosalind Chao (Keiko O'Brien), Hana Hatae (Molly O'Brien), Michael John Anderson (Rumpelstiltskin)

The imaginations of DS9 crew members start to manifest themselves in real life. O'Brien, who has read the tale of "Rumpelstiltskin" to his daughter, is suddenly confronted by the dwarf; Sisko meets up with baseball legend Buck Bokai, who for the first time has stepped out of the holodeck program created by the commander and is carrying on conversations with him as though they're the dearest of friends; and Bashir imagines a new version of Dax who is completely submissive and wants nothing more than to please him. At the same time, the station is threatened by a rip in space that seems to be sucking everything into it.

All of this turns out to be the work of alien beings who have tapped into the human imagination in order to gain a fuller understanding of the species. How's that for an original *Star Trek* concept?

••••

"It was a very hard concept to make work," says Michael Piller. "Somebody came in and said, 'Jake brings a baseball player home from the holodeck,' and that was the pitch. Basically, I said we just did the Moriarty show, where he walks out of the holodeck in *Next Generation,* and I didn't want to do another holodeck show, but I would like to do a show that celebrates imagination, since that's really what *Star Trek* is, a celebration of the imagination. We knew it was sort of a [*TNG* first season's] 'Where No One Has Gone Before' concept, but that was six years ago on another show, so why can't we do something where strange things are happening that people are imagining?"

One figment of Piller's imagination that never made it to the screen was his initial decision to have the story O'Brien reads to his daughter be that of a leprechaun, the folkloric Irish dwarf with a pot of gold. Says Piller, "We needed a reason for it to be happening and we came up with the idea that O'Brien would be telling a bedtime story about a leprechaun. We had the script written, and Colm Meaney called Rick and said, 'Every Irish actor I know has worked his entire life trying to overcome the stereotype of Irish people and leprechauns. It's really racist, and I don't want to do it.' We had no idea there was any sensitivity to leprechauns in the Irish culture and certainly we did not want to force Colm Meaney to act with a leprechaun, but what the hell do you do after you've got a whole story structured around a leprechaun stealing a child? Well, we went through story tales and Robert [Wolfe] came in with Rumpelstiltskin, and we went by it at least once, maybe twice, because Rumpelstiltskin wasn't exactly the same thing and wouldn't work in the structure we had. When I finally sat down to rewrite it, I said, 'OK, Rumpelstiltskin — let's see where it goes.' It was one of those scripts where I had no idea how to resolve it [or] where it was going to go. I wrote each scene to see if it worked and had fun with it."

Of the scenes of the romantic rendezvous between Bashir and his dream Dax, Piller notes, "I've saved the dailies of Terry's coming on to Siddig, and he doesn't know why, for my personal collection. There were twelve takes, and he kept breaking up and fluffing his lines."

Comments Armin Shimerman, who had the challenge of acting with two voluptuous fantasy girls created by Quark's vivid imagination in the story, "The writers were kind enough to give me every adolescent's fantasy. They gave me these two beautiful women who were very sweet. It was fun."

"This is an episode you've got to try and do," says Ira Behr. "We should be awarded brass balls for doing Rumpelstiltskin. It's an interesting show and it has a level of imagination and it's a high concept. Sometimes they work and sometimes they don't."

"I think 'If Wishes Were Horses' was the first time it all sort of jelled with Sid[dig]'s and my relationship," suggests Terry Farrell. "It took a long time before it all came together. I don't think it looked that way to anybody else, but I think this was the first time we were all really together and it all seemed to jell. It was an interesting moment where we realized we're like this basketball team — where we found our camaraderie — and felt comfortable."

Episode #17
"The Forsaken"
Original Airdate: 5/24/93
Teleplay by Carlos Dunaway and
Michael Piller
Story by Jim Trombetta
Directed by Les Landau
Guest Starring: Majel Barrett (Lwaxana Troi), Constance Towers (Ambassador Taxco), Michael Ensign (Ambassador Lojai), Jack Shearer (Ambassador Vadosia), Benita Andre (Anara)

When the Deep Space Nine computer is infected by an alien presence, all of O'Brien's attempts to get rid of it are fruitless. As a result, various items cease working properly, including the transporter and turbo-lifts, which in turn has an effect on Odo that he doesn't take kindly to: He is trapped aboard a turbo-lift with the amorous Lwaxana Troi, one of the ambassadors visiting the station.

••••

As O'Brien tries to figure a way out of this situation, Bashir handles three diplomats while Odo and Troi open up to each other in surprising ways, culminating in Odo's having to return to his original form and her promising to take care of him while he does so.

••••

"It started out being called 'Ghost in the Machine,'" says Evan Somers. "I was here back in the fall when the trio of ideas was pitched and sold — and it was quite a remarkable day — by a writer named Jim Trombetta. This is the first that had come to the point where a treatment had been submitted that was adequate to break. The story that had been initially pitched was relegated to B-story category, and a very interesting A story emerged involving Lwaxana Troi and Odo. Michael just did some brilliant work writing that."

"That was the only element of that story that really appealed to me when we first heard it," says Michael Piller of Mrs. Troi's first visit to *DS9*. "We were looking for A/B/C stories that gave us the opportunity to do lots of little stories in that same 'life on the space station' vein. We were also looking for bottle shows to save money. This does fit into the category of the season where it was time to start

paying the piper. I figured putting two people in an elevator has got to save money somewhere. The idea of having an enemy go into the computer is certainly not a new one, but I think we found a different spin on it and we got some very interesting comedy from Siddig and his tour of ambassadors. The ensemble seemed to be working much better for me by this time, and I just think that stuff in the elevator will be talked about forever. It's a wonderful performance by Rene, and Majel [Barrett] was at her warmest and most wonderful as Mrs. Troi. She goes from being the woman you can't imagine being stuck in an elevator with to the best companion you could possibly ever have."

Says Rick Berman, "I think here's another example of bringing a character from *Next Generation* that is delightful. Rene remains one of my favorite actors of all time and he does a wonderful job here. It's remarkably poignant."

"It was great working with Majel Barrett [Gene Roddenberry's wife, who played Nurse Chapel in the original series]," says Armin Shimerman. "I looked forward to doing that. She was sweet, she was kind and she was funny. She was so at home on these sets. It really looked like someone coming home to roost. The crew

adores her, and she was so considerate. Considering her position in the cosmology of *Star Trek,* she was a very, very considerate person."

And what did Marina Sirtis [*TNG*'s Counselor Troi] think of her fictional mother's latest sojourn in the world of *Trek*? "I was pissed." She laughs. "She's my mother; she should have been on my show."

Episode #18
"Dramatis Personae"
Original Airdate: 5/31/93
Written by Joe Menosky
Directed by Cliff Bole
Guest Starring: Tom Towles (Klingon), Stephen Parr (Valerian), Randy Pflug (Guard), Jeff Pruitt (Ensign)

The telepathic energy of a destroyed species in the Gamma Quadrant takes over the crew members of DS9, forcing them to reenact the Shakespearean power struggle that destroyed the alien world. What it basically comes down to is the Federation against the Bajorans, with Sisko heading one faction and Kira the other. Odo, the only person not affected by the alien influence, manages to manipulate Bashir into using a cure that rids the crew of the extraterrestrial presence, which is then blown out of an air lock.

••••

"It was a lot of fun," says Nana Visitor, who plots against Commander Sisko's life as Kira assumes a sexier, more vicious persona. "It was interesting to see how used to each other and the characters we've been playing we are. To see Avery behaving in a certain way and Siddig and Terry in a very different mind-set was fun. I came and watched scenes I wasn't involved with just to see what was going on."

"We got Joe Menosky back to do a script," says Michael Piller of the former *TNG* executive script consultant, who left *DS9*'s sister series to take a sabbatical in Europe. "It's somewhat of a low-budget affair, but a very interesting one with great performances. It's a very perverted little episode, and I think entertaining. Cliff [Bole], who very much wanted to direct *DS9* for us, came in and finally got to direct this one and did a wonderful job."

Says Visitor of first-time *DS9* director Bole, a *TNG* veteran, "Cliff was

Majel Barrett, who portrays Lwaxana Troi in both The Next Generation *and* Deep Space Nine, *seen here with Avery Brooks and Nana Visitor (copyright © 1995 by Albert Ortega).*

••••

wonderful because he's got a great sense of humor. He doesn't take himself too seriously and yet he commands respect, so you feel you're safe and are going to be taken care of and watched out for so that you can take some chances. Then you can do something that might be great and might be awful, but he'll be there to tell you that didn't work or it's great. That's the only way you can do interesting stuff. If you're always playing it safe, it gets boring, for me, anyway, and I think for most actors. He was great and he had a very low-key attitude, which I really enjoyed."

Offers the director on the first season, "Everybody was finding their character, but I compare that to the first season of [The Next Generation]. It's almost identical. I remember Brent Spiner was searching out his role [as Data]. I think Sisko was still playing with some things for a while. Fortunately for me, I had a show where I didn't have to deal with Avery and his normal character. I had ups and downs with him, which was great because he could do something different and didn't have to stay in character for the whole piece. We had a marvelous scene with Armin, when Quark and Odo were together. It's kind of the way I remember Charles Laughton and Peter Ustinov when I was doing script work on Spartacus. The screen just lit up when they were working together, and that's what happens with these two guys; they're marvelous."

Bole points out that the only major differences between directing the two shows is the sets. "They were marvelous new sets, and that was great fun for me," he says of DS9. "In its sixth year, everybody on The Next Generation was really in the groove. By contrast, Deep Space Nine was a little darker show. The characters are a little more ominous, and the sets are a bigger challenge. They're tough to shoot. So, from a directing standpoint, that's basically the difference."

Michael Piller didn't feel that having the characters take on new personas while they were still developing first season was a mistake. "It's dangerous, but the reason we were able to do that was because we had developed them so well the first half of the season," he says. "If you go back to the first season of Next Generation, people were changing, and you had viruses changing them into horny

people — so I suppose it's not that unusual."

"I loved this episode," says Armin Shimerman. "I love the fact that revolution broke out. Even though it wasn't a real revolution, I still love the conflict between Sisko and Major Kira, a person who is a national and who only thinks of her world first. I love those issues of nationalism because we go through that here in Los Angeles a lot. We had our riots because neighborhoods felt that they weren't getting a fair share of the wealth of Los Angeles, and there's the Bajorans who are fighting because they're not getting a fair share of what they think they deserve. That's very intrinsic to the life we live in Los Angeles, so when it's represented on television, I feel for that."

In shooting his first episode of the series, Cliff Bole consulted with some of the show's assistant directors to bring himself up to speed on the production routine. "I spent more time talking to the assistant directors than I did even with the producers," he says. "I was fortunate to get the actors together for the first time and have a read through. It just happened that they were all available at one lunch, so I was able to get them around a table and we read the script. I'd love to be able to do that every time, but you can't. It's just that time doesn't allow it."

Episode #19
"Duet"
Original Airdate: 6/14/93
Teleplay by Peter Allan Fields
Story by Lisa Rich
and Jeanne Carrigan-Fauci
Directed by James L. Conway
Guest Starring: Marc Alaimo (Gul Dukat), Ted Sorel (Kaval), Tony Rizzoli (Kainon), Norman Large (Captain), Robin Christopher (Neela), Harris Yulin (Marritza)

Kira is stunned when a Cardassian war criminal appears at the station, bragging of the atrocities he committed against the Bajoran people. She wants him sent to Bajor to stand trial and be executed, but Sisko isn't so sure that the man is who he claims to be.

All of the station's resources are utilized to investigate the man's tale and certain inaccuracies in his statements. What they eventually discover is that he is

actually Marritza, a simple filing clerk who, in his own words, did not have the courage to come out from under a table, where he wept upon hearing the screams of Bajorans being slaughtered. Ironically, just as Kira starts to feel sorry for him and starts to discuss possibilities for the future, a Bajoran stabs him to death. The cycle of hate continues.

••••

"Duet" is widely considered one of the best episodes of DS9 and was shown during the Museum of Television and Radio Broadcasting's Tribute to Excellence, held in Los Angeles in March 1994.

"I'd like to say that my performance as Marritza in Pete's office was absolutely brilliant," jokes Ira Behr of his animated breaking of the script with co-producer Peter Fields. "I only wish the cameras were rolling. I'm very, very proud of this show. Not in the sense it's a show for all humanity, but that it was a fun show to work on. You had a character who was larger than life and reveling in his evilness. It was just a blast. It was a lot of fun to write, but it was the end of the season, and we were all very tired, so neither Peter nor I were very happy doing it. We work very well together, and the show could have, literally, been another half hour if they would have let us. It was just mind games on top of mind games, and we could have done that forever."

Comments Michael Piller of the well-received bottle show, "We had to come up with some very creative ways to do shows that did not cost a lot of money. This was pitched to us by two of our interns, who wanted to do something about a war criminal. In the context it was pitched, it didn't turn me on. The idea of a war criminal found aboard DS9 seemed to me to be an interesting concept, but at first it seemed to me to be a Judgment at Nuremberg court show. We had done 'Dax' and didn't want to do another courtroom show. Ira gave us the twist that gave it The Man in the Glass Booth kind of feeling, where the guy isn't who he says he is but is doing it for more noble reasons. The writing is really quite powerful. The last two episodes of the season are very thought provoking."

"I've always been a big fan of Harris Yulin," says Armin Shimerman of the actor who portrayed Marritza. "We were acquaintances years ago when I first met my wife. We were all doing Broadway together. It's a fascinating episode dealing with Bajor and nationalism and with Cardassian war crimes. I love these kinds of scripts because they deal with social issues using the context of space to place them in."

Nana Visitor shares the enthusiasm of the rest of the ensemble for *Star Trek*'s tradition of addressing important contemporary issues in the guise of science fiction. "The action comes out of big issues on this show," she says. "There's action and intrigue, but the writing really lets us deal with issues we're not embarrassed to commit ourselves to as actors and people. On a sitcom, very often it's 'Should I let Johnny stay out after midnight or not?' It's an important issue, but not quite so much as Holocaust victims and facing evil in one person and how you deal with that, which is one thing that I had to deal with in 'Duet.' It was kind of harrowing to have to deal with that subject matter every day, but the harder it is, the more rewarding it is."

"Each episode puts different demands on me," says Marvin Rush. "That's one reason I've been in this line of work. I didn't want to stamp out parts in a factory; I wanted to do something that challenged me and was different every episode. New directors come in with a new idea and show you something you've never thought of before, so it's really good

to have a few new faces from time to time. [Director] Jim Conway came in and did a great job. He was real professional and had a difficult episode, because it didn't have a lot of action or movement. It's a small story."

Episode #20
"In the Hands of the Prophets"
Original Airdate: 6/21/93
Written by Robert Hewitt Wolfe
Directed by David Livingston
Guest Starring: Rosalind Chao (Keiko O'Brien), Philip Anglim (Vedek Bareil), Robin Christopher (Neela), Michael Eugene Fairman (Vendor), Louise Fletcher (Vedek Winn)

Shortly after the arrival of Bajoran spiritual leader Vedek Winn, who is vying to become the new Kai, on the station, a division begins to occur between the Bajorans and other races residing on Deep Space Nine. When Winn's views are not readily accepted, sabotage in the form of explosions and even murder begins to occur, leading to the attempted assassination of Vedek Bareil, who is Winn's primary competition for Kai. What unfolds is that Winn's rhetoric is more politically than spiritually motivated.

••••

In picking her favorite episode of the season, Nana Visitor notes, "One of the most fun things was the last scene of the last show between Avery and me when I am going, 'Wow, I can't believe

that just a year ago I was in such a different place and now I'm wearing this uniform.' It was fun because it was the last scene of the season and it was with Avery, and we looked at each other and kind of had a moment of realizing we really had gone through something here. The day we filmed that was my son's first birthday, and when I was going, 'Wow, I'd never believe I was wearing this uniform,' I could totally let that be truthful, because a year ago, at that hour, I was giving birth."

Says Ira Behr, "On one level, you could just say we're doing *Inherit the Wind,* but I think it enables us, as a specific television series, to explore the Bajoran spiritual life, which we haven't done too much of. It's one of the things we talked about, which is the rational, scientific bent of the Federation versus the Bajoran spiritual outlook on life, which is a clash that I think can give us episodes for quite some time."

"The episode is really the showdown between the humanist ideals of the Federation and the religious spiritual philosophy of Bajor," says Michael Piller, who did the uncredited rewrite on the teleplay. "It provides a bookend to the season that has a confrontation that seems to have been coming all along when we met these people and found out what their lives were like. You start to deal with religion in school, school prayer, the Scopes Monkey Trial, and fundamentalism, and it's very thought provoking."

••••

••••

Deep Space Nine: Season Two

As *Deep Space Nine* — which is budgeted at a reported $1.5 million an episode — entered its second year, its ratings were erratic. After the series premiered with the highest numbers ever posted by a show in first-run syndication, the Nielsens began to drop. Some blamed this on the show's dark and gritty tone, others on the fact that at the time, *The Next Generation*'s final season was getting the lion's share of attention, eclipsing its sister series.

The grim picture painted by some pundits failed to note that *DS9* was still one of the top-rated shows in syndication. Nonetheless, it was true that the series was not the unqualified hit that its progenitor had been. "I believe that because *Deep Space Nine* is a show that is grounded in a space station and is stationary, there are fundamental elements to the show that are going to be less attractive than a show like *Next Generation* or *Voyager* that takes place on a starship," says Rick Berman. "*Star Trek* has always been a show about people going forth and exploring the stars, so the minute you're locked down on a space station and a single spot, it isn't the same thing."

Berman admits that the perception that *DS9* has strayed from a strict definition of what *Star Trek* is may be accurate. "I think it's some great television, but I believe to a lot of people it's not exactly what *Star Trek* is," says Berman. "It wasn't like we said, 'Hey, I've got an idea, Michael. Let's not create a show that has to do with being on a spaceship.' This show is definitely a little darker and there's a lot more conflict."

"I really couldn't be prouder of what we did on *Deep Space Nine* second season," says Michael Piller. "I felt that it was as good a year of television as I have ever been involved with and I certainly would put it on the par with the experience of years three and four of *Next Generation*."

Adds Berman, "We had a slight falloff in the audience, and my guess is that it was a result of all the hoopla about *Next Generation*. I think knowing *Next Generation* had one season left, a lot of the fans decided to invest their time to watch it; and literally months before the last episode ended there was just so much commotion about the last year of *Star Trek* and about *Voyager* in the works and about *Next Generation* going to the movies that a lot of the attention was torn away from *Deep Space Nine*."

For Ira Behr, such questions are much ado about nothing. To him, what's important is the work and the quality of the episodes being broadcast. "We just do the best job putting it out there that we can and then whatever happens after that is almost beside the point. We are trying to please ourselves. We're obviously a grittier show and we don't quite have the rosy outlook [of *TNG*], although I think we're a very positive show in our own way.

"But I'm not talking about what's perceived — and usually what's perceived and what's real are two different things," he admits. "I think that *Deep Space Nine* will always be looked at by people as a very interesting take on *Star Trek*. We are getting about as 'out there' as *Star Trek* can get in terms of what we deal with and how we deal with it and the characters that we have."

Piller draws an interesting analogy between *Deep Space Nine* and its predecessor in the *Star Trek* universe by comparing them to two popular comic book superheroes. "*Next Generation* is like Superman and *Deep Space Nine* is like Batman. Clearly the complications and the psychological underpinnings and the quality of the storytelling and the angst is greater in Batman, but they both exist in the same DC Comics universe and they occasionally meet. The point is, if you think of all the pale imitations of Superman, they have all gone right out the window, but Batman has endured because it touches people in a certain, specific way. It is a more adult comic book. Somehow we have managed to do that with *Deep Space Nine*. Batman was never as popular as Superman was, but it has its own special audience. I think we've got that on *Deep Space Nine* — at least I hope so."

Going into second season, there were several problems with the first season Piller was intent on redressing. "I came out feeling that we still had a lot to prove to people who kept telling me, 'Well, you can't fly anywhere,' " he says. I was determined to say to these people, 'We can do everything that makes good television. We can have spaceships, we can fly into this station, we can have space battles, we can meet aliens. We can have anything you want on *Deep Space Nine*.' I thought we had done that first season, but as I went back and watched many of the episodes, I realized some episodes had credibility lapses in performance, in direction, in scripting, in the sets. The difference between having a credible hour of futuristic television and having an hour of unconvincing futuristic television is so slight. One wrong performance, one bad costume, can blow the whole thing.

"In the first year, there always seemed to be just enough credibility lacking in certain moments so that you'd never believe that you were in a futuristic space station," continues Piller. "I felt like we'd have to prove that in the second season, and we worked on the sets, but I think most of all we worked on the scripts. The first three-parter was a commitment to say, 'Hey, look at us. Look at what we can do.' It was, in a sense, supposed to do for us what 'Best of Both Worlds' had done for *Next Generation*. I think that we succeeded. Those three shows really did show the breadth of ambition of storytelling that we were able to do, and the special effects were terrific, the guest stars were great and the credibility was there." Piller was right in saying that the beginning of *DS9*'s second season was consistently strong, producing some of its finest episodes. "I think we started out with a terrific momentum," he says. "The first eight shows of *Deep Space Nine* were as strong a series of shows as I have been involved with."

One of the aspects of *Star Trek* that has often been cited as intrinsic to its nearly universal appeal is the family feeling of its crews. Some have criticized *Deep Space Nine* for lacking a warm, familylike ensemble, a notion disputed by its producers. "We get the same old stuff," says Ira Behr. "It's not a family. Well, it is a family — sometimes a dysfunctional family, but we have much more of a familylike the original series than *TNG*. Spock and

••••

Bones may not get along, but they love each other. These characters care about one another; Odo and Quark, Bashir and Garak, Kira and Dax, Dax and Sisko, Odo and Kira. I can't believe that it's such a hard concept to grasp. There are no unlikable people. I see that men are threatened by Kira, and they say they don't like her because she's too strong, but that's because we live in a screwed-up society, not because she's a bad character."

As Behr finds himself raising his voice, he catches himself, amazed at how caught up he's become in the mythos. "When I allow myself to think about it, I get extremely frustrated." He sighs. "I really like the show and so naturally I want other people to like the show. I want people to say, 'Hey, this is the only show on television that's dealing with religion.' What other show dares deal with religion on television? It's the same thing as *The Godfather, Part III*, which was a brilliant movie dealing with religion and big business, and no one seemed to mention that. *The L.A. Weekly* [a Los Angeles alternative newspaper] reviewed the final episode of *TNG* and they took a hit at us. They were reviewing them — but they

had to take a hit at us as well. And they were saying how lazy we are and how boring we are because all we do is Bosnia every week. I don't know if we do Bosnia any week, but I can't believe that people would take a shot at us for doing what I think is, for television, quite a sophisticated, subtle, multilevel look at nationalism and racism, but no one seems to care. It seems like, at times, we're in a vacuum."

Behr's faith in the appeal of the series was rewarded at a tribute the Museum of Television and Radio Broadcasting held in Los Angeles as part of its annual salute to quality television. Asked intelligent questions by the audience after a screening of "Duet," the producers and cast were all visibly moved by the acceptance of both their peers and the general audience.

"I think we have characters like Kira, Quark, Odo, Dax, Sisko and others who have such bright, clear character traits that it's easy to bring them into the lexicon of *Star Trek*," says Behr.

Offers Marc Alaimo, who portrays Gul Dukat, the former Cardassian commander of DS9, "It deals with conflicts we have as human beings that we can't really deal with human to human. The show can deal with prejudice and greed and hate and all that stuff in more interesting ways than human to human."

That may be the very element that has caused some of the vast *Star Trek* audience to tune out. The heavily politicized nature of the show — which weaves its intricate stories of political intrigue and Shakespearean theatrics on a tapestry encompassing the recently freed Bajoran world and the Federation's place in helping to maintain a stable political landscape while also tending off Cardassian aggression — isn't quite as simple as the *Enterprise*'s mandate to "boldly go."

"I think we do politics awfully well," says Piller. "The problem with that is there may be something to the fact that people would rather watch space monsters, enigmas and anomalies than politics. But one of the things I was proudest of with *Deep Space Nine*'s second season is that I began to realize during the course of the season that it takes a great deal more courage to stay and deal with the consequences of your actions and to deal with problems that don't get solved than it

is to go in, meet somebody, change their lives or have them teach us something and then zoom out to the next person."

Adds Ira Behr, "I think [story editor] Robert Wolfe explains it best: Unlike *TNG* and the original series, where you go out into the great void and explore and map and meet people and have adventures and then you leave, we know every move that Sisko makes, every thought he has, every action he takes, has repercussions that we can go back to and work on and play with. That's why we have the best supporting characters on television. From Dukat to Garak and Rom and Winn and all these wonderful people that we can continue to explore because they don't go away. We can leave as much as we want, but we always come back and the station is still there.

"And that's what I think Sisko's job ultimately is," continues Behr. "What we were trying to show without really articulating it while we were doing it was that Sisko's job is in a way more important, or certainly more complicated, than Picard's or Kirk's because they're explorers and he's a builder. What he has to do is basically build an alliance and build a relationship. It's a different thing than they get to do. They get to have fun. He gets to have fun too, but he has to make sure that his fun doesn't come and bite him on the ass three episodes down the line. That's what we realized second season, and I think it worked. There's a whole bubbling cauldron that just seemed to take on some new heat, at least for the writers. And we truly realized we were on a unique show with its own identity."

Says Piller, "I think we do politics very well, and politics is a lousy label to throw on certain stories because all of them have to do with the human drama. And if you don't like Klingons and you don't like Lursa and B'Etor fighting for control of the Klingon Empire, then maybe you didn't like the whole Klingon arc we did on *Next Generation*. Ultimately, we try to do a variety of stories and a mix of stories that really takes you to different places."

Armin Shimerman, whose character, Quark, represents the worst of twentieth-century avarice, comments, "They ask me to do scenes that are satires of current events, so I have a lot of stuff to work off of. Our show has been geared to always making comments on what's happening around us. If there is a difference between *TNG* and *Deep Space Nine* it is that we can involve ourselves in political issues. We *should* have our own arena. If we are more political, more power to us."

Interestingly, Sisko makes an impassioned speech in the episode "The Maquis" that could be considered defining for the show. In it, he points out how Earth may be a paradise in the twenty-fourth century, but the rest of the galaxy is not — positioning the show within the Roddenberry universe in a unique way. "We were able to give a speech about how it's easy to be safe in paradise," says Ira Behr, who wrote the episode. "The whole Roddenberry thing was believable when you're living back on Earth. We thought it was a fundamental thing to state. We're not pissing on *Star Trek;* it's a great view of the future. But we are on the frontier. It's not as simple as everyone behaving themselves. It's a difficult place to be.

"I am proud of the second season of the show," he adds. "I will always be proud of the show. The show is worth watching. There's always something to watch."

The success of the show's sec-ond year is echoed by many of those who worked on it. "There was wonderful development in several areas," says Shimerman. "Especially the interrelationships between a lot of the characters. There was further developing of the Sisko and Major Kira relationship. I believe the Lieutenant Dax character was more fleshed out in the second season than it was in the first. Both the writers and Terry Farrell found exactly who they think Dax is. I think we started out pretty well, and the second season furthered that even more. For myself, I didn't think necessarily the core character went that much further, but in 'The Jem'Hadar' a relationship that was first started in the pilot finally gets back on track a little and that's Sisko and Quark. I think there was a promise in the pilot that is being further fulfilled."

But even while the ensemble became better defined, the character of Sisko remained a bit of a cipher to the audience. In addition, nagging criticism of Avery Brooks's performance continued from some viewers as well. Piller, Behr and the writing staff dismiss these contentions but admit to being committed to continuing to define Sisko's role in future seasons. "I think that Avery is an amazingly interesting and talented actor," says Ira Behr. "We went to see him in his one-man show and it blew us away. He was charismatic, funny, talented. He sang, he danced, he told jokes, he made you cry. He did everything. We were dumbfounded at just how powerful he was as a presence. Some of that's not coming through in the show. I think some of it is us and some of it is that the pilot seemed to cover the character so well that after the pilot was over we didn't know what else to do with him. We've been talking about it a lot and we're going to be working on that. You're going to learn more about Sisko than just the fact he loves baseball."

Offers Piller, "We believed it's time that Sisko no longer lives in the past but in the present, and that we see what his agenda is — what he, as a hero, wants to accomplish here in this sector and in the Gamma Quadrant."

Despite the fact that *Deep Space Nine* entered its third season with a few slick additions, including a new briefing-room set and a powerful battleship to fight the Dominion — a new threat introduced in "The Jem'Hadar" — Ira Behr believes there will always be those unwilling to embrace the show. "I think it's part of this kind of sick need to have *Deep Space Nine* follow in the exact footsteps of *TNG*," he says. "It's just not going to happen."

••••

CHAPTER FIVE

Deep Space Nine: Season Two Episode Guide

"The Homecoming"

"The Circle"

"The Siege"

"Invasive Procedures"

"Cardassians"

"Melora"

"Rules of Acquisition"

"Necessary Evil"

"Second Sight"

"Sanctuary"

"Rivals"

"The Alternate"

"Armageddon Game"

"Whispers"

"Paradise"

"Shadowplay"

"Playing God"

"Profit and Loss"

"Blood Oath"

"The Maquis, Part I"

"The Maquis, Part II"

"The Wire"

"Crossover"

"The Collaborator"

"Tribunal"

"The Jem'Hadar"

••••

Episode #21
"The Homecoming"
Original Airdate: 9/27/93
Teleplay by Ira Steven Behr
Story by Jeri Taylor and Ira Steven
Behr
Directed by Winrich Kolbe
Guest Starring: Richard Beymer (Li
Nalas), Max Grodenchik (Rom),
Michael Bell (Borum), Marc Alaimo
(Gul Dukat), Frank Langella (Minister
Jaro)

When Quark gives Kira information that proves a famous Bajoran resistance fighter named Li Nalas is alive on a
Cardassian prison colony, she and O'Brien
take a runabout and implement a rescue.
The timing for the return of one of Bajor's
greatest heroes could not be better, as
there is much dissent on the planet. It
turns out that Li's reputation is based more
on rumor than reality, but it doesn't matter
when he finds himself caught up in a political web spun by the leaders of Bajor,
culminating in Minister Jaro's assigning
him as the Bajoran liaison officer to DS9
and reassigning Kira despite Sisko's objec-
tions. Simultaneously, an anti-Federation
movement known as the Circle begins to
wreak havoc on the station.

••••

"I'm not sure it was very smart
of us to do a three-part episode," says
Michael Piller of the Bajoran trilogy that
began the second season. "It certainly accomplished creatively what we set out to
do, but it got the worst ratings in repeats. It
scared a lot of people. I just have the feeling that perhaps it was not the strategic
thing to do in terms of ratings. In terms of
creativity, I couldn't be happier."

Adds Ira Behr, "Michael, back
from his days as a network executive, is
definitely a man who is into publicity, and
he said, 'You know, we didn't do a cliff-
hanger. Let's do a three-parter. Let's do
three and let's jump off from "In the Hands
of the Prophets." And since I have to relate
everything to either a book or a movie in
my life, it seems, I said, 'So in other words
"In the Hands of the Prophets" is The
Hobbit, and now we are going to do the
Lord of the Rings trilogy.' I don't know if
he knew what I was talking about, but
that's how I saw it."

Says series producer David Livingston, "It was like doing a movie or a

miniseries. It had a lot of gunfights and
space battles. Piller threw it all into the
mix. It was big. We knew we were going
to spend a lot of money for the first three
episodes and that we'd have to make it up
later, but Rick and Michael just wanted to
start off the season with a bang, and I think
we did."

Director Winrich Kolbe feels the
same way, believing that a lot was accomplished in "The Homecoming." "That was
the first episode of the three-parter, although Rick Berman didn't want to call it
a three-parter for some odd reason," he
says. "It started out with a bang because
we went out on location to shoot the
labor-camp sequence. We were shooting
in the beginning of July, and it was getting
hot. It was a quarry, or part of a quarry,
that the owner let us use for the prison
camp. It fit all of our purposes. We were
isolated from everything. The only thing
that bothered us was an occasional air-
plane.

"That was an interesting experience," he adds, "because we were tum-
bling all over. In good Kolbe tradition, I
refused to shoot everything in the same direction. I said, 'I'm paying for the same location whether I shoot it at an angle of five
degrees or an angle of three hundred sixty
degrees.' We get so much of the same
stuff. Shooting in the same direction, move
the walls but don't move the actors, is the
old Jack Webb tradition of shooting. It
was a lot cheaper than my style right
now or the style appreciated today. But
on the other hand, I think we do a little
more quality work than they did on
Dragnet."

One particular joy for Kolbe was
having the opportunity to spend a lot of
time working with Nana Visitor. "She's a
hell of an actress to work with and she's
wonderful for the part," he offers. "Very
often the males run the show, and you get
some sort of 'blah' but wonderful-looking
woman for a particular female part and
you really lose that character. But she is
the second in command and she's got to
have some — and I use the word very,
very carefully — balls to make that happen. Nana brings an aspect to the particular part which makes it believable. She's
loyal to the Federation, but she's also a
Bajoran, and that dichotomy comes
through and she will react to it."

Episode #22
"The Circle"
Original Airdate: 10/4/93
Written by Peter Allan Fields
Directed by Corey Allen
Guest Starring: Richard Beymer (Li
Nalas), Stephen Macht (Krim), Bruce
Gray (Admiral Chekote), Mike Genovese
(Zef'no), Philip Anglim (Vedek Bareil),
Frank Langella (Minister Jaro), Louise
Fletcher (Vedek Winn)

The political manipulation continues as Jaro's actions have Kira reas-
signed on Bajor and the influence of the
Circle begins to grow. Through various investigations, Odo and Sisko eventually
learn that the Circle has been supplied
arms by an alien race, the Kressari, and
that Jaro plans on using them to cause a
revolution that will put him in the ultimate
position of power on the planet. As the
layers of intrigue are peeled back further,
it is discovered that — unknown even to
Jaro — the true source of the arms is Cardassia, which wants to cause a revolution
on Bajor that will result in the Federation's
pulling out and the Cardassians' moving in
to reconquer. Starfleet orders Sisko to
evacuate the station, though he isn't quite
ready to give up.

••••

Louise Fletcher reprised her role
as the malevolent Vedek Winn from season one's "In the Hands of the Prophets."
"They just asked me to play this outrageous part, and I thought it was this one-
time thing," says the actress, who won an
Academy Award for her portrayal of Nurse
Ratchet in One Flew Over the Cuckoo's
Nest. "Then they kept coming back and
asking me to do more. As it turned out, I
was available most of the time. You just
run over to Paramount, put on the costume and you try and remember the
words, which is not easy. It's a lot of language and it's almost classical. I don't
want to say Shakespearean, but [Winn]
does have the tragic flaw of ambition and
pride. It's fun to play that high drama. Villains often come across as the nicest
people, and that's just pure fun to play."

As for shooting the surreal, mystical vision in which Major Kira envisions
herself stripped bare before Vedek Bareil,
who transforms into the visage of Winn,
Livingston laughs. "We just told Corey
[Allen] that he couldn't show breasts, and

STAR TREK
DEEP SPACE NINE
PROUD HELIOS

Deep Space Nine™
versus interstellar
pirates!

Melissa Scott

he guaranteed us that he wouldn't. He shot it discreetly and tastefully, and it came off. It was sexy, but it was certainly airable and not offensive."

Frank Langella (Dracula, Cutthroat Island, Doomsday Gun) returned as Minister Jaro, although he refused to take a credit on the episode.

Episode #23
"The Siege"
Original Airdate: 10/11/93
Written by Michael Piller
Directed by Winrich Kolbe
Guest Starring: Rosalind Chao (Keiko O'Brien), Steven Weber (Day), Richard Beymer (Li Nalas), Stephen Macht (Krim), Max Grodenchik (Rom), Aron Eisenberg (Nog), Philip Anglim (Vedek Bareil), Frank Langella (Minister Jaro), Louise Fletcher (Vedek Winn)

Everything comes to a head as most of DS9 is evacuated in preparation for arriving Bajoran troops. Sisko and his key officers remain in hiding on the station, and Kira and Dax seek out the evidence they need to prove that the Cardassians are behind the Bajoran revolution. While the former hold their own,

Kira and Dax get what they need and proceed to the Chamber of Ministers, where the truth is revealed. Jaro is stunned to learn that he has been manipulated by the Cardassians, the end result being that the provisional government will remain in place and the Federation will continue to supervise the space station. One rebel cannot accept this, however, and attempts to assassinate Sisko, but Li Nalas — turning out to be every bit the hero everyone had made him out to be — sacrifices himself to save the commander.

• • • •

"Michael had stolen a show from [TNG executive producer] Jeri Taylor that she had bought for Next Generation about finding an ex-terrorist who was imprisoned by the Cardassians," recalls Ira Behr. "What I got to do and what really got Michael interested was add another level to the show. 'Why don't we make this The Man Who Shot Liberty Valance?' he said. The guy isn't really a hero, but he shot a guy in his underwear. That's what made the show for me in my own mind. Then Michael said, 'Why don't we start with The Man Who Shot Liberty Valance and end with The Alamo? Let's do a siege and see how our people fight a guerrilla war. Let's see Bashir become Robin Hood,' and we did."

Interestingly, Behr fought against killing Nalas, an argument rejected by Piller, who insisted that the character die at the show's conclusion. "I thought he was a very interesting character that we never really got to explore enough," says Behr. "That's my only disappointment with the show. Michael felt he had to pay since a character like that can't live a lie."

Of working with Frank Langella, director Winrich Kolbe says laughing, "He scared the shit out of me. There's a mythology around him. He's a tremendous actor and he's got those dark brown eyes that seem to strip you bare of anything that you're wearing emotionally or literally. When he popped up on the first bit, and I know exactly what it was (it was the side entrance to the air lock that leads to the cargo bay), we started rehearsing, and I figured, 'This guy could be trouble,' because there's something in him that tells you, 'Watch that guy. If you tell him what to do, he might just tell you to fuck off.'

But he didn't. He was terrific. We talked about what we wanted to do. We're not talking about any very deep characterization here. There wasn't much there, and I figured whatever he brings into it, unless he's way out of the ballpark, can be handled. He's so good as an actor that you can't go wrong with him. And it was always, 'Would it be all right if I would be on this side? . . .' His instincts were perfect, and he didn't punch it in. He didn't say, 'I'm going to stop here and I don't care where you wind up with the camera,' which sometimes happens and you have to pedal very fast. He was also so shy. He didn't even want to announce that his last shot was done. He had said, 'Once we shoot the last shot, please don't say, "This is the last shot for Frank Langella."' He just faded away."

Kolbe admits that "The Siege" was not as intriguing to him as "The Homecoming" had been. "What was nice about [both episodes]," he points out, "is that when I started prepping the first episode, I had the script for part three in my hands and I had also read part two, which is a miracle. In order to do part three — Corey Allen was doing part two — I needed to figure out what that particular link was all about, what was evolving, in order for me to pick up the story in part three. To be very honest, I like 'The Homecoming' best. I didn't particularly care for 'The Siege.' It was more of a hardware show. The bad guys take over the ship. On an action level it was quite good, I think, but on a character level it did not measure up to 'The Homecoming.' "

He concedes that it's difficult to write what is essentially a three-hour episode. "I think the metaphor for any artistic endeavor, especially an endeavor that involves time, is Boléro. If you start too fast and too high, you have nowhere to go. If you start too slow, you might never get where you want to go. So it's a very precarious balance. With writing, the longer the writing stretches and the longer the arc of writing stretches, in this case three hours, the more difficult it is not to — pardon me — blow your wad in episode number one and say, 'We basically solved all the problems. What do we do for the next two hours?' It's not quite that extreme, but my feeling was that in

• • • •

'The Siege,' the last part, we were really vamping."

Episode #24
"Invasive Procedures"
Original Airdate: 10/18/93
Teleplay by John Whelpley and Robert Hewitt Wolfe
Story by John Whelpley
Directed by Les Landau
Guest Starring: John Glover (Verad), Megan Gallagher (Mareel), Tim Russ (T'Kar), Steve Rankin (Yeto)

Dax's worst nightmare comes true when a group of people led by the timid Verad board DS9 after it has been virtually evacuated due to an approaching plasma storm. Verad, it turns out, is a Trill who was rejected as a symbiont host and he is determined to fulfill what he perceives as his destiny by stealing Jadzia's symbiont. After sealing Odo in a specially designed containment unit, the group forces Bashir to perform the operation, which is ultimately successful. Jadzia is left feeling empty, and Verad senses that for the first time in his life he's complete. Sisko attempts to reverse the situation by tapping into his shared memories with Curzon Dax and, when this fails to elicit the proper response in Verad, he feeds into the paranoia of the man's lover, Mareel. Ultimately, Sisko stuns the Trill with a phaser blast, and Bashir reverses the operation. Jadzia is returned to normal — now having Verad's feelings and memories as well — while Verad is devastated by his loss.

••••

"I've been extremely pleased with the growth of Terry's performance," says Michael Piller. "I thought she was very touching in this episode, and the ensemble really worked together very well. John Glover was terrific. It was just a natural concept for us. We basically took our cue from shows like *The Petrified Forest* and *Key Largo*."

"This was the beginning of a concerted effort to make Dax's character more interesting second season," says Ira Behr. "We gave her more of a sense of humor. We said, 'She's not Spock. She's never going to be Spock. Let's make her more interesting.' And we're going to continue to work with that character. I think

Terry Farrell as science officer Dax (copyright © 1995 by Albert Ortega).

that whole Trill backstory is going to be explored."

One concern among the production team was showing the Trill symbiont as it was transplanted into Verad's body. "We didn't want it to look cheesy," says David Livingston. "It was always a problem showing it. It's that whole idea of *Alien*; you don't really want to see too much because the audience is either going to be repulsed by it or say it's too hokey."

"The makeup guys were gentlemen," laughs Terry Farrell of having the necessary pouch prosthetics and spotting applied to her nude body. "They didn't look, not even a peek."

"I had a grand time," says guest star John Glover. "The whole Dax thing was wonderfully playable. We had to reshoot the last scene, where they removed Dax from me, because I looked dead. I hope that I can come back someday. Maybe I can escape from the insane asylum and try again another season." Glover particularly enjoyed the part because it was so "psychological." "Those parts are actors' dreams," he says. "At the beginning he's so insecure about himself and has no self-confidence but wants that power so much — which is of course so

dangerous in a human being. In coming up with the variations for the character, I tried to work in a very human way. The fact that he trained all of his life to receive Dax was something I thought about. You know, the insecurity of the man and his need to have it. And then of course that incredible concept that when it does enter you, you've got all those other lifelong experiences of all those other people. Basically I just tried to imagine what was given me. That's another reason I thought the part was so good, because it was so well written with so many active, playable things. There was that great scene with Avery where we're reminiscing and remembering our pasts, and he brings up the one guilt thing, where I realize what I did was so bad and so wrong. It was just so rich and chock-full of great human things."

Dealing with phaser blasts that weren't actually there was easy for Glover. Probably the most difficult aspect of the show in terms of special effects from his perspective was Odo's entering the storage unit. "We spent a lot of time on that," he notes. "That was very bizarre as we did take after take of getting all of our eyes lined up as we followed him down. It's quite amazing how they put all those effects in. It just amazes me."

In addition to John Glover, Megan Gallagher from the first season of *The Larry Sanders Show, China Beach, Nowhere Man* and *Millennium* guest starred as Mareel. "Glover was great, but so was Megan Gallagher. I thought she was just wonderful," says Ira Behr. "It was one of my favorite shows of the season. I love the stuff with Verad becoming Dax and the scene with him and Sisko where he's suddenly his friend. It was very interesting material and well played. Les Landau did a wonderful job directing that show."

Episode #25
"Cardassians"
Original Airdate: 10/25/93
Teleplay by James Crocker
Story by Gene Wolander and John Wright
Directed by Cliff Bole
Guest Starring: Rosalind Chao (Keiko O'Brien), Andrew Robinson (Garak), Robert Mandan (Kotan Pa'Dar), Terrence Evans (Proka), Vidal Peterson (Ru-

gal), Dion Anderson (Zolan), Marc Alaimo (Gul Dukat)

When Garak is attacked by a Cardassian boy brought to the station by his Bajoran foster father, Bashir begins an investigation that reveals that numerous children were left behind when the Cardassians withdrew from Bajor. It turns out that the boy, Rugal, is actually being used as a pawn in a political struggle between Gul Dukat and Pa'Dar, Rugal's natural father.

••••

"I didn't have a lot of faith in this show at first," admits Ira Behr. "It was such an issue-oriented show that I thought we would oversimplify a complicated issue, but what got me into the show was when I realized this was not only a chance to bring back Garak but to do this whole weird little number with what's going on between him and Dukat. To me, that nailed the character and I knew after that happened we were going to see a lot of Andy Robinson, who's become quite popular on staff. What did not work for me was the kid and O'Brien. I thought that was very obvious stuff compared to the rest of the episode. Sometimes we have a tendency to overload the stories. Ultimately, who cared about this kid? It was weak compared to the rest of the episode."

"As an actor, when I got the script, I didn't realize Dukat was being set up to take the blame," says Marc Alaimo, who portrays Gul Dukat. "But I played him as a man who was being set up. A man who was taking the dive because he had wanted to remove the children but his orders were to leave them. I never really understood that story. It seemed complicated to me, and I never quite understood how he got blamed for it."

Episode #26
"Melora"
Original Airdate: 11/1/93
Teleplay by Evan Carlos Somers, Steven Baum and Michael Piller
Story by Evan Carlos Somers
Directed by Winrich Kolbe
Guest Starring: Daphne Ashbrook (Melora), Peter Crombie (Fallit Kot), Don Stark (Ashrock)

Ensign Melora Pazler, a cartographer whose task is to do some charting in the Gamma Quadrant, arrives at DS9 in a wheelchair. Melora is an Elaysian, a species that exists on a planet with extremely low gravity, so rather than walking they essentially fly through the air there. Bashir is captivated by her beauty and her mind, and the two of them almost immediately make a connection. To this end, Bashir begins a series of treatments that will enable Melora to walk in normal gravity situations, though the negative side effect is that she will from that moment on be different from all other Elaysians. Ultimately, she elects to remain as she is. Concurrently, Quark is doing everything he can — even going to Odo for help! — to stop one Fallit Kot, who has proclaimed that he will kill the Ferengi.

••••

"This was not an easy show to write," admits Michael Piller. "This script probably went through five or six rewrites. I was quite proud of what I wrote in that script because it turned out to be a delightful little show. And the interesting thing about it is that I knew, even when it was over with, that it had no real story to it. It had no real drama, but I thought there was a true romance going on between the actors on stage. It came through on film and I just thought that Daphne [Ashbrook] gave a wonderful performance. The result was a charming episode, a slice of life for Bashir, and I thought it was a warm episode."

Says Ira Behr, "We needed a love story for Bashir. We wanted to continue showing the audience why we were investing so much in Bashir, because we just thought it was a character who had a lot of things going for him, and I know there has been some resistance to him, which is just ridiculous. We wanted to do a strong show for him, and I thought it was a nice story. I loved the Klingon restaurant."

"We had a lot of discussions about it," says series producer David Livingston of sending Elaysian ensign Melora Pazler sailing into the air in the embrace of Dr. Bashir. "We did a lot less flying than we wanted to because we knew we couldn't pull it off on a television schedule. We used a digital wire-removal process that takes away the wires, and it was very successful, but it's also expensive and time consuming. It's hard enough when people are standing on the ground to shoot them, so when you have them flying around in the air and kissing and hugging, it's tough. But [director Winrich] Kolbe is very technically grounded, and the optical effects people were always there with him to make sure it came off."

"I think it turned out to be rather good, considering the technical difficulties we had," offers Kolbe. "If I like to shoot at three hundred sixty degrees, I also like to have everybody fly like real birds. The problem is that in episodic television you just don't have enough time to do that. The state of the art right now is kind of difficult to do because it's a very time-consuming affair. We did it with wires, no mirrors. The unfortunate thing is that I only had two rods to support the wires, so I had to decide, 'Which way do I want her to fly?' Basically straight, otherwise it would have required a totally different rig. The rigs that we had were used in Wayne's World 2. It was basically a situation where you could fly one way and then the opposite way, and that was about it. It was difficult to figure out what we could do so that it didn't just look like somebody going up and down. The image of Peter Pan going across the stage with one leg cocked and the other leg straight always went through my mind, and I said, 'Oh God, we can't do that.' We had the stunt coordinator there, and the actress, Daphne Ashbrook, did quite well. She was terrific. She was a good sport and didn't chicken out. One of the most enthusiastic actresses I've ever seen and a damn good actress in addition to that.

"Overall," he adds, "it was more of a romantic little story between two people. Siddig is a wonderful actor and is the type to fall in love with a flying woman. It's a little more restricted because it's a character piece."

As for the show's B story, in which Quark is threatened by an old partner, Piller comments, "It was always there because we needed to put these people in jeopardy. But the B story was a struggle. We never quite knew what it was going to be. The first-draft story had terrorists or something. We did whatever was necessary to bring the two stories together. Everything about that story did not work, including the fact that we were doing a story where an alien has to eat, which becomes a pivotal scene where he's feeding, and makeup designed this big kind of

••••

handle across his mouth so he couldn't eat. We had to kind of shove the food down his mouth. It was hilarious. We cracked up during dailies."

Episode #27
"Rules of Acquisition"
Original Airdate: 11/8/93
Teleplay by Ira Steven Behr
Story by Hilary J. Bader
Directed by David Livingston
Guest Starring: Helene Udy (Pel), Brian Thompson (Inglatu), Max Grodenchik (Rom), Emilia Crow (Zyree), Tiny Ron (Maihar-du), Wallace Shawn (Zek)

Grand Nagus Zek returns to the space station, where he tells Quark that he wants the Ferengi to be his chief negotiator in the Gamma Quadrant. Additionally, Zek talks Sisko into allowing him to hold a business conference with the Dosi on DS9. Quark is naturally thrilled over his good fortune, though one of his waiters, a Ferengi named Pel, warns him to be careful, for if Quark is successful, Zek will claim all the benefits, but if their efforts are a disaster, Quark will be the one blamed. So impressed with this advice is Quark that he asks Pel to be his assistant, which fills Quark's brother, Rom, with jealousy. Furious, Rom tries to find something that will discredit Pel in his brother's eyes and finds it when he discovers that Pel is actually a female who happens to be in love with Quark. By Ferengi law, females cannot take a part in business affairs, therefore Pel threatens all of Quark's potential profits. She does manage to keep Quark out of trouble with Zek, although she departs the station shortly thereafter. While admitting that he has fallen in love with her, Quark is forced to face the fact that when he gets married, he wants it to be to a traditional Ferengi wife.

••••

Michael Piller admits that he was a little unhappy with the Dosi alien makeup and headdresses of the episode. "Sometimes less is more," he says simply. "One of the aliens looked like Joe Piscopo in a *Saturday Night Live* skit. The credibility factor is so important. You had to swallow that to get into that episode."

David Livingston disagrees. "I personally felt that in 'Rules of Acquisition' these aliens were just right for the episode. Because whatever anybody may

say, I think it's a comedy. I keep being told that we don't do comedy on *Star Trek*, but I think it was a comedy. And that's why I think that the over-the-top nature of those aliens and their screwy makeup and their attitudes and their overblown posturing and stuff was right for the episode."

Says Behr, who wrote "The Nagus" first season, "I wasn't dying to write a Ferengi episode again, but Rick Berman caught me in the parking lot one night and said, 'What is all this? You know you're gonna write it eventually. Why don't you just do it and save us two weeks?' So I said, OK, I will. The thing that sold the show to me was coming up with the Dominion. I have mixed feelings about how it turned out. I think some of it is quite good. I thought they blew the big scene in the tent when [Pel] kisses [Quark]. It was not done the way I expected it to be. It was too schticky and slapstick and it should have been a wonderful, confusing scene. I was not a happy camper when I saw those dailies."

Livingston once again directed Wallace Shawn as the Grand Nagus, Zek. "I've always felt that 'The Nagus' was one of my better episodes and I think 'Rules of Acquisition' is even a better show because there's more story in it. It's more emotional. It's a love story. And I thought Helene Udy as Pel was just extraordinary. I've talked to people who've said that they didn't know she was a woman until she took off her vest."

Episode #28
"Necessary Evil"
Original Airdate: 11/15/93
Written by Peter Allan Fields
Directed by James L. Conway
Guest Starring: Katherine Moffat (Pallra), Max Grodenchik (Rom), Marc Alaimo (Gul Dukat)

When an attempt is made on Quark's life and vital information is gotten from Rom, Odo begins an investigation into the five-year-old murder of a Bajoran named Vaatrick, who had been a member of the Bajoran slave force held on the station by the Cardassians. The more Odo digs, however, the more likely it seems that Kira was involved in the murder. Eventually, Kira tells Odo that she was a member of the Bajoran underground and that she had played a role in sabotaging

the ore processor the night Vaatrick was killed. This turns out to be a lie, however, as she actually did kill the man because he was a Cardassian collaborator who tried to stop her from obtaining a list of names of other collaborators. Odo says nothing of this to anyone, though the bond between them may be damaged beyond repair.

••••

"I thought that this was as close to a perfect episode as we have done," says Michael Piller. "There was great stuff between Kira and Odo, and Katherine Moffat did wonderful work in the Lana Turner role as Pallra. The greatest regret I have about that show is that I allowed Rick to take out one scene that would have really made it better. That was a scene where Odo, having just talked to Kira, was going to see Pallra and he sees Gul Dukat coming out of her room and he kisses her good-bye, indicating that they just had sex. When Dukat walks away, we go around the corner where Odo was and there is now a picture that is crooked. Gul Dukat straightens it out and walks on, and then Odo goes to see Pallra. If we had left that in, that would have suggested that Gul Dukat, a red herring, might have also been involved in the murder and was involved in covering it up somehow. That would have been an interesting additional element for people to be thinking about during the course of the show. I have never been as sorry about cutting something out as I feel about that."

David Livingston believes this was one of their better episodes, if not actually the best show they've done. "Jim Conway is an extraordinary director, and it was an extraordinary script. Jim wanted to do film noir, and Marvin Rush delivered it. It has a terrific look and it shows you what the station was like under Cardassian rule."

"What I loved about that show is that it was left ambiguous between us," says Nana Visitor of the revelation that Kira is guilty of murdering a Bajoran collaborator. "Odo doesn't trust me the way he did and he never will, and that's so truthful to me. That's real life, and that's one of the things this show does very well. It doesn't tie things up in nice, neat little bows for the audience. It gives them more credit than that."

••••

Nana Visitor as Major Kira Nerys (copyright © 1995 by Albert Ortega).

Says Ira Behr, "It was an attempt to see how Odo and Kira met for the first time and see Odo as an investigator. Then it just grew. What nailed it was the sense of betrayal and the fact that this close relationship between Kira and Odo started out based on this lie, which just makes for fascinating storytelling. I think the director, who also did 'Duet,' Jim Conway, can take a lot of credit. It worked. All pistons were firing; it was a great show."

"I do think these characters grow and are continuing to grow," says Max Grodenchik, who plays Rom. "In 'Necessary Evil' Odo says to me, 'You are a hero, Rom. You saved your brother's life.' That feels good. I think Rom is torn between both sides of that — being a good brother and wanting the bar. He is very conflicted, and I think that is a good thing. We are all conflicted about something. It is more sophisticated and true to life than just saying Rom just wants the bar, because I think Rom also wants his brother's approval. He even says in that episode, 'I tried so hard to win my brother's trust, but now he is dead and I can never earn it.' He wants the bar to prove to his brother that he can make great profit. When Quark went away to the Gamma Quadrant with Pel, he did great business."

Episode #29
"Second Sight"
Original Airdate: 11/22/93
Teleplay by Mark Gehred-O'Connell, Ira Steven Behr and Robert Hewitt Wolfe
Story by Mark Gehred-O'Connell
Directed by Alexander Singer
Guest Starring: Salli Elise Richardson (Fenna/Nidell), Richard Kiley (Seyetik)

For the first time since his wife died at the hands of the Borg, Sisko falls in love. Her name is Fenna and somehow she is the exact duplicate in all ways but personality of Nidell, wife of Professor Seyetik, who has designed a means of bringing life to lifeless worlds. Sisko grows more and more confused when Fenna mysteriously disappears and reappears, and things only become clear when Seyetik explains that his wife is a psychoprojective telepath. Fenna, it turns out, is one of numerous images that Nidell has created, and, as she actually consists of pure energy, there is no chance of love between Fenna and Sisko.

••••

It's Michael Piller's opinion that "Second Sight" just doesn't work as an episode (and who are we to argue?). "It had a great premise," he says. "It's the old *Portrait of Jennie* idea where a mysterious woman keeps disappearing in front of your eyes, and we should have made it work."

"The character was supposed to be John Huston," says Ira Behr of Richard Kiley's Seyetik. "Someone who was bigger than life but not overbearing. What we kept saying was that the whole thing is going to depend on Sisko and this guy genuinely liking each other. When that did not happen, you had nothing. The dialogue was there, but it was played with grimaces and looks. The second thing that hurt a lot is that this was the closest we get to that dreaded *F* word. It was almost a *fantasy*. It had to have a light touch and be almost sentimental, but it was not that at all."

Richard Kiley, whose performances in *The Music Man* and *All My Sons* are legendary, guest starred as the egotistical scientist Seyetik.

Episode #30
"Sanctuary"
Original Airdate: 11/29/93

Teleplay by Frederick Rappaport
Story by Gabe Essoe and Kelley Miles
Directed by Les Landau
Guest Starring: William Schallert (Varani), Andrew Koenig (Tumak), Aron Eisenberg (Nog), Michael Durrell (General Hazar), Betty McGuire (Vayna), Robert Curtis-Brown (Vedek Sorad), Kitty Swink (Rozahn), Deborah May (Haneek)

A scout ship with four Skrreeans aboard comes through the wormhole, and they are beamed aboard DS9. The group's leader, Haneek, relays that there are three million of her people on the other side of the wormhole, all waiting to come through in order to find their homeland, Kentanna. Trying to help them, Sisko discovers a seemingly suitable planet, Draylon Two. At the same time, Haneek learns that Kentanna is actually Bajor. The refugees want to settle there, but the Bajoran government, which is already dealing with numerous problems, refuses to accept them and will go so far as using military force to keep them from immigrating. On a personal level, Haneek lashes out at Kira when she sides with the government on the issue.

••••

Of Kira's dilemma, Michael Piller points out that the character can easily be put in a situation where both sides have very clear arguments. "Sure, she's sympathetic with people who have a plight and are trying to escape," he says, "but the Bajorans also have a very serious problem: They have an economy that's broken and problems of their own, and how do you take care of a whole new group of people when you need to take care of yourself? Both arguments were meant to be as sympathetically presented as possible. Certainly you can understand Kira's position. She desperately relates to these people, wants to help them, but what do you do with them? There are no clear answers. I love shows when the audience can't say what's right and what's wrong. This is one of those shows. I thought it was quite effective."

From a production standpoint, the show was a difficult challenge. "The makeup was the main problem on the show," says David Livingston. "We had to put all these pimples on everybody's face, and [director] Les [Landau] had to wait for

••••

them to get ready. We also had to make costumes for them and budget enough money so that we could hire enough people so that you had the sense that the station was being overwhelmed with them."

"It was a show with a difficult history," says Ira Behr. "The writers who pitched it originally had a lot of trouble with the story. We never thought we'd get it. We were going with people who smelled and ugly people and so on. We went through everything we could come up with for a race. The thing that finally sold it was when we decided they would flake. There's something just disgusting and intrusive about an alien race that comes and leaves bits of themselves on your table and on your glasses. Michael insisted Kira be wrong, that we couldn't just make it easy and give the audience an easy answer. The last scene where the woman tells Kira she's wrong, I thought, had the impact of a physical blow. It was really well done. I liked doing the stuff with the language and the weird stuff with the two husbands who serviced her. It was a great show. Here was Kira, who fights for justice, facing a real problem of personal justice. And when it becomes a real tough decision, you can't make it."

Episode #31
"Rivals"
Original Airdate: 1/3/94
Teleplay by Joe Menosky
Story by Jim Trombetta and Michael Piller
Directed by David Livingston
Guest Starring: Rosalind Chao (Keiko O'Brien), Barbara Bosson (Roana), K. Callan (Alsia), Max Grodenchik (Rom), Albert Henderson (Cos), Chris Sarandon (Martus)

Quark's bar is given serious competition by the newest Deep Space Nine gambling establishment, Club Martus, which is owned and operated by a con man named Martus, who, it turns out, is using an alien device to cheat his customers. While Quark does everything in his power to expose Martus, the alien device is tied to O'Brien's feeling old when Bashir continually beats him at racquetball.

• • • •

Writer Jim Trombetta admits that writing the story for this episode was ex-

tremely frustrating "because there was this subplot of the racquetball game that they had wanted to put in a number of times and had not been able to, so they put it in this [episode] after I was gone because they felt it made the most sense since this was about games. I would have liked to have done more with the quantum-luck thing. I had the idea that if randomness could be managed, then you're in a lot of trouble. Basically, the universe is random; it's a mind-boggling thing. Eventually Quark would beat [Martus] by using Mr. Randomness. We never got into that, although I would have liked to. Ultimately, it seemed a little confusing. I never explained the quantum gambling device adequately. The problem is, after ten drafts there's always a problem that never quite gets solved. I've written six or seven outlines for some of these things, but then the problem gets to be part of the solution that might be plausible."

"When we did 'Rivals,' I thought that the character of Martus had a chance of being a recurring one," says Michael Piller. "It was like Harry Mudd or something like that. But I don't think it will. I thought it was an average episode, albeit with some great character stuff in it."

The idea of a device controlling random luck was one of several pitches bought from writer Jim Trombetta first season. "It was around for a year, and Jim came up with all these quirky science-fiction ideas," says Piller. "We had to figure ways to make them work as Star Treks. It was a little quirky for us, but you've got to take some chances."

Says Ira Behr, "I can happily say that 'Rivals' was not a show I did a lot of work on. I don't think we had a lead guest star who worked. We were looking for a Michael Caine, Dirty Rotten Scoundrels type, and Chris Sarandon was a lot more stolid and less effervescent. There were a lot of nice moments, and I loved Max [Grodenchik]. I think Rom is a great character, and he's someone we can keep exploring because the relationship between brothers is endlessly fascinating. I love the Bashir/O'Brien stuff also. I could have seen the whole just be about that. We bought the idea about random luck in a fit of needing to buy stories, which happens sometimes, but it never made any sense. We never cared about it. It's too much to

justify. I don't think there was an episode we did all year that didn't have something in it that was watchable, and this had the whole O'Brien and Bashir story, which was very watchable."

"It was another light kind of story with kinetic elements," says David Livingston, who directed the episode. "Working with Colm and Siddig was fun. I didn't have any time to shoot the racquetball match, so it was one of those things where you're just going on adrenaline and instinct. I was literally just shooting only the pieces that I needed. And when it was all put together, I surprised myself. It came out much better than I thought, because I had these horrible thoughts it wasn't going to work.

"It's a lot of work," he says of directing an episode of the ambitious science-fiction series. "I always say it's a lot of work, and nobody believes me. But when you have to stage a whole bunch of extras and also have big explosions and things like that it takes a lot of time — and I take a lot of time. I also tend to do stuff in oners rather than a lot of cuts, and that takes a lot of time to stage and make sure the camera works right. I know my deficiencies and it's that I do a lot of takes. I do ten to twelve takes a shot." Sharing a Star Trek directing secret, he adds, "What we do on the show when you go past ten or eleven takes is you change the slate number so you don't look like an idiot."

Lois & Clark's K. Callan plays Alsia and Murder One's Barbara Bosson, the wife of TV producer Steven Bochco, plays Roana. Chris Sarandon, of course, is well known to film fans from his villainous vampiric turn in Fright Night and The Princess Bride.

Episode #32
"The Alternate"
Original Airdate: 1/10/94
Teleplay by Bill Dial
Story by Jim Trombetta and Bill Dial
Directed by David Carson
Guest Starring: James Sloyan (Dr. Mora Pol)

Odo is reunited with Bajoran scientist Dr. Mora Pol, who studied the shape-shifter when he was first discovered. Claiming to have some knowledge of Odo's background, Pol lures him to a planet where he's exposed to a mysterious

• • • •

gas that, upon his return to the station, causes Odo to metamorphose into a rampaging creature. All of this has been orchestrated by Pol, who wants to continue his experiments on Odo, whom he considers more a thing than a person.

••••

Offers writer Jim Trombetta, "To be honest, the character I always wanted to write for the most was Odo. I gave him a multiple personality [in "The Alternate"] with the result that he kept taking a different shape, and nobody knew what he was or what he was doing, including himself. But that's a great character, because he's like a virus; he seems to be one molecule or something. He's just very interesting, and Rene is a great actor.

"It was a hard story to write," he continues. "I said, this is a matter of logic; if there is a toxic spill or something, and he's developed a multiple personality, psychosis or something, which they don't know anything about, he's going to have a different body when he has the other personality. Not only is he not going to know what he's doing, other people aren't going to know either. They're just going to find that there's a mysterious monster on board. I had that monster theme several different ways, and what they finally did was have this big monster be a different being. It was very intelligent; it expressed certain things in [Odo's] subconscious — things he wouldn't normally be able to express. It was also helpful, which they added later, to have his sort of mentor appear."

"I like this show," says Michael Piller of David Carson's last directorial effort prior to assuming the helm of *Generations*. "It's the closest thing we've ever done to a monster movie, and the hardest part was to keep the secret that Odo was the one who was actually doing it. I had to throw in a bunch of red herrings."

James Sloyan, the pitchman for Lexus cars who played Dr. Mora Pol, Odo's former caretaker, has also appeared in two episodes of *TNG*, "The Defector" and "Firstborn." "The character is exciting because he really doesn't want his protégé to succeed," says Piller. "He pats him on the back and says you can't make it out here with a warmth and sincerity a lot of people can relate to. There were a lot of

interesting psychological issues going on there."

"It was a cross between *Forbidden Planet* and primal therapy," says Ira Behr. "I think Rene [Auberjonois] is one of the best actors we have, and he not only plays dialogue, but he plays the spaces between the dialogue. You can give him a moment, and he's unbelievable. Originally, Rene was going to play both roles, but it would have been too difficult to have him in and out of makeup as Odo and Pol. We had to drop back at the last minute. As for his changing, don't ask me about that, because I still don't know. Was it the gas? The red herring didn't quite work for me all that much, but it's window dressing. Was there ever a John Ford movie that didn't have stuff in it that didn't work? But it doesn't annoy you because you're buying the package, and this package was just so rich. The scene where Odo starts losing it in front of his 'dad' broke my heart. Rene has the ability to break my heart."

So how does Carson compare directing his last *Deep Space Nine* episode to helming a big-budget feature film? "Well, it's just a different animal," says Carson. "One can't wish one had thirty million dollars [for a television episode]. You just tell the story as best you can within the confines of the budget. I've always believed that you can tell a good story whether you have five thousand dollars or fifty million dollars. You just have to scale your expectations down and use your ingenuity, if you have less money, to really make the story [work] well. I've often found, particularly working in the theater, that when people take money away from me, as they do in the theater, you come up with the most imaginative solutions sometimes because of the constraints that are put on you artistically. I think it just makes you look at things from a different point of view. I've never felt at all constrained by any of the budgets in *Star Trek*, even though, in the *Deep Space Nine*s or in the *Next Generation*s I directed, occasionally the appetite of the writers has been bigger than the budget could cope with, and therefore it has been a little frustrating."

Says David Livingston of the show, "It was cool because we got to do a

lot of stuff with Odo morphing as he turns into a creature. Rene was fabulous in the performance. We shot on Stage Eighteen and had to shoot a planet set. I think David [Carson] and [DP] Marvin [Rush] shot it successfully; you really believed you were on this ruined planet. It's hard to do that kind of stuff."

Episode #33
"Armageddon Game"
Original Airdate: 1/31/94
Written by Morgan Gendel
Directed by Winrich Kolbe
Guest Starring: Rosalind Chao (Keiko O'Brien), Darleen Carr (E'Tyshra), Peter White (Sharat), Larry Cedar (Nydrom)

O'Brien and Bashir use their respective expertises to help eliminate a biomechanical weapon known as "the Harvesters," which has been used for centuries by the Kellerun and the T'Lani. The hope is that with the weapon destroyed, their war will finally come to an end.

Unfortunately, O'Brien is exposed to the weapon, and he and Bashir must fight for their lives as the aliens are fearful the humans will try to duplicate the Harvesters. On DS9, in the meantime, Sisko and Dax investigate the supposed deaths of their comrades when the Kellerun's story has some discrepancies.

••••

"I thought it was an excellent show," says Michael Piller. "I was very pleased with the way it worked out. Those two guys [Colm Meaney and Alexander Siddig] work very well together. There is some great character stuff between Colm and Siddig. When you've got two actors working together and you give them good things to say and you're talking backstory and talking about the girl you left behind and decisions you've made and the real exploration of life in a marriage, that means so much to a show."

Ira Behr notes that the episode was considerably toned down from its original inception as a sprawling chase show. "We were in the office one weekend and [writer] Jim [Crocker, who did the rewrite] and I called up Michael, and I told him that the show was going to be as expensive as hell and we should have a fallback position. He told me to finish writing it, and we did. A week before we

••••

started filming, they said, 'We can't do it; you've got to put it all in one room.' I think it still works. I like the show. I think it takes the Bashir and O'Brien relationship another step, and Kolbe did a good job directing."

Director Rick Kolbe's strongest memories of the episode have to do with the three or four days spent in the bunker set with O'Brien attempting to fix the system. "It was a rather restricted show," he reflects, "but we got two damn good actors in there, and it actually worked. There was more humor in there than you saw on the screen, but I guess the powers that be eliminated a few things. To me, the challenge was shooting a very small room in such a way that it doesn't look like just one room. I think it turned out quite well. Give me two good actors in a room and I prefer that over six bad actors hanging from a rope on the Matterhorn."

Episode #34
"Whispers"
Original Airdate: 2/7/94
Written by Paul Robert Coyle
Directed by Les Landau
Guest Starring: Rosalind Chao (Keiko O'Brien), Todd Waring (DeCurtis), Susan Bay (Admiral Rollman), Philip LeStrange (Coutu)

A study in paranoia as O'Brien returns to DS9 from the Paradas system, stunned to discover that everyone is treating him as though he were an outsider. The scope of this seeming conspiracy continues to expand because everyone, including Federation admiral Rollman, is part of it. Escaping the station in a runabout, O'Brien heads back to Parada Two, where he gets into an altercation with a rebel leader before he's mortally shot. Just as O'Brien dies, he sees another O'Brien and learns the truth: He is actually a replicant that was created by the aliens as a tool in an assassination plot.

••••

Says Michael Piller, "I thought we came up with something very original. Paul Coyle pitched an idea that O'Brien wakes up one day and no one knows who he is. We worked on it for a while and we couldn't find a way to make it work to our satisfaction. During the course of our conversation, I made the suggestion, 'Well,

wait a minute, what if he wakes up and everybody's acting strange and we do the paranoia gag of *Body Snatchers,* and so forth. And it turns out that we're looking through the eyes of someone who is not O'Brien but thinks he's O'Brien. And the twist is that he opens a door at the end and sees the real O'Brien.' We couldn't think of anybody who had done that before. How many times in this life can you find a plot gag that hasn't been used?"

"Les made a decision to shoot it film noir, and I think he did a brilliant job on it," says David Livingston. "He shot it really fast and he came in way under schedule. We saved a ton of money. He kept telling me that he was concerned about what he was delivering because it was going so fast. I was watching the dailies and kept saying it was wonderful. I think it's a really good episode, but I'm not a real fan of the last scene and the denouement. Whether or not you buy the plot point, Les did a really nice job, and there is this sort of constant undercurrent of uncertainty that gives it a satisfying feel."

Episode #35
"Paradise"
Original Airdate: 2/14/94
Teleplay by Jeff King, Richard Manning and Hans Beimler
Story by Jim Trombetta and James Crocker
Directed by Corey Allen
Guest Starring: Julia Nickson (Cassandra), Steve Vinovich (Joseph), Michael Buchman Silver (Vinod), Erick Weiss (Stephan), Gail Strickland (Alixus)

Sisko and O'Brien find themselves trapped on a planet that has a duonetic field that makes it impossible to communicate with their runabout's computer or DS9. There they encounter a colony led by Alixus, a well-known proponent of life without technology. It's a lifestyle that she insists on imposing on Sisko and O'Brien, whether they like it or not.

••••

"We hadn't done a Sisko episode since 'Second Sight,' and I wanted to do another show that gave Sisko the opportunity to show courage and force of personality," says Michael Piller. "Cultism is an

issue I'm very interested in because I've got a family member who was involved in a cult, so I had to study the issues quite a bit. They are a very interesting phenomenon and greatly misunderstood. The thing about cults is that they are so often portrayed on television as something evil, but they really do address people's emotional needs on a basic level. When you go against the teachings of the cult, they can be brutal, and that is what the underpinnings of this episode are about. To explore how you can be brought in by what seems to be a warm, human bunch of people and suddenly see yourself coerced into accepting their standards. And frankly, if things had continued for another three weeks or so, it's very likely that Sisko and O'Brien would have fallen into this pattern to survive."

"It was a tough show because we had to create an exterior environment on Stage Eighteen," says David Livingston of the planet set. "The way that [director] Corey [Allen] and Marvin [Rush] shot it with long lenses and stuff was successful in selling that world. It was fun to build part of a ship on the surface so you really got the sense of size. We wanted it to be bigger, but we just didn't have the money, so the grand designs that we had for the set had to be severely truncated."

Julia Nickson, the wife of actor David Soul (*Classic Trek*'s "The Apple"), who starred in the first season of *Babylon 5* as Sinclair's girlfriend, played Cassandra.

Episode #36
"Shadowplay"
Original Airdate: 2/21/94
Written by Robert Hewitt Wolfe
Directed by Robert Scheerer
Guest Starring: Kenneth Mars (Colyus), Kenneth Tobey (Rurigan), Noley Thornton (Taya), Philip Anglim (Vedek Bareil)

While exploring the Gamma Quadrant, Dax and Odo pick up an unusual particle field that leads them to a society in which there is panic after twenty-two people have mysteriously disappeared. Odo starts up something of a rapport with the young Taya, granddaughter of colony founder Rurigan. Upon further investigation, Dax and Odo learn that the entire village is a holographic projection of Rurigan's homeworld, which was taken over by beings known as the Dominion. But now the holographic projector is beginning to malfunction and this seemingly real — in every sense of the word — society could disappear forever. For the sake of Rurigan, who is dying, the duo takes on the task of repairing the device in order to "save" this world.

••••

"The original premise was that someone would create a fantasy environment for themselves to replace one that was not satisfying their needs, and that someone could stumble into it and all these people would have no idea that they had lived decades in what they believed was a real community," recalls Michael Piller. "We didn't quite know how to make it our story, and that's always a critical problem of storytelling for *Star Trek*. How would you make it about us? When you put Odo there, we realized that we could deal with the idea of an odd life-form, and he could stand up for the values and survival of this community strictly out of his personal value system. We knew the way to do that was to connect him with somebody on that planet. The relationship between Odo and the girl worked remarkably well."

Noley Thornton, who played Taya, previously appeared in the *Next Generation* fifth-season episode "Imaginary Friend." And, of course, Kenneth To-bey is best known as the star of Howard Hawks's *The Thing (From Another World)*.

Episode #37
"Playing God"
Original Airdate: 2/28/94
Teleplay by Jim Trombetta and Michael Piller
Story by Jim Trombetta
Directed by David Livingston
Guest Starring: Geoffrey Blake (Arjin), Ron Taylor (Klingon Host), Richard Poe (Cardassian)

While Dax takes Arjin, an apprehensive Trill initiate, through the wormhole, their runabout gets caught on a small amount of protoplasm in a subspace pocket. When they return to DS9, O'Brien and Dax learn that this matter is a rapidly expanding proto-universe that threatens our own universe. The only hope is to bring the protoplasm back through the wormhole and return it before both universes are destroyed. Arjin, an expert pilot, volunteers for the mission, which earns Dax's fullest respect and proves that the man would indeed make an ideal host.

••••

"This was another interesting Jim Trombetta premise about an expanding universe and what do you do when a decision has to be made between destroying another potential civilization and your own," says Michael Piller. "We needed to do a personal story within the story of that science-fiction premise. And it was decided fairly early on that we would do a story that we always talked about, which was a student coming to be tutored by Dax in a sort of *Paper Chase* kind of way with Dax as Professor Kingsfield. The voles [Cardassian rats designed by Mike Okuda] were meant to be a little comedy relief. The problem with the script was always that nobody could find the balance between the three stories and nobody could find the relationship between the two characters. The kid was always a jerk, and Dax was harsh and unattractive, and nothing seemed to work about the episode. One draft would be full of technobabble about this universe, and the next one would be all about the relationships — except it wouldn't make any sense. One draft was thirty pages of voles."

Reflects Jim Trombetta, "Michael wanted me to add this thing where Dax was like Professor Kingsfield — but Dax can't be Professor Kingsfield. I wrote her like that because that's what he wanted, and he came back and said, 'I don't think we can do this.' Instead I concentrated on this poor guy who wanted to have a symbiont; he wanted to have a worm put inside of him and he wasn't sure he was going to pass the test. I had a little trouble writing that because I didn't really believe there was anybody that wanted to have a worm inside their body. So in one version I said the guy doesn't really want it. They said, 'No, we've gotta have it. It's an alien race; it means something different to them than it does to us.' I wasn't exactly sure what the guy was supposed to be doing to earn this. It was very hard to do."

Piller ended up responsible for the show's rewrite. "If you look at the status reports, it has ten names of people who have written drafts of the script," he says. "I had no idea of what I was going to do until I started thinking about what all of these personalities that Dax had been carrying around all these years could be doing inside her. I didn't know until I listened to Dax talk, which is the way I write a lot when things are going well, that Dax had this huge conflict with Curzon that we had never played before. Here was a wonderful opportunity for us to explore the differences between the two personalities and the many personalities that were in this one humanoid host."

Trombetta developed the B story involving an expanding proto-universe, which may or may not be a new form of life. "It was neat because it had a nice structural resonance. On one hand you had a subuniverse which you can't destroy because it's life. On the other hand you had these Cardassian voles infesting the station which you just want to get rid of as fast as you can."

This episode was one that science adviser Andre Bormanis made a major contribution to. "That script went through six drafts, which was unheard of," says Bormanis, who explains that the original idea for the story came from an article in *Popular Science* magazine. "According to some theories in quantum mechanics, these baby universes could be branching off from the universe all the time." While

••••

noting that the episode was not based on any real science as we know it today, Bormanis says that the conceptual problem for him was how the crew would come to discover that life was developing in the baby universe. Piller asked Bormanis to devise a scene in which Dax is having a conversation with the station's computer and makes this realization. "I kind of put that together last minute," he admits, adding that he had a chance to discuss the scene with Terry Farrell at the second-season wrap party. "She said she shot the scene at one-thirty in the morning, and it went fine and wasn't too much of a mouthful. I try to be very sensitive to the fact that real people who don't have any training in science have to say this stuff that I'm writing."

Episode #38
"Profit and Loss"
Original Airdate: 3/21/94
Written by Flip Kobler and Cindy Marcus
Directed by Robert Wiemer
Guest Starring: Mary Crosby (Natima), Andrew Robinson (Garak), Michael Reilly Burke (Hogue), Heidi Swedberg (Rekelen), Edward Wiley (Gul Toran)

Quark's former lover, a Cardassian named Natima, arrives at the station in a damaged vessel whose other passengers, Hogue and Rekelen, are her students. Seeing Natima, Garak claims that she is a terrorist, while Natima counters that she is leading an underground movement that is fighting the military government in order to establish a nonviolent future for Cardassia. Added to the mix are the feelings that Quark and Natima still have for each other and Garak's informing Gul Toran of the rebels' arrival on the station in the hope of getting Cardassia to end his exile.

••••

"This is the other disappointing episode in this season for me," says Michael Piller. "This was actually submitted by a speculative writer whom we hired to rewrite it. It was originally an homage to *Casablanca*, and the first draft was hysterically funny. It had the lines, it had the song, it had everything. We said let's do it. It would be fun and we'll do Quark as Rick and it will be great — and that was where we were going when we got a call from the law department saying, 'You know, you guys can't do this. This is *Casablanca*.' I said, 'Yes, it's an homage to *Casablanca*.' They answered, 'Well, somebody owns *Casablanca*, somebody wrote *Casablanca*. You will be sued for plagiarism.' 'Oh. We hadn't thought about it.' So we had to make fundamental changes that took out characters and made it clearly different than *Casablanca* until the legal people were satisfied. Having that accomplished, I don't know how else to say it, but the biggest mistake we made was to let it become mawkish. It gets right back to credibility again. I didn't believe the love affair for a second, and that, unfortunately, was why I was disappointed."

Ira Behr agrees. "The love story was meant to be bright, witty, and to show Quark like you've never seen him before," he explains. "As a guy who genuinely, sincerely, passionately wants something and is really out of control. What you got is Humphrey Bogart and these long scenes of soap opera. I thought it was terrible. I went down and discussed it with the director and said, 'Don't do it; this isn't what we had in mind.' I mentioned it to Armin, but they played it for sentimentality and they played it for gusto, and it was not good."

"Having read both, I think the second one is better," says Armin Shimerman of the script, which was originally entitled "Everyone Comes to Quark's." "If you're really into *Casablanca*, you get it; if not, it's just a normal *Deep Space Nine* episode that happens to have a love affair between Quark and a Cardassian."

Heidi Swedberg, who may be best known as George's fiancée on *Seinfeld*, was unrecognizable under her makeup as a Cardassian revolutionary.

Episode #39
"Blood Oath"
Original Airdate: 3/28/94
Written by Peter Allan Fields
Directed by Winrich Kolbe
Guest Starring: John Colicos (Kor), Michael Ansara (Kang), William Campbell (Koloth), Bill Bolender (The Albino), Christopher Collins (Assistant)

Jadzia Dax is obligated to live up to a blood oath taken by Curzon to aid three Klingons (Kor, Kang and Koloth) in their quest for vengeance against "the Albino," who murdered the son of Kang. Curzon became involved because he was the godfather to Kang's slain son. Sisko is completely against this, but Dax, feeling an obligation to something stronger than her duty to Starfleet, goes anyway. Dax and the Klingons arrive at the Albino's world and engage in a savage battle. Although it claims the lives of two of the three Klingons, their blood oath is fulfilled, and the Albino is killed.

••••

"Somebody pitched a premise to do a script that was about an over-the-hill Klingon gang, and somebody else read the script and said that it didn't work," recalls Michael Piller. "But I said to myself that it sounded appealing and I fed it to Pete [Fields], and we sat around and we talked about how we could pull Dax into it. I asked at the end of the meeting if there were any old Klingons that we could use from the original series, which would bring a resonance to the story and prove particularly sentimental to certain fans. It was a true Knights of the Round Table kind of show."

The Klingons they found were John Colicos, the first actor to ever portray a member of the Klingon Empire, who played the role of Kor in *Star Trek*'s "Errand of Mercy"; William Campbell as Koloth, who annoyed Captain Kirk in one of the most famous episodes (and *Star Trek*'s first comedy), "The Trouble with Tribbles"; and Michael Ansara's Kang, who was manipulated by an alien presence to lead a savage battle against *Enterprise* crew members in "Day of the Dove."

"It was the closest thing to *Beowulf* that I ever saw," says director Winrich Kolbe. "There was a mythological quality to it, and these guys were real heroes. I played Wagner in my mind the whole day, and it had a feel that was beyond episodic television. It really was *The Three Musketeers* on a smaller scale, and I loved it."

One of *Deep Space Nine*'s most challenging shows logistically, the episode took the characters from DS9 to a ship in space to the compound of a malevolent albino who was responsible for the death of Kang's son. "It was a killer," says David Livingston of producing the episode. "It was one of those shows where you decide

••••

to go for it all . . . and we did. It was a thrill to have all three [veteran actors] together, and Kolbe brought a real great German expressionist look to it, like Murnau or Fritz Lang. He always does great with the Klingons. We went to a Frank Lloyd Wright house in Pasadena, where we shot the exterior of the Albino's fortress and added a matte shot to it. The optical people blew up a miniature, and it looked fabulous. It was a tabletop miniature with fake trees and little bushes and when it blew up it looked like something out of *Lethal Weapon*."

Ira Behr recalls visiting the set during filming. "I went down to see some of the stunts and I couldn't imagine how they would edit it. Dennis Madalone, the stunt coordinator, told me they were giving me something like thirty hits [in the fight scene] so Rick could cut it down to fifteen or so. Two weeks later I saw Rick, and he was going, 'They didn't give me anything to cut to. I've got to put it all in there.' So it's pretty amazing stuff."

Adds Kolbe, "I don't consider myself an action director, so my instinct is to weasel out of the fight scenes as quickly as possible and just hope the rest of the stuff will overcome that deficit, but Dennis said, 'I've got it figured out; you just tell me where you want the camera, and I'm going to give you the action.' It just came together, and we shot the hell out of it."

One thing Kolbe did not do was go back to the original series episodes that featured these Klingon characters. "I thought about it," he says, "but I figured, 'What do I need this for?' They don't give me enough information about the characters to develop what I want to do, and I figured the actors knew what they had done, and they did. They were just wonderful. I had worked with Michael Ansara, although I don't think he would remember me, on *Quincy*. Not as a director. He was an actor, and I was an associate producer. I had worked with John Colicos, as Baltar, on *Battlestar Galactica*. When I heard he was coming in, I said, 'Oh shit, there goes the neighborhood.' He's extremely funny and wonderful to work with. Campbell, obviously, was wonderful. We had a wonderful time. I was, however, a little bit concerned that these guys could do all the physical stuff that was required. I had to convince them to put stunt people into it."

Terry Farrell (copyright © 1996 by Albert Ortega).

He also sings the praises of Terry Farrell. "She was excellent. Terry looks so beautiful that the first time you see her and until you get to know her, you think, 'Oh well, she's wonderful to look at but can't act,' and there are quite a few of those on the male and female side hanging around. But then there's the moment, as David Livingston says, that she explodes, and she just takes off and is right on the money and is wonderful. I think in 'Blood Oath' there were those moments. She took off. She had a hell of a time because there are some heavy, long speeches in there. And the writers don't make it easy on the actors, especially when they go into tech talk. We're talking about things that nobody really knows what they're talking about, so how you get emotionally involved with that I don't know. But the actors come up with it, and she was wonderful in that episode."

Episode #40
"The Maquis, Part I"
Original Airdate: 4/25/94
Written by James Crocker
Directed by David Livingston
Guest Starring: Tony Plana (Amaros), Bertila Damas (Sakonna), Richard Poe

(Gul Evek), Michael A. Krawic (Samuels), Amanda Carlin (Kobb), Marc Alaimo (Gul Dukat), Bernie Casey (Lieutenant Commander Cal Hudson)

When it becomes obvious that there are terrorist activities taking place in the Cardassian demilitarized zone, Sisko and Gul Dukat team up to learn the truth and see firsthand Federation vessels attacking Cardassian ships, which leads to Dukat's being kidnapped by a group identifying itself as the Maquis. Sisko, Kira and Bashir follow the kidnappers to an area within the zone identified as the Badlands. There, on a life-supporting asteroid, they are taken prisoner by a group of Federation colonists — part of the Maquis — led by Sisko's friend Lieutenant Commander Cal Hudson, who had been serving as Starfleet's attaché to the Federation colonies in the demilitarized zone.

••••

"DS9 is the true inheritor of the Maquis since there is no long-term benefit to them on *Voyager*," says Michael Piller of the Starfleet rogues who play an important part of the *Star Trek: Voyager* backstory. "What we get out of *Voyager* are a band of outlaws that are married to a group of Starfleet officers in order to survive. This turned out to provide a wealth of story material for us on DS9 in the second half of the second season that I was very pleased with. Although part one [of "The Maquis"] lacks a certain action quotient that would have been there if there had been more money in the budget, I still think it works in terms of storytelling very well."

Ira Behr recalls the initial meeting at which they realized "The Maquis" would become a two-part episode. "The way it got started originally was that Jim Crocker and the writing staff — including Michael — decided to do *Shane*. Don't ask me why. We were going to do a Jake show where we were going to have him get involved with an old friend of Sisko's, a mercenary or whatever, and it would ultimately be Van Heflin versus Alan Ladd, but this time Van Heflin would have a few more bullets in his gun. Well, we tried it and it did not go anyplace.

"Then Michael said do the Maquis, and we started doing them and we broke the story. No one knew where the story was going to go; it was really strange doing it that way. It was like, 'Let's just make it up as we go along,' and suddenly Michael says, 'We're not going to finish this episode, are we?', which is something everyone else had been thinking, but no one would say. We weren't close to finishing the story in an hour, and then Michael said, 'Let's make it a two-parter.' "

Bernie Casey, who guest stars as Sisko's friend Cal Hudson, is best known to genre fans as Felix Leiter in the Warner Brothers James Bond film *Never Say Never Again*.

Episode #41
"The Maquis, Part II"
Original Airdate: 5/2/94
Written by Ira Steven Behr
Directed by Corey Allen
Guest Starring: Tony Plana (Amaros), John Schuck (Legate Parn), Natalija Nogulich (Admiral Necheyev), Bertila Damas (Sakonna), Michael Bell (Xepolite), Amanda Carlin (Kobb), Marc Alaimo (Gul Dukat), Bernie Casey (Lieutenant Commander Cal Hudson)

Sisko must do everything he can to keep the volatile situation between Cardassia and the Maquis from exploding in full-fledged war. To this end, he tries to convince Cal Hudson to stop this madness — which the man refuses to do, citing the Maquis' feeling that the Federation has abandoned them.

••••

"We thought 'The Maquis' was the Cal Hudson Show," says Ira Behr of Bernie Casey's renegade Starfleet officer. "But as we were doing it, we realized the story was really about Sisko, and that was where the gold was, so we killed Cal Hudson at the end."

Or so was the plan until Piller vetoed Cal's offing. "Michael came to me and said, 'No, not this time. We need this character. We're not going to ruin another guest star; you killed Richard Beymer [in "The Siege"] and you're not going to kill Cal Hudson.' I said OK. Well, it got to the point during dailies where Michael looked up at me and said, 'We should have killed Cal Hudson.' "

Both "Maquis" episodes created a situation in which Sisko and Gul Dukat had to work more closely than they ever had, and one got the distinct impression that the writers were testing the waters to

see if Dukat should be a more frequent recurring character.

"I totally agree," says Marc Alaimo, who portrays the Cardassian. "I'd rather not just keep coming back to guest. If I'm going to do the show, I'd like to be a part of the team. And I think Dukat would be a really interesting addition, because he's got so much power. The Cardassians are incredibly intelligent and intuitive. I've tried to play him with some sort of sensitivity. I could have gone one-dimensionally aggressive and mean and ugly with this character if I'd chosen to. I have the feeling that's what they kind of wanted. I thought, 'I've done that a hundred and fifty times already.' So I wanted to give him some dimension, some depth, and I think it's worked very well. You suddenly find out he's got children and so on. Bad guy of the week is boring. I've really enjoyed it, particularly 'Necessary Evil' and 'The Maquis.' "

Prod the actor a little and he'll express more of his feelings regarding Dukat: "I think Gul Dukat even thinks that a lot of what his race does is evil. He understands the difference. Then again, in war — in a fight — Gul Dukat is unbeatable. He won't stop until he wins, and that's the Cardassian philosophy. They say all's fair in love and war, and in war I think he's pretty unbeatable. But when he's not in that situation, I would think he's a very reasonable, sensitive and thinking Cardassian, as opposed to some I have seen who are the one-dimensional idiots who are evil and screaming and yelling and want to eat people alive."

Episode #42
"The Wire"
Original Airdate: 5/9/94
Written by Robert Hewitt Wolfe
Directed by Kim Friedman
Guest Starring: Andrew Robinson (Garak), Jimmie F. Skaggs (Glinn Boheeka), Ann Gillespie (Nurse Jabara), Paul Dooley (Enabran Tain)

The slowly developing friendship between Bashir and Garak is put to the test when the Cardassian begins behaving erratically, his temper extremely frayed. The doctor learns that Garak was given an implant when he was a member of the Obsidian Order (essentially the eyes and ears of Cardassia) that would make

him fairly impervious to pain in case of torture. But since exiled from his homeworld and "trapped" on DS9, he has been using the implant constantly to deal with life away from his own people, and now it is beginning to malfunction due to continuous use. When it becomes obvious that this could result in Garak's death, Bashir does everything he can — including a trip into Cardassian territory — to remove the implant and save his friend's life.

••••

"It just so happens some of the best shows are the least expensive, because we're forced to be concise," Ira Behr comments. "Our conceptual thinking of two guys in a room who are struggling for survival, or against each other, frequently makes for very good drama. This episode was an opportunity to show Bashir with a real strength that he hasn't had before.

"[Story editor] Robert Wolfe talked passionately about doing this show, and we had always talked about the fact that Garak might have been George Smiley back in Cardassia and maybe we should explore that. Then I went to the movies and came back and said, 'He's Schindler.' Why don't we do Schindler and Smiley, and then Michael [Piller] said do all four stories, every one different. Robert came up with the idea that he tells this story about his best friend and it turns out to be him. Then you meet his mentor and best friend, who says, 'I hope he dies, but tell him I miss him.' That's perfect; it's all great stuff."

Admittedly, "The Wire" could be perceived as an attempt to repeat the success of first season's "Duet," and the staff was aware of the similarities. " 'Duet' was Kira's crisis as much as the guy's crisis, and this was much more Garak's show," offers Behr. "I thought that was a little dangerous, and we knew we were doing it, but let's face it, the Cardassian monologue is great and Cardassians like to talk. They're also great fun to write."

Says David Livingston, "It's a bottle show. It's basically Andy Robinson in a room, but it's very compelling because it's one man intervening. Kurt Cobain needed Siddig. If he had had Sid he might have pulled through, because Sid knocks some sense into Andy's head and says, 'You've got to get off this stuff.' "

••••

According to director Kim Friedman, " 'The Wire' was kind of a challenge because most of the episode was two people in a room, Sid and Andy Robinson. It's very hard to create pacing and energy for a show that is basically set in a room. But ultimately I was very pleased with the whole episode. I think my favorite moment was the implant withdrawal scene, which results in the fight between Bashir and Garak. It was just a very powerful moment."

Paul Dooley, who played the menacing Enabran Tain, returned in *DS9*'s third season two-parter "Improbable Cause" and "The Die Is Cast." He also is known for his role as Martin Tupper's gay father in the HBO sitcom *Dream On*.

Episode #43
"Crossover"
Original Airdate: 5/16/94
Written by Michael Piller
Directed by David Livingston
Guest Starring: Andrew Robinson
(Garak), John Cothran Jr. (Telok)

While traveling through the wormhole, Kira and Bashir find themselves in a parallel universe where the Cardassians and Klingons have joined forces to put the human Terrans under their domain. This follows the efforts of Captain Kirk nearly a century earlier to have the Empire (a totalitarian version of the Federation) soften its hold on the galaxy in the same parallel universe. Returning to the station, they are stunned to find that Kira's double is in command and that Odo hates human beings, who have been enslaved. Kira and Bashir must convince certain human workers on the station — including duplicates of Sisko and O'Brien — to rise against their inhumane masters while also finding a way back home.

••••

"Crossover" is a sequel to the original series episode "Mirror, Mirror," in which a transporter malfunction during an ion storm transports Kirk, McCoy, Uhura and Scotty to a parallel universe and aboard an evil incarnation of the *Enterprise,* where officers move up in rank via assassination. While Scotty attempts to figure out a way to get them back home, Kirk argues with that universe's Spock that compassion within the Empire is the only

thing that will allow it to survive. That Spock says that he will consider the captain's words.

"Mirror, Mirror" was written by genre veteran Jerome Bixby, who explains, "I wanted to do a parallel universe story. I had already done a fiction story called 'One Way Street,' which was a parallel universe story, and I thought that would make a good *Star Trek.* The universe I created was a very savage counterpart, virtually a pirate ship, into which I could transpose a landing party."

Bixby admitted to James Van Hise in *Sci-Fi Universe* magazine that he was upset over not being given on-screen credit for creating the original source material. "I have to watch myself here, because I have a temper and a casual mouth," says Bixby. "Yes, the fanzines advertised the source. It would have been appropriate if [Michael] Piller and crew had done that on screen. I don't know if money would have been an issue. They did refer to the visit by Captain Kirk and his landing party, and I perked up when they mentioned that.

"The Writer's Guild of America has a copy of 'Mirror, Mirror' and they're looking into it, but I don't really know how long that might take," he adds. All of

this derives from the Writer's Guild regulation that states that if a writer creates an original character on a series, and that character is reused, then the writer is paid a royalty for that. "It's arguable that the Mirror universe itself might be termed a 'character,' says Bixby. "In another [*DS9*] episode ["Blood Oath"] they did use a character I created — Kang, the Klingon commander from 'Day of the Dove.' In the long run that may be more damaging to them because they used the same character. Kang will probably mean some bucks for me, but I'm not sure that the 'Mirror, Mirror' spin-offs will unless the Mirror universe itself can be deemed a character. That was mentioned in passing by the guy at the guild."

"We've been pitched 'Mirror, Mirror' sequels since *The Next Generation* began, and I wasn't interested," says Michael Piller. "But I couldn't get away from the fact that it would be interesting to know what happened after 'Mirror, Mirror' finished. I couldn't escape the idea that Kirk's influence in the world that he left might have been profound and changed history. What would be more of a gross violation of the Prime Directive? Ira [Behr] said, 'What if he actually screwed things up?' Spock listened to what he said and then they turned this evil empire into a much more gentle empire that was conquered and taken over by the Klingons, the Cardassians and others."

In addition, Piller was fascinated by the what-if concept involved in the flip side of twenty-fourth-century Federation tranquillity. "I was watching *Schindler's List* and I was thinking if I were a little older, I could have been in one of those camps in Poland. If Germany had won the war, I would not be here doing what I am doing today. I guarantee you. That was what I was intrigued by. I was very pleased with the way the script turned out."

Frequent director and series producer David Livingston assumed the directorial reins of the challenging shoot. " 'Crossover' was a killer," he admits of the logistically daunting show. "I don't usually call Michael Piller to comment on the scripts, but when I read the draft, I just called him and said, 'Cool,' and hung up."

The episode, with its demanding production requirements in portraying the alternate universe, went one day over

••••

schedule and required additional reshoots along with extensive second-unit work for the split screen involved in shooting two Major Kiras. "It was not a pleasant experience for me because of all the pressure," says Livingston. "It was just not fun. I wanted it to be a lot more than it is, but I'm glad I got to do it. It's one of the most expensive episodes we've ever done. We had more prosthesis makeup because the station is inhabited by Klingons, Cardassians and Bajorans, and the humans are basically slaves so they're wearing different costumes. We had swing sets that were huge, like the mining set, and very complicated to shoot. The shooting time was long because of the look and because of special effects, like smoke and steam and that kind of thing. Plus, we did make changes in the sets themselves, like Quark's, in which we replaced the big graphic in the bar with the symbol that represented the Bajorans, Klingons and Cardassians melded together."

Another return to the mirror universe took place in the third-season episode "Through the Looking Glass," as well as the fourth year's "Shattered Mirror."

Episode #44
"The Collaborator"
Original Airdate: 5/23/94
Teleplay by Gary Holland, Ira Steven Behr and Robert Hewitt Wolfe
Story by Gary Holland
Directed by Cliff Bole
Guest Starring: Philip Anglim (Vedek Bareil), Bert Remsen (Kubus), Camille Saviola (Kai Opaka), Louise Fletcher (Vedek Winn)

Vedeks Winn and Bareil are running against each other in a Bajoran election that will determine who will become Kai. Winn plans on using information she has obtained that claims Bareil revealed the location of forty-three rebels, including Kai Opaka's son, to the Cardassians, who wiped them all out. Working with Odo, Kira, who had been developing a relationship with Bareil, is stunned to learn that the accusation appears true and she feels an acute sense of betrayal. Bareil withdraws from the election, allowing Winn to rise in power. Upon further investigation, Kira discovers that the actual betrayer was Opaka, who sacrificed the forty-three to save the thousands that would have undoubtedly been killed by the Cardassians if they had sought out the rebels on their own. To preserve the Kai's memory, Bareil chose to say nothing.

••••

"We're dealing with the fact that Bajor is a culture where people basically vote for their pope and sleep with their priests," Ira Behr states. "I think it's just fascinating."

Jokes Louise Fletcher, who returns as Vedek Winn, now Kai, "I'm the David Koresh of space. Maybe that's too horrible. I think I'd rather be pope. Kiss my ring."

"It was interesting to have her there," says Rick Kolbe of Fletcher. "This has nothing to do with her personality, but what she comes up with is the banality of evil. She doesn't go around gritting her teeth and chomping at the bit. The evil is underneath. She's a very normal evil person."

Says David Livingston, "It's a stunningly visual episode, and [DP] Marvin [Rush] did a fabulous job of lighting it and working with [director] Cliff [Bole]. Rene [Auberjonois] always astounds me. There is a wonderful moment where Kira reveals to Odo that she's in love with Bareil, and Odo flinches, showing us that it hurts him, and in one look he tells us that he's in love with her and he covers it up by saying, 'We all knew you were in love with him.' It's all in his looks, and it's a wonderful performance. Your attachment to Odo is so much greater just for that one moment where you realize that he's just like the rest of us; he's human. He may be goop in a bucket, but he's human. It's a wonderful piece of writing, and Rene nails it. [TNG's android] Data was always the observer, but you never felt with Data, because Data didn't feel. With Odo, you think that he's this cold fish, and then he surprises you in these moments and makes you feel for the guy. We've all been there. You know, when the girl tells you she loves the other guy, and you thought it was going to be you."

Michael Piller suggests that this character arc, further explored in seasons three and four, was one that had been simmering for a while. "There's a moment in 'Necessary Evil' where they look at each other across the room and he basically had to bust her and knows the truth. As I wrote that character at that moment, I knew that he loved her."

Episode #45
"Tribunal"
Original Airdate: 6/6/94
Written by Bill Dial
Directed by Avery Brooks
Guest Starring: Rosalind Chao (Keiko O'Brien), Caroline Lagerfelt (Makbar), John Beck (Boone), Richard Poe (Gul Evek), Julian Christopher (Cardassian Voice), Fritz Weaver (Kovat)

O'Brien is arrested and brought to Cardassia to stand trial on the charge of smuggling weapons to the Maquis. While much of the story is devoted to the seemingly twisted alien legal system, Sisko and Odo attempt to uncover the truth and learn that the Cardassians themselves were involved in the weapon smuggling to help fuel the conflict.

••••

Ironically, the genesis of "Tribunal" comes from a line in "The Maquis." "I wrote one line in 'Maquis, Part II' about the Cardassian judicial system," says Ira Behr. "Michael read the script and said, 'There's a story in this.' We did a whole show based on that line."

About making his television directorial debut, Avery Brooks has nothing but enthusiasm. "It was wonderful," he proclaims. "I've been a director in theater for an awfully long time, and this was something that I should have done some time ago. It was an extraordinary experience, and I know these people, so it was like being at home and closing the door. And the other thing is that we had an extraordinary script and great [guest] stars. Fritz Weaver was just wonderful to work with."

When Piller needed a technical term for a twenty-fourth-century camera, science adviser Andre Bormanis tried combining various syllables with the suffix "cam" to let the audience know it was something for taking pictures. Piller rejected his suggestions one by one. "I got the script back and I saw they had used 'holocam,'" Bormanis says. "I didn't think of that, but it's perfect. It made sense and it's a good word to use there."

Although being science adviser for two tech-heavy shows (DS9 and Voyager) seems like a full-time gig, it's only

••••

part-time for Bormanis, who also does research in his free time. Ironically, he has found that his work in the make-believe world of *Star Trek* may be having an effect on his experiments in the world of real science. "I'm probably a lot more open-minded," he admits, adding that the concepts of warp drive and holodecks may be completely beyond our abilities now, but there is nothing about them that is theoretically impossible by the standards of today's science. "The only thing I think is a real stretch is the transporter," Bormanis adds. "The Heisenberg uncertainty principle makes it impossible to know the exact location and energy of any particular subatomic particle. Therefore, were you to disassemble a person as the transporter does, it may well be impossible to put them back together again. We have reason to believe that this is because of some very basic physical facts about the universe and there's no way to get around that."

Naturally, the show's technical manual does mention "Heisenberg Compensators" as one of the elements of the transporter, which was apparently senior illustrator and technical consultant Rick Sternbach and Michael Okuda's ingenious way of acknowledging this problem.

Episode #46
"The Jem'Hadar"
Original Airdate: 6/13/94

Written by Ira Steven Behr
Directed by Kim Friedman
Guest Starring: Alan Oppenheimer (Captain Keogh), Aron Eisenberg (Nog), Cress Williams (Third Talak'talan), Molly Hagen (Eris)

On a camping trip to the Gamma Quadrant, Sisko, Jake, Nog and Quark encounter the Jem'Hadar, soldiers of the Dominion, who rule that area of space. Third Talak'talan, leader of this particular Jem'Hadar group, proclaims that the Dominion will no longer tolerate vessels coming through the wormhole. Sisko is held prisoner, and when word reaches DS9, the starship *Odyssey* and two runabouts containing Kira, Dax, Bashir, Odo and O'Brien are dispatched through the wormhole to retrieve Sisko and the others.

••••

"Ira and Robert and the staff worked very hard on creating a new group of aliens that are quite different than the others that we have had before," says Michael Piller of the genesis of the Dominion. "There's a symbiotic relationship where you have to peel back several layers to understand what they really are. What seems to be the most threatening is not necessarily the most threatening. I think it is a good show, and we have a good look to some of them, and it's only the tip of an iceberg. The Cardassians the

first time we met them were very undefined. They had a good look, but it took two or three years before I really felt good about them — and I still don't feel very good about the Romulans."

Details Ira Behr, "With the Dominion, we came up with characters, people, aliens and problems that impact not only in the Gamma Quadrant but the Alpha Quadrant as well. I came up with the idea for the Dominion, then the staff met every day for lunch for a week or two, and we would kick around what to do about this Dominion. Then we presented it to Mike and Rick, and they were receptive to it. People give Clinton a hard time because he's a president who's actually trying to do something. And we're trying to do something as well. We're trying to get away from the frontier as a big empty stage, and it takes time. It takes mistakes, and I think we're getting there."

Offers director Kim Friedman, "I thought it was a good show. There was a lot of laying the seeds for next season, so we had to lay down a lot of exposition, which is always a problem. I like the Jem'Hadar, although they're only the foot soldiers of the Dominion. They weren't the Borg, but they were good."

Alan Oppenheimer, who played the freighter captain, is best remembered as the original Dr. Rudy Wells in *The Six Million Dollar Man* TV series.

••••

• • • •

CHAPTER SIX

Deep Space Nine: Season Three

By the show's third season on the air, the producers of *Deep Space Nine* were beginning to feel like the ugly stepchildren. The ratings were down, other shows like the fledgling *Voyager* series were getting all the attention, malaise among the cast was growing and magazines like *Entertainment Weekly* and *Sci-Fi Universe* were eviscerating the show as having degenerated into "nearly unwatchable tripe."

Despite this, members of the production crew felt that they were doing some of their best work, though the sentiment was that it was getting lost in the preponderance of *Trek* available through various media outlets, including television, movies and multimedia.

"*Star Trek* is a phenomenon that people have not always been comfortable with," says Ira Behr. "I think the media has waited for what they perceive to be a weak point in the franchise and something they can kind of gang up on. I think this show was an opportunity to do that. Another reason is that Rick [Berman] and Mike [Piller], when the show was going on the air, gave many, many interviews in which they talked about the show being different and dark and gritty. People have kind of latched onto that. You would think we were doing this really lugubrious, depressing, dark show, which is not always the case or, instead, is a kind of shallow and simplistic way of looking at the series. The bottom line is we live in a media-haunted society where perception is always more important than reality. Because the show was perceived as a show about people who don't go anywhere, about a space station that is not off exploring the galaxy — which is what *Star Trek* seems to be — that in some way lessens the impact of the series.

"The fact is," he adds, "for good or ill, I think during the third season we had maybe nine shows out of twenty-six that took place on the station. Everything else is going off and doing things. Yet I still read things about ours being the show that has the setting of an airport lounge where you just wait around for things to happen. That's all perception. Here, we joke around that in ten years *Deep Space Nine* will become the cult within the cult, and people will look back and say, 'What a weird and different and strange, funky show that was. Look at all the things they were trying to do.' Maybe that will happen; maybe it won't. The one good thing about working on a TV series where you have twenty-six episodes [a season] is you don't really have the time to brood over the possible inequities that may be flung your way; you're too busy trying to get a show on its feet every week. When we do the show, we try and please ourselves and what we perceive to be the *Deep Space Nine* fans, and there are certainly a lot of them out there."

Michael Piller believes that *DS9* was suffering from the "middle-child syndrome" during its third season. "There was *The Next Generation,* which was a media phenomenon — there was nothing like it," he offers. "When people realized that it sold magazines, the coverage went crazy. *Deep Space Nine* got a great launch, with a lot of publicity, but then Paramount decided that they wanted to do *Voyager,* so the baby came into the family and took attention away from the middle kid. At the same time, *The Next Generation* ended, which got a great deal of press. And since *Voyager* was getting ready to start, people viewed it as [*TNG's*] replacement. *Deep Space Nine* just got overlooked. I feel it's been treated unfairly for a show of such quality."

Behr agrees with Piller's assessment. He feels the situation has obscured the show's unique place in the annals of sci-fi history. "The show is different from the show that came before it and it's different from the show that came after it," he points out. "Even though people talk about science-fiction fans having vision and being able to embrace the different and the odd and the slightly more esoteric type of show, I don't think that's true when it comes to television. I think people like to find something that's comfortable, and *Deep Space Nine* does not always fit in that way. I think that makes some people uneasy. I really believe that there are a lot of people who don't 'get' the show."

Piller emphasizes that *DS9* was created not as a show about space exploration, but as an interior exploration, a character-based series that deals with humanistic issues such as loyalty, commitment and personal responsibility. "That's exactly what these characters are forced to do," Piller explains. "They are forced to stay in one place and face the consequences of their actions week after week. Going on a trip in the *Enterprise* is like cruising your favorite hang-outs on Friday nights. You can always go on to the next one — it's a one-night stand. I would say that *Deep Space Nine* is a much more adult series than any of the other *Star Trek* shows. It's much more psychological and it forces people to confront things that aren't always comfortable."

"Everything we do," interjects Behr, "six episodes later comes back to haunt us. Everything is interwoven and interconnected. I keep saying that this is a very fluid show, which is what I like about it. Everything — the relationships, the political ramifications — are all very fluid and change. For me, what's nice is I get calls from Pocket Books, and they're always complaining good-naturedly about how tough it is to assign *Deep Space Nine* novels because of the lag time between somebody selling a premise to the time the book is released. By that time, we will have changed the show, and I think that's wonderful. The show is alive. That's the appeal to us as writers."

One cannot, however, ignore the fact that the show's ratings were eroding, leading to concern from Paramount Pictures, which foots the bill for the pricey series. "Clearly, there's been a ratings deterioration that cannot be ignored," says Piller. "We think we're doing a great show and we're trying to find a way to get people to come back to see it again, so we want to do some things that will attract an audience."

"I think the third season was very rewarding," he adds. "The mix of stories has been much more interesting than it was in the second season, and I think that we got to stretch a lot more. The criticism of *Deep Space Nine* is that it's not as easy as other shows to just jump into because people are carrying a lot of backstories. One of the things I've counseled Ira [Behr] on again and again is not to assume the

• • • •

audience already knows something and to make sure each episode introduces a subject and resolves it. You can have backstories, but you're going to have to make sure it's clear."

The party line on *Deep Space Nine* is that it's a show that offers a view of Federation officers in an ongoing, evolving situation as gatekeepers of the wormhole and guardians of Bajor rather than in fleeting missions going from planet to planet. "There is a true connection from episode to episode that shows the characters growing, changing, developing, learning and being responsible," says Piller. "The idea of being in a committed relationship to a new planet or any kind of new relationship, and the struggles and difficulties and conflicts and dysfunctions that it takes to grow through that relationship is a terribly interesting and relevant contemporary issue for a franchise to explore. I just think it's a wonderful series. It is not as comfortable and attractive in a popular way, and I can live with that as long as it gets good enough numbers to stay on the air."

"Ira feels it's going to end up being like *The Prisoner*," says David Livingston. "It's going to become this classic, and people are going to sense they're missing something. I don't know if that's the case or not. I just think it's good television and it's got a lot of meat to it."

"To me, being popular has never been the signature of success," offers Piller. "The original *Star Trek* was supported by a small, dedicated group of fans that kept it on the air and kept it in syndication until it turned into this phenomenon. I believe that *Deep Space Nine* had the difficulty of being on at the same time as all the other *Star Trek* series and during this huge new rebirth of the science-fiction genre. But in time, the quality of the writing, the ambitiousness of what we try to do, will become clear, and it will be seen as one of the great *Star Trek* series because it really will stand out from anything else that's ever been done on *Star Trek.*

"There is a hardcore group of fans who call themselves the Niners who like their *Deep Space Nine* and are happy that it's not a ship show and that it's not like any of the other *Star Treks*," Piller continues. "If that dedicated fan base can be strong and coax their friends in front of the set, I believe that we'll see an appreciation of *Deep Space Nine* that we haven't seen in the past. But we're not willing to rest on our laurels."

Producer Rene Echevarria, who produced *TNG* and joined the *Deep Space Nine* staff at the beginning of the season, was impressed by the richness of characterization that had been established during *DS9*'s first two years. "They laid a lot of pipe, and I came in at a really great time in terms of a creative flowering," Echevarria observes. "To me, these are really fun characters to write. I find them more real than the *Next Generation* characters, who were almost iconic. They were having a fantasy life where between adventures they would all do theater. *Deep Space Nine* feels more real to me in terms of the characters and the setting. One of the things I remember talking to Jeri Taylor about when they were developing *Voyager* is that it would be really helpful for the show to have a couple of young guys who are close enough friends that Harry Kim can drop by Tom Paris's room, walk in, say 'Hey,' flop down on the couch, pick up a newspaper and read for five minutes and say, 'See you later,' and walk out. On *Next Generation* you had to have an excuse for someone to be in [someone else's] quarters. You'd write a scene, and the notes would say, 'Why is Riker visiting Geordi?' There had to be a reason. Thankfully, there was always the crew evaluation report. On *Deep Space Nine* you find people having coffee together or walking along the Promenade. There are so many types of stories you can tell on this show. If this wasn't an action-adventure show for young men eighteen to forty, we could easily do an entire season on life on a station where nothing much happens except everyday life."

Supervising producer Ron Moore, who also made the move to *DS9* from its first sister series, found his greatest challenge to be dealing with new characters. "By the time *The Next Generation* ended, I'd written those characters for four years," says Moore. "I cowrote the movie; I'd written a lot of shows for them. We knew more about Worf's family than I cared to know. Just moving over to a new series that was starting a third year and looking at these characters made me realize that there were all kinds of possibilities for filling in their backgrounds."

Another intriguing difference for him was the change in setting and the possibility of providing "embroidery" for existing story lines. This he contrasts with *The Next Generation,* where an excuse had to be made for a past plot line to be picked up. "You had to have a gimmick to get back into an old plot line," Moore explains. "Whereas on *Deep Space Nine* we're there, and the Bajorans aren't going anywhere, so that always has to keep moving along storywise. Garak's tailor shop is still down the Promenade, so anytime we feel like it, we can have a Garak show. It just gives you different storytelling abilities. I also like the format of the show because we don't have the *Enterprise* on a serious mission every week. Without that looming over your head, you can do shows that are lighter. You can do things that aren't quite like, 'Ooh, the *Enterprise* is investigating a space anomaly.' That would always hamstring us on *Next Generation.* Joe Menosky and I wrote 'In Theory,' the Data romance, and we had to come up with some stupid subspace anomaly that the *Enterprise* had to be battling at the same time. It was annoying storytelling, but that was built in to the structure of that show. While you were

• • • •

downstairs with Data, you always kind of wondered what the ship was doing. On *Deep Space Nine* you don't have that looming over your head all the time, so it expands the kinds of stories you can do."

Expanding the *Deep Space Nine* universe was a primary goal during the third season, which is why the station was equipped with the starship *Defiant*, a prototype vessel designed to battle the Borg but now being utilized to battle the Jem'Hadar from the Gamma Quadrant.

"At one point, [executive story editor] Robert Wolfe and I were sitting around after the 'Jem'Hadar' episode had been filmed," recalls Behr. "We were looking at dailies and said, 'Jesus, we're blowing up Galaxy Class starships; these guys are tough, and all we have are these freaking runabouts that no one likes and are very difficult to shoot in.' You had these little piss-ass ships going up against what we were saying was the greatest force of the Gamma Quadrant. We had to come up with a ship to combat them, and that's when we talked to Michael Piller and Rick Berman and said, 'We need something with teeth to it so it doesn't seem ridiculous that this space station is the only thing between the Dominion and the Alpha Quadrant,' and that got us through the first couple of episodes."

Also in the first two episodes — "The Search," parts I and II — Odo comes to answer one of his seemingly eternal questions: where he comes from. It turns out that he is a member of the Founders, a society of shape-shifters who rule the Gamma Quadrant and look at the so-called solids as a threat to them. The Jem'Hadar, audiences learn, are actually the foot soldiers of the Founders, who, along with the Vorta, make up the Dominion. Given the opportunity to stay with his people, Odo chooses to return home to DS9.

In some ways, it was surprising that the staff "solved" one of Odo's basic questions, which would seem infused with the kind of longevity that Data's quest to be human had on *The Next Generation*. "We just changed his quest a little bit," explains Robert Wolfe. "We took him from someone who wanted to find out who his people were to someone who knew who his people were but still felt lost. A lot of *Deep Space Nine* is about the

quest for self-discovery, and I think the truth of the matter is that there really aren't magical answers to the things people are looking for."

According to Behr, when the staff was discussing the Dominion, one of their thoughts was that as a joke, in the last episode of the series it would be revealed that Odo was the once and future king of the Founders, who were going to turn out to be shape-shifters. "We always said that with a laugh," says Behr, "because we figured it would be too big a character thing to spring on both the audience and Rick and Mike. But one day Michael said, 'I've got a crazy idea. You're all going to think I'm nuts: what if the Founders turn out to be shape-shifters?' We had lunch with Rene Auberjonois to clue him in, and that's how it came down."

Explains Auberjonois, "When I first read the pilot script, even though Odo's character was quite sketchy, the fact that he didn't know where he was from and didn't know if there were any others like him was what was most fascinating to me. When they told me we were going to find out, I was concerned about where the character would go. But I must

say that I was and have been very satisfied with the solution they've come up with, which is something equally complex. To me, not only is acting a challenge, but the character has to have a challenge to make it interesting to play."

Ron Moore points out that another seasonal goal was to create more of a family feeling among the characters. Although there was a general feeling that the staff didn't want to lose the conflict between the characters — as that's what made *Deep Space Nine* different — there was a need for a transition from the people who met each other in the pilot to those who had been working together for several years. "After so much time, they are going to genuinely like and care about each other," he says. "Even in 'The Search' we were trying to get that feeling. Sisko comes back to the station and Jake says to him, 'DS9 is becoming home,' and Quark is showing that he actually cares about what happens to these people when he says good-bye as they go off to the Gamma Quadrant in the *Defiant*. There was a sense we wanted more family third year, for the cast of characters to come together."

He agrees that an appealing aspect of the characters is that they can "get in each other's faces" without damaging their overall relationships. "That was one of the most charming elements of the original series," Moore offers. "Then came *Next Generation*, which took a couple of years to grow on people and then people began to love it, and it's become one of the icons of *Star Trek*, but those characters were really bland with each other. They loved the shit out of each other, and that got boring to write. We were always desperately trying to find ways to get Riker and Picard into conflict, to have Picard chew Worf out about something. Those were great moments, but they were so rare, and we were always hunting for more. When people were criticizing the show, they were always saying, 'The characters are getting along too well; it's all so touchy-feely.' Along comes *Deep Space Nine*, and you get some of that friction, and people are saying, 'Oh my God, these people are yelling at each other all the time,' and it's this complete overreaction. It's a weird criticism to say that conflict is bad. Conflict is the root of drama."

Beyond character development — and there was a lot of it in season three — there was also an attempt to expand the scope of the storytelling in more ambitious adventures.

In the two-part "Past Tense," a transporter malfunction sends Sisko, Bashir and Dax back in time to San Francisco circa 2024, where the homeless are imprisoned in areas known as Sanctuary Districts. The trio has arrived at a precipitous moment in history: A series of events — sparked by the anti-Sanctuary activist Gabriel Bell — has just begun that will define humanity's future. "There are people who just want their escapism," muses Robert Wolfe. "I'm not a big space-anomaly fan myself. I definitely think that it has its place in *Star Trek,* along with exploring scientific theory and making it come to life. But to me, the shows that deal with reality — human anomalies — are more interesting. No one is ever going to see a black hole, but I see homeless people every day."

In the two-part "Improbable Cause" and "The Die Is Cast," when Garak's shop explodes, Odo begins an investigation to determine who is trying to kill the exiled Cardassian and why. Eventually, the evidence suggests that Garak blew up his own shop in an attempt to join up again with his onetime mentor,

Enabran Tain. When Odo and Garak's runabout — which has been launched to investigate the situation — is caught in the tractor beam of a Romulan warbird, the duo eventually learns that the Cardassian Obsidian Order and the Romulans are going to lead a fleet of vessels through the wormhole in a surprise attack to destroy the Founders. Shortly after being told of this, Garak is invited to join Tain, which he is happy to do. He is not so enthusiastic, however, when he's ordered to torture Odo to learn anything he can about the Founders. In the end all is for naught, as Tain and the Romulans discover that they have been completely manipulated by the Founders and are under attack by a fleet of Jem'Hadar vessels.

Says Ira Behr, "I know we took some hits in the media — which pisses me off — about the shows being too complicated and you need to know too much about them. Some guy from *USA Today* gave us a review where he listed what he thought were twelve things you need to know going into the episode. That's a little frustrating because you never know what people are going to react to. When we did 'Past Tense,' I expected all this media attention and the little media attention we got was almost entirely negative. The fan reaction was great. Then we did the 'Improbable Cause' two-parter, and I thought

we were going to get great media reaction, and basically nothing again. It's amazing, because I think it's really quality TV. I liked everything about the episodes. They're about as good as *Deep Space Nine* gets."

The season finale, "The Adversary," had Sisko and his crew aboard the *Defiant,* being manipulated by a Founder who is trying to trigger a war and ominously lets Odo know that the changelings are omnipresent. "It was meant to be a paranoid, tension-producing show," offers Behr, "and represented an interesting way to use the changelings, making them more of a threat."

As far as Behr is concerned, it will be the next generation, literally, that will appreciate all of the creative effort that has gone into the series. "If you think people were writing articles and college papers on *TNG,* wait until they sit back and take a look at all the stuff on *Deep Space Nine,*" he emphasizes. "All of the political situations, the social situations, the personal interaction. If that's your rice bowl, if you actually care enough to treat it seriously, there is just acres of stuff to pick over and study. All kinds of little facets in each jewel." Behr pauses for a moment, then adds — not quite jokingly— "I just hope that I'm not too old to enjoy it when it happens."

• • • •

CHAPTER SEVEN

Deep Space Nine: Season Three Episode Guide

"The Search, Part I"

"The Search, Part II"

"The House of Quark"

"Equilibrium"

"Second Skin"

"The Abandoned"

"Civil Defense"

"Meridian"

"Defiant"

"Fascination"

"Past Tense, Part I"

"Past Tense, Part II"

"Life Support"

"Heart of Stone"

"Destiny"

"Prophet Motive"

"Visionary"

"Distant Voices"

"Through the Looking Glass"

"Improbable Cause"

"The Die Is Cast"

"Explorers"

"Family Business"

"Shakaar"

"Facets"

"The Adversary"

• • • •

Episode #47
"The Search, Part I"
Original Airdate: 10/1/94
Teleplay by Ronald D. Moore
Story by Ira Steven Behr and Robert Hewitt Wolfe
Directed by Kim Friedman
Guest Starring: Salome Jens (Female Shape-Shifter), Martha Hackett (T'Rul), John Fleck (Ornithar), Kenneth Marshall (Lieutenant Commander Eddington)

After a prolonged debriefing at Starfleet Command, Sisko returns to DS9 with the starship *Defiant,* a prototype vessel equipped with a Romulan cloaking device designed to combat the Borg, but one that will be used instead to head off a potential attack by the Jem'Hadar. Sisko leads his key officers through the wormhole to find the Dominion — actually, the Founders — leaders of the Gamma Quadrant. What they discover is that the Founders are changelings — and Odo has found his people.

••••

Kicking off the third season of *Star Trek: Deep Space Nine,* "The Search" was fairly significant in what it introduced to the series, not the least of which was the starship *Defiant.*

"The major thing we wanted to accomplish in year three was to take the Dominion, which we had been teasing the audience with throughout the last half of the second season, and really bring them to some kind of fruition," says executive producer Ira Behr. "We needed to show that there was something worthwhile in the Gamma Quadrant, which for the first season was this big empty piece of space. I think that's what we went in thinking: How do we make this Dominion the next big enemy or antagonist of the *Star Trek* franchise?"

Supervising producer Ron Moore notes that it was important for the series to begin the season in an attention-grabbing way, as it represented the first time that *DS9* essentially had the franchise to itself. "Everyone acknowledged that with *The Next Generation* off the air, *Voyager* three months away and *Generations* not due until Thanksgiving, there was a window of opportunity for *Deep Space Nine* to really grab an audience and establish itself. To really say, 'This is us, by ourselves, and there is no other *Star Trek* floating around

at the moment.' We really wanted to do an opening two-part episode that would do a lot for us. We threw the dice and did as much in those two episodes as we possibly could."

The roll of this particular pair of dice resulted in some answers to Odo's seemingly perennial quest to find out where he heralds from. The answer is that he is one of the Founders, a race of shape-shifters that rules the Gamma Quadrant. This revelation was a surprising one, particularly considering that it took Data from *Star Trek: The Next Generation* seven years and a feature film before he was given emotions, thus solving a major part of that character's quest.

"It was a risk," admits Moore, "but less of a risk than doing it with Data. Data's thing is an internal character quest like Spock's. There's internal conflict all the time as he tries to figure out how to be more human. The Odo thing had a danger of running out of steam early anyway. How many times can you play 'I don't know where I'm from, but here's another clue on this planet. Will this show where I'm from? Oh, not this week.' I think you would get tired of that after a while, because it is an external mystery, and you can only appease the audience for so long and then you start building traps for yourself. I think it was ultimately a good decision to just go for it, because now we can play all the things with Odo and his people out there who want him back. That's a complex emotion. Who are his loyalties to?"

David Livingston comments, "It was very arduous shooting. Shooting the *Defiant* was tough initially because we hadn't been in there a lot, and it's cramped; anytime you shake the camera or move the camera it takes a lot more time. The crew had moved over from *The Next Generation,* so on the first bunch of shows we had crew burnout. Rick was putting down the dictate 'No working past midnight or shooting late on Fridays,' but there was just no way to do that. The shows were so heavily written, and there was so much action and stuff happening, it just took a long time to do it. The crew was working just as fast as the previous crew [which had gone on to *Voyager*], but the material was difficult, and the people were really suffering."

Episode #48
"The Search, Part II"
Original Airdate: 10/8/94
Teleplay by Ira Steven Behr
Story by Ira Steven Behr and Robert Hewitt Wolfe
Directed by Jonathan Frakes
Guest Starring: Salome Jens (Female Shape-Shifter), Andrew Robinson (Garak), Natalija Nogulich (Admiral Necheyev), Martha Hackett (T'Rul), Kenneth Marshall (Lieutenant Commander Eddington), William Frankfurter (Male Shape-Shifter), Dennis Christopher (Borath)

Odo spends time with his people — eventually discovering that he doesn't belong with them — while Sisko heads back to DS9, where he finds that Starfleet has quickly established a peace treaty with the Dominion and the Jem'Hadar has placed a strong military presence on the station. Not willing to be led like cattle, Sisko and company launch a counterattack, going so far as to destroy the wormhole to stop invading forces. In the end, it turns out that the entire scenario has been programmed into the crew's minds so the Founders can see just how far the humans will go to preserve their freedom.

••••

Ira Behr reveals that when penning the "Search" two-parter, the staff's approach was to handle it differently than a traditional two-part episode. "Usually you do an opening show that is setup," Behr explains. "You have all the plot elements happening, but basically the show is a setup for part two, which is where you really spend the big bucks, go for it, blow everything up, tie up the loose ends and really have a resounding climax. We said, 'No, fuck that. What we're going to do is do a show, the first part of which is we're going to go out there and find the enemy and deal with it. Then, in the second show, it's going to be "Wait a second, when you go looking for the enemy, sometimes you find out that the enemy is you."' In other words, it's a much more subtle and intimate show. So instead of being about who's going to beat whom, it's a show about character revelations and a deepening of character and what happens when you find the truth about yourself. How do you deal with it? We

••••

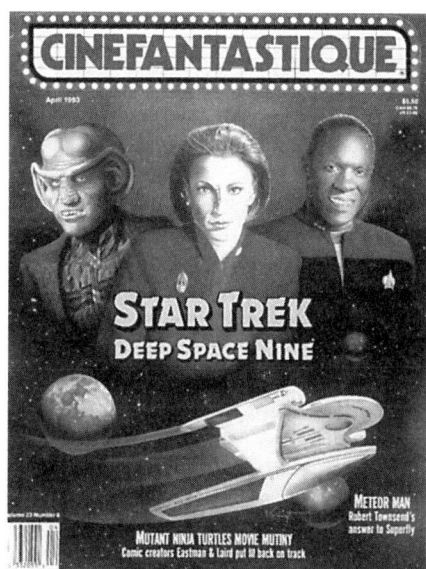

thought that was a clever and interesting way to deal with it. It's one of those shows where I get a lot of feedback from fans who say, 'I didn't like "The Search, Part II" when I first saw it, but now when I see it in repeats I see what you guys are going for.' The expectations of what should have happened aren't there."

There was some criticism of the episode's ending, which many compared to Bobby Ewing's being in the shower on *Dallas,* signifying that an entire season's worth of events had been nothing more than a dream. "The so-called Bobby Ewing aspect of part two was the least interesting part of it," says Behr. "We said, 'OK, we're going to give the audience what they think they want,' which is what happens if the Dominion gets into the Alpha Quadrant. What's the truth? Who's good? Who's bad? What happens if Starfleet itself gets turned in some way? Then we're going to say, 'That's not what happens; it's what's happening to Odo that's important.' I thought that was interesting and that Rene [Auberjonois] did a wonderful job. All in all, I thought it was a nice opening for the season and did what *Deep Space Nine* does well, which is give you a lot of bells and whistles, but ultimately these are small shows about our characters."

According to Ron Moore, the staff knew that some viewers would be annoyed at the revelation at the end of the

episode, but they felt it was intriguing to watch the characters being manipulated by aliens powerful enough to run entire scenarios in their heads just to see how they would react. "We tried to keep the whole dream sequence as real as we could," he says. "What would really happen if these things occurred? How would the characters react? Ultimately, that's what the Dominion was trying to find out."

"We also didn't want to spend the whole season with Deep Space Nine under siege," adds producer Rene Echevarria, "where we would have to evacuate the station and every time we use the wormhole it's battle stations. We basically wanted to set up what the Dominion was and establish that they had a different strategy. It wasn't going to be them sending the Jem'Hadar to battle us, but they were going to have a long-term strategy of destabilization. We wanted to show how far our people would be willing to go. I think people enjoyed it because they were primed for another epic battle. They love that shit because it's not what we set out to do every week. This show isn't *Battlestar Galactica.*"

With production having concluded on *The Next Generation* and the *Generations* feature film, actor-director Jonathan Frakes [*TNG*'s Commander Riker] was freed up to helm his first *Deep Space Nine.* "The nature of the show is different," says Frakes, contrasting the series with *TNG.* "*Deep Space Nine* is not on a ship. The *Star Trek* adherence to the Prime Directive is certainly in *DS9* or is similar. Jonathan West, whom I did a lot of years on *TNG* with, became the DP on *Deep Space Nine* third season, so we had worked together quite a bit and we work together quite well. You can tell that you're watching a *Star Trek* show within seconds, as with our show when it was on. *Voyager* and *Deep Space Nine* are the best shows on television; you see where the money goes. You see it on screen, and that's not always the case."

Episode #49
"The House of Quark"
Original Airdate: 10/15/94
Teleplay by Ronald D. Moore
Story by Tom Benko
Directed by Les Landau

Guest Starring: Rosalind Chao (Keiko O'Brien), Mary Kay Adams (Grilka), Carlos Carrasco (D'Ghor), Max Grodenchik (Rom), Robert O'Reilly (Gowron), Joseph Ruskin (Tumek)

After Quark accidentally kills a drunk Klingon in the bar, he starts bragging about his prowess, which leads to his being forced to marry the widow of the Klingon he killed. Suddenly he is trapped in a bitter feud between a pair of Klingon houses and finds himself in a battle to the death — a battle he has no chance of winning.

••••

The original story pitch for this episode came from series editor Tom Benko, who suggested that a Klingon comes into Quark's bar, Quark accidentally kills him and gains the reputation of "Quark — Slayer of Klingons." Naturally, Klingons come to the station and bring all the problems associated with them.

"I didn't get it when Tom Benko pitched it," admits Rene Echevarria. "If I had been alone, I would have said no. But Ron Moore immediately fell to it, and it turned out to be a delightful episode: a great pairing of two races that you usually can't see coming together."

"It reminded us of some film classics like *The Paleface* and *The Shakiest Gun in the West,* a really great setup," says Moore. "I really liked it because it gave me a chance to revisit the Klingons, whom I had done so much work with on *Next Generation,* and play it differently. I could have fun with them, keeping them true to who they were while not making buffoons of them. Really, to throw Quark into the mix and have fun with some of the ridiculousness of their whole system. Whenever we were doing Klingon shows, there would be knife fights, people would challenge each other to duels, and Rick Berman always said, 'How do you guys run a car factory let alone an entire planet like that?' They always seemed a little strange. I enjoyed the episode; it was a lot of fun to write. If I had any complaints, it's that the show ran long, and there were jokes and scenes that got cut out."

Perhaps the most satisfying part of the episode is its conclusion, in which Quark manages to save his life by bowing in front of the Klingon warrior and offering himself up for a kill that has no honor.

••••

Armin Shimerman as barkeep Quark (copyright © 1995 by Albert Ortega).

"That was a moment a long time in coming," says Ira Behr, "because at first we went through all of the easy choices. At one point, we were going to have Rom fighting Quark, and Quark falling out the window and you think he's dead. We went through all these hokey ways of getting out of the fight and we realized that that wasn't the way to do it. The way to do it was to ask ourselves, 'How would a Ferengi do it?' We wanted to be true to the character. Whenever you're true to the character, you're on better footing than if you're trying to maneuver the character into waters they won't go [into]."

"The makeup created time problems," admits David Livingston. "Because Armin was in so much of it and we had the Klingons that were in so much of it. In order to get the actors nine hours' of turnaround time so they could at least go home, take off their makeup, go to bed for a couple of hours and get up the next morning, we had to keep pushing the calls later each day. The crew likes to start coming to work at seven in the morning and when they have to come to work at noon, their bodies are all thrown off. By seven that night, their bodies say it's time to go home. Instead, they have to work till two or three in the morning. It's very debilitating on the crew, and ["The House of

Quark" was] another one of those shows that took a long time, not necessarily a lot of extra hours but just in terms of having to push the call each day. It became very arduous and tough on the cast and crew. And, of course, when you have the Great Hall and Klingons and stuff, it always takes extra time."

Episode #50
"Equilibrium"
Original Airdate: 10/22/94
Teleplay by Rene Echevarria
Story by Christopher Teague
Directed by Cliff Bole
Guest Starring: Lisa Banes (Dr. Renhol), Jeff Magnus McBride (Joran Belar), Nicholas Cascone (Timor), Harvey Vernon (Yolad)

Dax begins experiencing hallucinations involving a mysterious figure in a mask and blacks out as a result. Worried for her mental and physical health, Sisko and Bashir take her to the Trill homeworld, where they hope to uncover exactly what is wrong with her. At first there seems to be a conspiracy to keep something secret, but upon further investigation they learn that Dax has suppressed the memories of a host she didn't even know she had — Duran, a deranged killer.

••••

A difficult show to bring together, "Equilibrium" began as an attempt to write a script for magician Jeff McBride. While the original story by Christopher Teague just didn't feel right for an episode of *Deep Space Nine*, it did feature a mysterious figure in a mask that intrigued the writing staff.

"The whole thing with the mask is what interested Michael Piller," says Ira Behr. "I remember getting into this question about identity and the idea of Dax having another host inside her that she doesn't know about. That seemed to bring the episode into clarity. We all started spinning on this thing, and it became an interesting show. But it was a medical show and a mystery, and at the end it had a kind of talk-out with Sisko explaining everything to the audience — which are always difficult to write. It was complex. What worked for me was that Terry Farrell was quite good in showing Dax's vulnerabilities. I also thought it was a good show for Bashir, showing him caring in a med-

ical way, but also in a human way for Dax going far beyond whether he's going to screw her or not. We've kind of lost that element of the character, thankfully."

Explains Rene Echevarria, who penned the script, "I had had one story idea that I wanted to do, in which Dax is visited by Curzon in her own mind, and there is a deep, dark secret in her past that she doesn't know about. That's how we came up with the idea of another host that she didn't know about. I think there were a lot of interesting things about the Trill homeworld that you found out in the episode. I'm not sure how well it played out as a mystery, though. In order to be satisfying, you want the audience to conk themselves on the forehead and say, 'Why didn't I think of that?' and I'm not sure if they do. It was a troubled script in that we were writing stuff that was filming the next day three or four days into the shoot. We had locked down certain scenes that we would have liked to have changed to fit the new climax, and so on."

"I think everyone was in love with the idea of one of Dax's previous host's being a psychotic killer," says Ron Moore. "But the more the script was rewritten over and over again, it just kept losing focus and regaining focus. It's just one of those things where you're trying real hard to make it work, but ultimately you're not satisfied with the end result. It's an intriguing idea, and the episode holds up pretty well in some of its elements, but it's not quite satisfying in the last couple of acts. It becomes too much of Bashir and Sisko running around investigating the mystery rather than concentrating on the character of Dax."

For Robert Wolfe, the intriguing aspect of "Equilibrium" was the opportunity to explore Trill society in general and Dax in particular. "Dax comes across as being very human to me, despite her many lifetimes of experience," he explains. "In the same way that Troi came across as being very human. You sort of feel, 'OK, she's a humanoid and you know what to expect,' but I think the culture is more complicated than that and I think this show demonstrates that complication, which I like."

In the episode, the crew visits the planet Trill for the first time, making it the fourth in a group of expensive episodes. "The first couple of shows did cost a lot of money," admits David Livingston, "and the studio was concerned. My point to them always is 'Hey look, guys, we end up being on budget or under budget every year. We always go through this, but we always end up being OK.' The unfortunate part about that is that in the middle of the season we ended up doing some big battle shows and we had to change scripts to take out some of the production value that in hindsight we really didn't have to do. But it's all part of the game you play at a studio. I can never complain about money because the money that was given to us to do these television shows is a lot more than anybody gets to do any kind of TV show. So if they tell us they want to cut the budget, fine. But it does hurt the shows in the middle of the season because every season you want to start with big shows and a bang and then you begin to realize later you're in trouble."

Some of the Trill planet exteriors were filmed in Huntington Gardens. "It's this beautiful, pastoral kind of place," says Livingston. "We shot there on the pilot, we did some *TNG* there and we went there several times for *DS9*."

One of the problems with the episode was showing the Trill parasites themselves as Dax wades through a pool of them. "We built up a little pool area on Stage Eighteen," says Livingston. "It was fun trying to figure out how to make these things mechanical because it always looks cheesy. The idea is to shoot it like you'd do *Jaws* or *Alien*. You want to shoot it in a lot of shadows and make it go by real fast. I think it was pretty successful."

Episode #51
"Second Skin"
Original Airdate: 10/29/94
Written by Robert Hewitt Wolfe
Directed by Les Landau
Guest Starring: Andrew Robinson (Garak), Gregory Sierra (Entek), Tony Papenfuss (Yeln), Cindy Katz (Yteppa), Lawrence Pressman (Ghemor)

A lesson in self-awareness, "Second Skin" has Kira kidnapped by Cardassians who try to prove to her that she is actually one of them, taken from her parents by the Bajorans and turned against her own kind. In truth, her Cardassian "fa-

ther" is attempting to use her to replace his real daughter, who died.

• • • •

Surfing the Internet, one can see that many *DS9* fans feel that "Second Skin" is a remake of the *Next Generation* episode "Face of the Enemy," in which Deanna Troi is surgically altered to look like a Romulan.

"I don't agree," says writer Robert Wolfe. "The central concern of *Deep Space Nine* is the search for identity, the search inward to figure out who you are, where you come from. It's my opinion that in ["Second Skin"] at the end it didn't matter whether Kira was a Cardassian genetically or not. I think she would have gone back to *DS9* at the end of that episode because that's where she feels she really belongs. I think the episode is different from 'Face of the Enemy' because that show is just an episode about spying. There was never a question of who Troi was. It was a nice way to show the inside of a Romulan ship, and, if anything, you can say 'Face of the Enemy' was a rip-off of 'The Enterprise Incident' from the original series."

Comments Rene Echevarria, "A real triumph for Robert [Wolfe]. It was a real important show about healing and acceptance for Kira to suddenly see her lifelong enemy in a different light and realize, 'My God, these people have families and love each other just like we do.' I've heard several pitches where people want to find the real daughter, so obviously quite a number of people were struck by it. Originally, Robert wanted to say that Kira was Cardassian, that the arc of the show was that the real Kira died, but she is essentially Kira now and it doesn't really matter. I think Rick and Mike considered it and thought that it was too weird, too alien a notion for the audience to really hold on to a character they had invested themselves in. You want to believe they are who you think they are. It's very similar to when we wanted to kill Will Riker and keep [his double] Tom. The writer's impulse is to do something daring like that, but it's up to the creators of the show or the supervisors to take the long view and ask, 'Is this really what's best for the show?' They were probably right in that decision."

"Gregory Sierra was great," says David Livingston, "and I thought Larry Pressman was very good. In fact, we

brought him back to play a changeling in the final episode of the season. Nana's performance was phenomenal. I just have the utmost respect for her as an actress. I think this and 'House of Quark' were two of the strongest episodes we did all season. It was a high-concept show, which are always the best in my mind. You have something to latch on to."

Episode #52
"The Abandoned"
Original Airdate: 11/5/94
Written by Thomas Maio and Steve Warnek
Directed by Avery Brooks
Guest Starring: Jilly Sayre (Marta), Bumper Robinson (Teenager), Leslie Bevis (Boslic Captain)

An infant Jem'Hadar is discovered on the station and begins aging rapidly. Odo — feeling an obligation to the growing child — tries to teach the youth to control his aggressions and realize that he does not have to be a killing machine for the Founders. In the end, though, the youth cannot deny what he is and departs the station for his destiny.

• • • •

"We wanted to keep the Jem'Hadar alive on the series but not do another battle show," Ira Behr explains. "The trouble with coming up with a villain is they lose their ability to strike fear in your heart if you're able to kick their ass too quickly. One of the things we also came up with in the very beginning with the Dominion was the idea of drug-addicted villains. We really wanted to play that out, so we gave some backstory to the Jem'Hadar and wanted to see where Odo was as a character in order to play off what had happened in the past. We see that Odo is no longer using the bucket; we see that he has his own quarters and the impact the first two episodes of the season have had on him."

Adds Rene Echevarria, "A good show for Odo. I think people may have started seeing shades of [*TNG*'s] 'I, Borg,' but the twist on it was that you just can't turn this Jem'Hadar. People felt [that] Hugh [on 'I, Borg'] had turned, and it was more of a tragedy that he must go back and sacrifice himself for us. This is a different type of tragedy, where we see that there is no turning this type of creature."

• • • •

Rene Auberjonois as the shape-shifting Odo (copyright © 1995 by Albert Ortega).

"The Jem'Hadar are basically killing machines," says Robert Wolfe, "and it's not their fault. They're just drawn that way. It's the reality of who they are. They are another alien race I'm fond of because we worked really hard in creating them. Like the Cardassians, they started off as nice makeup, and we wanted to use them again. With the Jem'Hadar, we sat down and tried to design from the ground up this race so they were fully formed from the first time we saw them. Usually that doesn't work, but this time it did. In terms of Odo, he was thinking he had found some family, but he was wrong again, poor guy. It's a hard life."

It's Ron Moore's opinion that not enough was done with the young alien; that the relationship between him and Odo was not as fully developed as it should have been. "It's a good episode," he says, "and an important one to tell things about the Jem'Hadar that were different than we had dealt with before. I thought it was a good opportunity to show Odo's feelings for his people, but the scenes should have been deeper. Act five is particularly rushed and it doesn't pay off as satisfyingly as it could have."

"Avery's always been a good director," says David Livingston. "He has a firm grasp of the process, and I think often

the actors are more simpatico with another actor because a lot of episodic television directors come and do a show, and their approach is they're going to put the camera down and everybody else has to do their job because the permanent cast should know their characters, but I don't like that type of director. I think it's good to *direct* the people. I think when the actors say they like working with an actor-director it's because they're being paid attention to and respected. I don't like directors who come in and are just traffic cops and don't communicate with the actors."

Episode #53
"Civil Defense"
Original Airdate: 11/12/94
Written by Mike Krohn
Directed by Reza Badiyi
Guest Starring: Andrew Robinson (Garak), Marc Alaimo (Gul Dukat), Danny Goldring (Legate Kell)

An automated Cardassian security system is accidentally activated, putting the station on a self-destruct mode that seems impossible to stop as every time the crew finds a solution to one problem, another one develops. Gul Dukat arrives, gloating over the situation until he finds himself trapped as well and must work with Sisko to stop the station from being destroyed.

••••

A difficult teleplay, according to Ron Moore, because it kept running the risk of getting lost in technobabble, as is wont to happen when you're battling a machine. "We kept paring it back and trying to have vignettes of character things, and then lost track of the ticking clock," he says of the script, which was redolent of *TNG*'s "Disaster." "It became difficult to balance the two of them. Production problems, things we couldn't shoot, resulted in our having to change locations. There was a lot of internal turmoil to get it filmed, though ultimately it came out very nicely."

Notes Rene Echevarria, "A lot of the stuff we wanted we couldn't afford in the episode. We had a lot of opticals originally that had to be cut out. And to maintain the level of tension and to keep it building was not easy, but I really think they pulled it off. It's a great 'the-familiar-

becomes-dangerous' kind of story. The hidden program on the station and the stuff with Dukat, and then having the tables turned on him, were all very satisfying to watch. The episode was also filled with a lot of fun little character asides, wry dialogue in the middle of the tension. Ira [Behr] hates tech more than anyone who has ever written for *Star Trek*. Some people might fill those scenes with tech, but he'll strip it down to the minimum and fill it with 'Will you stop breathing so loud?' type of banter. It's just a lot of fun."

"A show that almost killed us." Behr laughs. "Michael Piller bought the show, and it was not one I would normally have been interested in because there was not a lot of character on the surface. It just ended up being a really good show. In fact, one of the best of the season. What was great was the whole key to that show: Every time they come up with a solution, it leads to a greater problem, and it's just a succession of victories and defeats."

Interestingly, Gul Dukat, who had become something of a nice guy in season two's "The Maquis," was back to his more sinister ways in "Civil Defense." "We were making him a little too friendly," Behr admits, "and we definitely did not want to do that. I don't want him to become the friendly neighborhood Cardassian."

"Cool episode," says David Livingston. "And poor [director] Reza [Badiyi] had no prep time. It was very tough for him. We put the screws to him in terms of scheduling and everything. And he has a system where he tells you where he's going to be each minute of the day and he hands it out in the morning and he sticks to it. I have a lot of respect for his getting it done. He pulled it off even though it was tough going on the station, which included going back into our ore processing room. The logistics of trying to figure out how to get from point A to point B were a struggle in the production meetings, but we solved it all. [Production designer] Herman [Zimmerman] built enough of the set that we could make it all happen."

Episode #54
"Meridian"
Original Airdate: 11/19/94
Teleplay by Mark Gehred-O'Connell

••••

Story by Hilary J. Bader and Evan Carlos Somers
Directed by Jonathan Frakes
Guest Starring: Brett Cullen (Deral), Christine Healy (Seltin), Jeffrey Combs (Tiron)

Dax falls in love with the inhabitant of an alien world that only becomes corporeal in our dimension for short periods of time. Before he departs, she decides to leave with him, but it nearly costs her life and those of the aliens, as she cannot exist on their dimensional plane.

••••

"Another one that was the low point of the year, with 'Meridian' and 'Civil Defense' back to back," says Ira Behr. "Rene Echevarria and I ended up doing the rewrites on 'Meridian,' and I have to take the blame because it was my idea. I happen to like *Brigadoon* and I thought it would have made a good episode. There are some nice things in it, but to make that show really work, we would have needed another $200,000 for opticals. There were some sweet things in the show, some nice moments, but it was tough to do. We were trying to create a society that was not tech oriented, yet there were all these tech questions that had to be answered: What do they wear, how do they live? How do you tell a love story in thirty minutes? It's really difficult. I can't say as a love story the show was really successful. Besides, no one got to sing, 'Go Home with Bobby Jean' [from *Brigadoon*]."

Echevarria explains that a major problem in the various drafts was defining the story's overall focus: Was it about Dax staying with the planet or her lover joining her on DS9, and what was the overall conflict? "The opticals weren't what we wanted, and there were too many things that had to be serviced in the story to really get a line on this culture or that relationship," he offers. "The original idea was that the planet was always corporeal, but it existed in another dimension. We came up with the idea that it was only corporeal in our dimension to give them a much more alien feel, which I think helped a lot. Some of the love scenes are sweet and kind of funny, especially Dax doing a classic stage double take when she leaves, comes back and says, 'Later, we'll count my spots.' I think Ira's sister is the one who said it seemed like an original series episode, and I'll take that as a compliment. On the original *Star Trek* they often asked the audience to accept a love story, a huge premise or a tragic separation — sometimes all three — in a single episode."

Notes Ron Moore, "An episode the staff does not look back on fondly. For whatever reason, romance has always been a difficult area in the *Trek* franchise. It was a concept left over from the second year, and no one is real pleased with it. It was kind of blanded out and not very interesting. But I like the concept. That's the thing. At the heart of every episode, whether or not they ultimately work, there is always something about it that we found attractive. There was a reason we were doing these shows. That was always a cool concept and an interesting idea to build a love story from, and to go to tragedy and pathos. There are always good intentions; they just don't always work out."

"It was mostly talking," says David Livingston dismissively. "Jonathan got some really nice performances out of Terry and our guest actor. We went back to Huntington Gardens and we found this tree that was great. It was a sweet scene."

Jeffrey Combs, who starred in the episode's Quark B story, is, of course, best known from his sinister turn in Stuart Gordon's *Re-Animator*.

Episode #55
"Defiant"
Original Airdate: 11/26/94
Written by Ronald D. Moore
Directed by Cliff Bole
Guest Starring: Jonathan Frakes (Tom Riker), Marc Alaimo (Gul Dukat), Tricia O'Neil (Korinas), Shannon Cochran (Kalita), Robert Kerbeck (Cardassian Soldier), Michael Canavan (Tamal)

Tom Riker (from *TNG*) arrives on Deep Space Nine pretending to be his duplicate, Will, and steals the starship *Defiant* with Kira on board. His plan is to deliver the vessel to the Maquis, who have received word of a military buildup by the Cardassian Obsidian Order. Sisko teams up with Gul Dukat to either bring Riker to justice or destroy the *Defiant*.

••••

"Defiant" picks up many of the plot threads left open in the "Second Chances" episode of *Star Trek: The Next Generation,* which introduced Will Riker's duplicate, Tom, who was created through a transporter malfunction a decade earlier.

"We had talked early in the year about doing an episode with Tom Riker," says Ron Moore. "Early on we had played with the idea of Tom being the leader of the Maquis movement; that we would suddenly notice that the Maquis was getting a lot better out there and kicking some serious butt. Why? Because Tom Riker has defected; he's their general. We played with that for a while, but we couldn't come up with a story line that was satisfying.

"When Ira asked me to come up with a Tom Riker show," he adds, "the first thing that I came up with was the gag of him impersonating Will, because that's the most obvious thing between the two men. I had the whole stealing of the *Defiant* sequence before I even knew why he was stealing it. I thought that would be a great way to open an episode. It was relatively late in the creative process that we came up with the mysterious buildup of the Obsidian Order, but it was a chance to take a character from *TNG* and make him an adversary for an episode, which I thought was a great idea. The great thing is we were going to be able to do some serious character stuff. Here's a guy who knows that there's someone else out there with his face and career and woman. What does that do to you? In this case, it was a different direction. We'll probably see a return-of-Tom-Riker episode. What's nice is he's not really a part of *Next Generation,* so he's ours, and we can do what we want with him and not worry about what the movies will do with Will Riker."

Adding to the scenario, Ira Behr notes that "the whole idea was basically Sisko stuck in Cardassian Central, looking at a blip on a screen and knowing that he's going to have to shoot down one of his own people. That's where the body of the show was conceived. What happened was, again, we had a lot of trouble with shows that were too ambitious. We write scripts we have to then cut pages out of. There were some good things that didn't make it to the screen because we didn't have time. What I do find interesting, though, is that Jonathan in some ways was

••••

more interesting as Tom than as Will. The role gave him a little more of a chance to be more like Jonathan Frakes, who's a wonderful guy and not at all as formal or stiff as Will Riker could be. Tom gave him more of a little spring to his step, a little cockiness, which I like. A good, exciting episode."

And an episode hurt by the budget crunch, particularly in terms of computer opticals of Cardassian war vessels in pursuit of *Defiant*. "It wasn't supposed to be a money-saving show," says Robert Wolfe, "but we didn't realize how much money it would have been. You need to spend almost as much money doing those graphics as you do on the actual effects. I think that was a mistake to save money. The truth of the matter is, it didn't look good."

"[DP] Jonathan West had already shot a show on the *Defiant* and he asked for some changes in terms of paint scheme and lighting, and now it was pretty together," recalls David Livingston. "The show went very quickly. It was one of our higher-rated shows of the season and the reason, obviously, was Jonathan Frakes."

Episode #56
"Fascination"
Original Airdate: 12/13/94
Teleplay by Philip Lazebnik
Story by Ira Steven Behr and James Crocker
Directed by Avery Brooks
Guest Starring: Majel Barrett (Lwaxana Troi), Philip Anglim (Vedek Bareil), Rosalind Chao (Keiko O'Brien)

It's Love Potion Deep Space Nine when the arrival of Iwaxana Troi — whose hormones are always on overdrive to begin with — triggers a mysterious virus that results in passionate responses in all the crew members of DS9, who start pairing off with each other.

••••

"The show that now and then runs the risk of pissing everyone off," admits Ira Behr. "It was a show that we had developed for the second season and never got around to doing. What I like about the episode is I thought Avery did some nice work with the direction. Another nice thing was the Keiko/O'Brien relationship. I think it was one of the most

interesting threads we've ever done on the series, and some of the most real dialogue between two married people who have expectations but at the same time can't quite sync up with each other. I remember when we were watching dailies, everyone was uncomfortable because it really did strike close to home. Everyone had something in their lives they could relate it to, how a relationship could seem to be bad over such small things — what seem to be small things but are not, really. I thought it was a nice human story. I thought Jake was very sweet with Kira, wanting to go out with her. Dax going after Sisko was kind of fun. I didn't think the Bareil stuff worked that well. The show was better than it had any right to be."

While Ron Moore acknowledges that every incarnation of *Star Trek* has done a similar story, he nonetheless feels that "Fascination" manages to be effective. "We thought it would be fun to come up with all these pairings and see what happens," he says. "It got a lot of divided opinion in the mail that we got. People either loved it or hated it. We think you have to have a mix of shows. They can't all be with the fate of the universe hanging in the balance. Sometimes you just want to kick back and have a little fun."

"I'll take the blame for that show," Robert Wolfe proclaims. "What we wanted to do was *Midsummer Night's Dream*, the show where everybody falls in love with the wrong person but still reveals some things about themselves. I think we learned some things about Odo and his feelings for Kira. I think that's the justification of that. We tried a lot of different ways to do that show and putting Lwaxana Troi in not only gave us a little bit of an emotional bottom, because she really is suffering, but it also, we thought, was a nice way to explain all of these strange things."

Impressing Rene Echevarria more than anything was the direction of Avery Brooks. "There are some really nicely staged scenes," he says. "There are these beautifully orchestrated tracking shots through the Promenade — really impressive stuff. A change-of-pace episode. A lot of fans just despised it, and a lot of people thought it was very funny and enjoyed it."

Majel Barrett Roddenberry, who returned to portray Lwaxana Troi, the Auntie Mame of space, says of the show, "It was marvelous. It was great being with everyone again and it was also kind of nice doing a part that wasn't just the lead character all the way through. I loved the idea of working with all the other characters. It was the first time since the show

The cast of Deep Space Nine *(copyright © 1993 by Albert Ortega).*

••••

started that all of the *DS9* characters were together on the same show."

Comments David Livingston, "All I can say is that it was cute."

Episode #57
"Past Tense, Part I"
Original Airdate: 1/7/95
Teleplay by Robert Hewitt Wolfe
Story by Ira Steven Behr and Robert Hewitt Wolfe
Directed by Reza Badiyi
Guest Starring: Jim Metzler (Chris Brynner), Frank Military (B.C.), Dick Miller (Vin), Al Rodrigo (Bernardo), Tina Lifford (Lee), Bill Smitrovich (Webb)

A transporter malfunction sends Sisko, Bashir and Dax back in time to San Francisco, circa 2024, where the homeless are imprisoned in areas known as Sanctuary Districts. The trio has arrived at a precipitous moment in history: A series of events — sparked by anti-Sanctuary Gabriel Bell — has just begun that will define humanity's future. But Bell is killed while trying to save Sisko and Bashir in a brawl, and Sisko must take Bell's place in history or the prosperous future the Starfleet officers know will be lost forever.

● ● ● ●

" 'Past Tense' was a real highlight of the season," says Ira Behr. "I've always said that I don't like issue-oriented shows because it's really tough to deal with an issue in an hour, to say something that is worth saying that doesn't just simplify a difficult problem. But Robert Wolfe wanted to do a show about the homeless and he came up with all these ways to do it."

Wolfe says his initial idea had Sisko waking up on a Santa Monica beach in 1995, disheveled and disoriented. He knows he's a Starfleet commander, but everyone around him thinks he's crazy. "The problem with my concept," says Wolfe smiling, "is that Brannon [Braga] went and did it with Riker in an insane asylum [in *TNG*'s "Frame of Mind"]. So we kept fighting for other ways to do this show with Sisko as a homeless guy. We were trying really hard to avoid time travel because of all of the pitfalls that time travel brings with it, but we didn't succeed."

"We certainly didn't want to do a Martin Luther King, which would have

been an obvious way to go," says Rene Echevarria. "We didn't want to have Sisko leading a march or a protest. That's when Ira came up with the idea of 'Past Tense.' It was sort of a twist on [*Star Trek*'s] 'City on the Edge of Forever,' where he has to take someone else's place in history. This was not meant to happen, but now that it has, Sisko has to step into history. You don't know what's going to happen and when you cut to the future you see that history has changed."

Ron Moore was intrigued by the notion of Sisko's taking Bell's place, feeling that it separates the commander from Captains Kirk and Picard. "They always sort of shied away from interfering with the past and being instrumental," says Moore. "We wanted Sisko at the heart of the action."

"The only time we shot night for night on the back lot on *Star Trek* was for [*TNG*'s] 'The Big Goodbye,' " says David Livingston of actually shooting night shots in the evening, an uncommon occurrence for network television due to its expense. "Subsequent to that we had not shot night for night anywhere on the back lot until we got into 'Past Tense.' It was surprising to me, because I'd walk around the back lot saying, 'Why aren't we using this?' Especially since we shot 'Big Goodbye,' they rebuilt the back lot, and we have used it for some day stuff [*TNG*'s "Time's Arrow" and "Emergence"]. Thank goodness we had [director] Reza [Badiyi], because he has so much experience doing this kind of stuff, and we all wanted to do night for night, but everybody was kind of scared because we don't do it often. We planned it out real carefully. We took a lot of street walks and decided where we were going to prerig lighting and where the crew would be. We did it all in preproduction so that by the time the sun went down on that first night of shooting, we were ready to go and everything was in place. A light broke the first night, and we lost some time, but Reza is so quick on his feet that he was able to adapt. He got it all done and got some big shots. We also budgeted for a lot of extras, which we kept adding. Rather than taking away, we had to keep adding because we needed it to feel like something special. We probably could have used another fifty extras, but we didn't have the money to do it. He maxi-

mized it all. It was really a matter of all the departments coming together and saying, 'Hey, look, we don't do this every day, but let's make sure that we're going to be able to do it again by pulling it off.' And we did."

In addition to depicting the weathered and dilapidated Sanctuary Districts, where the homeless are interned, the production team needed to portray the stark, near-utopian world of the twenty-first century as well. "Right around the corner from our exterior locations — which was all this dilapidated stuff — was this modern office building on the back lot and that's where we shot," says Livingston. "The part where Dax comes out of the underground and you see this modern facade is all on the back lot. We then built an interior of the guy's office that she visits. The contrast was really good, and Herman Zimmerman did a really good job of contrasting the two looks so you got the real sense of the haves and the have nots. We also put up a gate because Ira was very insistent that we show the Sanctuary Districts were really like a prison camp. ["Past Tense" parts I and II] definitely were two of our strongest shows ever."

Episode #58
"Past Tense, Part II"
Original Airdate: 1/14/95
Teleplay by Robert Hewitt Wolfe
Story by Ira Steven Behr and Robert Hewitt Wolfe
Directed by Jonathan Frakes
Guest Starring: Jim Metzler (Chris Brynner), Frank Military (B.C.), Dick Miller (Vin), Deborah Van Valkenburg (Preston), Al Rodrigo (Bernardo), Clint Howard (Grady), Richard Lee Jackson (Danny), Tina Lifford (Lee), Bill Smitrovich (Webb)

Sisko must defuse a hostage crisis in the Sanctuary District to prevent time from being changed, while Kira hopelessly tries to find the commander before the future is irreparably altered.

● ● ● ●

To weave the homeless issue into a dramatic and exciting action story, Ira Behr decided to plumb his memories of one of the "big" events of his life, the Kent State shooting in 1971. "Once they started shooting down American college students, everyone I knew who was still

Avery Brooks as Commander Benjamin Sisko (copyright © 1995 by Albert Ortega).

pro-war said, 'Maybe we should just end this damn thing.' And many of the counterculture kids, ironically, said, 'If they're going to shoot us, screw the revolution. Let's become accountants.' It had a big impact on me, and I got the idea of doing a combination of Kent State and an Attica [prison]-type siege, starting with the question: What would happen if the government started putting these people in camps? How would society deal with that or rationalize it? How would the homeless people deal with it?"

Shaking his head in disbelief, Behr adds, "The frightening thing is that when we started shooting here in L.A., the mayor [Richard Riordan] came out and said something like, 'We want to take part of the factory district and throw people into camps.' That proposal, or remark, was on the front page of the *Los Angeles Times,* and everyone on the show went insane when they saw that. Here we are shooting this thing, and it might actually happen. I don't think we showed anything in that episode that isn't a very possible future for this country."

"That was an epic, truly an epic," says Jonathan Frakes, who directed the second part of "Past Tense." "That was the best *DS9* episode that I got and that was Ira Behr. When you are a director, you

are assigned a show and you don't have any say; it's very much the luck of the draw. Some are better than others; some are great. This was great."

After the massive scope of the first part, the more intimate nature of the conclusion may have proved disappointing for some viewers. "I did find being in that room all the time a little disconcerting," says David Livingston. "But that was intentional. They wanted this feeling of claustrophobia, of being trapped. The one thing that we did that helped pay it off was having the searchlights come across the window and the crowd sounds from outside. You really got the sense that there were forces outside, both good and bad."

Episode #59
"Life Support"
Original Airdate: 2/4/95
Teleplay by Ronald D. Moore
Story by Christian Ford and Roger Soffer
Directed by Reza Badiyi
Guest Starring: Philip Anglim (Vedek Bareil), Aron Eisenberg (Nog), Lark Voorhies (Leanne), Ann Gillespie (Nurse), Andrew Prine (Legate Turrel), Louise Fletcher (Kai Winn)

An injured Vedek Bareil arrives on the station to negotiate a peace treaty with the Cardassians, but the possibility exists that he could die before the mission is completed. Backed into a corner by the significance of the Vedek's mission, Dr. Bashir must use various technological means to keep him alive, even when it becomes apparent that the man's body is ready to die.

• • • •

When this episode was at the story level, it was about a Federation ambassador — a young JFK-type diplomat — who was negotiating with the Romulans and trying to get rid of the Neutral Zone. As in the aired episode, a shuttle arrived, damaged, and the ambassador was dying. "We do the whole deterioration of the man as Bashir is desperately trying to keep him alive and we're dealing with the same issues of how far do you go and what's humanity and all that," explains Ron Moore. "As we were breaking the story, I felt that the problem was you just didn't care. It was a Bashir show, front and center, about a medical problem, medical ethics and Bashir's struggle, but the guy

whose life was at stake was just a guy who came to the station. The issue at hand — peace with the Romulans — just wasn't a big deal in *Deep Space Nine* because it's not like we're on the Romulan border; they don't come raiding the station all the time. It just seemed like there wasn't enough at stake emotionally. As the audience I said, 'This guy should be Bareil. He's dying, you've got Kira who's in love with him, peace with Cardassia, which means something for the show,' and that's the way we went. We came to the conclusion that it was time to move away from the Bareil/Kira relationship anyway, because some people loved it, some fans, but we just didn't see it going anywhere. It didn't seem to have a lot of magnetism coming across on screen. Once that decision was made, that changed the whole complexion of the show.

"The last scene with Kira is very moving," he elaborates. "At one point, we were going to take the whole positronic thing even further. We were going to have Bareil's body completely collapse, and they were going to put his brain in an android body, to go the next step and go for Frankenstein. But we decided that it would distance the audience from the show, emphasizing the science fiction at the expense of the emotional impact of the story line." (Probably a good thing, since that scenario seems one step removed from the original series' "Spock's Brain.")

One gets the sense that Robert Wolfe is only half joking when he announces, "Ron butchered my character, what can I say? I think it was a good episode, but that's a character payment I'll never see again. I do think the episode works well because [Bareil] was an important part of Kira's life, so it had impact on the audience, which had gotten to know Bareil."

For Ira Behr, one problem with the show was Louise Fletcher's health. "She was really sick during shooting," he says, "and on screen she just doesn't have that same nasty little streak that we normally get out of her."

Explains Rene Echevarria, "Michael Piller really wanted to do a medical-ethics show about Bashir, and when we made the victim Bareil it became a Kira show, and there was always a tension there between whose show it was going to be. I don't know if it ever became a Bashir show. I'm not even sure if we ever got to the place we wanted, where he had to say no to the requests to keep Bareil alive. I think the audience was already saying no by the time he was. It didn't have that 'My God, what a bold and brave and unexpected thing he's doing' feel to it. But when all is said and done, I think the end of the show had some real impact."

While feeling he helped the episode with the addition of Bareil, Moore believes that he brought something negative to it as well. "I just got nervous writing the show," he reflects. "I said, 'This show is going to be irredeemably grim, such a downer that the audience will hate it and I'll hate writing it.' The guy just gets worse and worse and he dies. I said, 'We need a B story that's a little lighter,' so we came up with some situations for Jake and Nog that, when tied in to the A story, is a weird combination. You literally have cuts in there where you're going from a gag with Jake and Nog that's really funny to a hard cut to Bareil in agony. It's kind of disconcerting. I wish we hadn't done that."

"It wasn't my favorite show due to the fact that we shot it in six and a half days," says director Reza Badiyi. "Everything was either in the operating room or the recovery room, and they were saying I should be able to do it in four days. I tried to use different lenses, since basically the entire episode occurs in the infirmary. Some of it worked and some of it didn't. The only thing that worked for me was the ending of the show. We broke a wall and then we just pull back forever as [Kira] says good-bye. It was one of those shows that they would call a throwaway. They wanted to do it with very little money, and I think Paramount was putting a little pressure on them since it was coming near the end of the season and they wanted to come out ahead."

Since the episode aired, a vocal movement in fandom has lobbied the producers to bring Bareil back, to no avail.

Episode #60
"Heart of Stone"
Original Airdate: 2/11/95
Written by Ira Steven Behr and Robert Hewitt Wolfe
Directed by Alexander Singer

Guest Starring: Max Grodenchik (Rom), Aron Eisenberg (Nog)

Odo and Kira pursue a Maquis renegade to a small moon, where they are temporarily separated. Responding to Kira's cries, Odo finds that she has been entrapped in a crystalline structure that is slowly enveloping her body and will undoubtedly kill her. During what should be her final moments of life, Odo proclaims his love for Kira, but her response makes him realize that he's being manipulated by — it turns out — the Founders.

••••

"One of my favorite episodes," announces Rene Echevarria. "I found it absolutely heartbreaking for Odo to finally proclaim his love to Kira, thinking she's going to die, and then realize that she's not who she says she is when she says she loves him too. How much do you want to hear that? Imagine the anguish he had to go through hearing that, and then his responding, 'That's not true.' To me, that's wrenching stuff. I think it was surprising for the audience, and it allowed us to set up the element of paranoia that would come into play later on. It's the first time we see the shape-shifters do people. Odo can't — he doesn't have the skill — but they apparently can. They touch and not only do they look like you, but they copy your brain and know what you know. That's very dangerous. Basically, the show was two people in a room. A money saver that had a lot of impact and a lot of heart."

Recalls Ira Behr, "That story came about because Piller walked by and said, 'Remember the movie *Sometimes a Great Notion?*' I said, 'Gotcha, Michael,' and that one line was the basis of the show." (He is referring to the famous scene in the film where someone is trapped under a log on a river and the tide is slowly rising, ultimately drowning him.) "It's a great scene in a not so great movie," says Behr. "It just shows you how shows can grow out of nothing. The 'Tribunal' episode from the second season grew out of one line about how Cardassian trials have the same outcome: Everyone is guilty."

"Ira and I had two different stories that we combined in one episode," adds Robert Wolfe. "Ira really came up with the Kira/Odo story, and the Nog story was mine. It just struck me one day that

out of Wesley, Jake and Nog, the one who will really become Starfleet and stand on a bridge to say 'Engage' twenty years from now would be Nog. There was a nice irony, and something cool to do with that character, especially after Jake said he did not want to enter Starfleet."

As much as he enjoyed the A story, it was the B story that captured Ron Moore's attention. "It was an arc that could have easily gone in a different direction," he says. "Nog could want to do this because he's not satisfied, but he learns to like his father after all and appreciates being a Ferengi. We decided not to take it in that direction and said that he really was embarrassed about his father. He loved him but didn't want to end up like him. He wanted something better in his life. I think that was an interesting direction. Somehow, Captain Nog sounds cool."

"The real challenge of this show was making the audience believe that [Kira] was really getting trapped inside this stone," says David Livingston. "We went to the makeup effects lab to build the different elements that she was going to go through, and it took a lot of research and development and a lot of discussion and money to build. Those things are always tough because you never have the time you want and they never look as good as you really want them to, but I believed it, and Nana played it really well. One thing she did was have her hands above the thing. It wasn't always her standing straight up and erect. Seeing her body positions and her hands exposed and sticking out made it believable. It was tough for her to play it. We built a little stool for her so that she could sit down at times, and it was easily detachable, but still, it's tough to

Max Grodenchik with his "son," Aron Eisenberg, who portrays Nog (copyright © 1996 by Albert Ortega).

••••

play thirty to forty pages standing inside a rock."

Episode #61
"Destiny"
Original Airdate: 2/18/95
Written by David S. Cohen and Martin A. Winer
Directed by Les Landau
Guest Starring: Tracy Scoggins (Gilora), Wendy Robie (Ulani), Erick Avari (Vedek Yarka), Jessica Hendra (Dejar)

A joint effort by the Federation and the Cardassians to install a communications relay in the Gamma Quadrant goes directly against a Bajoran prophecy of doom that Sisko cannot seem to stop from coming true, although the results are ultimately far from deadly.

••••

"A story left over from second season," Ron Moore points out. "It just took us a while to figure out how to do it. We wanted to deal with the Emissary [Sisko], we wanted to do a Bajoran-oriented show. We also wanted a communication relay in the Gamma Quadrant anyway, and since it was following 'Life Support,' we could make the Cardassians integral to it and include the peace treaty. It all just started to come together for us."

Notes Robert Wolfe, "A rare case where we actually did produce a spec script from outside writers. We really fell in love with the idea that the prophecy, no matter what you do, ends up coming true. We had a lot of trouble making it work because the concept was difficult, but I think it was Rene [Echevarria] who finally cracked the show."

For his part, Echevarria explains that he had done an uncredited rewrite on the teleplay. The story originally pitched was one that told of a prophecy of joy, wonder and happiness, and eventually the prophecy comes true. "It just didn't quite work," he says, "because it really needed to be a prophecy of doom. When we decided we were going to do the show, we were rebreaking it entirely, and Ron came up with that notion, and it all of a sudden fell into place. The twist would be, of course, that the prophecy comes true in a different way in that there is no doom, and it still gives you a smile. The reason I think we initially resisted the prophecy of doom

is that we wanted this to be a smile the whole way through. Every time another piece of the prophecy would come true, you would say, 'Sisko, you can't fight this.' But it just didn't work dramatically. I like the show a lot. It's really interesting regarding the Bajoran religion, Kira and her beliefs and Sisko trying to walk the line — is he the Emissary? It's a real *Deep Space Nine*. I'm very happy with it."

Lois & Clark's Tracy Scoggins guest starred as the Cardassian who develops a crush on O'Brien during her mating cycle, an amusing B story, and *Twin Peaks's* Wendy Robie (who played Nadine) also appears as a visiting member of the Cardassian delegation.

Episode #62
"Prophet Motive"
Original Airdate: 2/25/95
Written by Ira Steven Behr and Robert Hewitt Wolfe
Directed by Rene Auberjonois
Guest Starring: Max Grodenchik (Rom), Juliana Donald (Emi), Tiny Ron (Maihardu), Wallace Shawn (Zek)

When the Nagus arrives on Deep Space Nine, Quark and Rom are horrified to learn that he has decided to turn the Ferengi Rules of Acquisition inside out and wants Quark to spread the word. Upon further investigation, Quark learns that the wormhole aliens (introduced in the first episode of the series) have found the Nagus and his philosophy distasteful and have altered his personality. Quark must convince them that what they have done is wrong before his whole world falls apart.

••••

"Prophet Motive" owes its origins to the sitcom *Taxi*, which turned down the original story line. "Ira had written a spec script that they didn't buy," reveals Robert Wolfe. "In that story, Louie De Palma's uncle, who is the guy Louie modeled his life after, shows up and he's gotten religion and become this really nice guy. Louie spends the whole episode trying to turn him into a bastard again. They were fools not to do that episode on *Taxi*, so we did it on *Deep Space Nine*."

Says Ron Moore, "I think Wallace Shawn is a great actor. He always has a ball playing the Nagus, and we've tried

to give him different things to play. The whole concept of turning the Rules of Acquisition inside out is great. This is an episode you could not have done on *The Next Generation* or *Voyager*. It's a unique ability we have to say, 'Who cares what's going on in ops in this episode?' You just don't give a shit."

Ira Behr explains that back in the first season of the series, Michael Piller said he never wanted to see the wormhole aliens from the pilot again unless they meet Quark. That thought was kept in the back of everyone's mind until this episode.

"I have a reputation here of being a Ferengi maven," admits Behr laughing. "They are fun to write sometimes, and we've done a lot with them compared to where they started off. Of all the Ferengi episodes, 'Prophet Motive' was by far the lightest. It was also nice to see the wormhole aliens again, although if I were them I wouldn't want to deal with any of these people. Who wants to deal with humanoids and their petty problems?"

Of Rene Auberjonois's direction, Rene Echevarria says, "Rene brings a real comic sensibility to the show. A real theatrical, physical comedy. He works it a different way than a lot of the other directors. He would have the actors in his home, and they would rehearse for hours and come up with new material. It was more like you would rehearse for a play or a film."

"I think Rene has an incredible visual sense," adds David Livingston of Auberjonois's directorial effort. "He has a great sense of pacing and energy as well as a great comic sense. I think the fact that he got to do the two Ferengi shows is great, because he was perfectly suited to that material. It was another high-concept show and it was very funny."

Episode #63
"Visionary"
Original Airdate: 3/4/95
Teleplay by John Shirley
Story by Ethan H. Calk
Directed by Reza Badiyi
Guest Starring: Jack Shearer (Ruwon), Annette Helde (Karina)

Through a bizarre disruption of the space-time continuum, Chief O'Brien finds himself projected a short time into the future, where he witnesses his own death and the destruction of Deep Space Nine. When he returns to the present, it's a race against time to stop the future from occurring as he witnessed it.

••••

"A very cool story," says Ron Moore, "because it was a different way to do time travel that we hadn't really played yet, which was going a short distance into the future and returning with that knowledge. Seeing yourself die and the station explode — it just became fun to try and play those scenes out, to enjoy the plot and not get bogged down in 'Oh my God, we're changing history.' You can play the gag of seeing yourself dead and bitching to the doctor because he didn't save your life."

Moore has heard comparisons of this episode to *The Next Generation's* "Time Squared," but he doesn't agree. "I watched the episode again, and it's so ponderous," he offers. "They agonize about what to do the whole show. All right, already! We just quickly decided we weren't going to be that concerned and just went forward."

"A pitch I took from a schoolteacher in Texas," recalls Rene Echevarria, "and it just struck me as a nice twist on a time-travel show that could be a bottle show to save money. Originally it was an Odo story, but we had done quite a number of Odo shows so we changed it to O'Brien. It turned out pretty well, although it may have been a little confusing. Overall, it was a straight-on *Star Trek* that could have been done on any of the series."

Offers director Reza Badiyl, "The challenge was creating two people. Colm played two parts, which is kind of tough. He is such a wonderful actor, and I really like him, but you cannot keep him on the set. He has to go outside and get a little fresh air. So when he's in every scene twice, and we have to shoot it three times and lock the camera, and then he's coming to do this part and then he has to do the other part, it's very difficult. They didn't want to do it all in blue screen because it's so time consuming, because it would take nine days. They gave us seven, and we shot it in seven and a half days. I

felt it worked, and the effect and the relationships worked fine. I liked the show."

Episode #64
"Distant Voices"
Original Airdate: 4/15/95
Teleplay by Ira Steven Behr and Robert Hewitt Wolfe
Story by Joe Menosky
Directed by Alexander Singer
Guest Starring: Andrew Robinson (Garak), Victor Rivers (Altovear), Ann Gillespie (Nurse)

After an alien attack, Bashir is comatose and dying. To survive, he must access different aspects of his subconscious mind, which are personified in the form of other crew members. What follows is Bashir's surreal journey back to consciousness and survival as he seemingly ages decades in a short matter of time.

••••

"More bad sushi for Joe again," jokes David Livingston about the latest of a string of offbeat premises from former *TNG* staffer Joe Menosky. "Certainly we have such a wonderful ensemble that they play the hell out of it when they have something to play. I thought Sid did a fabulous job."

"I thought it worked very well," agrees Ira Behr. "It hit on a lot of levels that we wanted the show to hit on. It was a station show, but it was an interesting station show. It used all of our characters in interesting ways and was a wonderful episode for Bashir and Siddig. It has Bashir dealing with a difficult situation and dealing with it in a heroic, interesting manner. I thought he did some wonderful acting as he aged. The villain was interesting; Garak was a lot of fun. We had some alien chick D'abo girl singing in a saloon. . . . Overall, a fun show."

Sharing Behr's opinion of Alexander Siddig's performance is Ron Moore, who notes that the actor "aged believably." "A lot of times," he says, "when actors age it becomes a caricature, and you don't believe it. It's always a bit of a sell to the audience, because you know the guy's not really old. As soon as you do it, you're asking the audience to accept an artificial construct, but Sid carried it off very well. The scenes between him and Garak really

Chase Masterson, who plays a D'abo girl, Leeta, one of Quark's employees, who was featured in DS9's "Facets" and "Bar Association" (copyright © 1996 by Albert Ortega).

pulled that off. It was a cool idea and a show that was long in development. Joe Menosky had written the story long ago, and it went through various permutations until we could figure out what the handle of the show was. Basically, it's about your consciousness: splitting up your mind and passing on the different phases of your personality to the crew. Once you kind of reduce it to that, it's a little easier to understand, and from that point on it was an easier development."

Cowriter Robert Wolfe is surprised the show turned out as well as it did, because he went into it "kicking and screaming because I didn't know how to make it work. In the end, I was pleased. The idea of its being Bashir's thirtieth birthday, that he was going through some self doubts about himself, and making it a chance to show in a lot of ways how far he has come since the first episode — how much he's grown up — is what I'm proudest of in that episode. Sid did a terrific job. I totally believed that he was aged, which is not easy. Acting in that makeup is never easy, though Armin [Shimerman] and Rene

••••

[Auberjonois] are able to push themselves through it."

David Livingston says of Michael Westmore's old-age makeup, "[Siddig] was totally believable as the old guy, and the makeups were great. Michael always makes them a bit older. When we say seventy, the guy looks a hundred. If we say a hundred, the guy looks a hundred and fifty. Michael says you've gotta go for it in order for the audience to really get it. I think it was very successful and well directed by Alexander Singer. He shoots in a very interesting way with a lot of wide-angle lenses and low angles."

Episode #65
"Through the Looking Glass"
Original Airdate: 4/22/95
Written by Ira Steven Behr and Robert Hewitt Wolfe
Directed by Winrich Kolbe
Guest Starring: Andrew Robinson (Garak), Felicia M. Bell (Jennifer Sisko), Max Grodenchik (Rom), Tim Russ (Tuvok)

O'Brien from the "Mirror, Mirror" universe arrives on Deep Space Nine and convinces Sisko to come back to the alternate universe to help save the rebellion by taking the place of his recently murdered counterpart. Their mission: to rescue Jennifer Sisko (who died in this universe) before she is forced to develop a weapon to be used by the Bajoran-Cardassian alliance.

••••

"Through the Looking Glass" is, of course, the third *Star Trek* episode to look at this parallel universe. The first was "Mirror, Mirror" on the original series, and the second was the *DS9* second season episode "Crossover."

"At the end of last season I came to Ira and said, 'I've got a way to do a sequel to "Crossover,"' and it was the idea of Sisko's going to the other side to replace himself," explains Robert Wolfe. "From there we went back and forth about whom he should rescue, until Ira came up with the idea that it should be Jennifer [Sisko's dead wife], which I thought was a stroke of genius. From there, it was just 'Let's spend a lot of money on phaser fire and do a swashbuckling episode where Sisko can kick some butt and fire two guns at the same time.' If only we could have had

a sword fight, but we just couldn't get it in there."

Exclaims Ron Moore, "It's a cool universe, and it's kind of fun to go over there and see the world turned inside out. I didn't have much if anything to do with the episode, but I loved it. Avery did a great job over there, and, if anything, you want to see more and more of that world. I want to know more of what happened. It loosens up the characters a little bit, and Nana really sinks her teeth into those scenes. There are some great undertones to that stuff."

Indeed, Nana Visitor truly seems to be enjoying the alternate Kira's sexuality, sensuality and bisexuality — in fact, in "Crossover" she came damn close to kissing herself. "Nana is fearless with that stuff," says Ira Behr with a touch of disbelief. "We were wondering how far we could push the envelope, but when she plays it, she takes it further than we thought. Not just the bisexuality but the overall sexuality. I think the next thing we want to do without a doubt is bring some of that sensuality and sexuality to the real universe and not have to keep it there. We need to have some healthy romance in the *Star Trek* universe."

Behr points out that he is generally happy with the show, although he

Avery Brooks and Tim Russ (copyright © 1995 by Albert Ortega).

wishes the episode had been two hours in length. "We certainly had enough stuff that could have kept that show going another hour," he says. "I thought the Sisko/Jennifer relationship was interesting. It was a nice way to bring Jennifer back, and I think we'll have to meet her again. Jake is going to have to see her at some point. The action stuff was pretty cool. I thought that the look of the show was good.

"My biggest complaint is that we had to cram too much into too little time," Behr continues. "In the original outline we had a lot more with Bashir and the whole thing back at the camp. Sisko had a longer decompression period where he was studying the other Sisko. That is one of the great unfortunate things about forty-three minutes of television. That stuff can still make me cringe when we have to do it. It makes me angry at the medium and angry at ourselves for not being more deft in the available time."

"It was Rick Berman originally who wanted to put me in," says *Voyager's* Tim Russ regarding his cameo as the mirror-universe Tuvok. "They were looking to cast that role with somebody else, and he decided, or one of the writers decided, why don't we use Tuvok, because it is an alternate dimension? They thought it was a great idea, and so he gave me a call in my trailer and said, 'Do you want to appear in the mirror universe as Tuvok on *Deep Space Nine*?' I said, 'Yeah that would be great to do that. Let's do it.' It was such a neat thing because both shows were on at the same time, and you're dealing with a basic physics concept, theoretical physics — the concept of an alternate universe — and I thought it was wonderful. I wouldn't have done it if it didn't make any sense. But the character made perfect sense. I thought it was going to be something like this character would be sort of an evil version of what my character was, but, in fact, it was the same."

"Terry [Farrell] never looked better," says David Livingston. "She looked so sexy with her hair down. I was lobbying to have her keep that hairstyle permanently because she looked so fabulous. I also loved Nana — it's too bad she can't wear that leather suit all the time."

Of course watching the episode was a joy for Livingston, who had helmed the first "Mirror, Mirror" sequel, "Cross-

••••

over," which had proven his most arduous directorial assignment. "I told [director] Rick [Kolbe] exactly what was going to happen and I said, 'Guys, it's not going to happen. It's not an eight-day show. It's going to take longer.' I told Jonathan West that. These shows have to be shot in a certain style because it's an alternate universe. Even though Deep Space Nine is already moody and dark, this universe has a certain sinewy look to it, and Jonathan said, 'If you want it then I have to take the time to do it.' We all kind of bit the bullet, and it went over tremendously. It was not a surprise to me. It might have been a surprise to some people, but I had been there, and Rick also had to deal with more action than I did. At least he didn't have to do the split screens that I had, which is what really killed me. He had to deal with a lot of firefights, and it just takes time."

Episode #66
"Improbable Cause"
Original Airdate: 4/29/95
Teleplay by Rene Echevarria
Story by Robert Lederman and David R. Long
Directed by Avery Brooks
Guest Starring: Andrew Robinson (Garak), Carlos LaCamara (Retaya), Joseph Ruskin (Informant), Darwyn Carson (Romulan), Julianna McCarthy (Mila), Paul Dooley (Enabran Tain)

When Garak's shop explodes, Odo begins an investigation to determine who is trying to kill the exile from Cardassia and why. Eventually, evidence points to the fact that Garak blew up his own shop in an attempt to rejoin with his one-time mentor, Enabran Tain. When a runabout containing Garak and Odo — which has been launched to investigate the situation — is caught in the tractor beam of a Romulan warbird, the duo eventually learns that the Obsidian Order and the Romulans are going to lead a fleet of vessels through the wormhole in a surprise attack to destroy the Founders.

••••

Life for this two-parter began when DS9 editor Tom Benko pitched the notion of Garak's tailor shop being blown up and Odo's leading an investigation and discovering that it was Garak himself who was responsible for the bombing.

"It started as a one-part episode,"

says Rene Echevarria, "and it was fun to write the characters of Garak and Odo. That was my first big Garak show, and it was enjoyable to write that kind of articulate person who speaks eloquently and largely. In any case, I wrote the entire draft, and it all boiled down to the final scene with Tain and Odo and Garak. We had constructed a situation that was basically Garak and Odo had left information with Bashir, and when Tain heard that, he thought his attack would lose the element of surprise, so he canceled the mission. It just wasn't satisfying. Everything was building to this, and we felt the audience wouldn't be satisfied just having Odo pull something out of his hat. We bandied around some other solutions, and none of them worked."

Continuing the scenario, Ron Moore adds, "Basically Tain was blackmailed into letting them go. The first draft came out; it was a good episode. The relationship between Odo and Garak up until that point was good, and it was pretty much the episode it is now, but we were all pretty dissatisfied with the ending. We stayed late after work and tried to come up with a better way to get them out of that room. The gag of 'I have the secret information; if you don't let us go you'll die' just seemed kind of a cliché and didn't work very well. We kept coming up with more and more elaborate gags for Odo to morph quickly into the ceiling, to do action beats and things like that. The joke was we could never get Odo out of that fucking room."

It was Michael Piller who suggested that they turn it into a two-part episode to allow the resolution to "Improbable Cause" to develop naturally in "The Die Is Cast." "That was kind of a bold thing for him to say," Moore notes, "because 'Improbable Cause' was in prep; we were getting ready to start shooting in about a week or so. 'Through the Looking Glass' was going to be shot the next week. We didn't even have a story for the second part, but it made sense. We rewrote the ending of 'Improbable Cause' as a two-parter and we shot 'Through the Looking Glass' next, which gave a little bit of a breather for me to do 'The Die Is Cast.'

"I like the episode," he says of the end result. "It was probably one of my two favorites, the other being 'The House

of Quark.' We had set up all of this stuff about the invasion, the attack and all of those things in the first episode, and when we got to the production meeting, we emphasized that we were really going to do a big space battle here and wanted to see it and have it blow our socks off. We didn't want to go cheap on this one. The visual effects guys kind of blanched a little bit, but they went for it. It's one of the best space battles we've ever done. It was also fun to put Tain and Garak in a room together after all the talk we'd had and go through their characters. It was all about shifting alliances throughout the show: the change in the relationship between Odo and Garak, and Garak's being the interrogator again and Odo's flipping the interrogation back on him."

Episode #67
"The Die Is Cast"
Original Airdate: 5/6/95
Written by Ronald D. Moore
Directed by David Livingston
Guest Starring: Andrew Robinson (Garak), Leland Orser (Lovok), Kenneth Marshall (Lieutenant Commander Eddington), Leon Russom (Toddman), Paul Dooley (Enabran Tain)

Garak is invited to join Tain in the attack on the Founders, which he is happy to do. What is not so pleasurable is his assignment to torture Odo to learn anything he can about the Founders. In the end, all is for naught, as Tain and the Romulans discover that they have been completely manipulated by the Founders and are under attack by a fleet of Jem'Hadar vessels.

••••

The interrogation scene, where Garak utilizes a device to prevent Odo from returning to his natural state, resulting in the shape-shifter's body starting to flake away, had a profound effect on Robert Wolfe. "I saw that in dailies and I was horrified," he says. "It was so disgusting. But really cool. One of those moments where they outdid themselves. I kept watching the dailies as if I were watching the episode, I was so caught up in it." An interesting moment during that interrogation scene is Garak's apparent reluctance to torture Odo. Muses Moore, "You get the sense in that episode that Garak's experiences on DS9 have changed him, that Bashir's lunches had not gone for naught."

"This two-parter and 'Past Tense' were really the highlights of the season for me," says Ira Behr. "I think they're great shows. They ["Improbable Cause" and "The Die Is Cast"] tend to get a little talky at times, but you're dealing with Cardassians, and Cardassians love to talk. When you have Rene Auberjonois and Andy Robinson, you're not going to get a bad performance. They were terrific. I also thought the whole Tain thing worked nicely. There were some shaky things in the plot — again, because you're rushing to get to places, even in two hours sometimes. I wish we had had a little more time setting up the ambush so they weren't caught with their pants down so badly, but it moved. I liked everything about the episodes. They're about as good as *Deep Space Nine* gets.

"We had to make cuts on the two-parter," admits David Livingston. "It's not as big as it was originally. I think shooting this was the best experience I've had as a director. I think it's one of the better scripts I've been able to do. I had incredible actors, and it was a joy. [DP] Jonathan West told me after the show, 'We had heard horror stories about you, David, and how you work these horrible hours and you don't let go and you drive everybody crazy and do a million takes and make life miserable,' but after the show he told me that I was delightful and that everybody loved working with me and none of it was true. That made the wonderful experience for me into this fabulous experience. People came up and said what a delight it was. I don't know if they were just sucking up to the boss or not, but I felt they were genuine, and that meant a lot to me."

Episode #68
"Explorers"
Original Airdate: 5/13/95
Teleplay by Rene Echevarria
Story by Hilary J. Bader
Directed by Cliff Bole
Guest Starring: Marc Alaimo (Gul Dukat), Bari Hochwald (Dr. Elizabeth Lense), Chase Masterson (Leeta)

Trying to see how much truth there is in a myth, Sisko constructs an an-

cient Bajoran space vessel with solar sails so that he and Jake can re-create a legendary journey from Bajoran history. As much as it is an adventure, it is also a rare opportunity for father to bond with his growing son.

• • • •

"A pitch I took from Hilary Bader," Rene Echevarria says. "She was talking about an old space ship with primitive engines. I loved the idea and suggested solar sails, and she loved *that* idea. I think the production design was gorgeous — a Jules Verne fantasy type of thing. It was a softer, smaller story. I think Avery and Cirroc [Lofton] are very good together, creating a believable father/son dynamic. I'm very happy with the show."

Adds Ron Moore, "After Hilary's pitch, I wrote up a memo that said, 'Let's make this about the Bajorans and let's tie it in to the treaty that was established in "Life Support" and see a different side of Sisko.' That he's really into something for a personal reason and wants to make it a father/son project. So they go out and bond on this ship as Jake is getting older, and Sisko realizes that Jake has other interests. He wants to be a writer, but, ironically, the thing holding him back is he's worried about his dad. I thought that was a nice

Cirroc Lofton as Jake Sisko (copyright © 1995 by Albert Ortega).

character moment. Rene did a wonderful job with the script."

"I want to pay special homage to Rene Echevarria, who I thought wrote a really wonderful script and gave Sisko his best role in the history of the show," proclaims Ira Behr. "Avery was wonderful; for the ship itself I also have to give a nod to [production designer] Herman Zimmerman. When we went on stage and walked the ship, it was probably how they felt about the time machine from the 1960 movie — a great little piece of equipment. I said, 'Don't throw this thing out; don't trash it. Keep it somewhere, because this goes in the *Star Trek* museum someday.' It's just a great prop.

"I thought the relationship between father and son was lovely, showing a nice side of Sisko," he continues. "I really liked Sisko in this show. Of course, it also had my favorite scene in the history of *Star Trek*, Colm and Siddig singing 'Jerusalem,' which started out to be 'Louie, Louie,' then it was going to be 'Rocket Man.' There were all these things we couldn't get permission for. Colm suggested 'Jerusalem.' The only thing I miss is that the scene was actually longer, but we had to cut it for time. I thought the whole scene was hilarious. Again, it was a male-bonding relationship that was never seen on *TNG*. I'm hard pressed to remember ever seeing it on the original series. Two guys just hanging out rang true to me. And then Bashir saying, 'That's a beautiful song; let's go down to Quark's and sing it for everybody.' That's the kind of knucklehead thing you would really do. O'Brien is admitting he likes Bashir, obviously, and I love that relationship. And for this episode to come after the two-parter and to shift gears like that is great stuff."

Says David Livingston, "It was a bottle show, but an interesting bottle show with a father-and-son relationship and some interesting computer graphics of the sailing ship. We were reluctant to do computer graphics, but [producer] Peter Lauritson finally came around. He recognized how valuable it is. You can do more stuff with the ship, but you have to do it right. Not to pick on other shows, but *Babylon 5* looks like computer-generated imagery. On *Voyager* and *Deep Space Nine*, you might not know some of these shots are

• • • •

not motion-control shots. They're really, really good if done properly. You have to spend a couple of extra bucks and get really good artists, but CGI just allows you to do more and you can build more elements into the shots."

Episode #69
"Family Business"
Original Airdate: 5/20/95
Written by Ira Steven Behr and Robert Hewitt Wolfe
Directed by Rene Auberjonois
Guest Starring: Penny Johnson (Kasidy Yates), Max Grodenchik (Rom), Jeffrey Combs (Brunt), Andrea Martin (Ishka)

Quark and Rom return to the Ferengi homeworld (Fereng) when they learn that their mother, Ishka, has broken a Ferengi law prohibiting females from earning profit. Once there, the brothers begin exploring old conflicts and start to come to grips with who they are.

• • • •

"I don't think it was quite the Ferengi version of *Long Day's Journey into Night,* but it's about as pure a Ferengi show as you can get," says Ira Behr. "This season we've accomplished two very good episodes for the Ferengi. 'Prophet Motive' was a flat-out comedy with nothing else but humor. Then we did 'Family Business,' which was much more serious. I thought there was some wonderful stuff between Rom and Quark, and the fight was good and surprising. I thought Andrea Martin was very good. The relationships were all nice, and it was an interesting look at the Ferengi homeworld. Things like 'My house is my house and so are my contents,' which is a nice riff whenever you visit someone — promising you're not going to steal anything. You have to pay money when you enter someone's house. We were also able to develop Rom's character and Quark's character, and it gave some insight as to why Quark is the way he is. It worked on a human level as well as a Ferengi level. It's family, and family stuff has to be dealt with. I'm not sure we'll be going back to the Ferengi homeworld, but I enjoyed the episode."

Robert Wolfe has high praise for guest star Andrea Martin *(SCTV)* as Quark's mother. "She was great," he says. "We also wanted to find out why Quark is

the way he is, why he's so fanatical about his Ferengi values. It's been my experience that a lot of people are fanatics because they're reacting against parents who were a certain way. The most liberal kids come from the most conservative parents and vice versa. Quark is reacting against his father, who was basically not a very good Ferengi, and that's something he's ashamed of and has always blamed his mother for. The show was as human as you can get with a show about people with those big ol' heads. It's nice to have a regular character who looks at the Federation and thinks, 'What a weird, in some ways horrifying, way to do things.'"

"Andrea Martin is a fabulous comedian and gave a fabulous performance in a very moving show," says David Livingston. "We had a hard time finding someone, and I suggested Wallace Shawn [Zek, the Grand Nagus] in drag, which didn't go over real big. It was tough finding somebody. In fact, she didn't even read for the part. We just offered it to her, and she delivered it. Ira said it was Eugene O'Neill, with the compelling family kind of stuff, and it was very moving. [Director] Rene [Auberjonois] did a great job. The stunt sequences he did showed that he could do action, and the fight between Quark and Rom I thought was wonderful, flying over tables and stuff. It seemed like a seasoned television action director working instead of a guy doing a second episode."

Penny Johnson, who appears in the episode as freighter captain Kasidy Yates, is a regular on *The Larry Sanders Show* on HBO and previously appeared in the *TNG* episode "Homeward."

Episode #70
"Shakaar"
Original Airdate: 5/27/95
Written by Gordon Dawson
Directed by Jonathan West
Guest Starring: Duncan Regehr (Shakaar), Diane Salinger (Lupaza), William Lucking (Furel), Sherman Howard (Syvar), John Doman (Lenaris), Louise Fletcher (Kai Winn)

When asked by Kai Winn, Kira agrees to go to Bajor to meet with her former leader, Shakaar, in the resistance movement to try and get him to cooperate

in the rebuilding of Bajor. Discovering that Winn is — once again — attempting to manipulate people as though they were chess pieces, Kira decides to join Shakaar as a fugitive — all of which could lead to civil war on Bajor.

• • • •

"We developed the idea of doing an episode based on *Zapata,*" says Robert Wolfe, "who rose up to overthrow the unjust government of Mexico and then put in a government that he rose up to overthrow as well. He kept fighting well after the war was won. I think that was the idea here, just to see Kira's mentor and the fact that it's not so easy to end a war even when your side has won. We also wanted to continue playing out some of the stuff going on on Bajor.

"Don't you just hate Kai Winn?" he adds rhetorically. "She's just another member of our beloved dysfunctional family, which seems to get bigger and bigger every year."

"Shakaar" sat on the shelf for well over a season, largely because Paramount had asked the staff to pull back a bit on stories involving Bajor. As Rene Echevarria explains it, market research indicated that those stories were the least interesting to the fans. "Things like the three-part story that kicked off season two," he explains. "That's asking a lot, to expect people to sit through three hours. I guess the feeling is that there is so much politics in our daily lives, so much to read about, do you need to see made-up political situations unfolding? A lot of people just don't have the interest. So we put it aside for a while and then found where we thought it would work in the season and where we could sneak it past Paramount without their getting upset. We also focused it more on this being a homecoming for Kira and brought Kai Winn into it, which she wasn't in the beginning. It turned out to be a good episode. Duncan Regehr [who also played a ghost in the *TNG* episode "Sub Rosa"] did a nice job."

Ron Moore says that the story line was reconceptualized several times. "At one point," he explains, "it was going to be about a new gigantic Alexandria-esque library that the Bajorans have rediscovered and are reopening. That's prompting the rebellion because the farm-

• • • •

ers are angry that their needs are not being met, but people are putting all this money and effort into raising these old libraries. Who cares about culture when it's food on the table? It was that kind of show, and that didn't work. We just went at it over and over again. It wasn't until we'd seen Kai Winn doing the peace treaty with Cardassia that it became obvious she was rising to more political authority on Bajor. If it's the Kai and Kira and Shakaar, then the players are all in place finally. The Kai becoming the president of the United States and coming to Kira with a new veil of authority and saying, 'I need your help. Help me.' Shakaar has done something that was questionable. Yes, he has a legitimate grievance, but you could see Kira's point as well, so we had to put Kira in a tough position and take her back home. Overall, I'm pleased with the episode. I wish we'd had more money and could have done a bigger battle sequence. I feel a little short-changed, but when you're doing a show with that much location work and building all the sets, it just gets expensive real fast."

The episode marked the most extensive use of location work of the season, with the crew once again trekking out to Bronsan Canyon, a frequently used outdoor venue for *Trek* (as well as hundreds of other series). "We built the farmhouse on one part of Bronsan Canyon and then went around the corner and shot the rockquarry stuff," says David Livingston. "I defy anybody who's not being perverse to say that it's Bronsan Canyon. We use Bronsan all the time, and I take a lot of shit for it, but it worked, and Jonathan West photographed it fabulously. It's a strong episode. It was tough for Nana because we went on location for three days in a row and shot night for night, which is tough because it was freezing cold and Nana had this flimsy little outfit on at night and was freezing her ass off. It was tough, cold, and it gets very windy up in Bronsan."

"Without a doubt, an episode that was severely truncated by time," says Ira Behr. "It ended way too abruptly, and I thought that hurt the show. I do, however, think that Duncan Regehr is a much worthier love interest for Kira than Bareil. I also think it was one of Louise Fletcher's best performances, and Jonathan West did

a nice job directing. Ultimately, I'm not sure if the show works. We have very fertile imaginations, and our reach sometimes exceeds our grasp — so sue us."

Episode #71
"Facets"
Original Airdate: 6/17/95
Written by Rene Echevarria
Directed by Cliff Bole
Guest Starring: Jeffrey Alan Chandler (Guardian), Max Grodenchik (Rom), Aron Eisenberg (Nog), Chase Masterson (Leeta)

Dax engages in a Trill ceremony, the object of which is for her to meet her previous hosts. This is accomplished when a Guardian from her homeworld comes to the station, and Dax chooses her closest friends to embody those hosts. Things heat up when Sisko is taken over by Duran, the psychotic, and actually get worse when Curzon takes over Odo's mind and doesn't want to go back.

••••

Recalls Rene Echevarria, "Ira said he wanted to do *Sybil* with Dax and he threw that into my lap. I was sort of kicking it around and I thought that *Sybil* leads to a revelation, a deep, dark secret. I

The original Star Trek's *Nichelle Nichols (Lieutenant Uhura) and* Deep Space Nine's *Terry Farrell (copyright © 1996 by Albert Ortega).*

felt we had done that with the host bubbling to the surface earlier in the season with 'Equilibrium.' Then I came up with the idea of a weird Trill ceremony where hosts are embodied by your friends, and that's how that ball got rolling."

"Kind of a difficult script to bring together," says Ron Moore. "I think at one point it was Dax herself having to become each of the hosts as she reexperienced them, but that didn't seem like it was going to become very much, so we came up with the idea of pushing the hosts into our other characters and seeing how they reacted. The trouble with the whole Dax thing is trying to figure out where the lines are. There were lots of debates. When Curzon is in Odo, does Dax even remember who Curzon is? No, she kind of knows who he is and remembers being Curzon, but she doesn't remember Curzon being Curzon. A lot of ambiguity, and we weren't quite sure how to define it. I think there was difficulty in that we also wanted to tell an Odo story, with Odo experiencing Curzon and wanting to retain that zest for life that Curzon had and that Odo finds appealing. It kind of takes the focus off of Dax in the later acts, and I'm not sure if that works as well as it should have. It sort of becomes two episodes. There's the Dax thing going on, which is very important to her, and Curzon, and toward the end of the show it becomes an Odo ministry. I don't know if we paid enough attention to Odo. It was there and they talked about it, and it is definitely taking up screen time, but I don't think we gave it enough justice, or the Dax one. I think it meandered a bit at the end."

Ira Behr points out that "Facets" is "all over the place. The story doesn't really get going until act three. Before then, you don't know what it's about. Is it about Dax? Is it about Odo? Is it about Curzon? I dare anyone to figure it out until the show is halfway over. It's filled with scenes that exist just for the hell of having the scenes. They don't all advance the story. We do a whole act of meeting these hosts, one after the other. But the fact that the story moved so fast, and so many outrageous things are happening every two minutes, it works a lot better than I thought it would. I actually wound up liking the show much more than I thought I would when I was watching the dailies. It has all the idiosyncrasies and eccentricities of a *Deep Space Nine* episode. Terry really does her best work when she's vulnerable, worried and trying to wrestle with problems.

Episode #72
"The Adversary"
Original Airdate: 6/24/95
Written by Ira Steven Behr and Robert Hewitt Wolfe
Directed by Alexander Singer
Guest Starring: Lawrence Pressman (Krajensky), Kenneth Marshall (Lieutenant Commander Eddington), Jeff Austin (Bolian)

Starfleet sends Sisko and his crew on a mission aboard the *Defiant,* during which they learn that the admiral accompanying them is actually a shape-shifter and control of the starship has been seized in an effort to trigger a war. What follows is a study in paranoia as they try to stop the changeling before it changes form again. The episode culminates in a battle to the death between the changeling and Odo.

• • • •

"Originally," reveals Rene Echevarria, "we were planning a big two-part episode where we go back to Earth — maybe the Academy — and realize that there has been changeling infiltration. It was supposed to be a big, big show. That was also when, simultaneously, the first conversations began about [*TNG's*] Michael Dorn's joining the show, so we realized we couldn't do this two-part episode. Everybody was very disappointed, though I have to admit that the story we were conceiving was too political, too 'them out there.' What's really interesting to me about the Founders is thinking that it's us, that it's you, it's Sisko, and containing the story."

Ira Behr points out, " 'The Adversary' was, at the time, the biggest budgeted, longest scheduled of any *Star Trek* episode in history. It was a very difficult show to do, although I thought it worked well. I thought it was a nice season finale. It was meant to be a paranoid, tension-producing show and represented an interesting way to use the changelings, making them more of a threat. The fact is, that show was written in five days after we were told we could not do a cliff-hanger. I think it worked nicely. It was, again, a very

strong Sisko show, although it wasn't an actor's show. This was a director's show, and I thought Alex [Singer] did a good job."

Ron Moore sees the episode simply. "The attitude was 'Let's go for it,' " he recalls, laughing. " 'Let's get on the *Defiant,* let's get a monster and hunt it down. None of this 'Should we negotiate with it?' shit. It's a shape-shifter, it's on our ship, let's kill him! I respect that. Enough playing around."

Echevarria found the episode to be taut and suspenseful, with interesting twists and turns. "It also provides another opportunity for Odo to deal with who he is, being the first of his people to kill another shape-shifter and setting up in the minds of our fans that this — the changelings — is an ongoing, very dangerous problem. To a certain extent, it's felt in the fourth season. We've had a lot of internal debates about what this would mean."

He points to the two-hour fourth-season opener, "Way of the Warrior," in which a Klingon boards DS9 and demands a meeting with Sisko and Kira. "There's a great scene early on," Echevarria smiles, referring to the fact that the one way to determine if someone is a shape-shifter is whether or not he or she has blood, "where the Klingon says, 'Let us see that we are who we say we are,' and he slices his hand open and bleeds on the table, and Sisko and Kira have to do it as well. They have to prove they are who they say they are or the Klingon won't talk. So it's something we'll keep alive but will be careful not to overdo."

The element of paranoia appeals to Robert Wolfe as well. "Hopefully, people were surprised by some of the events of the episode, if it wasn't ruined on the Internet," he says of the episode, which some have accused of being redolent of John Carpenter's *The Thing.* "When you're dealing with shape-shifters, paranoia is the natural thing to play. I think paranoia is one of humanity's scarier emotions, and it's good to remind ourselves of that once in a while."

"Something else I liked about the episode," adds Moore, "is that the *Defiant* has developed nicely over the course of the year. That episode introduced the engineering section and the mess hall and now we have a fully functioning starship.

We can now basically tell any stories we need to. If need be, we get off the station and do a story in the Gamma Quadrant with the ship."

Echevarria concurs: "We can start an episode, 'Captain's log: We're deep in the heart of the Gamma Quadrant, where no man has been before.' We can do a shipboard episode if we want and cut back to the station for a B story. We really feel we have the best of all possible worlds with the *Defiant.* We're freed up. We can basically do *Next Generation, Lost in Space,* whatever."

"We basically did *The Thing,*" says David Livingston, referring to the Carpenter classic about a metamorphosing alien killer. "We had a ton of morphs. You're never going to see more morphs in forty-three minutes than you will on this show. It was our first official nine-day show and it went a day over plus a couple of days of blue-screen shooting. It was the most complicated, time-consuming episode we'd ever done on *Deep Space Nine* or any of the other series. Next to the pilots, it took the longest to shoot of any of the other series simply because of these elements and all these morphs that go on."

As Moore noted, new standing sets built for the episode included an engine room for the *Defiant* as well as a mess hall. "If you counted all the costs involved in this episode, it's the most expensive show we've ever done on any of the series," says Livingston. "What we did is we amortized the set costs in our amortization account since they're permanent sets."

Another highlight of the episode was the promotion of Sisko from commander to captain. "It was about time," says Behr simply. "I think we should have made him a captain long ago. It was a mistake to have him be a commander, though it seemed good when the show was created. I would have made him a captain at the end of season one, but certainly by the end of season two we were all feeling we should do it. I think it's going to change a lot of audience perception, just making him a captain. I know it sounds silly, but we're no longer the junior show. We are as much the franchise as *Voyager* is at this point and we deserve the captain, and he deserves to be the captain. It was a nice way to end the season."

• • • •

••••

CHAPTER EIGHT

Deep Space Nine: Season Four

Ira Behr began the fourth season of *Star Trek: Deep Space Nine* in a *really* foul mood. After news had been leaked that Michael Dorn would be reprising his *Next Generation* role as Lieutenant Commander Worf on *DS9*, Behr found himself inundated with letters and postings on the Internet from people thinking that the addition of the character was going to change the entire series and result in the elimination of other characters.

"It simply wasn't true," says Behr. "I think people should have waited to see the work we were doing. We had a couple of really great Worf stories and developed a lot of interesting shows for all of our other characters. I just wish people would stop getting so fucking hysterical. We live, eat, sleep and breathe this television show. Do they really think we're going to flush it all down the toilet? It's just so nuts."

Obviously Worf was the big news for the new season. While some people looked upon the event as a desperate means to pump up the ratings, others saw it as a new means of creative exploration, tapping into and expanding upon the declaration at the end of season three that the so-called changelings are everywhere. "That episode, 'The Adversary,' was meant to be a paranoid, tension-producing show," says Behr. "It represented an interesting way to use the changelings, making them more of a threat."

That threat carried over to season four's two-hour premiere, "The Way of the Warrior," in which the treaty between the Federation and the Klingon Empire is on the verge of breaking down thanks to the concerted efforts of the Founders. It is also the episode that reintroduced Worf to the *Star Trek* universe. "It was very clear to us that the ratings for *Deep Space Nine* had eroded over the last two years," explains Michael Piller, "but we're very proud of the show. We believe it's a very good show, but clearly some

people have made the decision early on to leave it or not make the time to watch it. We wanted those people to watch again so that they would see what a great show it is. Worf was one of several things we were using to say 'Hey, come on back. Check out what we're doing.' With a character as beloved as Worf played by as good an actor as Michael Dorn, we thought this would be a nice addition."

Behr explains there had been some talk of doing an episode in which the Vulcans pull out of the Federation, which was how the fourth season would open. "Then I watched the tape we have of 'The Die Is Cast' and the line the Founder said, 'The only thing we have to worry about in the Alpha Quadrant is the Federation and Klingon alliance, and that won't be a threat for much longer.' That just leaped out at me. Suddenly the light went on. I called Ron Moore into my office and said, 'You know the line,' which he wrote, 'think about it. Maybe we're making a mistake. Maybe the Vulcans should not be the ones leaving the Federation. Maybe it's the Klingons who should break off diplomatic relations. That might have more heat to it.'"

Behr then brought the idea to Rick Berman. "And Rick said, 'Boing! The Klingons. It's gotta be Klingons,' " he explains. "We met with Paramount, and they said, 'It's OK, but you guys don't understand. We want something even bigger than the Klingons.' Rick said, 'What if we bring Worf along with them?' and they said, 'Bingo!' "

Negotiations began with Dorn, who says he joined the show because Berman asked him to. "Rick has a way of making me do things just in the way he asks me," says the actor. "I've got to be honest, though; when we heard that *Next Generation* was coming to an end, I said, 'I'm ready for it to be over. I'm ready to move on.' It was scary in that I was suddenly out of work after seven years, but I was prepared for it. It's truly amazing that I'm back. More amazing is that I'm not freaking out about it."

In fact, he seems intrigued by Worf's new position. "Inserting Worf into their universe upped the tension level a little higher than it was before," he says. "And it was pretty tense already. The tension that I wanted to insert into this is the

same tension that Worf felt when he first came on the *Enterprise* — a fish out of water. These are brand-new people, and a lot of them he does not like. But he recognizes rank and privileges, so he does not go too far, though he definitely lets these characters know how he feels. That's the beauty of Worf. All of these things he's not used to seeing, you never know what he's going to do or how he's going to react. His reaction isn't a lot of words; just let me look at you with that glare. He's *always* pissed."

Of Worf's character arc, Ron Moore notes that "DS9 is a station of people who are all outsiders coming together. They're all people who stand alone among their own. That certainly suits Worf. The character dynamic that we went for is that, basically, following the destruction of the *Enterprise* [in the feature film *Star Trek: Generations*], his home was destroyed. He had a home and a family there for seven years and then it was taken away from him, which has brought about a reevaluation of his life. In the opening episode, he's talking about going back to Borath, the place we established where there are Klingon clerics and religious monks. He wants to go there to check out his life and see what he wants to do.

"We're picking up a Worf who doesn't have a direction," he adds, "who doesn't know what he wants to do next. There is no new starship *Enterprise* yet. He doesn't have a clear goal that he wants to accomplish anymore. Ultimately he decides that he wants to go into command, so he wears the red uniform. He wants to be a captain someday. I think we can get into darker territory with Worf on *DS9* than we could on *Next Generation*. Some of the fun of the season was his adjusting to the station, bumping into some of the stranger conventions of Deep Space Nine. It ain't a starship and it doesn't run like one. What's with the Ferengi bartender-smuggler thief criminal that everyone seems to put up with? Obviously Odo is the chief of security, and Worf used to be security. At the same time, I think there is an interesting contrast between Odo and his notion of justice and Worf, who stands for honor. Sometimes those concepts are closely tied together, but they can also conflict with each other."

For his part, Dorn enjoyed the

••••

The cast of Deep Space Nine *with Michael Piller and Rick Berman (copyright © 1995 by Albert Ortega).*

challenges of the character's new setting. "With the destruction of the *Enterprise,* Worf's world is gone. That's an interesting acting choice for any actor. You've got to play a guy who's just lost. Before, he had his comrades around him, at least he was on the best ship in the galaxy, and he had the opportunity to fight and be honorable. But DS9 is like a station in Alaska or something. He doesn't consider it a punishment, but it's not the choicest assignment, either. I think he brings a lot of different things we definitely haven't seen yet. It's all very exciting."

There was reportedly some concern from fans that breaking the Klingon-Federation alliance would cause the Klingons and the Federation to resume their old militaristic posturing, going directly against one of Gene Roddenberry's personal triumphs in creating *Star Trek: The Next Generation.* "I thought it was a necessary step forward," says Moore. "The Klingon alliance was cool and interesting because they had been villains on the original series. Well, that alliance was established ten years ago. We haven't seen the Klingons as true villains; they sort of got defanged. All you could really play with them was the internal politics and the

Worf family material. Ultimately, though, they're just great villains, worthy adversaries and very interesting. I think that's why we brought them back that way."

Robert Wolfe agrees. "I wouldn't call the idea retro *Star Trek,"* he muses. "I think what Gene wanted to do was portray a better society where problems could be worked out. I think we're still portraying that vision. The Federation is still the good guys; they're still going to try and find the peaceful solution. But this is history. Our perspective, in a weird way, is that *Star Trek* in particular, and science fiction in general, is about history. It's showing you what has happened and what can happen again. In the real world, friends become enemies and then become friends again. Sometimes seemingly overnight. Right now, the Russians are our friends. God knows how that can change after their elections. There is certainly a possibility that the relationship can dramatically change. So what we're doing is trying to take a more realistic approach. The more realistic you can make the universe, the more powerful you can make the message. If things are real bad but there's still a way to work things out, then that makes a more powerful statement. It

reminds me of the Deep Space Nine manifesto: It's easy to be a saint in paradise, but this ain't paradise! It's easy to be a saint on the *Enterprise,* but it's a little bit harder to be a saint on DS9. Our guys still manage it. Sisko is still kind of a saint, but he's a saint that just has to work a lot harder."

The same can be said for the staff of *Deep Space Nine,* though the results have been pretty obvious throughout the fourth season. For the first time in the thirty-year history of the *Star Trek* franchise, a season's worth of episodes was produced with a large percentage being solid storytelling. In terms of consistent quality, *Deep Space Nine*'s fourth season is the one by which others will be measured. "I think our batting average has been very good," Moore concurs. "I know the feeling on the staff is that there are episodes that we're not as happy with as we could have been, but there's nothing we would point to and say, 'Ooh, that's an embarrassment,' which is unusual. In all the years I've been on these shows, there are always a couple where you groan and say, 'What happened there? What were we thinking?' The key to the show is that the characters keep on getting better, and we're finding different things to play all the time."

Producer Hans Beimler, a veteran of the first few seasons of *The Next Generation,* notes the differences between writing for the two series. "This is a very different show," he muses. "*Next Generation* did very well and was very popular with the fans, but it had a different dynamic. On *Deep Space Nine* the focus on the characters is sharper, and I don't think anyone would disagree with that. I think you know more about this ensemble than you do about the ensemble of characters on *Next Generation,* which was a show about going where no one has gone before. You were encountering the situations and the focus was a little different. The addition of the *Defiant* has given us the ability to every once in a while do a show that's dynamically similar to *Next Generation,* but I think this always will be a character-driven show. When we talk to freelancers about stories, that's really the glasses we're wearing. What does this do or say about our characters?"

••••

"Take Bashir, for example," Wolfe interjects. "That, to me, is a real guy in a way that [*TNG*'s Dr.] Crusher was never really a person. I think part of it is just the idea of the franchise. On *Next Gen* everybody got along. They all woke up in the morning, brushed their teeth — except for Worf — went to work and they were all very polite to each other — except for Worf, which is why he works so well on *DS9*. He's one of us; he's a dysfunctional person with his little bad habits and peculiarities."

As usual, the characters were at the forefront of the season, with former enemies working together (Major Kira and Gul Dukat), friendships frayed to the point of breaking but somehow managing to survive (O'Brien and Bashir), characters facing retribution for perceived crimes (O'Brien and Odo) and romance (Sisko and Kasidy Yates, Kira and Shakaar, Dax and a female Trill). Most surprising of all, however, was Avery Brooks's Captain Benjamin Sisko, who has come to life in a way that he never had in seasons past. As strange as it would seem, much of the "new" Sisko can be attributed to the fact that the actor has been allowed to shave his head, thanks to Behr's determination to "make the actor comfortable."

According to Wolfe, the studio was reluctant to allow Brooks to look more like his other famous television alter ego, Hawk, from *Spenser: For Hire*. With his mustache, goatee and, now, bald head, the image is fairly close, missing only the trademark sunglasses. "He's actually a little scarier looking," says Wolfe, "but the point is: That's what Avery looks like, so why shouldn't you let the guy look like himself? I think it lets him identify a little more with the character. The key to a good performance, especially in television, where you do it every day, is to be able to really find where you and the character intersect. When you make someone radically alter their appearance in a way they don't identify with, that can be restrictive. It's a subtle, psychological thing. But, hey, he's been terrific. If anyone's to blame for the fact that he may have had some trouble, it should be us. He's very talented, and his performances this season have been terrific."

What amuses Moore is the presence the actor has been bringing into sequences ever since the change in his appearance. As an example, he refers to a moment in "The Way of the Warrior" when Sisko is sitting in a room with a Klingon general and Worf. "It's a tense scene, and they're looking at each other," says Moore, "but you get the impression that *Avery* is the guy in the room you've got to worry about. Sisko, suddenly, is the most threatening presence and the guy who is just going to kick your ass. There are two Klingons with him, and he's just blowing them away. I think it's really given him an edgy presence, which is great. He's a comfortable actor, and that makes a difference."

"Hey." Behr smiles wryly. "Maybe we're writing a little better too."

With the close of the fourth season, the staff eagerly anticipated picking up plot threads and moving them forward. "We're playing with the relationships of the major powers of the Alpha Quadrant," offers Moore. "Obviously the cliff-hanger is going to send us into a big situation with the Klingons again. As a result, the relationships of the Cardassians and the Dominion will be changing toward us. Odo losing his powers will be a big threat that

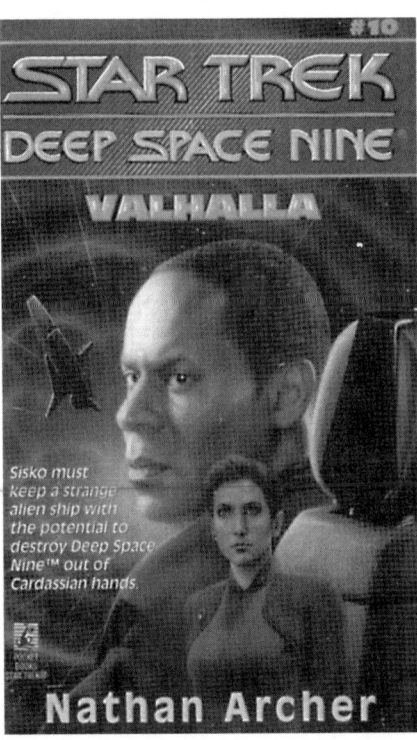

should carry him through a number of episodes. We've got Kira's pregnancy; Odo's search for his shape-shifting abilities; Kurn, Worf's brother, has now become somebody else; Gowron is a shape-shifter; Jake is becoming a writer; Nog has gone to Starfleet Academy — there are a hell of a lot of plot threads that we're still following."

Wolfe is hopeful that season five will explore more of the problems that face Sisko on a daily basis. According to the writer, Sisko has the hardest job in the galaxy and it's something they want to continue to explore. "Additionally, if you take a step back and take a real look at it, the Klingon problem is just one part of the vast problem Sisko's got to deal with," he explains. "Just because you put one little fire out, it doesn't mean the forest is safe. *DS9* in many ways is about real life. There aren't any easy solutions, but that doesn't mean you stop trying to find solutions. That's part of the nobility of what Sisko's doing. He's got a tough job, but, damn it, he's going to do it. By the time the series is over, in all likelihood he will have achieved some of his goals. Bajor is pretty much stable now, which was not true when he came in. The Cardassians are on the way to being our buddies, and that wasn't true when he came there, either. The Dominion threat is being dealt with, largely because of Sisko. The guy's not going to give up until he gets what he wants. That's what heroes are all about, and we'll keep going down that road."

Perhaps the most interesting shift that occurred between the end of the third season and the end of the fourth is the staff's realization that *Deep Space Nine* is *not* the bastard child of the *Star Trek* franchise, which is the kind of label that has often been applied to the series. "I think *Deep Space Nine* was an imaginative leap almost of the same order as the original *Star Trek*," offers Rene Echevarria. "*Star Trek: The Next Generation* was an evolution of the original series — basically a new *Enterprise* out there having adventures. I think it was an inspired and bold move on Rick Berman, Michael Piller and Ira Behr's part when they started *Deep Space Nine* on a space station. People criticized it for not going anywhere, but now, as we're going into the fifth season, we've had a solid year where we proved there are many stories left to tell, and that continuing story lines can make great *Star Trek*."

Behr too feels that they have finally proven without a doubt that they are a legitimate part of the franchise. "*Deep Space Nine,* by being a show which is about a family facing the crises they encounter on the edge of the frontier, shares a kinship with Kirk, Spock and McCoy, which really made that part of the franchise work in the first place. For a long time we kept talking about its being a darker show and a dysfunctional family — which it is on occasion — but I think we've really grown those relationships, that sense of unity and the sense of people working together. It's what *Star Trek* is all about. Just working to make something better. On at least one fundamental level, that's what the show seems to be about. But we are the franchise as much as *Voyager* is the franchise. I've stopped feeling like the bastard black sheep of the family."

Wolfe applauds this attitude, which is shared by his fellow writers. "The beautiful part of all this," he adds with a laugh, "is that we're making it all up as we go along. That's the secret. There is no vault with five years' worth of stories. It's basically the five of us tap-dancing as fast as we can."

• • • •

CHAPTER NINE

Deep Space Nine: Season Four Episode Guide

"The Way of the Warrior"

"The Visitor"

"Hippocratic Oath"

"Indiscretion"

"Rejoined"

"Little Green Men"

"Starship Down"

"The Sword of Kahless"

"Our Man Bashir"

"Homefront"

"Paradise Lost"

"Crossfire"

"Return to Grace"

"The Sons of Mogh"

"Bar Association"

"Accession"

"Rules of Engagement"

"Hard Time"

"Shattered Mirror"

"Muse"

"For the Cause"

"To the Death"

"The Quickening"

"Body Parts"

"Broken Link"

Episodes #73 & #74
"The Way of the Warrior"
Original Airdate: 9/30/95
Written by Ira Steven Behr and Robert
Hewitt Wolfe
Directed by James L. Conway
Guest Starring: Penny Johnson (Kasidy
Yates), Marc Alaimo (Gul Dukat), Robert
O'Reilly (Gowron), J. G. Hertzler (Gen-
eral Martok), Obi Ndefo (Drex), Christo-
pher Draga (Kaybok), William Dennis
Hunt (Huraga), Andrew Robinson
(Garak)

A fleet of Klingon ships appears around Deep Space Nine without warning. Upon boarding the station, Klingon general Martok informs Sisko and Kira that Gowron has sent him to support the Federation against the Dominion, which they believe has overrun Cardassia. When the Klingons interfere with the normal functioning of the station, Sisko recruits help in the form of Lieutenant Commander Worf, who arrives just in time to witness the Klingon invasion of Cardassia. This prompts Sisko to embark in the *Defiant* on a mission to rescue Gul Dukat, leading to a Klingon attack on Deep Space Nine.

••••

"When this show first aired, after Paramount told us we could do a two-hour episode — which I think has now become just a two-part episode in reruns — it was more like a little movie than an episode of the series, and that really energized us," says Ira Behr. "We got to play a lot of different levels from the politics of the Klingons and Worf coming on; we were able to do scenes with Garak and Dukat, and Kasidy Yates and Sisko. We had a real canvas; plus we knew we were getting the bucks to do some pretty spectacular stuff, which I think we managed to do. I thought it was a real strong opening to the season. It had all the typical *Deep Space Nine* elements: It had action, comedy, relationships, and it was actually kind of fun. Very well directed by Jim Conway. I thought the scene at the end between Sisko and Worf was as finely an enacted scene as you're going to find in the franchise. I would point to that scene for anyone who has any doubts about Sisko. I thought he was strong, understanding, and told it like it was. I was very proud of that scene and I'm proud of that episode."

"Violence. Cool," jokes Robert Wolfe regarding the episode. "We had a totally different season opener, but then Paramount started talking about getting some attention, and the way to do that was to bring Worf. As a result, we had to come up with a whole new season opener. I think the Klingons were talked about first and then Worf's name came up. We basically came up with the notion of making the Klingons bad guys, bringing Worf onto the station as an adviser on how to deal with Klingons and just doing a kick-ass, shoot-'em-up, cool show that appeals to the thirteen-year-old boy in all of us.

"What makes me proud about that episode," he continues, "is that we managed to find the time to do something nice for every character on the series. Everybody got a moment or two that was very true to their characters; that was fun and exciting, and we used it as a chance to showcase all of our characters, not just introduce a new one."

Ron Moore notes that the episode presented a creative challenge. "The tough thing about this was how we were going to do everything we set out to do. Paramount was going to give us a big amount of money to do a big two-hour premiere, and the question was 'How do we make this transition work? How do we bring the Klingons onto the series for the first time?' Although we'd seen Klingons and interacted with them on DS9, the Cardassians have kind of been our bad guys for a long time. So it became bringing the Klingons in in a plausible way and tying them in to Worf. I thought the show came out really well. The end battle is the biggest and best you're ever going to get on any of these shows. It was spectacular. To me, my favorite moment in the whole episode is the scene between Quark and Garak where they draw comparisons between root beer and the Federation. A great scene. Andy and Armin played it so well, and it's one of the stand-out moments of the season, if not the series. That's always what *DS9* is good at, these characters. This was a big action/adventure mythic tale, but it's scenes like that that make you really love the show, that really make the show work. They added that scene for time and then they realized for some bizarre reason that the show was long, and there was some

debate about cutting it. There was no way it was going to be cut. When the show was cut into a two-part episode, there was again some consideration about cutting it, and I screamed, 'No, you cannot cut that scene; it's too good!' "

Episode #75
"The Visitor"
Original Airdate: 10/7/95
Written by Michael Taylor
Directed by David Livingston
Guest Starring: Tony Todd (Adult Jake),
Galyn Gorg (Korena), Aron Eisenberg
(Nog), Rachel Robinson (Melanie)

An aged Jake Sisko is a reclusive writer living in the backwaters of the Louisiana bayou when a young woman visits his home. The woman, Melanie, claims to have been caught in a storm but is actually searching for advice from the famous writer and trying to learn why he gave up a brilliant writing career. In a series of flashbacks, Jake tells the story of the death of his father, which he wants to share before he dies.

••••

"Quite a tour de force," says Ron Moore. "It was great in concept. When we were breaking that show, we knew that was going to be a special episode. The format we chose — doing the flashback from the beginning and the old Jake telling the tale to the young writer — was just a great concept, a great idea. It was a departure, which was another thing that was really good for us because you need to do different things, keep stretching the muscles so the show doesn't get boring. Just a great show, and Tony Todd's a great actor."

Rene Echevarria, who did an uncredited rewrite of the teleplay, explains, "The concept was really a challenging one. As Michael Piller would say when you're breaking a story with him, 'If you're not crying when you write this scene, it's not working.' I'm very happy with the way it came out. In my rewrite, the story didn't fundamentally change except that I tried to give a character arc for the old Jake and Melanie so that that story had some kind of arc to it other than just telling you what had happened in the past. I wanted to give them a relationship. The other major change is that I had Jake actually write the book. Originally, the way we broke the story and the way Michael wrote the first

••••

Tony Todd, who played an older Jake Sisko, and Rachel Robinson, Andrew (Garak) Robinson's daughter, guest starred in "The Visitor" (copyright © 1996 by Albert Ortega).

draft, Jake never got back to writing, and I realized as I was rewriting it that that was very bitter. In a sense, Sisko had failed as our hero to change Jake's life. So I restructured it and brought Sisko back one last time in limbo and I had him impact Jake and get him to go back to it. That became his gift to his father, and his gift to Melanie, in a sense. I also thought Tony Todd was just lovely as the old Jake. The show worked on every level. The only thing I thought was disappointing was the future *Defiant* sequences. There was originally a little more interaction between the old characters that had to be cut for time. O'Brien was there as well [originally], but Colm wasn't available, and that was a shame, because we had some fun stuff between O'Brien and Bashir. But all in all, it's a show I'm proud of. It's very emotional and a tearjerker."

Says Ira Behr, "What can I say that other people haven't? It's another kind of episode we can do and another of those *Star Trek* episodes that fans love — [*TNG*'s] 'The Inner Light,' 'Duet' — a sensitive little episode. The script is terrific. Rene [Echevarria] did a terrific job on the rewrite. He really understood that show. [Director David] Livingston was really

jazzed by that show, and it shows. Cirroc [Lofton] and Tony Todd did some wonderful things. Avery did some wonderful things. A really good show. It's a nice, sensitive, interesting, complicated little tale."

It was also a budget saver. "I don't think the budget was a big consideration in that show," observes Behr. "Sometimes you definitely don't need it; sometimes you do."

Todd, who gives an extraordinary performance in this episode, is better known to *Trek* fans as Kurn, Worf's Klingon brother, from *TNG* and *DS9*.

Episode #76
"Hippocratic Oath"
Original Airdate: 10/14/95
Teleplay by Lisa Klink
Story by Nicolas Corea and Lisa Klink
Directed by Rene Auberjonois
Guest Starring: Scott MacDonald (Goran-'Agar), Stephen Davies (Arak'Taral), Jerry Roberts (Meso'Clan), Marshall Teague (Temo'Zuma)

Bashir and O'Brien are returning from a biosurvey in the Gamma Quadrant when they detect a plasma surge on an uninhabited planet. Investigating on board their runabout, they are struck by a plasma

discharge and crash on the planet's surface, where they are taken prisoner by the Jem'Hadar, who are also stranded there. With waning supplies of "White," the drug that all Jem'Hadar warriors are addicted to, Bashir sets out to cure their addiction, while O'Brien secretly tries to find a way to escape.

••••

"I thought it was interesting in the ongoing O'Brien/Bashir relationship," says Ira Behr. "That worked really well. I was a little disappointed in the Jem'Hadar as presented in that show. Since then we've done some adjustments to their makeup; we've gone a little bit into their backstory. I think we might eventually do even more adjustments to their look. But in this episode the Jem'Hadar themselves did not quite make it for me. I thought the *potential* was there; it just wasn't really achieved. It left me wishing that the Jem'Hadar had been a little more clear in terms of who they are, how they are and how they reacted. It's not easy coming up with new alien races, especially with complicated backstories like the one they have. But I thought it was a good episode. That's the only thing I can say about it on a negative level. I thought the acting was really nice."

Rene Echevarria explains that the original story concept featured an alien race that was not the Jem'Hadar. "It was a planet where we end up in this camp; we think these are the people who live here, but it turns out they are not native to this planet and that they are fighting the natives off. We realize we are on the wrong side and that we have been helping fight off some kind of aliens living in the forest, when in fact they are the natives who are fighting a war of rebellion. Somehow we realized that it could be about the Jem'Hadar and freeing of them of their drug addiction."

"A great concept from the beginning," adds Ron Moore. "Lisa Klink had pitched it as something like *Bridge on the River Kwai*, where you've got the doctor involved with the Jem'Hadar, doing something that he gets lost in and suddenly wants to defend. O'Brien is William Holden out in the jungle, coming to him and giving him an 'Oh my God, what have I done?' kind of moment. That was the concept. We worked that out and decided to make it more of a Jem'Hadar-specific episode with the drugs and this and that. It was a cool episode. I think if it has any shortcomings, it's that the Jem'Hadar blanded out between themselves. Part of that was the makeup, part of it was maybe the final polish on the script. They didn't come off quite alien enough, yet it was hard to tell them apart. But there are some great moments in that episode. My favorite moment is when the central Jem'Hadar is talking about the Founders and the fact that they're like gods, but these gods don't talk to them even though they die for their gods. I thought that stuff was pretty interesting."

A real highlight was Bashir's pulling rank on O'Brien, and even the aftermath, when a tangible tension hangs between them. "I think one of the things we've been able to do, and one of the things we don't get enough credit for, is that we have established relationships on this series that are pretty sophisticated for *Star Trek*," says Behr. "Kirk, Spock and McCoy were great relationships, really terrific, but Kirk was the leader and he had the guys he depended on. The relationships here are much more across the board. Bashir and O'Brien have been equals; they've become friends, with relationships that ebb and flow like relationships in real life. I'm very proud of that aspect of the series."

Ron Moore agrees. "That moment when they're confronting each other and Bashir pulls rank was a great scene. Sid and Colm made that work. It's nice that we took those guys, who didn't like each other at the beginning of the series, and made them friends. Now they're kind of buddies, and then you put that relationship to the test and you realize that they are — still — two very different guys with different agendas. You kind of put a strain on that relationship, and at the end, instead of everything being OK, they're still buddies. You have to realize that some damage has been done, but they will ultimately get over it."

"The thing we try to do in terms of conflicts," explains Robert Wolfe, "is make everybody right, and that makes it even worse and more difficult. O'Brien is totally right and justified in what he does,

and so is Bashir. For that reason, I really like that episode and much of what we do on this show."

Episode #77
"Indiscretion"
Original Airdate: 10/21/95
Teleplay by Nicolas Corea
Story by Toni Marberry and Jack Trevino
Directed by LeVar Burton
Guest Starring: Penny Johnson (Kasidy Yates), Marc Alaimo (Gul Dukat), Roy Brocksmith (Razka)

An old friend of Kira's, Razka, sends word that he may know the location of the *Ravanok*, a Cardassian ship carrying Bajoran prisoners of war that disappeared six years before. Sisko allows Kira to take a runabout to the Badlands on the condition that she accept the help of a Cardassian observer, who turns out to be Gul Dukat. Arriving in the star system where debris from the *Ravanok* was found, Kira learns Dukat's real reason for joining the mission: to find his missing half-Cardassian/half-Bajoran daughter.

••••

Notes Ira Behr, "A very nice show that was well directed by LeVar Burton. We wanted to do a show about Dukat and Kira. Robert and I took a pass at that and I think we moved that relationship forward quite a bit. It's an interesting relationship, and you got to see it in ways that in season one you never thought it would go. There's obviously still a lot of distrust and a level of animosity that Kira feels toward Dukat. What's interesting is that Marc Alaimo plays Dukat like he's the hero of the TV series. You listen to Marc talk about Dukat, and it's totally different than I see the character, but he brings that to it and adds a whole other level to it. It was nice to be on location for that show. I thought it worked."

The way the episode dealt with Gul Dukat was something that Robert Wolfe, who rewrote the script with Behr, was proud of. "I think we've really come to understand the Cardassians a lot better than anybody expected us to. I think they started out as very much stock heavy bad guys and have evolved into people. But they can still do some pretty rotten things, which is good too."

Episode #78
"Rejoined"
Original Airdate: 10/28/95
Teleplay by Ronald D. Moore and Rene Echevarria
Story by Rene Echevarria
Directed by Avery Brooks
Guest Starring: Susanna Thompson (Dr. Lenara Kahn), Tim Ryan (Bejal Kahn), James Noah (Dr. Pren), Kenneth Marshall (Lieutenant Commander Eddington)

A visiting science team led by Dr. Lenara Kahn visits the station, much to the chagrin of Dax, since Kahn's symbiont was once married to Dax when the two were in previous hosts. Ignoring Sisko's hope that she will take leave, Dax is reunited with her old love despite the fact that "reassociation" is shunned and prohibited by her people, as it has potentially devastating consequences. Despite arousing the suspicions of those around them, Dax and Kahn initiate a tempestuous relationship, unsure of what their future together will be.

••••

Emphasizes Ron Moore, "A key episode of the year. I felt strongly about this one all the way through. When we were working on that show initially, Rene [Echevarria] was working on a story in which one of Dax's wives shows up who's now a man. So it was going to be he's a woman now, she's a man, and they've switched genders. It was the same kind of story, where the past mate shows up, they're still in love, but Trill taboos prevent them from getting together. It kind of played out the same way. I remember I was driving home after reading the story and giving notes on it, and I thought this would be so much better if we played it with the idea that this was a woman and you played that relationship. I called Ira [Behr] from my car — being a Hollywood producer — and he liked it. The next day we sold it to the rest of the staff. We knew this was going to be a big thing, very controversial. I knew this was going to be a great episode. You had the opportunity to do something different, to advance an interesting story in the *Star Trek* universe that we had never done before, and it wasn't a gratuitous episode. I thought, 'This is a love story about two people who cannot be together because of a societal

••••

107

taboo.' It's a great metaphor for today, but it wasn't hitting it over the head. What I really respect about that episode is that in the final analysis we never, ever mention the fact that these are two women. That is the part that no one even raises an eyebrow about in the episode, yet it is the one thing that the audience cannot forget. You had this taboo, which sounded so ridiculous, on Trill, yet it makes you think our own taboos are ridiculous. I thought that was a great way to go.

"Having said that, we really had to sell the idea to everybody," he adds. "We had to approach Rick Berman and get him aboard very early. He wanted to know how we were going to handle this, how far we were going to go, why we wanted to do it. He made us answer some hard questions. Then he was on board and *he* went to the studio and said, 'Look, this is what they want to do.' The studio had some concerns too, but they were willing to go for it. We shot it, and right along the way everybody was watching the episode to see what we were going to do, how far the kiss was going to go. It was pretty much Avery, Terry and Susanna Thompson on the set, and we said, 'Make this

real, just don't make it salacious. Just make it a real moment.' And that's what they did. The studio supported the episode, we all stood by it and I'm very proud of that show. I think that show is an important one in the *Star Trek* pantheon and I think it's one we'll all stand by. I get hate mail about it. We've gotten negative reaction and a lot of good reaction. That was our choice. That was our statement, and we chose to make it, and I won't apologize for it. I think a lot of credit goes to Terry and Susanna, who played Lenara. Those two really had to carry a big burden. They had to make that a love story without it being a real cliché-ridden lesbians-in-space story. They did it; they made you feel for them."

"It was a great kiss," says Ira Behr. "It was banned on some station in Canada. I thought [the episode] was good, though it did suffer from what all those shows — those issue shows — tend to suffer: It was a little too black and white. It wasn't as complicated as it could have been dramatically, but I don't think it could support that, because the issue is such a polarizing one. That would tend to confuse it. As a result, we had to put it pretty much in your face. On that level, I think it worked. I don't think it was a really sophisticated hour of television, but I think it was a well-done issues show. I thought Avery did a bang-up job of directing, really got it and worked well with the actors. Terry had some great moments. I was a little disappointed in some of the special effects, but it certainly was a topic of discussion on the Internet. I'm still amazed, though, how conservative a large part of the *Star Trek* audience is. A lot of people really didn't like the idea of that episode, which of course makes me want to do more of them."

In a better world, Robert Wolfe muses, people would get more uptight about the violence in an episode like "The Way of the Warrior" than the fact that two women shared a kiss in "Rejoined." "We got flak," he admits, "but we got more flak from killing Vedek Bareil [in season three's "Life Support"]. The kiss has blown over, but the Bareil fans still write us letters. We didn't get as much flak as we expected, though I don't think it should be a big deal. At the very least, I think it's a thought-provoking episode. Any time tele-

vision can make people think a little bit and question things a little bit, wonder a little bit where they're coming from, that's a good thing."

Episode #79
"Little Green Men"
Original Airdate: 11/4/95
Teleplay by Ira Steven Behr and Robert Hewitt Wolfe
Story by Toni Marberry and Jack Trevino
Directed by James L. Conway
Guest Starring: Megan Gallagher (Nurse Garland), Charles Napier (Denning), Max Grodenchik (Rom), Aron Eisenberg (Nog), Conor O'Farrell (Carlson), James G. MacDonald (Wainwright)

Now that Nog has been accepted to Starfleet Academy, Quark and Rom decide to accompany him to Earth. Not surprisingly, Quark has a secret agenda to ferry an illegal load of kemasite, which is inadvertently ignited in the ship's hold. This leads Rom to create an inversion wave that propels them back in time to Roswell, New Mexico, in 1947, where the U.S. Army mistakes them for invading aliens.

••••

"When Toni Marberry and Jack Trevino pitched this story, our response was 'Try and stop us from doing this story,'" comments Robert Wolfe. "Great pitch, great concept. They didn't pitch much more than Quark, Rom and Nog are the Roswell aliens. We just took it and ran with it, and had a lot of fun — and I think that shows. We wanted it to be a real homage to all of the movies that we loved when we were younger."

Ira Behr smiles. "I have only fond things to say about this episode. We wanted it to be a clever, witty episode and tell the truth finally about the Roswell incident, even though the government was very unhappy with us for coming out with the true story after all these years. We're coming to the millennium; it's time to clear the air of these twentieth-century mysteries, because we're going to have to deal with twenty-first-century mysteries, so it was time to lay the Roswell mystery to rest once and for all. Sometimes you've just got to stand up and speak the truth in a loud, clear voice.

"Anyway," he removes tongue from cheek, "the only thing I would have

done differently on that episode was that we should have gotten Quark heavily addicted to cigarettes and given him a cigarette jones to deal with back home. Have him kick it, but have that to deal with. The reason we had everybody in the episode smoking was that in the 1950s the whole shared concept of the cigarette reached its apex in a movie called *The Lost Continent,* which starred Cesar Romero and dealt with a dinosaur on a Pacific island, where the sharing of cigarettes in the face of death as a bonding moment became so incredible that every two seconds someone was smoking a cigarette or lighting up. It just stuck in my mind forever, and, to me, that was part of the tribute we were paying to those movies. You had to have cigarettes. It was a cultural touchstone of the times. I just really felt like it would be a mistake to leave that out, because now it's the nineties and people don't want cigarette smoke near them.

"I thought the performances from everyone were great. In a way, I felt it was the best cast show — in terms of the guest cast — since 'Past Tense.' When people get to play humans in contemporary time or close to contemporary time, you just get a wider range of actors you can use. The casting sessions for those shows for me were just great because we had a lot of actors in from science-fiction movies of yore. So it was a lot of fun."

Notes Rene Echevarria, " 'Little Green Men' and 'The Trouble with Tribbles' are probably the two best *Star Trek* comedic episodes ever filmed. It was just a delight. I couldn't believe it when I read the first draft, because it was so magical and operated on so many levels as a parody of that genre film, a social satire of our own time and a story about the brothers, Quark and Rom. By the way, I somehow recall it being pitched to me while I was on *Star Trek: The Next Generation.* The writers said something about Quark being the Roswell alien. I remember mentioning it to Robert Wolfe and somehow it came back up. When *Deep Space Nine* became Ira's show and he could do what he wanted, he said, 'We're doing that one, baby.' "

Episode #80
"Starship Down"
Original Airdate: 11/11/95

Written by David Mach and John Ordover
Directed by Alexander Singer
Guest Starring: James Cromwell (Minister Hanok), F. J. Rio (Muniz), Jay Baker (Stevens), Sara Mornell (Carson)

The *Defiant* hosts a secret meeting in the Gamma Quadrant between Quark and Minister Hanok of the Karemma. Sisko hopes to use the Ferengi as the intermediaries in opening trade relationships with the local population to avoid incurring Dominion hostility to the Federation. Unfortunately, Hanok suspects that he is being taken for a ride by the Ferengi, and as the truth comes out, the ship is attacked by the Jem'Hadar, sending the *Defiant* into the atmosphere of a gaseous planet in an attempt to protect the Karemma.

••••

"My least favorite of the season," admits Ira Behr. "As I like to tell people, I was sick during the making of that episode. I don't think it's a bad episode, but it is definitely the weakest. We were trying to do a submarine movie and if we want to, we can try again sometime. That was script problems and a lot of other problems. We all have to take the blame for that one."

Ron Moore concurs with the criticism of this episode. "We all felt we could have done that one better," he says. "We wanted to do a submarine movie and play these little dramas out throughout the show. The submarine movie was not as exciting as it should have been; the Worf story did not play very well — we did not give that a lot of drama to play. It was about things that weren't that interesting, the issues of command, how to deal with the enlisted men — it just got short shrift. That was one we were rewriting while it was shooting, which is always difficult. The Bashir/Dax thing in the corridor with the gas didn't play well. . . . Basically, the show just came up a little short."

Says Robert Wolfe, "We wanted to show the *Defiant* in action and pushed to its limits. We always said that the *Defiant* wasn't good at certain things — that there's a cost for designing a pure warship, and why doesn't the Federation just crank out thousands of these things? — and this was a case where another ship like the *Enterprise* or *Voyager* would have been just fine. They would have had the labs and at-

mospheric sensor equipment and things like that. The *Defiant* was just meant to go around and shoot people, and that's a bit of a drawback when you're going into a difficult atmospheric situation. That's what our goal for the show was, to show there are some disadvantages to having a ship like that. It's an episode that was a little rushed, and we tried to push too many B stories into it. We did have a great performance by James Cromwell, who was nominated for an Academy Award [for *Babe*]. He was a great person for Quark to play against. We just wanted to have a lot of fun this season. Maybe we weren't suffering enough."

According to Rene Echevarria, the staff may have lost confidence in the concept of this story and the feeling that they could successfully deliver a submarine movie set in space. "I'm thinking of one scene in particular — before Sisko's hurt, and he's on the bridge of the *Defiant.* They're out there, sensors are down, he's relying on instinct and he destroys a ship with a torpedo," he says. "There could have been more of that and that kind of tension. I think we backed off a little bit from that concept and got closer to the model of 'Disaster' on *Next Generation,* where we isolated people in different situations and tried to do little story arcs with them. That was a show that came in as a first draft from some freelancers. I did a second draft which was much more of a submarine movie, then we decided we had to pump up some of the little story arcs. Basically, I think two of them worked OK and two of them didn't work at all. The other part that I liked — even though there wasn't much going on — was having Kira pray. I think that's something we've never seen on *Star Trek.* We've seen people talk about their spirituality and pray for spiritual things, but to really hunker down and say, 'Oh my God, you're really going to die and I'm going to pray,' is a nice new color that we've just never seen. I was very glad to have that in the show. But basically, the script just kind of got away from us in terms of time."

Until November of 1996, James Cromwell was best known as the beloved Farmer Hoggett from the Oscar-winning film *Babe,* for which the actor was nominated for an Academy Award for best supporting actor. Of course, he is now better

••••

109

known as Zefram Cochrane, the inventor of warp drive, in *Star Trek: First Contact.*

Episode #81
"The Sword of Kahless"
Original Airdate: 11/18/95
Teleplay by Hans Beimler
Story by Richard Danus
Directed by LeVar Burton
Guest Starring: John Colicos (Kor), Rick Pasqualone (Toral)

The Klingon Kor returns to recruit Dax on a quest for the legendary Sword of Kahless. Dax convinces Kor to reluctantly enlist the aid of Worf on their mission to retrieve the ceremonial weapon for the emperor in the hopes that he can use it to unite the Klingon people. Once they have begun their mission, though, Kor and Worf find themselves feuding almost as violently between themselves as with the antagonists they confront on their quest.

••••

"I thought it was an interesting show, a fun show, and it was great having John Colicos back — he can certainly deliver it," says Ira Behr. "It was an interesting show for Worf and Dax. I thought we had some production problems in terms of the fact we were in those caves *a lot,* and that could get tiresome after a while. That's one of those shows I wish we would have had a little more money for and could have been done on a bigger canvas. You try to do an adventure show and you're limited. Some of the fight scenes I felt weren't as we saw them originally. They were originally a little more filmic. I did, however, think the whole idea of the sword — the whole *Treasure of Sierra Madre* thing — was really nice."

Notes Ron Moore, "That's a show where we took Worf and pushed him. That's not a show they would have done on *Next Gen.* I think Worf would not have behaved quite that way in *Next Gen.* We wanted to push this guy and give him a passion — almost a psychosis — about this sword and really play the *Treasure of the Sierra Madre* thing, with these guys on this quest and how the quest fucks all of them up. I thought that was a good episode. Very mythic, the old warrior and the young warrior. Great stuff."

"We just wanted to do a big, fun, dumb Klingon show," Robert Wolfe

smiles, "with a twist, because this is *Deep Space Nine.* What would be a Klingon Holy Grail and would you want the Klingons to get ahold of it? That was the idea behind it. And the answer is no, you wouldn't want them to, because they're psychos. It was fun turning the quest on its head a little bit. I don't think Worf and Kor were unattractive in this show as much as they were alien to everyone; they have their own kind of ethics and culture, and there are things they would kill for that we don't quite understand. Or we do understand and that's what scares us. Like the Ferengi, they can sometimes embody some of our negative qualities."

Rene Echevarria opines, "We pushed Worf to the wall and had him do something we've never seen on *Star Trek:* a character who, for a moment, seemed to be willing to kill somebody to get something. I think John Colicos was just great fun to write. Hans [Beimler] and I had a real good time doing it. I think this is a big hit-or-miss show with the fans. Some people have just loved it and some people just didn't care for it at all. We were very pleased when it reran and the L.A. TV guide said it was a 'best bet.' It's the first time we've ever had a 'best bet' for a rerun. It was nice to hear that some people thought it was great."

Michael Dorn's idea for an episode tag was to cut to Worf's quarters after the sword has been transported into space and have the audience see that he has actually kept the *real* Sword of Kahless. "It's an interesting idea on a lot of levels," says Echevarria, "but ultimately I think it would be a cheat to the overall concept of the show. This Holy Grail is just too dangerous for the Klingons now; put it to destiny and maybe someday their people will be ready to do it honor. After having nearly killed a man, you would have to ask why has [Worf] changed? I guess the fear was that it would be saying that Worf *hasn't* learned anything from what he's been through. That would have been dicey."

Episode #82
"Our Man Bashir"
Original Airdate: 11/25/95
Teleplay by Ronald D. Moore
Story by Robert Gillan
Directed by Winrich Kolbe

Guest Starring: Max Grodenchik (Rom), Kenneth Marshall (Lieutenant Commander Eddington), Andrew Robinson (Garak)

Garak intrudes on Bashir's holosuite program, where he finds the doctor relaxing as a suave secret agent working for England in 1964. Bashir is upset over the intrusion, but soon both he and Garak have their hands full when Sisko and the senior staff are stored by the computer in the holosuite buffers when they are beamed away from an exploding shuttlecraft. As a result, they take the form of the various characters in Bashir's 007-inspired adventure, including Major Kira as Russian agent Colonel Anastasia and Sisko as the Dr. No–like supervillain who wants to plunge the Earth into a watery grave by melting the polar ice caps.

••••

Deep Space Nine script coordinator Robert Gillan came up with the original story premise for the episode. Naturally there were some significant differences in his version, most notably the fact that Bashir was originally sharing his holosuite adventure with Kira. "He wanted her to experience it with him," Gillan explains, "so she was with him, not Garak. I had her playing one of the Bond-type girls, and Kira, being kind of a headstrong person, was kind of put off at the sexist role she was supposed to play, so she kind of modified her character. It was a very vague story; the whole first draft of it was very vague. But I definitely had Kira less than enthused at the type of character she was playing and wanting to make it a more active type of woman. But to keep up with the Bond thing, Bashir couldn't really have a woman partner because the women were always treated differently. He doesn't really have a woman partner like a *Remington Steele* type of thing. We kept saying, 'What is Kira's role; what is she doing here exactly?' With Garak, he had been a spy before, so it worked for him."

"One of my all-time favorites," comments Ron Moore, who turned the story into a teleplay. "I had so much fun writing it. It was just a real joy because I am a fan of that genre, from *Man from U.N.C.L.E., The Wild Wild West, The Avengers,* to, obviously, James Bond. That whole era of secret agents and the gad-

Real-life lovers and costars Nana Visitor and Alexander Siddig, seen here at the Sci-Fi Universe Awards (copyright © 1996 by Albert Ortega).

real moments there between Garak and Bashir, that it said something about Bashir as a man and as a character. It was interesting that you had the [John] Le Carré character Garak portrayed involved in something from Ian Fleming. I thought that was kind of a cool idea."

Says Ira Behr, " 'Little Green Men' and 'Our Man Bashir' were a nice one-two punch so close together. 'Our Man Bashir' was an incredibly expensive show, but I thought it worked like gangbusters. I think it does help to have an appreciation of the sixties spy movies. I don't know if you don't have that how the show works. The whole Bashir/Garak thing was fun and interesting. Nana did a wonderful job; Avery did a wonderful job. If there was anything about the episode that I felt did not work, it was the stuff on the station. You didn't want to cut away to any of that stuff because it didn't play. We lost the humor that we thought was inherent in those scenes; they just kind of lay there. The whole point was we wanted to be able to cut away but not lose the feeling of the episode, and I think we did [lose] a little bit. But as long as you were in that holosuite, it worked. Sid was dashing and debonair, and I liked it. We want to do it again, but it would have to be a terrific episode to bring that back, because you just don't want to blow it on a nothing story."

Rene Echevarria was pleased that the episode was budgeted higher than most others. "Plus we had Rick Kolbe, thank God, one of our best directors. The actors were clearly engaged, and I think everybody had a lot of fun doing that episode. I think part of the spark that it has is that it's clearly a lot of fun. That's the first time in years that I heard a holodeck pitch that had a new twist, that allowed us to do something like that."

On *The Next Generation*, the audience got little bits of Picard's "Dixon Hill" holodeck adventures every so often. Behr doesn't think the same could be done with Bashir's adventures. "We might be able to do that, but this was pretty expensive. A little moment in any of those sets would not work productionwise. 'Our Man Bashir' had an impact, unfortunately, on some shows that followed, and I think we got hurt because we were so aware that we were behind the eight ball a little

bit. 'Paradise Lost' is a show that really comes to mind."

Episode #83
"Homefront"
Original Airdate: 12/30/95
Written by Ira Steven Behr and Robert Hewitt Wolfe
Directed by David Livingston
Guest Starring: Robert Foxworth (Admiral Leyton), Herschel Sparber (Jaresh-Inyo), Susan Gibney (Commander Benteen), Aron Eisenberg (Nog), Brock Peters (Joseph Sisko)

With mysterious wormhole anomalies ongoing, Sisko is recalled to Earth after the assassination there of twenty-seven people when a bomb exploded at a high-level diplomatic conference between the Federation and Romulan officials. Learning that the changelings are responsible for the terrorist action on Earth, Sisko and Odo consult with the highest echelons of Starfleet and the Federation to solve the crime, which also allows Sisko and Jake the opportunity to visit New Orleans, where Sisko's father, Joseph, runs a restaurant.

••••

The hour was rife with lots of faces close to the *Trek* saga, including Brock Peters as Grandpa Sisko, Admiral Cartwright of *Star Trek VI: The Undiscovered Country*; Susan Gibney as Captain Benteen, onetime *Enterprise* design engineer and Geordi LaForge crush; and Robert Foxworth as Admiral Leyton, who'd been the lead in Gene Roddenberry's promising yet unsold pilot *Questor*.

Director Livingston noted in *Sci-Fi Universe* that as part one of a two-parter, the show didn't have a lot of action, just talk. "The suspense was built in to the script, but in order not to let it lie there, I had to try and keep moving, even though you want to have some moments among the father and son and grandson. But I didn't want to get maudlin either." Livingston registered some disappointment with Jaresh-Inyo, the United Federation of Planets president, who seemed a little too soft for the plot role he played, and the marriage of his makeup with character. "My responsibility is to make him compelling, but that's how the character was written, and I wonder in hindsight if he should have had more of an edge. Maybe

gets, the women, the megalomaniacs. I thought that was a great idea when Bob [Gillan] pitched it. As we worked through it, I knew it was going to be a real fine walk because I didn't want to just do a big silly parody of all that. I wanted to make that story on the holodeck true to those stories and make it all work and make it interesting, and at the same time have fun with the conventions of those pieces. I think it worked wonderfully. I think Sid sells the agent so well; you can completely see him as a British secret agent. The apartment in Hong Kong, the assistant who has all the degrees in chemistry and biology and speaks all these languages *but* wants to be his valet — all of that was so great. We spent a lot of extra money on that episode and we got all of it on the screen. The production values are tremendous, from the casino to Dr. Noah's hideaway to the wall that comes up to reveal the map . . . all of the beats just worked. [Director] Rick Kolbe did that and understood what we were going for and the tone we were going for. What I really liked too was that we were able to play something real at the same time, that there were

••••

I should have fought against that in terms of directing his performance."

Once again, the Tillman Water Reclamation Plant in Van Nuys masqueraded as the live facade for the Starfleet Academy and Headquarters complex — although this time a quick-and-dirty model provided a direct look at the never-seen HQ building itself, complete with a high-speed shuttle-train. The effect includes mini-blinds, a tie rack, a veggie chopper, miniature Starfleet ships, and a CD rack with alternating slots removed for the shuttle tube.

Episode #84
"Paradise Lost"
Original Airdate: 1/6/96
Teleplay by Ira Steven Behr and Robert Hewitt Wolfe
Story by Ronald D. Moore
Directed by Reza Badiyi
Guest Starring: Robert Foxworth (Admiral Leyton), Herschel Sparber (Jaresh-Inyo), Susan Gibney (Commander Benteen), Aron Eisenberg (Nog), David Drew (Riley Shepard), Minda Badie (Security Officer), Rudolph Willrich (Academy Commandant), Brock Peters (Joseph Sisko)

Sabotage of the Earth's power grid plunges the planet into a nightmare of catastrophic proportions, prompting Starfleet to mobilize its forces against a possible changeling attack. Initiating blood tests, Sisko discovers that Earth is not going to be invaded by the Dominion but is rather being manipulated by the traitorous Admiral Leyton and his unwitting accomplice, Commander Benteen, who are terrified of what the Dominion could be capable of without increasing Earth's vigilance, even if it means sacrificing personal freedoms.

••••

"If we had not done 'Way of the Warrior,' these shows may have been the opening part of the season," says Ira Behr. "Not exactly these shows, but the idea of shape-shifters on Earth really did interest us. I thought that was a nice, paranoid kind of show to do. It said some interesting things without being too pedantic about it. I liked Sisko's relationship with his father; I liked Nog at the Academy. I thought Robert Foxworth was just terrific as Admiral Leyton. The shows worked, but

they needed more extras. We had to paint that world a little better and we were really feeling the budget crunch. We just needed more people. We needed more Starfleet officers. But those blood screenings are such a scary and effective thought. I think we did get that across, and the fact that fear will make people do all kinds of strange things. I liked the scene very much with the changeling O'Brien, which was intended to be somewhat surreal. We knew that scene was going to be in the show way before we wrote it. I guess it was our little salute to Oliver Stone. Just how far into paranoia do we want to dip? Colm was a strange little changeling. It was a well done little scene.

"Like I said," he adds, "I thought 'Paradise Lost' got hurt. There should have been more space scenes. This is where we shot ourselves in the foot. We literally kept cutting stuff out. Again, I blame myself for that. I guess we should have pushed the envelope and made the studio pay the money, but you can only do that so much."

Despite the budget crunch, as was often the case with the original Star Trek, well-written scenes of two characters in a room were more powerful than a space battle. "Maybe," Behr muses. "I'm aware that I look at the shows not quite the same way the audience does. It's easy for us to see the failings. It was a two-parter, and Paramount hates when we do two-parters. But if you're going to do them, you want the two-parters to work like gangbusters. I thought we had the story, I thought we had everything, and I think we just took our fingers off the trigger; we blinked. If we had it to do all over again, that I would have done differently."

Ron Moore explains that there had been an idea for a two-part episode dealing with the idea of the breakup of the Federation bouncing around. This story had Vulcan seceding from the Federation and the Federation suspecting that there are shape-shifters there. "The Vulcans are saying that they're just getting fed up with the Federation becoming more and more security concerned about the shape-shifters," he says. "There's martial law, various transgressions of personal liberties that the Federation is taking — certain elements that are still in the episodes. The Vulcans objected to this, and we thought,

'Well, they're shape-shifters.' From the beginning we had posited an old friend of Sisko's father, a Vulcan, who had been coming into his restaurant for years, and he was going to be our voice to the Vulcans. At some point, there was going to be a standoff between the Defiant and a Vulcan ship in orbit. They were going to probably fire on each other and have this confrontation. So there was this whole big political scheme going on with the Vulcans, and ultimately it turned out that they weren't shape-shifters.

"When it came time to do 'Homefront' and 'Paradise Lost,' " he elaborates, "a lot of that had gone to the wayside because we had just taken different directions in terms of the Klingons and the political makeup. We didn't feel like doing another show on geopolitics. We thought it was a better idea to go for a little smaller story, focusing on Earth and humanity, and being on Earth. We started talking about making it more of a coup rather than a planet seceding from the Federation.

"As we got closer to a coup, we realized that this was a little closer to Seven Days in May, and that was a cool archetype to think about," Moore continues. "It was a cool idea: a military takeover of a democratic government and how it would work. What I really liked about that episode is that [in] the first part you're really on the side of what turns out to be the bad guy. You are with them as they're dealing with these security problems. You think the admiral is on the up-and-up, and Sisko totally buys into it, thinks his dad is a stick-in-the-mud and so on. It's just so easy to buy into that mind-set. You have a security problem and you start chopping away at these personal liberties and it all seems perfectly reasonable and rational, until suddenly you say, 'My God, where are we going?' That's what I really liked about part one. You take the audience on a journey and by the end of the episode you've got troops on the street, and you think that's cool, that it makes sense. I thought it was an important show that demonstrated that the best of governments have to be watched. You can't allow our fear of outside forces or interior threats to chop away at our own democratic institutions."

Muses Robert Wolfe, "At what

••••

112

price liberty? If the United States became a fascist state to fight fascism, would that be worth it? I would say no and most Americans would say no, and that's a special thing about the United States and a special thing about the Federation. We really wanted to explore the idea of whether or not you would destroy the village in order to save it. We know that the *Star Trek* answer is no. There was some nice acting in that episode as well. We spent a tremendous amount of effort on casting. We've been wanting to use Robert Foxworth for a long time but hadn't been able to work it out before this."

Episode #85
"Crossfire"
Original Airdate: 1/27/96
Written by Rene Echevarria
Directed by Les Landau
Guest Starring: Duncan Regehr (Shakaar), Bruce Wright (Sarish)

Odo, whose feelings of love for Kira have been previously established, finds himself in the ironic position of having to protect both Kira and the Bajoran first minister, Shakaar, whom she has feelings for, from a would-be assassin.

••••

"It was a warm and fuzzy show," says Ira Behr, "and Rene [Echevarria] is a warm and fuzzy guy. What this show did have was Rene Auberjonois, and Rene just plays the hell out of everything. I just thought he was terrific. The guy I thought we should not have turned into such a warm and fuzzy character was Shakaar. Maybe it was in the dialogue or the way it was played, but the intent was he was supposed to be a gruffer, much more plain-speaking guy, more of the bull in the china shop. Unfortunately, we had two sensitive guys, and that was wrong. But I like that episode. I thought it was a show that only *Deep Space Nine* could do in terms of the franchise. Sometimes we say, 'OK, people are watching this show and we've got to figure they like the characters. If they like the characters, let's give them characters and see if they'll buy it. We'll give them the best characters we can give them in the best situations that we can.' You've got to watch the show, you've got to care about the characters in a way that not all TV shows make you care about the characters. So I think it

Nana Visitor (copyright © 1996 by Albert Ortega).

worked. Unfortunately, if I'd known we would have saved so much money on 'Crossfire,' I definitely would have put more into 'Paradise Lost.' "

Rene Echevarria admits, "Yes, that was one of my touchy-feely episodes. I think it was pretty effective for what we were setting out to do. It was a small story, and with Rene Auberjonois, what you ask for you get — and more — in terms of just his face. There was a lot of heartbreak for him in that. It's a softer show, finally forcing Odo to put aside these feelings he's got and face the fact, 'I can't be human, I can't risk emotion,' which is an interesting spin. That's all Data wanted, and here's a guy who gets burned in his first love and decides he just can't handle it. There was also some interesting stuff with Quark, revealing a side to their relationship of friendship and mutual respect that was kind of unexpected. Quark was really there for him."

"Pretty cool" is how Ron Moore describes the episode. "We really needed to get Shakaar going again after last season. We wanted to get a relationship between him and Kira, and we wanted to keep that story going. We started feeling we had lost sight of Bajor and some of the issues that were going on there, so it was

important to get him back on the show. It was also important for Odo because we'd been playing this forbidden love of his for quite a while and we thought we should move it to another level somehow. Just making him the bodyguard to these two people put him under such a vice that it was a lot of fun. The struggle with that episode was how much of the mystery we should tell. The temptation was to spend a lot of time ferreting out who was trying to kill Shakaar and make it Odo tracking down the assassin, and that threatened to overwhelm the story at a few points. Ultimately someone pared that down so even the capture is off screen. Worf gets the guy. That really was able to hit Odo where it hurts."

Admits Robert Wolfe, "We had neglected Rene Auberjonois, and that was bad. We needed to give him a good show and [the way to do] that was to give him a character piece, a piece where he could be both the constable and the tragic figure that everyone knows and loves. It was sort of a quieter episode in a way. I think that's good. It was a show that did follow a lot of very heavy thinking about the Federation and politics. So it was nice to do a show about broken hearts and love."

Episode #86
"Return to Grace"
Original Airdate: 2/3/96
Teleplay by Hans Beimler
Story by Tom Benko
Directed by Jonathan West
Guest Starring: Marc Alaimo (Gul Dukat), Cyia Batten (Tora Ziyal), Casey Biggs (Damar)

Although he has been demoted in rank, Gul Dukat nonetheless believes that he can regain his former status within the Cardassian Empire by using his strategic abilities in a military situation. To accomplish this goal, he actually turns to Kira Nerys for help.

••••

Upon watching "Return to Grace," Ira Behr says, he mused to himself that he wasn't sure if it was a good hour of science fiction, but it was definitely a good drama about two people and their twisted relationship. "I thought that Alaimo was terrific. It was sort of like a sequel to 'Indiscretion.' As the episode took form and became real, we realized that we had

••••

thrown the episode a little bit too much toward Dukat and away from Kira. Dukat had all the major decisions, but it was just so great to put him out there. It was a Sitting Bull moment: 'I am the last Cardassian; I will never retreat.' It's a great little moment. You can go off with that. It was fun."

Ron Moore notes, "A difficult show productionwise because it takes place almost entirely off the station on two alien ships that we didn't have that we had to create — a Klingon ship and a Cardassian transport. Again, *DS9* has all these dangling plot threads going. There are certain ones we are happy to get rid of and others we happily continue to lay out. Turning Dukat into Captain Dukat of the Spanish main seemed like a great idea. He takes that ship and off he goes."

"An action show with Dukat and Kira on another adventure," says Robert Wolfe, "and it sort of turns the relationship on its head a little bit. We've always wanted to do a show about the Cardassians fighting a war that didn't have anything to do with us but that Kira could get in the middle of. It was also an opportunity to see Kira and Dukat in another kind of way."

Rene Echevarria points out, "It was an attempt to look at Dukat and have him realize that regaining his glory in a hollow empire isn't quite worth the undertaking. More important is getting back to his roots as a military man and being a sort of freedom fighter, so that he and Kira are becoming more alike in some ways. It's another step in that relationship, which was important to us."

Episode #87
"The Sons of Mogh"
Original Airdate: 2/10/96
Written by Ronald D. Moore
Directed by David Livingston
Guest Starring: Tony Todd (Kurn),
Robert Doqui (Noggra)

Thanks to the fury of Gowron, Worf's family has been disgraced on the Klingon homeworld. As a result, Worf's brother, Kurn, arrives on Deep Space Nine demanding that his brother restore his honor by taking his life. Worf finds himself torn between the tradition of his people and his oath to the Federation.

••••

This was an episode discussed early in the season and put aside until the time was right to deal with the Klingons again. "That was a good show," says Ron Moore. "I think the best decision we made in that one was the change in the opening of act one. Originally we had broken the show so that Worf never tried to kill his brother. It was more of a traditional story where his brother comes on and he wants Worf to kill him and he won't do it. The whole show is about his trying to convince Worf to do this thing, and at the end of the show Worf almost does but finds a way out. As I was writing it, I began to feel that that was just too predictable and didn't have any juice to it. Ira and I decided that the best thing would be for Worf to try and do it right up front. Kurn asks Worf to do it. As a Klingon, it makes sense and he does it, which is something that would jolt the audience. It would not only get the story going, but it would tell us how seriously Worf took this request. Once you did that, the whole rest of the story had that 'Oh, my God' overtone to it, so I think that was a good decision. I also like the ending, where Kurn has been stripped of his memory.

"The only thing that's not there," he adds, "that's a little disturbing on some

Tony Todd returned as Worf's brother, Kurn, in "The Sons of Mogh" (copyright © 1996 by Albert Ortega).

levels, is that we didn't do the scene that we assume took place off camera, where they talk to Bashir and say, 'Look, this is what I want to do,' Bashir struggles with it a bit and asks questions and decides he'll do it because it's a Klingon thing and otherwise Kurn is going to have to die, and so on. That scene is not there, we never structured that scene there, but when you walk away from the episode, you go, 'Wow, Dr. Bashir's House of Horrors. Bring 'em in; I will wipe your memory or bring you back from the dead.' The way it's presented, you kind of show up and it's 'Oh, sure, where's the knife?' I think we can assume they had that ethical discussion."

Robert Wolfe concurs. "That's the one sticking point for me," he says, "because I don't think the audience is sold on the necessity of doing this, and we needed a scene about that. If we had done a scene weighing our options and trying to convince a very reluctant Bashir to go through with this, I think we could have used that moment to convince the audience that what Worf was doing was right. I don't think we did that and I guess I take the blame for that as much as anybody else."

"It's Tony Todd and Michael Dorn, so you know it's not going to be bad," says Ira Behr simply. "That relationship is really rich. I thought it had a great ending and a great conundrum to put Worf into. The fact that he stabs his brother — what a moment! Ron [Moore] did a really bang-up job on that show. I think it's possible that Kurn will return."

Episode #88
"Bar Association"
Original Airdate: 2/17/96
Teleplay by Robert Hewitt Wolfe and Ira Steven Behr
Story by Barbara J. Lee
Directed by LeVar Burton
Guest Starring: Max Grodenchik (Rom), Chase Masterson (Leeta), Jason Marsden (Grimp), Emilio Borelli (Frool), Jeffrey Combs (Brunt)

Quark's abusive behavior toward his employees — particularly his brother, Rom — reaches its zenith when the employees of the bar, led by Rom, decide to go on strike to demand fairer treatment. At first Quark is resistant, but he eventually finds himself with no choice but to give in. In the end, though, Rom decides to leave Quark's to strike out on his own.

••••

"The next step in the Rom/Quark relationship," observes Robert Wolfe, "which is a great relationship with two terrific actors. The premise may not have seemed like much, but watching the episode you see that it's about people, and when it's about people, about the brothers, it takes on a whole new meaning. When we do these shows we make sure we've got an 'in' to the character element, otherwise we don't do them."

Rene Echevarria admits that "Bar Association" was a story that began one way and went through an amazing transformation in its development. "It became a much deeper character study of the brothers," he says. "Always when we sit down to write things, Ira will say, 'What's it *really* about? Let's dig and think. What's at the heart of this story, and how will we tease it out of this premise?' And that's when we realized we couldn't just go back to the status quo at the end of the story after what Rom has done, that he needs to move on. And that's a totally satisfactory conclusion."

Ira Behr points out, " 'Bar Association' was a show that was very popular among the staff. The staff really loved that episode. What we were trying to do is what we tried to do with 'Family Business' third season, and that was to take Rom and Quark one step further. Although 'Family Business' was fun, in 'Bar Association' we did want to make some more dramatic points. We wanted to take the audience on a ride they weren't really quite sure they were going to go on; they didn't quite know where we would end up. I thought LeVar [Burton] did a wonderful job of directing; the action was terrific, and Jeffrey Combs was great as Brunt. He was the first Ferengi that I really thought was a threat. We knew the whole union thing would piss some people off because unions have gotten to be such a negative thing. I don't know if unions are so bad. Life before unions was not so wonderful for the workingman — if I can get on my soapbox for a second. But I really liked the show. I thought it was one of the more successful Ferengi shows that we did."

"I like that episode a lot, personally," agrees Ron Moore. "I thought it was a cool thing to do with Rom. It made him stand out a little more, and the conflict with the brothers and the love between them has turned out to be a real strength of the show. I think the Quark/Rom relationship is not a PC 'Oh, he's my brother' kind of thing, but you nonetheless get the sense that there's an underlying bond between the two men, and I think they play really well off of each other. The Ferengi are turning out to be a pretty interesting race."

Episode #89
"Accession"
Original Airdate: 2/24/96
Written by Jane Espenson
Directed by Les Landau
Guest Starring: Rosalind Chao (Keiko O'Brien), Robert Symonds (Vedek Porta), Camille Saviola (Kai Opaka), Hana Hatae (Molly), Richard Libertini (Akorem Laan)

When a legendary Bajoran poet, Akorem, comes through the wormhole after having vanished two centuries earlier, the man claims to be the true Emissary,

Max Grodenchik, who portrays Quark's brother, Rom (copyright © 1996 by Albert Ortega).

usurping the title given to Sisko by the Bajoran prophets. As the Bajoran people — including Kira Nerys — voice their willingness to do whatever this man says (no matter how illogical), Sisko is forced to consider whether or not he should step forward and fulfill his so-called destiny as the Emissary.

••••

"This is a show that I'm told worked better than I thought it did when I watched it," says Ira Behr. "Personally, I wanted David Warner as Akorem. He wanted to do it, but his wife talked him out of it because he was on vacation and she didn't want him to work. To this day, I still wish David Warner was in it. I think it's a really interesting script and idea, and it leaves us with a nice, interesting mystery. It's a good show, and Avery was great, but I wanted him to have a better opponent."

Admits Ron Moore, "That was a difficult show to bring off. Anything having to do with Bajoran religion is always kind of difficult to make interesting and exciting for the audience. I think the notion of another Emissary popping out of the wormhole is a great idea. That was a really cool high-concept idea. After that, it went through a lot of permutations of what is the impact, politically, on Bajor and what is Sisko's role? As we were struggling with it, we were struggling basically with what do we want Sisko's character to be vis-à-vis the Bajorans? What is he? Is he truly some kind of mythic figure that is destined by fate to be involved with the Bajorans? Does he want that? As we struggled with it, we realized that the character was struggling with it as well, because there wasn't a real clear answer to us. The 'You are of Bajor' line used in the show is a great line. It's really opaque. God knows what it means, but it must mean *something*. Where that will take us is open to question. It seems like an interesting follow-up to last year's 'Destiny,' which dealt with the Bajoran prophecies and Sisko being really uncomfortable with it and wringing his hands in his quarters about his role in the whole thing. Now we bring him to a place where he's saying, 'OK, maybe this is about something and maybe I am connected with these people somehow or some way and why not embrace that?' "

••••

Notes Robert Wolfe, "Every once in a while we've got to revisit that Bajoran religion and make sure that everybody knows that we still care. This was our episode for that purpose. A nice performance by Avery; a really nice performance by Nana. It's also the first time in a while that you actually feel that the Bajorans are kind of alien rather than just being people with bumps on their heads. The idea that a whole society would say, 'OK, I'm going to quit my job and do something completely different because this guy says I should,' makes them alien and not human. That was what we were going for. It was also an important episode for Sisko. He's definitely a character with an arc over the past four seasons. One of the things I really like about the character is that he's really grown and changed and learned a lot of things by coming to a place he didn't want to come to in the first place and calling it home by the beginning of the third season. By the fourth season he's 'All right, I'm the Emissary. Worship me.' Avery has done a really terrific job this year. Couldn't ask for a better actor."

Sharing the enthusiasm, Rene Echevarria, who did an uncredited rewrite on the episode, comments, "As soon as I heard the pitch, I immediately knew it was a great idea. In fact, it's a story I hold out when people come in to pitch and I sense that they're not on the right track. People often come in and pitch Klingon and Cardassian wars — something big that we probably are working on ourselves. This, on the other hand, is the kind of oblique angle on our series that only an outsider can bring us. And as soon as you hear it, you say, 'Wow, that's perfect. Why hadn't I thought of it?' The pitch was rather general, but our response was, 'Yeah, he's from the past, what does he want to do? What if the Bajorans have a caste system?' And we just spun it out. This is one I really enjoyed working on, with some nice stuff for Sisko and Kira. We were lucky to have Les Landau as director, who's good with the actors. One moment that sticks out in my mind that wasn't in the script is the end of Akorem's speech to the people, when he first announces his intentions. I basically wrote, 'Some people clap, some people don't, the room is divided.' But Nana sold that beautifully when Les had

the camera push up on her. You see her hesitate, look around and decide, 'OK, I'm going to clap. I have to clap and support him because he's the Emissary.' Then you see the intensity of her clapping increasing when she's saying, 'Hey, everybody else, why aren't you clapping?' It saved the act-out. A couple of people felt we didn't have an act-out, but they just found it during the shooting."

Episode #90
"Rules of Engagement"
Original Airdate: 4/13/96
Teleplay by Ronald D. Moore
Story by Bradly Thompson
Directed by LeVar Burton
Guest Starring: Ron Canada (Ch'Pok),
Deborah Strang (T'Lara)

When Worf accidentally has the *Defiant* destroy a civilian vessel that mysteriously decloaked in front of them in the midst of a battle, he suddenly finds himself on trial, accused by the Klingon Empire of the honorless slaughter of innocents. Sisko defends Worf against a Klingon attorney named Ch'Pok.

••••

Ron Moore admits that he had been wanting to do a courtroom show throughout the fourth season, and one finally presented itself in the form of "Rules of Engagement."

"The idea of putting Worf on trial was pretty cool, since he had just arrived, and I thought in some ways it was a bookend to Worf's character, the other bookend being 'Sons of Mogh,'" he explains. "In 'Sons of Mogh' we go out of our way to have Worf say, 'I've always assumed I would go back to the Klingon Empire one day. My family is there and maybe I can always revisit my heritage.' But in that show he says, 'Maybe that's not for me. Even if I did, I've changed so much that I don't belong there anymore. The Klingon Empire is not part of me.' Then he looks at his comm badge and says, 'This is all I've got left.' In 'Rules of Engagement' we almost take *that* away from him, which I thought was really cool because now you've got a character who's been kind of shaken a bit. The two foundations of who that character is in the Klingon Empire and in a Starfleet uniform were both shaken up pretty heavily in the same season. Now it becomes, where does he find himself?

What's his personal journey now, and how does he figure out where he fits? The only place he fits at the moment is Deep Space Nine, home for the outcasts.'

"The stylistic conceit of the characters looking at the camera during the flashback was an idea of Ira's during the break session," adds Moore. "I think if there's a flaw in that show, it's that we don't give Worf a scene early on in the picture. He, as the defendant, is not someone we're really with. He doesn't have a lot to say for quite a while, and that's something we only realized in reflection upon viewing the final episode. We purposely structured that show to take place *after* the incident. We wanted to tell you about the incident slowly over the course of the show to build interest and suspense and keep you in there, instead of just a dry recitation of facts. So I liked that, but if I had to do it again, I would give Worf a scene in act one just to get us inside his head and understand what he's thinking and feeling. On the good side, I think Ron Canada was excellent. I thought he was one of the best Klingons we've ever cast. I think he really got inside that character and he, along with LeVar Burton [who directed], liked the character. In the script I had written he was described as a 'warrior of the mind,' and they both jumped on that and were able to give us a Klingon who was different. He was a warrior, but a warrior on a different battlefield than we were used to seeing. An interesting color to play in terms of the Klingons."

Ira Behr isn't quite as enthusiastic, offering the opinion that "it's an interesting show that doesn't quite work. The trouble is that we did a trial show and kind of lost the defendant's point of view. Yes, we had a nice performance from Ron Canada and some nice, interesting things that we did, and we told an interesting story, but some of the meat was missing. When we looked at it, we said, 'Oops!' I think we could have used a little less Ron Canada and a little more of Worf's dilemma."

"A little wrinkle I'm not sure we pulled off was Odo's investigation," says Rene Echevarria. "That wasn't enough of a through line. It felt contrived, that Worf was just kind of rescued and off the hook. I don't think we built that puzzle quite right. But a solid show anyway."

••••

Moore notes that there was a trial sequence featuring Kira that was cut for time. In this lost scene, the character gets on the stand and relates her version of the events and says that she completely supports what Worf did and she has no doubts at all about it. "This takes place before the O'Brien scene," he says. "Then Ch'Pok stands up and says, 'Well, weren't you a terrorist?' She says, 'Yes, I was.' 'Weren't you involved in the bombing of an administration building on Bajor where twenty-five innocent people were killed?' She quietly says yes, and he says, 'No further questions.' It was really interesting. Worf's biggest supporter gets up there and says, 'God damn it, he did the right thing!' Then he knocks the wind out of her sail, and it also would have reminded the audience that Kira had been a terrorist, that this character has some edges to it."

Robert Wolfe notes, "We've accused people of crimes on *Deep Space Nine* two or three times, and I think it's nice that sometimes they're guilty, which is unlike any other television show on the face of the earth. Worf made a mistake, and people make mistakes. Yeah, he was set up, but I think it's nonetheless cool that our characters can make mistakes and learn from them. It makes them a little more human. On the original series, Kirk made mistakes and Spock mutinied, for God's sake. Guilty as charged. It just makes for a little bit more interesting canvas if you've got people who are prone to failings."

Episode #91
"Hard Time"
Original Airdate: 4/13/96
Teleplay by Robert Hewitt Wolfe
Story by Daniel Keys Moran
Directed by Alexander Singer

When O'Brien is charged with a serious crime by an alien race, he is found guilty and sentenced to a twenty-year prison term. His sentence, however, actually only lasts a couple of hours, while his brain is filled with two decades' worth of prison memories. Once "released," he must readjust to the life he thought he had left behind.

• • • •

"Hey, who better than O'Brien to put through hell?" Ira Behr smiles maniacally. "I love O'Brien. He's one of my fa-

vorite characters. That was a show that we wanted to do in the second season that Michael Piller didn't want to do; he didn't feel it was going to be a show. We just kept it hanging and then we said, 'Let's take a shot at it.' I thought Robert [Wolfe] did a really nice job with the script. When you have O'Brien, you just put him through hell. It's an interesting idea and it was a sweet show, a sad show. I felt for the guy. It was a hellish thing to do to a man. . . . But we're going to put the man through hell again in the fifth season. You always put the big hurt on O'Brien."

Adds Robert Wolfe with a good-natured laugh, "So vulnerable and human, it's really fun to torture O'Brien. He is everyman, so when we do a show that sort of hits home with real trials and tribulations, he's just a natural choice. Colm is such a good actor that he always comes through. I think he did a terrific job on that show, and we asked him to do a lot. The story itself was pitched to me in the first season, and everybody said no. In the second season I said we should do it, and everybody said no. In the third season I gave up on it, but in the fourth season I said we should do the show, and everybody, for some reason, finally went for it. We had to track the guy down who originally pitched it to us, who, as far as we could tell, had dropped off the face of the earth. We managed to find him eventually, and he was kind of pissed off at *Star Trek* in general because we didn't buy the story and *Voyager* did an episode with some superficial similarities to it, and he was kind of grumpy about that. But we didn't do anything wrong, just bought the story from him. Then we took it from there, and I wrote it over a period of time. There were a lot of things that were in there internally that we kept working around as a staff in terms of what to do, whether to let O'Brien actually have hallucinations or not, where to leave him in the end, which is basically that we have him on maintenance medication. There was some feeling that we make sure he didn't have these memories anymore, and there was another feeling that he should just work through them and feel better. My wife is a psychotherapist, and I knew that wasn't really true. That's not how things really work. It was important to me to show that sometimes there are things that you

just need to go see a doctor for, and that's OK."

Ron Moore notes, "A difficult show to bring into focus. We didn't know how it was going to work, the whole way to use the hallucination character, just how much he was going to be involved with the show, whether he would be used at all or if he would only be used in flashbacks. That was a pretty contentious break session, as I recall, but after a couple of drafts it worked out for the best."

"The right mix of elements of science fiction and emotion and the kind of show I really like," says Rene Echevarria. "Robert wanted to do one himself and did a bang-up job on it. Colm Meaney is an actor you can rely on to give you everything. Again, here's another example where we pushed one of our characters to the brink, like Worf in 'Sword of Kahless.' If you look back at the season, we put some of the characters in really interesting boxes. 'Hippocratic Oath,' Bashir and O'Brien are at odds; 'The Visitor,' Jake kills himself to save his father at some level; Dax and this woman from her past in 'Rejoined'; Worf and the sword. Here we pushed O'Brien all the way to killing someone who was supposed to be his best friend. Just a really strong show. I would have loved to have written it."

Episode #92
"Shattered Mirror"
Original Airdate: 4/20/96
Written by Ira Steven Behr and Hans Beimler
Directed by James L. Conway
Guest Starring: Felicia M. Bell (Jennifer Sisko), Aron Eisenberg (Nog), Carlos Carrasco (Klingon Officer), Andrew Robinson (Garak)

Jennifer Sisko from the so-called mirror universe comes to Deep Space Nine and manipulates Jake and his feelings of loss for his mother in order to get him to follow her back to her realm. Sisko has no choice but to follow them and finds himself having to help the resistance fighters put the finishing touches on their own *Defiant*, which will be used against the Klingons and the area "regent," Worf.

• • • •

"One of the most fun episodes of the season," Ira Behr says. "What we started to realize halfway through is that

Felicia Bell, who portrays Captain Sisko's late wife, Jennifer, and her parallel universe counterpart, with Richard Biggs (copyright © 1996 by Albert Ortega).

it's one of the most outrageous episodes. Every scene started to have something going on. Nana, who does that role unbelievably; Michael was having fun with the mirror-universe Worf — that relationship with Garak was great; plus the sweet story with Jennifer — it was really the kitchensink episode. It was a very dense story, plus it had the special effects. That show was great. Really just flat-out ballsy fun with some nice, sweet moments. Sisko loses his wife again, which shows that O'Brien isn't the only one we put through hell. If we go back there again — and it's something we'll probably do — the obvious thing I'd like to do is something with the Worf character over there. He can be a lot of fun. But you have to find a worthwhile story. There's also a big push to have them come to us. . . . We'll see."

"Some of the best visual-effects sequences I've ever seen," adds an exuberant Ron Moore. "It's a great battle sequence. The *Defiant* flying through the station, underneath those Klingon ships, was worth the price of admission. It's a fun universe, and I can see still going over there. It's just such a fun place to be. You

go over there and everybody's playing different roles. You've got evil Kira in sexy outfits — it's just wild fun. The logic of this parallel existence, where all our people look exactly the same but play other characters, is tenuous at best. Rick has always kind of stumbled on it. He always stumbles on it, then he always likes the episode. I think it's how we all feel. It seems like a place to go and relax and have a good time."

Rene Echevarria points out, "We got great reaction to Worf's character, so he might be the focus of the next 'crossover' episode. Just a show filled with fun references. Ira said, 'Well, we kill a Ferengi every time we go over there, so we have to kill Nog.' When you see those characters, you see how much fun the actors have getting to play these shadow versions of themselves. This is a piece of the franchise we want to do every year, but we're always looking for an in that is more than just playing games. The Jake angle was a great one, realizing that there would be a mirror Jennifer and that he would be drawn there. Losing his mother again was pretty deep stuff. People always say they want those guys to come to our universe, but the idea of them impersonating one of our people, unfortunately, is an angle we sort of cover with the changelings. So what does that really give you? That's why we keep going there."

Episode #93
"Muse"
Original Airdate: 4/27/96
Teleplay by Rene Echevarria
Story by Rene Echevarria and Majel Barrett Roddenberry
Directed by David Livingston
Guest Starring: Majel Barrett (Lwaxana Troi), Michael Ansara (Jeyal), Meg Foster (Onaya)

An odd mixture of story lines makes up the episode. First off, Jake continues his writing efforts, inspired by a mysterious alien woman who seems to be something of a vampire and has, in the past, served as a muse for other writers. At the same time, the "relationship" between Odo and Lwaxana Troi is taken a little further.

••••

Ira Behr explains that "Muse" had the longest gestation of any episode of the

season. "When we came up with the story, it was such a wacky idea — the danger of creation. History is filled with self-destructive writers. It would be nice to find out why writers can be so self-destructive, and we did. It was kind of a demented yet interesting attempt. It's a weird show. It's a show that we enjoyed. I haven't heard much reaction from the fans. I do think we give Majel some good stuff to play, and I think Odo helps. Rene really helps sell those scenes."

"Kind of an odd show," admits Rene Echevarria. "At least they were both serious stories; one wasn't a comedy or anything. Here was a show that took many incarnations. It originally started as four romances on the station. One was Odo and Lwaxana, one was Bashir and O'Brien and Keiko and Leeta, some kind of weird double date, Bashir having an infatuation with Leeta . . . or something like that. We just realized that was too soapy, so we kept the Odo one because that's a story we had originally put into development and it was an idea of Majel's, who the fans seem to enjoy seeing. We skipped her for a year, and I think Rick really wanted to use her. Ultimately she comes together pretty well on *Deep Space Nine*. We were just spitballing, and somebody started talking about Jake, his writing and a vampire, the dark muse and this kind of stuff, and we decided to go for it. It has a real original-series feel to it in a lot of ways, which is both a compliment and can be an insult. It has a certain sense of fun to it. When you look back at it, you can say, 'Wow, an entity who has inspired writers throughout history!' I watched the show and was a little worried about it and how it would come off, but I always had Meg Foster in mind and was delighted when we got her. She struck all the right notes and was totally creepy. You just knew from the minute you saw her that Jake was getting himself in trouble. That was kind of fun, [as was] tying it back in to 'The Visitor' in that the story Jake is working on will eventually become his novel — at least in a different time line. It's the story that has Jake's imagination. It was kind of a sweet show, and here, once again, is Odo reaching out to someone after resisting. When he is forced to speak to the crowd and talks about Lwaxana, he realizes, or at least he talks himself into believing, that maybe he's in love with her. Here's someone who wants him, and he's been rejected by someone who doesn't. Can he let her into his life? Then he's told that he doesn't love her, he just needs *someone*. Just another piece of Odo's character for the year."

"What a show." Ron Moore laughs. "This is a real writer's show. The idea that you would sit someplace and write, and as you're writing a woman is getting off on your writing — that is the most inside writer's fantasy you can imagine. I don't know if anything else is quite like those scenes. He's writing, putting words on paper, and she's coming on to him. These are like our fantasies. But it was a cool concept. I love Meg Foster. She's one of my favorite actresses and she just brings a real inhuman quality to that part. It's also nice to keep Jake moving along as a writer. Now we've really taken that on ever since 'The Visitor,' and I think we're going to continue to do it."

Robert Wolfe points out, "We basically had the B story, which was the Odo/Lwaxana show, and we had no A story to go with it. We finally came up with the idea of this space vampire, but to do it with a twist. To do what they would have done on the original series. She's a goddamn muse, that's what she is. A fun episode, and I think Rene and Majel play well together. We try and give her good stuff to do."

Episode #94
"For the Cause"
Original Airdate: 5/4/96
Teleplay by Ronald D. Moore
Story by Mark Gehred-O'Connell
Directed by James L. Conway
Guest Starring: Penny Johnson (Kasidy Yates), Kenneth Marshall (Lieutenant Commander Eddington), Tracy Middendorf (Ziyal), John Prosky (Brathaw), Steven Vincent Leigh (Lieutenant Reese), Andrew Robinson (Garak)

Putting the paranoia about the shape-shifters aside for a moment, suspicions of a different kind arise when it seems that Sisko's love, Kasidy Yates, as well as DS9 crewman Eddington, may be a part of the Maquis, former Starfleet officers protesting the Cardassian demilitarized zone.

••••

Ron Moore explains, "I thought that was really well directed by Jim Conway and that Avery gave us a really wonderful performance. It was time to give the Kasidy/Sisko relationship some juice. It seemed like we didn't know a lot about Kasidy; we'd never introduced any conflict into the relationship, and this was the time to do it. What I think I liked about the episode the most is that from the teaser you put Sisko into a vise between his responsibilities and his personal life, and that pressure never lets off all the way through. Avery really had to bring that out in his performance. Every scene he's playing a couple of things — what do I do about this smuggling thing, and my personal relationship? It was just fascinating. I think the scene with him and Jake, where he starts to tell Jake how important the situation is, that things change but not their relationship — he's trying to tell his son something, he can't tell his son something and he just gives up and walks away. I thought that was just a wonderful moment. A very *real* moment. There are a lot of little moments in that episode that I like a lot. There's a moment in the teaser when Kasidy gets out of bed and leaves. Sisko is there, he reaches over, sniffs her pillow, throws his away and takes hers. It was a moment the guys wanted me to cut over and over again. To me, that was a very key bit of business that I wanted. That said something about the relationship that goes beyond what you can say in dialogue. It was such a real moment. I also don't think that you expect Kasidy to truly be guilty. You suspect that someone else is going to be setting her up, so it's a nice surprise when you learn the truth."

"A really good, dramatic story," says Ira Behr. "I thought it made the Maquis interesting and Kasidy Yates interesting. Also, Eddington is not a shapeshifter — maybe people will finally put that to fucking rest. People have said that since season two's 'The Adversary.' He's just a member of the Maquis."

Robert Wolfe explains, "We wanted to remind people that the Maquis are still around, because they're part of our franchise. Part of what we wanted to do was point out that Kasidy Yates was a Maquis, and hopefully her relationship with Sisko will survive that — depending on the availability of the actress, whose

primary responsibility is *The Larry Sanders Show*. Avery gave us a nice performance in that show."

"Lots of twists and turns," muses Rene Echevarria. "I think Kasidy came a little more alive here than we've seen her before, and it was a very good show for Avery. Very subtle, all on his face. There was some controversy about starting the episode with Sisko and Kasidy in bed together. Rick wasn't sure whether or not he wanted to do it because it had never been done on his *Star Trek* — the idea of an unmarried man, a father, with his girlfriend in bed. The reason I think he balked at it was that we had a scene in a previous episode, which was actually filmed, in which Jake was at the door knocking; he knows what's going on in there, and they're talking to him through the door. That was a scene that pushed some of Rick's buttons, so we took out the Jake angle."

Episode #95
"To the Death"
Original Airdate: 5/11/96
Written by Ira Steven Behr and Robert Hewitt Wolfe
Directed by LeVar Burton
Guest Starring: Brian Thompson (Toman'Torax), Scott Haven (Virak'Kara), Clarence Williams III (Omet'Iklan)

A strange alliance forms when Sisko leads a team of his officers in conjunction with Jem'Hadar soldiers in an effort to stop Jem'Hadar renegades from strengthening their power base.

••••

Ira Behr notes that this marks the first episode of *Star Trek* that was actually edited for television. "Thirty-two seconds of violence were cut out," he says. "Lots of violence between Jem'Hadar and Federation people. Thirty-two seconds of nothing but action, and I wish it had happened. It kind of restored my faith in the Jem'Hadar, and I think it really makes them interesting. I thought Clarence Williams was good; we finally had Jeffrey Combs back. I thought it really filled in a lot of the Dominion backstory that I thought was really necessary. It was really a tense little episode. I just wish it had been thirty-two seconds longer."

"We wanted to do a show for the

••••

thirteen-year-old boy in all of us." Robert Wolfe laughs. "We wanted to spend some time with some Jem'Hadar who weren't screwed up, because the two times we spent any time with the Jem'Hadar was the kid who's so young and doesn't know what he's feeling ["The Abandoned"] and also the ones in 'Hippocratic Oath.' So we wanted to show what a functional Jem'Hadar society is, because we know so much more about them than anyone else does and we wanted to get some of that information out there so the audience could understand them a little better. It seems that the more you learn about the Klingons, the less scary they are. The more you learn about the Cardassians, the less scary they are in some ways. What we want with the Jem'Hadar is that the more you learn about them, the *more* scary they are. These are not the kind of guys you want to party with."

"The only criticism that I have about that show," says Ron Moore, "is that I wish we had been able to get the location that we used for 'The Quickening' and use it there, because that was a *tremendous* location. A lot of production value, and it looked wonderful. 'To the Death' was much smaller, not quite as sweeping. I liked Clarence Williams III, I always have, and I thought he really personified the Jem'Hadar for the first time in a way that the audience could grab onto. The Jem'Hadar in a lot of the episodes tended to kind of bland out. Sometimes it's hard to differentiate between them, and [Williams] brought something to that performance that made him at least stand alone among that race. Also, chopping and hacking has always been one of my favorite things. Not since 'Blood Oath' has there been so much chopping and hacking."

Rene Echevarria emphasizes, "A hugely important episode for us, and I think we learned some really fascinating things about the Jem'Hadar. It was a show that I was very skeptical of, wondering what we were going to do for three acts on the *Defiant* with the Jem'Hadar. Robert and Ira were saying, 'We'll find stuff,' and they really did find some great, fascinating stuff about them. Finally we fleshed them out in a believable way that's a real important building block."

Episode #96
"The Quickening"
Original Airdate: 5/18/96
Written by Naren Shankar
Directed by Rene Auberjonois
Guest Starring: Ellen Wheeler (Ekoria), Dylan Haggerty (Epran), Michael Sarrazin (Trevean)

For the first time in his career, Dr. Bashir is put to the ultimate test in his effort to save the remnants of a Gamma Quadrant alien society infected with a seemingly incurable disease by the Jem'Hadar. As far as he's come as a physician and as vast as his knowledge is, it may not be enough. Indeed, he may be making things worse.

••••

"It's a grim episode with some terrific performances," says Ira Behr. "When those people start dying, I think that caught a lot of people by surprise — that old Bashir screwed the pooch big time. We don't usually make those kinds of mistakes, mistakes that cost people lives, though it was realistic. I thought Michael Sarrazin was interesting as Bashir's foe. Rene [Echevarria] did a great job with the writing on that one."

Rene Echevarria, who once again performed an uncredited rewrite, admits that this was an episode he was truly intrigued by. "I thought it came out right from my typewriter the first time," he says. "We had Michael Sarrazin, who was wonderful. I thought it was a moving episode, and powerful to see Bashir fuck up, in a sense, and be really taken to task by Dax, who points out that just because *he* couldn't cure it doesn't mean it can't be cured. Pretty happy with it."

"Such a downer of a show," adds Ron Moore. "We were watching the dailies, and I remember saying, 'Man, I don't know if I can sit through this show. It's such a downer. All those people suffering and in agony.' But it's a good show. It really works on a basic level in terms of Bashir's character, which we don't see that often. He's trying to do his job, getting out there healing and curing and struggling with medical issues. On that level, I think it was a nice showcase for Sid[dig]. The production values were tremendous. The sets were great, the location was fabulous, the whole look of that planet was

good. I thought it was an interesting back-story that said something interesting about the Dominion and how they deal with dissent. That they weren't just berserkers that went around killing everybody, they actually make examples of you and make you suffer quite a bit. They do it in a really nasty way, which adds more to the franchise overall."

Robert Wolfe says, "Every once in a while we've got to give Sid some doctor stuff to do. Rene Echevarria did an uncredited rewrite on the episode. In fact, he wrote two terrific episodes this year, both exceptional, neither one of which has his name on it: 'The Visitor' and 'The Quickening.' Maximum respect for Rene. We spent too much money on the episode, though. What happened is that we budgeted 'The Quickening' and 'To the Death' and switched the order they were to be shot, but forgot to switch the money from one to the other. As a result, the matte stuff in 'To the Death' is not so great, but the mattes in 'The Quickening' are really good. We probably could've used them more in 'To the Death,' but we kind of screwed up, and as a result, 'The Quickening' is a beautiful show. That shouldn't be forgotten. It looks great and has great performances. Some really gross makeup."

Episode #97
"Body Parts"
Original Airdate: 6/8/96
Teleplay by Hans Beimler
Story by Louis P. DeSantis and Robert J. Bolivar
Directed by Avery Brooks
Guest Starring: Rosalind Chao (Keiko O'Brien), Max Grodenchik (Rom), Hana Hatae (Molly), Andrew Robinson (Garak), Jeffrey Combs (Brunt)

Quark finds himself bound by a Ferengi contract when he is misdiagnosed with a deadly disease and decides to sell his body parts on the open market in an effort to pay off his debts. When he learns that he will not actually die, he may be forced to live with one of the most serious Ferengi laws: A contract is a contract, particularly between Ferengi.

••••

"Avery [Brooks] did a really nice job directing; Hans did a nice job writing," says Ira Behr. "Brunt's back; Armin does some terrific things. A really good show. I was really surprised that it takes you places, and it's a good Quark show."

Observes Ron Moore, "The guys described this as a breaking ball. It comes at you and just keeps changing. You think you're going to get it and know where the show is going, and it just keeps changing. Right from the teaser on, where Quark comes in in such a good mood but at the end of the teaser he's saying, 'I'm dying.' Then he's a loser, he hates his life, he's going to lose all his properties and so on. To me, this really brought home Quark's sense of Ferengi honor: that he's a Ferengi businessman living by a code and he takes that as seriously as Worf takes his Klingon heritage or Sisko his oath. There's something there that mattered very much to Quark, and that was a great step to take."

Rene Echevarria says, "It's a really effective show. Robert Wolfe said it's like an episode of *The Simpsons,* unfolding and changing course in ways that are very organic but unexpected. Ultimately it's really sentimental, but it's totally effective at the end. It becomes almost *It's a Wonderful Life,* and there's some dropdead hilarious stuff in it. Avery directed it, and I think he got one of the most subtly shaded performances out of Armin that I've ever seen. Sometimes Armin plays really tough — he's the toughest little motherfucking Ferengi you'll ever find — but here he shows a lot of vulnerability as well as toughness and resolve. It's a real wonderful insight into how far Quark is willing to go for what he values."

"Ah," says Robert Wolfe, "the show in which we had to deal with nature's natural effects on one of our actresses. We could have hidden Nana's pregnancy, which felt like cheating, or incorporated it into the show. We realized we already had a pregnancy, having started the notion of Keiko O'Brien being pregnant (designed to make O'Brien's life more miserable), and we figured we'd incorporate it into the show by having Keiko's baby placed in Kira, which is a crazy science-fiction thing to do. I was really pleasantly surprised at how well it worked. I thought it would be an OK

Armin Shimerman (copyright © 1996 by Albert Ortega).

episode, but I actually found it to be a very moving episode, very sweet."

Episode #98
"Broken Link"
Original Airdate: 6/15/96
Teleplay by Robert Hewitt Wolfe and Ira Steven Behr
Story by George A. Brozak
Directed by Les Landau
Guest Starring: Salome Jens (Female Shape-Shifter), Robert O'Reilly (Gowron), Jill Jacobson (Aroya), Leslie Bevis (Freighter Captain), Andrew Robinson (Garak)

Picking up plot threads from the season-two cliff-hanger "Adversary," "Broken Link" finds Odo suddenly losing his shape-shifting abilities and forced to return to his homeworld. There he learns that he has been stripped of his powers by his people due to the fact that he broke the changelings' most honored commandment, against killing a fellow shape-shifter. Now Odo must live among humans in a humanoid form. At the same time it is revealed that Gowron — who has led the Klingon Empire in its aggressive strikes

against both the Cardassians and the Federation — is actually a changeling. Odo is forced to return to his homeworld and face judgment for killing one of his own.

••••

"The episode gives us the opportunity to open up season five with a really nice episode," says Ira Behr. "We have to deal with Gowron being a shape-shifter, Odo's loss of powers. I think it's a strong ending to a strong season. On a certain level it is a strong character piece. We were a little worried about that, whether we should go bigger. 'Way of the Warrior' became such a burden, to an extent because we did have such a big budget for that, and the audience expected us to go out with a bang. Well, we did, but it was a different bang, and, as I said, we wanted to do something that brought the season around full circle. I think we did that and I'm glad we did. Let's face it, we're never going to have the bang of 'Way of the Warrior,' we're never going to have a two-hour episode, we'll never have an extra half a million dollars, but there will be all kinds of different bangs for the buck in the fifth season."

Robert Wolfe explains that the idea for the show was pitched by a freelance writer, and the staff felt it would make an effective season ender. "We saved it for months and then incorporated it with the Gowron revelation," he says. "When we were talking about 'To the Death,' we talked about twenty different missions the Jem'Hadar could go on with Starfleet. One of the missions we talked about is that they would have to go and kill Gowron because they find out he's a renegade shape-shifter. We played with that for a while and it didn't quite come together, so we went back to the original story. That idea — that Gowron was a shape-shifter — made a lot of sense to us, so we incorporated that into the ending to give the season ender a kick. Every year we sort of manage to end the season with some kind of 'Oh, shit!' ending. The second season was 'Oh, shit, the Jem'Hadar,' the third season was 'Oh, shit, they're everywhere,' and the fourth season is 'Oh shit, they're running the Klingon Empire and are going to start a war.' "

••••

CHAPTER TEN
Voyager: Season One

In the mid 1970s Paramount Pictures had hoped to launch a fourth network using a show called *Star Trek II* as its cornerstone. That series never materialized — thanks to its transformation into a feature film — and neither did the network. But twenty years later, the studio has seen its dream become reality. *Star Trek: Voyager* debuted along with Paramount's United Paramount Network (UPN) in January of 1994, representing the third spin-off of Gene Roddenberry's original 1960s television series.

Stranded on the distant fringes of the galaxy, the starship *Voyager* has begun its trek homeward. The creative team behind *Voyager,* executive producers Rick Berman, Michael Piller and Jeri Taylor, have taken the bold step of creating a series that is inherently unable to take advantage of the voluminous *Star Trek* backstory that is intrinsically part of the more familiar regions of the *Trek* universe. "The challenge was to find something that was fresh and original," says Jeri Taylor. "That's the main reason that we took the very risky move of throwing our people to the opposite end of the galaxy and cutting ties with everything that's familiar. No Starfleet, no Klingons, no Ferengi — all of those things that have been very comfortable for the audience. It was a universe that they knew well and that they loved exploring, and we turned our backs on that. It was very scary, but we felt that we would force ourselves into having a fresh slant on things and fresh storytelling. It was tough to make that decision. We swallowed and gulped a few times."

Adds Michael Piller of devising *Voyager's* new *Star Trek* premise, "We needed to do something that was unique and hadn't been done before but at the same time create the kind of environment that a spaceship provides. It was the same process of going through decision making that we did on *Deep Space Nine:* 'What can you do in a spaceship that is not the same as *The Next Generation?*' One of us said, 'You know those [*TNG*] shows

where Q sends the *Enterprise* off to some strange quadrant and we meet the Borg, but we solve everything in an hour and get back home? Well, what if we don't? What if we get stuck there in space and it is completely unknown to us and this is the story of that journey and of our trying to find our way back?' "

The producing troika immediately gravitated to the idea, particularly when they realized some of the allegorical underpinnings to the premise. "When we hooked on this idea we realized, in a sense, that we were talking about a journey that is very much like the journey that all of us in this country are embarking on today," says Piller. "We were sort of in the afterglow of the last presidential election, and it seemed clear the kind of problems that this country is facing are not problems that are going to be easily solved in our lifetime. We have to begin on solutions that may take more than one generation to see the final result of and that, in fact, our children might be the ones who get to see the results of our hard work, if we start now. In a sense, the ship franchise of *Voyager* is that kind of journey, because we are on a ship of men and women who are beginning a journey that conceivably we may not see the end of — and we are working in the best interests of everybody on board to try to solve our problem and to make the best life we can for ourselves on this ship to find the way back home.

"But in the end," he adds, "we realize we may have lost what we really love forever and that the journey back is seventy-five years, even at our best speed, in the hopes that our children may be the ones to benefit. The bottom line is that we felt that this was a very contemporary kind of message to be dealing with. We said to ourselves this is what Roddenberry had to deal with back in the original days when he was trying to figure out what *Star Trek* was going to be, because the original *Enterprise* really was about being alone out there. It was about being in a ship in space facing unknown aliens, and if you look at the years since, it's gotten very crowded out there in our part of the galaxy. We know all the political scenarios there are in *Star Trek*; we know the Bajorans and we know the Klingons; we know the Vulcans and we know the Cardassians. When we sent this ship out to the Delta Quad-

rant alone out there, the canvas is clear, and the same things Roddenberry had to do are the things we're going to have to do. It's really back to basics, and that's a huge creative challenge and should produce creative rewards."

Of course, once the premise was established for the new series, the creative team had the equally daunting task of creating the characters that would inhabit this new universe. "There was just a wide array of combinations and aliens both male and female that had already been used," says Taylor. "Every time we said 'What about A?' we'd realize that we were re-creating Data or re-creating Odo. It seemed like all the good people and good species were used up. It took weeks and weeks, if not months, to create a tapestry of people."

The premise of the show has the starship *Voyager,* under the command of Captain Kathryn Janeway, pursuing a vessel into an area of space known as the Badlands. The other ship is crewed by members of the Maquis, Federation renegades opposed to the Cardassian demilitarized zone, and it is Janeway's mission to bring them to justice.

However, both ships are spirited seventy thousand light years away by an alien hoping they can help him preserve a race he has sworn to protect, the Ocampa. When the alien "caretaker" dies, the crews of both ships realize they must put aside their differences and work together to get back home — a journey that will take them a minimum of seventy years at maximum warp.

If *Deep Space Nine's* premiere could be likened to the cerebral original *Trek* pilot, "The Cage," then *Voyager's* premiere, "Caretaker," could be considered more akin to the action/adventure of "Where No Man Has Gone Before," *Star Trek's* second pilot. "I think what we have concocted is a wonderful action/adventure romp," says Taylor. "It's very different in character from [*TNG's* finale,] "All Good Things." It's very different from the first movie and very different from the premiere episode of *Deep Space Nine,* which was sort of heavily metaphysical and philosophical and intensely devoted to one character. This is a romp and it's a true action/adventure."

Notes Piller, "We thought that

the best thing we could do right now was to have a pilot and a show that really concentrated on adventure. *Deep Space Nine* was a show that went straight to character. It's a much more internal, psychological show — and for some viewers it's been too taxing. I think what the audience is asking for is a slam-bang adventure show, and that's what *Voyager* is. Having said that, you know from my contributions to *Star Trek* that we will never lose sight of character."

According to Rick Berman, who co-created the series with Piller and Taylor, the intention was to make *Voyager* different from the previous *Trek* incarnations. First of all, the show would allow inter-character conflict and confrontation, which was something Roddenberry had been opposed to. "The fact is," says Berman, "that conflict is what drives drama. So, without breaking Gene's rules, we're always trying to find ways of creating conflict. This show features the inherent conflict between Captain Janeway's crew and that of the Maquis vessel *Voyager* was chasing. The Maquis become provisional Starfleet officers when they come abroad the *Voyager,* but there will always be conflict between them, and that gave us something new and unique."

Taylor points out that particular attention was paid to the creation of characters for this new series. *"The Next Generation* characters were deeply beloved,"

she says, "and the obstacle we faced when we created *Voyager* was 'How do we create fresh, interesting characters that haven't been done before in the previous three series?' We spent a lot of time in development working on that, and I'm pleased that we came up with really unique, individual and lovable people. We're hoping to capture both the spirit of camaraderie and some of the action elements of the original series. I think *Next Generation* was really a slightly more buttoned-down approach to space travel."

The second change in direction was to put *Voyager* in an area of space where there could be no contact with the Alpha Quadrant or Starfleet Command, thus providing a fresh new canvas upon which adventures could be placed. "The Alpha Quadrant was getting a little bit like Mr. Rogers' Neighborhood," muses Taylor. "It was very cozy, very comfortable, and you knew everybody. That sense of the unknown, of the wonder, the excitement, wasn't necessarily there. So it's our responsibility to populate the Delta Quadrant with fascinating new aliens which will be just as interesting to the audience eventually as the Klingons are to them now."

"That's a commitment we've made," interjects Piller, "to really open up and meet the aliens and the canvas of this quadrant. We met the Kazon the first year and we have been formulating quite a deep investigation of their culture that will turn them, I think, into perhaps one of the top five adversarial alien races in *Star Trek*'s history."

A third difference was placing a woman in command of a starship. "It's something we felt it was time to do and it gave us a new direction," says Berman. "Gene [Roddenberry] was never averse to the idea of having female captains in guest roles, but this was something that we never did get a chance to discuss with him. Jeri, Michael and I all agreed when we took this on that it was the next logical step for us. I'm sure Gene would agree."

As for the question that has dominated the show's media coverage: How does actress Kate Mulgrew, who plays Captain Janeway, feel about being *Star Trek*'s first female captain? "Well, after a few alterations to my stretch uniform, mi-

nor changes in my hair, it feels absolutely terrific," says Mulgrew. "I'd say I average fifteen-, sixteen-, eighteen-hour workdays and I'm aware that the work schedule will continue to be difficult, but I think the price is worth it. It's a wonderful role, and I'm very grateful to have it."

It's an opinion shared by the so-called first lady of *Star Trek,* Majel Barrett Roddenberry. "I am delighted, of course," she says of the Janeway character. "And I am particularly delighted with Kate. She's the greatest gal in this whole wide world. She's a real honest and down-to-earth being and she just owns the screen when she's on it. She's magnificent. She has eyes that sparkle, and her whole presence just kind of says, 'I'm here; this is my ship.'"

Certainly one limitation of being stranded in the Delta Quadrant that is not lost on the distaff Roddenberry is the fact that several familiar Trekkian staples, including her own character Lwaxana Troi, will find it hard to make recurring appearances. "I feel very badly about that, but I am hoping with modern mechanics, some of our great writers can think of a way to get me there, because I wouldn't want to give up the Lwaxana character."

In the series' gestation period there was probably more attention drawn to the fact that a woman would be captain than any other aspect of the show. For Mulgrew, this was not surprising. "I'm not even remotely surprised," she says matter-of-factly. "This is the human condition. It's a novelty. I think that it piques a mass kind of curiosity and it's very typical of our nature as human beings. I do suppose that one has to always refer to the gender in this regard. I am a woman, and that lends itself to maternity, to compassion, to warmth — to a lot of qualities which our culture has encouraged in women. Men, of course, enjoy them and reveal them as we do, but I think that women are encouraged to reveal them and express them more. I think I've been able to take this character into greater dimensions emotionally as a woman than perhaps a male captain would feel as free to do. I think that's the best way to put it."

Driving home this point, Taylor points to the first-season episode "The Cloud," which ends with Janeway's joining her crew in a game of pool in the holodeck. "In that episode," she explains,

••••

123

"we saw Janeway concerned about the morale of the crew and questioning her role as captain and how she would be able to hold things together in this environment. Then, when she comes in to play pool, we show that she's not necessarily going to be the captain of captains past. She is willing to have a different kind of relationship with the crew than Kirk or Picard."

The success of Mulgrew in the lead role is probably surprising to some, considering that the making of the series pilot was marked by the arrival and rapid departure of actress Genevieve Bujold, who offered an unexpected interpretation of the character during her few days on the set. "Genevieve had a certain approach to the role that was very low key and — who knows? — it might have been effective," says Taylor. "Kate came in with a very solid sense of command and authority, and it really seemed like the way to go. Considering that Kate came in after it had already started shooting, she was astonishingly good and professional. She is the captain not just of the crew but of the cast as well. She is so professional and so prepared that everyone is afraid not to be as prepared as she is. Nobody is late because she's never late. Everyone knows their lines because she always knows her lines. She's got such a high standard that she sets the caliber of everybody else's work, and that was obvious from the first day."

"I think people are excited about the show because we are," offers Mulgrew. "We've found some pretty good interpersonal angles in the stories, and we're a very inquisitive crew, full of energy and drive, wanting to explore."

Roxann Biggs-Dawson, who plays the role of the half-Klingon/half-human chief engineer B'Elanna Torres, adds, "Kate is very much one of the group, but she also knows how to take control and get into these scenes. There's not a question among any of us that in all the scenes she's in control."

"I think Kate has a natural strength," says Robert Picardo, who plays the ship's holographic doctor. "She has another great asset that all captains on Star Trek have had — she has a terrific voice. That's very important. You do all this nar-

ration, 'Stardate blah, blah, blah.' Imagine Edith Bunker as a starship captain."

Comments Robert Beltran, who plays Commander Chakotay, "Off the set, Kate's like Kathryn Janeway with about five whiskey sours in her."

In writing her, Jeri Taylor admits that she has made Janeway a fictional surrogate for herself — even to the point of proclaiming during a television interview, "I *am* Captain Janeway!" "I am concerned about character and relationships and personal stories and how we flesh out our people," says Taylor. "I've become enormously protective of Janeway. I really am careful that the character is not put in a light where she might come under siege from anybody. We have a strong male demographic, and Janeway has managed to be somebody who is the ideal blend of authority, command and believability as a captain, and yet is not threatening to the male audience. They buy her, they accept her and they like her. Kate has also managed to endow the role with a lovely femininity. She's attractive, she's nurturing, she's sensitive, she's caring. She really owns the whole package, and I am enormously respectful of what she has brought to the character."

Immediately obvious from the first day was the fact that this cast — including Tim Russ, Ethan Phillips, Robert Duncan McNeill, Garrett Wang and Jennifer Lien — came together as a unit remarkably quickly; jelling on camera in a way that took the casts of the previous *Star Trek*s at least a full season to do. "The actors are wonderful," says Piller. "I think we learned from our mistakes on *Deep Space Nine* and, to a lesser extent, on *Next Generation* that we needed to immediately find these people as individuals and as a crew. And it's paid off handsomely."

Populating the bridge of the *Voyager* is a wide array of characters blending both Starfleet officers and Maquis renegades. "It was a short, grueling pilot schedule, but it was fun," says Robert Beltran, who was cast as Chakotay, the Maquis captain who now serves as Captain Janeway's first officer. "The cast came together like magic. I don't know if they could have chosen a better ensemble as far as camaraderie and support goes. It's fun to come to work."

"The cast has gotten along fantastically," agrees Ethan Phillips, who laughingly attributed his character Neelix's being pegged as the show's "breakout" star to a potential allergic reaction to his makeup. "It feels like we've been working together for years. They really took their time with the pilot and treated it like a feature. There was never a sense that you were rushing. I guess this show has a reputation for having very, very long hours and I'm seeing that in more of the episodes now. They'll keep you there forever until they get it right."

And considering the show's heavy demands on an actor, it's probably a good thing that the cast had already achieved that easy rapport. "It's been just nonstop work, work, work," says Garrett Wang, who plays the young ensign Harry Kim. "People on the crew told me, 'You're going to make a lot of money, but you're going to have no time to spend it.' And they're right. I get home at two in the morning and I'm out like a rock for the whole weekend to rev up for Monday. But I have no complaints." In fact, Wang couldn't be happier with the reception his already beloved character has received.

Garrett Wang, who portrays Ensign Harry Kim, fresh out of the Academy and lost in space with the Voyager *(copyright © 1995 by Albert Ortega).*

"Overall, I think Harry Kim is well liked," he says. "There are conflicts between Chakotay and Paris, and Janeway and B'Elanna, but everyone loves Kim, which is a good thing."

He does have one qualm, however. "In the early episodes, Tom Paris was in all the holodeck programs, where he gets all these babes around him because he's the macho man of the show." Wang laughs. "I jokingly complained to [director] David Livingston during a scene we were filming in a pool hall. All these women were coming up and fawning over [Paris], and I asked, 'David, why doesn't Harry get any women?' 'Because you're the nice guy,' he answered. And then Robert McNeill turned to me and said, 'You know, I used to play innocent and naive in my early twenties, and you're going to have to go through that for a while before you can be this stud guy like me.' "

Wang acknowledges that he's going to remain, in his words, "green around the gills" for a while. "Whenever they need a reaction shot of somebody being amazed by something they go to Harry Kim," he observes. "As the seasons go on, I'm sure that they will add more depth and more color to my character. In fact, in the episode 'Emanations' I actually died and came back to life."

Robert McNeill, a veteran from the *Next Generation* fifth-season episode "The First Duty," shares Wang's enthusiasm for the new show. "Every character has a great backstory, and I don't think that they've all been completely explored yet," he says. "That's what makes it interesting. Everybody's got this sort of dark side, which is different than the other *Star Trek* shows that have gone before. Another great thing about this show is that as an actor, sometimes you do work and then it's forgotten or you do a play and fifty people see it. One thing that's great about this is that for the rest of our lives, people will know this part of our work, and it's great to have that sort of longevity."

One performance that has impressed most *Trek* aficionados has been that of Tim Russ, who portrays Tuvok, the first regular Vulcan character since Spock. "I've learned from Nimoy's character [Spock] and from Sarek [Spock's father] and from all the Vulcans that we've seen

up to this point," says Russ, one of the only cast members who was an avowed *Trek*-aholic prior to beaming aboard. "I've read a lot of the books based on the original series and so I've gained more insight into Vulcan. They were very useful because this is the first opportunity I think anyone might have to play an autobiographical character based on a prior performance in a feature role on television. If I walk into a scene and I'm not Vulcan, somebody's going to know it. It's going to have to be right, and the character can't sound monotone. The differences will come from the tonality of my voice compared to Leonard Nimoy's. We will not speak in the same rhythm."

The fact that the cast members have become major television stars allowed the show to take more risks in a shorter period of time than most shows would. Taylor points to market research that indicates that the show's audience has quickly embraced the characters and performers. "That," she says, "is the most important thing you can have in a series, that the audience bonds with the people, feels they know them already and wants to welcome them back into their living rooms again."

Producer Brannon Braga adds that since *Star Trek* has grown from a cult show to a cultural mainstay in the past decade, the *Voyager* actors entered the series with an advantage. "With *The Next Generation*," he says, "most of the actors had never seen *Star Trek* before being cast. Now we have a group of people who know what *Star Trek* means. They're good actors, and we have a writing staff and production team that have been producing these shows for years. *Voyager* definitely felt fully formed almost from the start, born as an adult instead of as a child. Basically, we have a good feel for what works and what doesn't."

Getting there, according to Braga, who had been on the staff of *The Next Generation*, was an interesting process. "Certain challenges of changing shows are the same," he says. "What we tried to do was find new voices, and that's a very fascinating process. The challenge that remains the same is coming up with good sci-fi ideas. The first few weeks were me, Jeri and Michael getting together each day

and brainstorming. Who are these people? Where are we going to take them? What are the little arcs we can take them through during the first season? All very basic things. During those five weeks, the one character we didn't really talk about was the [ship's holographic] doctor. We didn't know what the hell we were going to do with him and were terrified. This guy wasn't going to have anything to do because he's stuck in sick bay. He's going to be neglected. What a drag. As it turned out, though, out of all the characters, he's the best one so far. But you never know how things are going to turn out. I was writing scripts for this show before it was even cast. I didn't know what these people looked like, which was a challenge, but you just have to go with it. When the actors come in, you get a better feel for speech patterns. Once Kate Mulgrew was cast, for example, I had someone I could imitate just like I did with Picard. You take the voice and it helps you with the writing."

Executive story editor Kenneth Biller, a veteran of shows such as *Beverly Hills 90210* and *The X-Files,* points out that one of the greatest challenges facing the show is that expectations are inevitably high when it comes to *Star Trek.* "What gets forgotten," he muses, "is that the franchise may be around for so long, but this is a whole new show with a whole new set of characters and a premise that has its own set of complications and difficulties. I think in the first year we did some really great episodes and others that weren't quite as great, and I think that's true of any show. If you look back at *Next Generation*, which when taken in its totality is a wonderful show with some of the best stuff done on television in a long time, it's because we only remember the best episodes. I think when people look back at the first two seasons of *Voyager,* there will be a few episodes that you can look back upon as being really good *Star Trek* and really good television."

Most importantly, *Voyager* seems to have had an impact on the audience, with the cast already feeling the effects of the *Star Trek* phenomenon drawing them in and raising them to the level of cultural icons.

Mulgrew gratefully notes that for

her it has been rather slow in terms of being identified in public. "I hope that I have developed and helped make Janeway a very different character from who I am in my own life," she says. "So I enjoy an anonymity and the same sort of comfortable life I've always lived. The [Star Trek] conventions were very interesting to me. I mean, you're carried on this cloud of such love and support. It's quite extraordinary. But the attention has only affected me in an extremely positive way, because I love Janeway so much. I can't wait to get to work, so for me it's a laboratory of excellent proportions, and my life, as I said before, is my life, so I've considered certainly since I got this job that I have absolutely the best of both worlds."

Tim Russ has found the reaction from people to be endlessly surprising — particularly friends of his and friends of friends who have "come out of the closet" to admit that they are Star Trek fans. "I had no idea that they watched the show at all." He laughs. "And I kept getting responses from my family members that were the same thing. That was the most striking thing to me, that I noticed that there are a lot of people out there who watch the show. When you say, 'I'm on Star Trek,' or anything Star Trek related, people immediately tune in. Even if they've never seen the show before, they know it; they know what it's about. And that is really incredible."

Roxann Biggs-Dawson feels that the biggest difference in her life has been her family's response. "When I first brought a picture home to my parents and showed them a Polaroid of a test makeup of B'Elanna as we were developing it, going through the many stages of finding her, I sat down at dinner and my father started laughing hysterically. He said, 'Who got you this job?' And now I go home and he shoves about ten pictures in front of me to sign before I even say hello. So it's really changed my relationship with him."

In its inaugural year, Star Trek: Voyager presented a number of episodes that really established what the show could be. The pilot, "Caretaker," efficiently set up the premise of the show. "When we started the pilot," says Michael Piller, "I felt that after all the psychological stuff we had done on Deep Space Nine, we could

let loose and have a wild ride and adventure with this. My push on the pilot was to let it all hang out in a real old-fashioned adventure story. I think we accomplished that pretty well."

While deemed an overall success, there were a few negatives for Voyager's first season as well. For one thing, the season only ran fifteen episodes, resulting in a high number of reruns and, in turn, ratings that dropped significantly from those of the premiere. Four additional episodes that had been shot to wrap up year one were held back for the second season.

"It's very important to note that we didn't hold back any of the episodes, UPN did," explains Taylor. "It's important that people start understanding that there is a significant difference at this point between the network and the studio. The studio produces the television series, and the network buys it and runs it as they would from any other studio. The network has control over when and how they schedule the episodes. We and Paramount and the studio were not in accord with that decision to hold back episodes, but it was UPN's right to do so. I was uncomfortable with it because all the feedback I've gotten is that people were

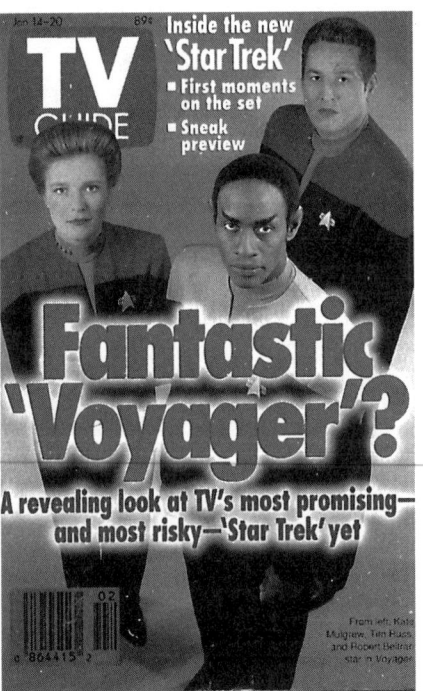

distressed with the high number of reruns during the season, and by summer we were having the third run of some shows, giving the impression that people are seeing the same shows over and over again and that there is no fresh programming. I would much rather they had used those extra four episodes to provide more fresh programming so the audience wouldn't feel the show had gotten stale in its first season. Also, we had planned those four shows as a build that would take us out of the first season on a triumphant, uplifting note. As it was, the season just ends."

From the network's point of view, Lucy Salhany, president and CEO of UPN, explains that they wanted the second season of Voyager to begin at the end of August. "I didn't want to wait until the middle of September, when all the other networks — the 'big' networks — are premiering," Salhany points out. "In order to do that, we needed to hold some episodes back. The shows that we held back would have run two in June and two in July. They would not have run earlier because they wouldn't have been done to go on in May. So we've had some reruns. We knew that was going to happen."

In fact, the original plan had been to produce twenty-four hours of Voyager in its first season, but only twenty were shot with fifteen aired. "We actually had directors booked through twenty-four episodes and were going to shoot until the end of June, which would have been crazy," says former supervising producer David Livingston. "As a result, they decided to change the schedule around."

Not everyone expresses reservations about the idea of holding back episodes. Piller believes that Salhany's strategy, which effectively launched Fox into the big leagues when she was there, worked for UPN as well. "I don't think it's frustrating at all," he offers. "And I'm the only one. When I was called I said, 'Of course it's a good idea,' because look at the job that UPN has to do in premiering in the fall. You have to understand the stations we're on. In most markets we're on channel forty-eight, and Star Trek is the one thing that's driving this network. It's a good strategy, and they asked us to help them launch their fall season. The only problem for us, the only reason we balked, was because we were afraid that they were going to premiere the second season with the end of our first season, in which case we would have had no money left to pay for production values and tired writers. Fortunately, I can say three out of the four episodes were terrific."

A creative complaint leveled against the show involved certain similarities between some of the *Voyager* story lines and those featured in previous *Star Trek* series, particularly the original. "Most of us are not that familiar with the original series," admits Taylor. "I think you know that there are only so many stories in the universe, and what's important is the way they're told. And while we did want to return to the original series in the sense of being out in the unknown — that sense of adventure that you're going out there where no one has gone before — that's the reason we put them in the Delta Quadrant, to get away from the familiarity. That was a conscious attempt to rekindle that sense of adventure. But in terms of story lines, we try to tell fresh stories as uniquely as we can."

"There have been over three hundred fifty hours of *Star Trek* produced," adds Berman, "and I would challenge anybody to come up with a story that would not relate in some way to one of those three hundred fifty stories. There are always going to be comparisons and similarities between stories about a group of people on a spaceship that last approximately forty-five minutes. We've had stories that have been pitched and discussed that we all like — and some of them come out of our own heads — and then we realize, 'My God, that's episode twenty-four of the original series, called "The Blossoms of Katiria Three," ' or something like that, and none of us ever saw it. The potential for similarity is always there when you have so many episodes."

"The bottom line is that for writers and producers it is very hard to find new science fiction that hasn't been touched before," argues Piller. "In *Star Trek* we've done two hundred and something episodes at this point. We sit in rooms every day of the week with ideas and story lines, and as soon as they start to veer into something we've done before, we have to pull them out of it and go in

another direction. [Story editor] Ken Biller is the new guy on staff and he is always coming up with ideas that we've done before that he wasn't around for. It's very painful. I think we've done a very good job of coming up with twists on old themes so that they aren't carbon copies. *Next Generation,* for all the remarkable imagination that went into making that series, started off by stealing directly from the original series.

"But, you know, time travel shows and alternate universe stories are subgenres to themselves," he adds. "You can't avoid them when you're in space."

A bigger problem for the staff was having the *Voyager* come into contact with societies that are too Earth-like for comfort. Taylor points to first-season episode seven, "Ex Post Facto," as a prime example. "What I did not care for [in that episode] was how Michael Piller rewrote the script, though he was extremely pleased with it. I thought it was a mistake for an early episode of a franchise which says we're in a new, different, unexplored part of space that's unfamiliar to us to do an homage to a 1940s American film style. He wanted to do film noir. The setting, the situations, the dialogue, all sounded like something that would come from Ross Macdonald. To see in essence a suburban home where the husband comes in and essentially says, "Hi, honey, I'm home,' she complains because he hasn't told her he's bringing guests home, they have a dog for a pet, she smokes a cigarette — it was Earth. To me, that was not the way to go."

In a similar vein, Piller refers to the ninth episode, "Prime Factors," in which aliens seeking nothing but pleasure in life manipulate the *Voyager* crew with promises of getting them much closer to home. "We had set a goal first season to create three alien races in this quadrant that provided different story material as antagonists. The Kazon, the Phage aliens and the pleasure aliens. Well, two out of three is not bad. I was very disappointed in how this alien race turned out; plus it was a mistake casting a French actor as an alien villain. I think the idea of an alien race seeking new pleasures wherever they go, and they can be extraordinarily dangerous in the pursuit of that pleasure, is a

great idea. I just don't think we realized our goals."

Among the goals for the second season were the beefing up of certain characters who were neglected in year one — particularly Lieutenant Tom Paris and First Officer Chakotay — and mixing up the types of shows presented more effectively. "We tended toward the end of the season to do more internal, contained ship shows and didn't deliver the kind of action, excitement and new alien quotients that we would have liked to," says Taylor. "The reason for that, frankly, is that we did a lot of high-production shows early on and overextended our budget and had to make good on it. We had to come out even at the end of the year, so we had to do some bottle shows that would bring the budget back down again. That's why it happened, but we're very aware that it sort of trickled down toward the end of the season. Our goal in the second year was to provide the action, the adventure and the production values, but to scatter it throughout the season rather than front-loading it."

In an ensemble the size of *Voyager*'s, it's not surprising that some characters would be better serviced than others over the course of the first season. "Paris and Chakotay are the two characters that went largely underdeveloped in the first season whom I want to take on and make more interesting in the next seasons," says Taylor. "I wanted to explore the emotional baggage that Paris brings with him about his family and his father and letting people down, not about being a womanizer."

Adds Taylor, "I'm not happy with the way Tom Paris was originally developed. I think the worst thing we have done for him is to characterize him as a womanizer. It seemed that in the first part of the season that was the only part of his personality that was ever hit, and I think that is a severe disservice to him. I think that is unattractive and shallow and one dimensional and I began excising that from the latter part of the season.

"With regard to Chakotay, we certainly did not want bitter blood between [him and Paris] because we also felt Paris has been given a chance at redemption," she continues. "Janeway has given him something that he felt was lost to him forever. And he is probably going to jump on board and do anything to justify that. He's not going to screw up; he's not going to pick fights with Chakotay. It just doesn't seem like a smart thing to do. We might be able to get some resonance from that down the line."

"It's sort of the Sisko syndrome," says Piller of Paris's disappearing act, referring to the development of Commander Sisko in the early seasons of *Deep Space Nine.* "We developed Paris a great deal in the pilot and then we went off and started developing the characters who hadn't gotten so much attention in the pilot and we haven't really come back to him.

"Jeri and I had a real argument over what the impact of 'Ex Post Facto' was," adds Piller. "She felt we had assassinated his character in that picture, and I thought he came off very well in it. The idea that he would even consider a relationship with a married woman she found quite distasteful. She felt he looked like a low-life womanizer. I think that he has a character flaw, a weakness, that I can appreciate. I think a lot of men can appreciate that and that he fell victim to that flaw — but rose above it to achieve. Jeri can forgive some flaws and she can't forgive other flaws. Infidelity is one that she can't forgive. George Clooney, who is the heartthrob of the season — who gets on all the covers of *TV Guide* — is the worst adolescent betrayer of faith and love there is in the history of film in *ER,* yet people find him attractive. It's a difference of opinion."

Taylor also expresses concern about the way Chakotay was developed over the course of the series' first year. "Women love Chakotay," she comments. "He is a wonderful character and he started out very strong in the first part of the season. He is a very demanding presence: overbearing, powerful, very sexual, and none of that has been taken advantage of in the last part of the season. He has been reduced to 'Aye, Captain.' He was wonderful in the pilot, and I want to develop some heroic stories for him."

For freelance writers, the lack of character development represents an opportunity to focus their pitches on characters the staff is looking to service better. "I look at Chakotay and I see him as a young Brando. He's got that quiet intensity. I

would love to do more with that character," says Ron Wilkerson, a freelance writer who wrote the first-season episode "Learning Curve" with Jean Matthias.

Adds Jim Trombetta, another frequent contributor to both *Trek* series, "He was like this neoprimitive, but he didn't swing with the neoprimitives that much because he really wanted technology anyway. That's a truly complex person, and a culture in the future that might happen. Indians going back and having planets which they want to settle is a very interesting way to look at the future."

Despite any shortcomings, the entire staff is proud of what it managed to accomplish in year one and looking forward to improving as the series continues. Brannon Braga in particular supports this when he scores half of the first season's episodes as "great," a quarter as "solid" and only the remaining quarter as "slightly disappointing." "They're not all winners, but all of them are pretty damn close. There's not a single episode that I'm embarrassed about," he says. "I admit that we had a lot of shows about planets with people that look just like humans. I feel that one of the promises of this premise —

Robert Beltran as First Officer Chakotay (copyright © 1995 by Albert Ortega).

and one we're hoping to deliver on — is to be *The X-Files* of *Star Trek:* expect the weirdest, blackest, most dangerous shit you can imagine."

In assessing their first year, Piller is enthusiastic about the show. "We wanted the *Star Trek* audience to feel the rewards of a ship show, and I think we were very successful. There were some shows that were better than others, but by and large I was very happy with the mix. And at the same time we did the high concept, we were able to do remarkably strong character development that I think defines these characters as well as any group of *Star Trek* characters have ever been defined in the first season. I think we're way ahead of *Deep Space Nine* or *Next Generation* on *Voyager.* I think we've got a quality show that I'm very proud of."

"I feel pretty good about the season," says Jeri Taylor. "I wish that we hadn't shot our wad financially in some of the early shows so much that we then had to make up for it quite so drastically at the end. Certainly there are some episodes that I haven't been terribly fond of, but that's been true every season of any *Star Trek* I've worked on. I'm very pleased with the premiere and the franchise. I think it's working, and it does not feel restricted. Coming up with the stories is nonetheless always a chore."

Finding those stories remains a challenge in light of *Star Trek's* ever more voluminous history. In generating *Voyager's* first-season missions, Piller admits there was a temptation to try new approaches, including introducing story arcs, à la Steven Bochco's *Hill Street Blues,* which proved unwieldy for the writers as they evolved and were dropped from the plans early on — despite the inclusion of one story arc involving Seska, a traitorous Cardassian spy, as well as the continuing dilemma of naming the doctor.

"We had these early conversations about Bochco having these character arcs that last the whole season and why can't we do something like that," admits Piller, who had been inspired by the Bochco template when designing *Deep Space Nine* in its first season. "When we started getting into it, we abandoned our noble plans as soon as we realized that some of our best shows were penciled in to be episode twelve. We didn't want to wait that long to do the science-fiction story that we were really excited about, for instance. We talked about themes to characters, but there were really no stories that took us into multiple episodes. Part of that is there has also been a new concern expressed by the studio that multiple-part episodes are not necessarily in the best interest of the show. If a viewer misses part one, they will often not tune in to see part two."

Adds Jeri Taylor, "We try not to preplan too much; we don't set a point where we want to be at the end of the season because if you do that, you are kind of locked into it. And we've always found that serendipitous things happen. There's a seed in one scene and all of a sudden it's expanded into a whole thing that becomes quite marvelous, so we like to keep ourselves open and kind of on the balls of our feet and ready to move in any direction. We realize that one of the emotional overtones of the series would be the way in which the people grapple with being so far away from home. And we felt it was very important that we not just start doing encapsulated action/adventure stories, especially in the beginning. We wanted to explore what it means to be so far away from home. How does that impact us? How are we all going to get along? Janeway questioned her relationship with her crew. Should she get closer to them because of this? Should she be more remote? People were dealing with these kinds of issues that had never been addressed in *Star Trek*. So we did have a lot of discussions about that and pairings that we might sort of look for in our characters' relationships."

Ron Wilkerson, who, along with his partner Jean Matthias, wrote some of *TNG*'s finest episodes, comments, "I would give the first season a B plus. It was overall very well done, and if you compare the first season of *Voyager* with the first season of *Next Generation,* the difference is like night and day. *Voyager* really has its act together. The cast has really come together and moved into those roles wonderfully. I don't think there is a weak member in the cast and I am really excited about the potential of the show."

One of the important concerns in creating *Voyager* was to avoid the perceived mistakes of *Deep Space Nine.* Re-gardless of its successes on a creative level, *DS9* has failed to measure up to *TNG*'s remarkable success from a ratings standpoint, prompting the network and the show's creators to cut a different path in the creation of the newest *Trek.*

Many have attributed *DS9*'s failure to engage viewers to its inherent character conflict. "We don't want this to be *Deep Space Nine,*" admits Taylor. "That's a separate show. We don't want people to be unpleasant and not liking to be with each other. We think people watch *Star Trek* because it's uplifting and it's positive and it's hopeful. We have the possibilities for some conflict, but we're just being careful about it. 'Learning Curve,' in which Tuvok runs a boot camp for Maquis, is a warm, positive story which starts out with a lot of conflict, so if we're careful, we can have our cake and eat it too."

"We learned a great deal from *Deep Space Nine* so that we did not make the same mistakes again this time," says Piller. "When we started *Deep Space Nine,* I said we're going to start this series with confidence. We're going to start this like this was the third season of *Next Generation* and we're going to focus in on the characters. We're going to tell intimate stories that really focus on the characters. We came out of the pilot with a belief system that the show could be sort of *Hill Street Blues* on a space station. If you took a lot of little stories and brought them together and saw life on a daily basis in a sort of crowded, difficult, challenging environment and really focused on the characters, it could be fascinating and, at the same time, save money, because the overages on the pilot were astonishing. I think a result of that was a lack of scope in the early shows. I really thought we were going to be a show about life in the future on the space station and all the people who interact. I thought that the breadth of the station itself was going to be interesting enough to carry a lot of the stories and, frankly, I am very happy with those, but the audience seemed to be telling me very early on that they felt claustrophobic on this space station, and I believe that is the result of this decision to get intimate in the very early storytelling of *Deep Space Nine.* It's been very hard to shake that perception even though since then we have gone all over the place."

As a result, the producers chose to begin *Voyager* with several high-concept stories rather than focus on intimate character drama in the earliest episodes of the season. "The development that we decided on was that rather than getting intimate with these characters so quickly, perhaps the audience will have more of a stake in who they are after they have gone through a number of adventures together as a family," Piller remarks. "That's the other thing *Deep Space Nine* seems to have been lacking in some people's point of view, a sort of family bonding environment like in *The Next Generation.* People watch *Star Trek* for adventure and space mysteries and excitement, so in the planning for *Voyager* I said we are not going to try to get even [financially] on the pilot. I don't care how much the first ten episodes cost, we are going to do visually exciting, challenging, high-concept shows."

Not everyone shares that view, however. According to David Livingston, who left *Voyager* after its first season to pursue a directing career full time, "*Deep Space Nine* is my favorite now because I think it has more of an edge and there's more conflict. I was hoping that *Voyager* would have the combination of *TNG* going off to explore new worlds and galaxies but also have more of an edge. In some ways it's paid off with the Maquis being aboard, but I think there should be more kick ass going on. It needs to be bigger and ballsier, with more jeopardy. I think the stories have seemed to be a little bit soft, but part of that was money. In the middle of the season, we had to fight severe budget overruns, and some of the shows by nature had to be written smaller."

Because the show is set on board a starship, the launch of the series proved much easier than its predecessors from a production standpoint since many of the craftspeople involved had years of experience working on *The Next Generation.* "Of all three series, *Voyager* hit the ground running more than any of the others," says Livingston. "It had fewer of the problems associated with the start-up. The first and second seasons of *Next Generation* had some well-documented problems, and the first year of *Deep Space Nine* had some problems, but I didn't think we had those problems on *Voyager.*"

Explains Livingston, "We had

• • • •

done a pilot for *The Next Generation* where we had a spaceship and *Voyager* had a spaceship and we had done space stuff for seven years. *Deep Space Nine* wasn't a spaceship, and when you're on a station which different alien species come to, you've got to define those aliens, you have to define the wardrobe for them, you need crowd scenes to make it look like it's a real place. You need to make the space station come alive. It's not just the bridge of a spaceship. With *Deep Space Nine,* all the architecture was Cardassian and was complicated, convoluted and multiplaned and dark, mysterious and moody. Right away, you're going to have a more complicated pilot. It's going to be more expensive because the building costs are huge and it's going to take more time to shoot it because we just hadn't done that kind of stuff before. Then you get a director like David Carson, who is one of the most tenacious people in Hollywood, and he's asking for the moon all the time, and it's going to be tough. We had to try out new makeup. Odo's makeup was very complicated. We were also dealing with extraordinarily late casting. With *Voyager,* the casting problems were only the one person, but on *Deep Space Nine* it was more complicated. We got one shot after about seven hours the first day and everything had to be reshot. Also on *Deep Space Nine* it took some time for the cast to find their roles, but on *Voyager* it was like everybody had been doing it for years."

Preproduction supervisor Lolita Fatjo, who oversees preparation of the scripts for shooting, agrees that *Voyager* was easier for the writers as well. Says Fatjo, "I have a feeling that it was probably like that all the way across the board because we all knew what it was like to produce two shows at the same time, and the pilot experience overall, except for the casting of the captain and all that craziness, for everybody was real smooth compared to the pilot on *Deep Space Nine.* The whole season just kind of flew by without too many hitches."

"I credit the cast with a lot of that," says Jeri Taylor. "They stepped into these characters like comfortable slippers. They just seemed to know who they were and they bonded with each other and played in an ensemble way as if it were a

seventh season. They felt like a family, and I think that in the pilot it looked like a show that had been on the air a lot longer."

"You have the same kind of writing, although there's even more at stake in terms of the plot, which is kind of nice," says Robert Scheerer, who directed *Voyager*'s "State of Flux" in the first season. "No matter what the story is, they're also trying to find a way back, and that adds to the impetus of the show, and I think it kind of moves it along well. *Deep Space Nine* was a separate experience, whereas *TNG* and this one are quite similar. Of course, the sets are very similar too, but they're updated. The writing is always good and they're always striving to make it better, and I think that's very evident. Frankly, I think there's a certain formula involved in all of these series. Their final choices obviously make things different, but I think that it's very similar in all cases."

One way in which *Voyager* sought to differentiate itself from its progenitors was to create an eclectic mix of new characters unlike those previously seen in the *Star Trek* universe. But ultimately it is the stories on which *Voyager* will soar or sink. "I kind of like just showing up and reading the script week by week and seeing what's in store for my character," offers Robert Beltran. "I was not a big *Star Trek* fan at all. In fact, I was not a science-fiction fan. I only got into it while I was preparing to audition for this role. And then I realized what a lot of people had been talking about. People in my family, my friends, people that I had a lot of respect for, seemed to be in love with this show. I never could figure it out until I really got into it and then I realized It's the stories, it's the writing, and that's the main thing. People have their theories about the success of *Star Trek:* Well, it's because humanity is seen in a very positive light or it speaks about the human condition in a very scooby-dooby way and all this. I just think it's good stories."

"All this stuff dealing with what people go through is the essence of what Roddenberry was doing; questioning our values and our concepts and traditions is what I think is most important," adds Tim Russ.

"I thought of *Star Trek* as more of

a cartoon before I got involved and then I realized, 'My God, it's almost like these are the myths of our times," admits Roxann Biggs-Dawson. "I realized there was all this depth here. It was really shocking to me. I didn't realize that I missed so much of this lore. From the moment I got the role, I would watch *Next Generation* every night, and if I missed it, I'd tape it. I just became completely taken by these shows."

For Garrett Wang, who is a fan of the original *Star Trek* like Tim Russ, getting used to the fervor of its fans took some doing. "They said you will not believe it," says Wang of his fellow *Trek* actors' advice to him before he embarked on the convention circuit. " 'You're just going to be inundated by people who will laugh no matter what you say. Why did the chicken cross the road? I haven't said the punch line yet. They'll still laugh.' I think that's amazing, because people just love this show. It's their life. Some people live their life according to *Star Trek* ideals, you know. The Prime Directive is there, and I find that absolutely incredible. You don't see anybody wanting to live their life like *Seinfeld.*"

Piller shares Wang's bemusement over the way *Trek* has penetrated the popular zeitgeist. "Jonathan Frakes has appeared as himself on *Cybill,* and people poke fun at *Star Trek* all the time," he says. "I wanted to get away from *Star Trek* for an afternoon, so I went to see *Crimson Tide.* And what do they do? You get twenty minutes of them talking about *Star Trek.*"

But even with the unbridled enthusiasm among the cast and crew, one has to question whether the franchise can sustain its incredible growth and what the future holds as *Star Trek* prepares to enter the next century. Based on the eroding ratings, one wonders if there is such a thing as too much *Trek,* or if it's time to put the brakes on the merchandising machine that has led to the show's logo being slapped on everything short of condoms.

"I think that if people had tried some of the [merchandising] things that they try now when Gene was alive, he would have had some people crucified," says Taylor. "It is so much against what he believed. He wanted to hold *Star Trek* as this pure, unexploitable entity and he

••••

made very sure that was adhered to, to the limits of his ability. Now it has become such a cash cow that everybody is trying to milk it for everything that it can give, and I think that can ultimately cheapen it in a way that will make it lose that special magic and luster that it has always had."

But as for the future of *Voyager,* everyone has hopes and dreams for a long and prosperous run on the new United Paramount Network. Robert Beltran smiles when referring to one of his noted progenitors, Captain James T. Kirk. "I just hope that when I meet my demise thirty years from now, I can say 'It was fun,' " he says.

• • • •

CHAPTER ELEVEN

Voyager: Season One Episode Guide

"Caretaker"

"Parallax"

"Time and Again"

"Phage"

"The Cloud"

"Eye of the Needle"

"Ex Post Facto"

"Emanations"

"Prime Factors"

"State of Flux"

"Heroes and Demons"

"Cathexis"

"Faces"

"Jetrel"

"Learning Curve"

• • • •

Episode #1
"Caretaker"
Original Airdate: 1/16/95
Written by Michael Piller and Jeri Taylor
Story by Rick Berman, Michael Piller
and Jeri Taylor
Directed by Winrich Kolbe

When a Maquis ship vanishes into an area of space known as the Badlands, the USS *Voyager* is sent in pursuit, but that vessel, under the command of Captain Kathryn Janeway, disappears as well. The crew finds itself seventy thousand light years away, meaning that at maximum warp it would take over seventy years to get home.

In its new locale, the *Voyager* crew hooks up with the Maquis, captained by Chakotay, and together they decide to investigate the situation, ultimately learning that they have been brought here by "the Caretaker," an alien whose sworn duty is to protect a race of people known as the Ocampa. He is dying, though, and is looking for someone who can take his place as their guardian. When he does cease to exist, Janeway finds herself in the position of having to destroy the alien's technology — which represents the only means of getting home that they know of — or allow it to fall into the hands of another race called the Kazon, which will surely use this power to wipe out the Ocampa.

At episode's end, the *Voyager* and Maquis crews elect to work together to find a way home.

••••

The creative staff of *Star Trek: Voyager* has nothing but praise for "Caretaker," feeling that it effortlessly established all that it had to in launching the new series.

"When we started the pilot," says Michael Piller, "I felt that with all the psychological stuff we had done on *Deep Space Nine* we could let loose and have a wild ride and adventure. My push in the pilot was to let it all hang out in a real old-fashioned adventure story. I think we accomplished that pretty well. The cast came together remarkably quickly, and I think we accomplished some good stuff right out of the gate. A necessary evil of pilots is exposition, but thankfully we had done a lot of backstory on *The Next Generation* and *Deep Space Nine* with the

Maquis and so forth, so we didn't have to do a lot of work in that regard."

Adds Jeri Taylor, "It also managed to be about something and delivered the franchise. The actors walked into that pilot as though they had been living the lives of their characters for years."

The making of "Caretaker" was marked by the ignominious arrival and departure of actress Genevieve Bujold as Captain Janeway. During the early days of shooting, Bujold offered a very different interpretation of the character. "The search for the captain was a long and difficult one," says Taylor. "This is the person that gets the white-hot glare of publicity as the first female ever to head one of the *Star Trek* series and she had to be just right. We considered, auditioned, looked at tapes of what seemed like every actress between the ages of probably thirty and fifty-five in Los Angeles, New York, Chicago, Canada, London and Europe. We had several people we were happy with. Some of the studio executives didn't necessarily share our feelings. Finally, with days to go, we were made aware that Genevieve Bujold was interested and we were ecstatic. So we went ahead with that and thought, 'Wow, we've got it,' and, of course, when that didn't work out it was distressing for everybody. I am deeply grateful to her that she did this after a day and a half instead of after six weeks or two months, because that would have destroyed us. She did what she knew in her heart was right, which is the way she functions as a person and as an actress, and she was right."

The reason for Bujold's departure was attributed to "the rigors of episodic television," which were more than the actress, who had worked primarily in film, was accustomed to, although one source on the show says that "she just wasn't getting it," pointing out that "the dailies of her were terrible." In fact, Bujold was hired without a screen test in deference to her stature.

Now, with shooting already under way, the producers needed to find a new actress . . . and quickly. Revisiting many of their previous candidates, they agreed to look at Kate Mulgrew — who had been sidelined by a cold on a previous audition — for the third time. "The third time she absolutely nailed the part," says Taylor. "She was so right and in all of

her work she has continued to validate that choice."

Ironically, the character's original name was Elizabeth Janeway, which was changed for legal reasons. "There is a prominent Elizabeth Janeway, and we're not allowed to use names of prominent people because it can be sticky, although we heard sort of secondhand that Elizabeth Janeway was flattered about it," says Taylor. "It then changed again to Nicole at Genevieve Bujold's request, because that is in fact her given name and she wanted that. For two days it was Nicole Janeway and then when Kate came on board, it was Kathryn — in fact the name we'd already chosen even before Kate was cast in the role."

Taylor dismisses the contention that Paramount was reluctant to have a female captain aboard *Voyager*, but admits there was initial trepidation as to whether a woman in command would be universally embraced. "The most pressing concern about a female captain, of course, is will people buy that she's a captain?" says Taylor. "Will they accept that a whole crew would follow her, report to her, trust her in battle? This is the most important selling point in a woman. Kate Mulgrew has that without even working at it — as a person, as a human being, she is everything that we envisioned Janeway being. She has power coming out of her genetic code and the moment she walked out on that bridge the first day, she owned it."

Adds Taylor, "I have always said during this whole process that surely by the twenty-fourth century women can assume roles of leadership without acting like men. We have created and will continue to explore the softer, nurturing side of her. She can be a caring and compassionate person. We are going to see that she interacts much more easily on a social level with the crew in a way that Picard never did."

Despite the snafus involving Genevieve Bujold and the subsequent hiring of Kate Mulgrew, most of the telefilm's other casting by Nan Dutton (regular *Trek* casting director Junie Lowry-Johnson was off on maternity leave) went fairly smoothly.

"It was one of the easier jobs I've ever gotten," says Roxann Biggs-Dawson. "I know that it hasn't been like that for other people in the past on other shows or

••••

on this one here, but I just went in for my first audition and I was one of the first people to read. I didn't hear for a couple of months and then I went back and they gave it to me. It wasn't full of all this kind of angst. If I had known all the

implications, I might have been more nervous and unable to do the work I needed. I thought it was just another show. I didn't know what I was stepping into at the time."

Interestingly, director Winrich Kolbe hasn't seen the premiere episode in its entirety. "The feedback has been very positive, and everyone is happy with it, so I guess I'll have to check it out one of these days." He laughs. "I guess I'll have to agree with those who say it's terrific."

In the wake of *The Next Generation*'s less than stellar two-hour premiere and *Deep Space Nine*'s critically lauded kickoff, it was decided that *Voyager* would start off with a visceral action/adventure that would immediately engage viewers. The job of crafting the premiere fell to the series co-creators, Rick Berman, Michael Piller and Jeri Taylor.

In retrospect, Piller expresses some reservations about the effectiveness of their strategy. "I remember feeling that ["Caretaker"] was passionless," he says. "As an audience member, I was ready for a real rock-'em, sock-'em adventure and I really wanted to have this crew off on this remarkable adventure and spend all the studio's money in creating a really neat adventure, but when it was over a couple of people said, 'You know, it's got the kitchen sink in it but no heart,' so we really had to get the audience to care about these people and Janeway's plight. I think the hardest part of the process was making anyone care about Neelix, so we had to rely a great deal on the character of Kes to make us care about him."

Unexpected fallout from the pilot involved the producers' seeming Gingrichian sympathies, most notably Janeway's final speech, in which she tells the Caretaker that the Ocampa no longer need to be looked after and should be allowed to fend for themselves. In many ways this was redolent of the Speaker of the House's tub-thumping about Boys Town and his antiwelfare platform. "I think that we were certainly cognizant of the issue of taking responsibility for oneself," says Taylor. "It was after that the whole Newt Gingrich Contract with America issue came along, and, unfortunately, in my mind they have been lumped together. I think we weren't talking about anything as drastic and dra-

conian as he seems to be; we were thinking as speaking to our children and saying you must learn to take responsibility for yourselves. If we do too much for you, this does not prepare you to go forth into the world. Now, of course, many people assume that we are part of the New Right, which is anything but the truth."

In addition to shooting on the standing *Trek* sets on the Paramount lot, the production shot on several exterior locations, including the El Mirage Dry Lake Bed for the Kazon encampment. "I thought it was nuts to go all the way out there, but Rick [Kolbe] totally insisted," says David Livingston. "I wanted to go back to the rock quarry where we shot the second-season premiere of *Deep Space Nine*, but in hindsight Rick had a vision and he successfully executed it. It did have a large scope. You really felt that these guys were out in the middle of nowhere."

Matters were complicated by director Kolbe's getting ill during the shoot. "He missed a day of shooting, and I got a call the night before saying I may have to come in and fill in for Rick for a day," recalls Livingston. "I had to direct a couple of scenes and I was real concerned he wasn't going to be well enough for the dry lake bed, because there was no way I could shoot that out there. It takes a director a long time to plan out all that stuff, and fortunately he got better. He was a point man in Vietnam, so he has a lot of intestinal fortitude and pulled it off."

Additional location shooting took place in Norwalk, California, where the Caretaker's farmhouse was filmed.

Perhaps the most inspired location of the shoot was the Ocampa's underground city, which was actually the Los Angeles Convention Center. "When you get an I. M. Pei building that's worth a couple hundred million dollars, that's pretty good production value," says Livingston laughing. "I told [production designer] Richard James if he won the Emmy, he would have to share it with I. M. Pei."

Unfortunately, some reshooting was necessitated by a change in Janeway's hairstyle midway through production, forcing the crew to return to the convention center to shoot retakes with Mulgrew to maintain ever-important hair continuity.

••••

Back on the lot, the pit built for *The Next Generation* on Stage Sixteen, now *Voyager*'s swing set, was used for the shaft leading from the Ocampa city to the surface of the planet. "We never used the pit again; in fact, we covered it over and built a set on top of it," says Livingston. "Any time we need a cave set, we've gone over to *Deep Space Nine*'s cave sets on Stage Eighteen."

Of shooting the pilot, Biggs-Dawson comments, "I was basically just kind of jabbing in the dark and hoping I was in the right ballpark. I was just kind of praying that when the thing finally aired and I saw it up on the screen that I would see a character. I still had no idea how to work my face under that rubber and I really wasn't sure who [Torres] was at the time, so I was just taking some jabs, and some of them were right and some of them weren't."

"It was such a great thing to see some of the other players do the scenes they did, not knowing how they did them or what they did at the time," says Tim Russ. "It was such a great surprise to see some very fine performances and scenes come to life that I had only read in the script. Some of the opticals and special effects were very impressive. I watched the show a couple of times through and what I do notice and what I think has gotten better since the pilot is a sense of pace and story detail."

Offers Robert Beltran, "I didn't start work until after the first week, so the whole Genevieve Bujold fiasco had passed by already. The feature quality of [the premiere] was evident."

Episode #2
"Parallax"
Original Airdate: 1/23/95
Teleplay by Brannon Braga
Story by Jim Trombetta
Directed by Kim Friedman
Guest Starring: Josh Clark (Lieutenant Carey), Martha Hackett (Seska), Justin Williams (Jarvin)

The *Voyager* encounters a quantum singularity after receiving a signal from another vessel that seems to be in jeopardy. Their attempts to rescue this other ship all meet with failure, and they eventually learn that it is actually the *Voyager* that is trapped in this strange time-space anomaly.

In the B story there is a debate over who should be the ship's chief engineer: Janeway wants a Starfleet officer, and Chakotay believes his Maquis engineer, the human-Klingon hybrid B'Elanna Torres, would be better suited for the role. What starts off as an antagonistic relationship between Janeway and Torres develops into one of mutual trust and affection.

••••

As Michael Piller explains it, the dual purpose of the first group of episodes was to showcase the formation of the *Voyager*'s crew as well as high-concept science-fiction premises. "I wanted the ship out there and into danger to see how the crew reacted," Piller notes. "So we created this strange time-space anomaly that we were involved with, and then we were going to see how this crew would work together. What appealed to me most about 'Parallax' was how it illuminated the relationship between Chakotay and B'Elanna and Janeway: how Janeway was going to deal with this first issue with the Maquis, how Chakotay was going to be the man in the middle and how, ultimately, B'Elanna was going to fit into this crew. Essentially she went from being the most outside force on the ship to being brought into the inner circle."

A gag involving two *Voyager*s within the quantum singularity was part of the original pitch by Jim Trombetta, who had successfully pitched a number of tech-heavy installments to *Deep Space Nine*. "That story was very complicated and possibly wasn't completely doable," admits Trombetta. "The way it should have come out was there really shouldn't have been two *Voyager*s, there should have been three. I wanted them to send the hologram doctor to each ship by crushing him into a burst of energy, sending him to the next one to warn them. It would have started out with him arriving on their ship trying to warn them but not being able to do it because he's all garbled. The original idea was more metaphysical and less character. It was what's going on and how do I figure it out?"

Says Piller, "What made this show work for me was that this was a show about a crew coming together and not about a ship in jeopardy. Ultimately, what worked was the triangle between Chakotay, Janeway and B'Elanna. The more time we spent with that, the better the show became."

Originally, B'Elanna was promoted to chief engineer in one of the tags written for the pilot episode, which was cut for time from the teleplay. "We bought the idea of the quantum singularity and then tried to make a story out of it, and several people added to it," recalls Jeri Taylor. "The original writer had a vision for it and Brannon [Braga] took it over. We had planned originally to make B'Elanna the chief engineer and Tom Paris the con officer in the pilot, and then it just seemed overkill, so we lifted that out and attached it to this. I think a nice arc occurs between B'Elanna and Janeway from conflict and skepticism to a real bonding, problem solving and, ultimately, affection. I also liked the fact that Brannon set up the conditions of the crew and the ship, giving us things that we were able to have fun with. For instance, the replicators are not fully functional, so people are on replicator rations. They have to get food and grow food."

Although "Parallax" established conflict with the Maquis, Trombetta is dubious that this will remain a recurring source of tension on board the ship. "I think that this idea of the Maquis is great," he comments. "To have this nebulous group of people that are freedom fighters in space seems very real and plausible. Something like that will be almost inevitable. The only thing about it is that the setup of *Star Trek* is that the Federation and Starfleet tend to assimilate everything to themselves. Even if you have these Maquis that aren't Starfleet and they're a little tougher, more sarcastic and nonperformers, maybe even mentally ill, you know once they get on that ship they're part of Starfleet, even though they may argue about it once in a while.

"Look at Paris," he continues. "They treat him a little too much like he's a juvenile delinquent who needs to have his wrists slapped to get on the straight and narrow. It's like the first time I came in to pitch and I said something about a luxury liner, and Michael Piller said there's no luxury liners in the Federation, there's

••••

135

no money, they don't need money. I said to him, 'Boy, I sure wish I lived there, because if I did, I wouldn't be sitting here.' They're real big on those virtues of the Federation. I just have a horrible feeling that the Federation will really turn out to be the Soviet Union, and everybody would be sitting around black marketing and the insulation coming out of the corner and people saying like, 'Oh, you mean you don't like the Federation? I thought you liked it.' That's just my own personal opinion. I think that if you're gonna have the Maquis then you can't really do them because you're saying there's a problem with the Federation and it really isn't all that great. *Babylon 5* has a much more realistic kind of a government where the president has been killed by the vice president and so forth."

For Brannon Braga, the "Parallax" script was a difficult one to pull together. Initially, he feels, he had written the characters a little too hard edged for their own good, and it took some time to find their proper "voices."

"Too much tech," he says of the finished episode, "but some clever twists and some great character work. All in all, a good episode. [Writer] Jim Trombetta came up with the idea of our finding a ship in a quantum singularity and there were aliens trapped in there that we helped. What I did was cut the aliens out and say, 'Wouldn't it be cool if in fact it wasn't another ship, it was us and we've been trapped all along?' "

Episode #3
"Time and Again"
Original Airdate: 1/30/95
Teleplay by Michael Piller and David Kemper
Story by David Kemper
Directed by Les Landau
Guest Starring: Brady Bluhm (Latika), Ryan McDonald (Shopkeeper), Joel Polis (Terla), Jerry Spicer (Guard), Nicholas Surovy (Makull), Steve Vaught (Officer)

The *Voyager*'s sensors pick up a shock wave in space generated by an explosion on a nearby planet. An Away Team beams down to investigate the situation, only to discover that all life-forms have been wiped out. Shortly thereafter, subspace fractures transport Janeway and Paris back to a time shortly before the

explosion and they discover that they themselves — albeit accidentally — are responsible for what happened.

••••

"The original pitch," recalls Jeri Taylor, "was what if you were in Dresden twenty-four hours before the fire bombing and knew it was coming? What would you do? That just seemed like an irresistible kind of a premise. We weren't necessarily thrilled with the way it came out for a variety of reasons. I also think this is the one where people have the response, 'Oh, another time-travel or screwing around with time story. Haven't we seen a lot of that?' We have gone to the well too many times with the time-travel thing, and I sort of wish that this episode would have been shown second season. It was just a compelling story with a high-concept idea that we couldn't resist. The major dissatisfaction was that I don't think anybody knew what happened. The end was so confusing that most people said, 'Huh?' I don't think we did our most effective job. I think that was the script and not the production in selling exactly what happened."

"I was a little disappointed with the location stuff we did," adds Michael Piller. "We got caught in the rain, and it looked kind of bleak. I think the director was under a great deal of pressure to get everything done. I liked the idea of it and I liked what we did, but on the Altman scale I give it two and a half stars. It didn't really deliver the goods. I liked the idea of going back and forth between the two time periods."

Piller admits that putting Janeway at the center of the action was a concerted attempt to develop her character early on in the series. "We did it deliberately," he offers. "It's another experiment from *Deep Space Nine* I think we learned from. It was terribly important for us to establish this captain's anchor position, and we didn't do it that well in the first season of *Deep Space Nine*."

Story editor Kenneth Biller doesn't consider "Time and Again" one of *Voyager*'s brighter first-season moments, primarily because of the nature of the aliens utilized. "They looked human," he emphasizes, "except they have different hair and costumes. It's unfortunate that our first episode of a show, where we're seventy thousand light years away, had aliens that

looked completely human. I also think that to a lot of people the time anomaly was very baffling. The good things in the episode were getting to see Tom Paris and Janeway develop their relationship, but the show also suffered from child-actor syndrome. If you remember, there's a kid that Paris is accused of threatening, and you ultimately wish he had."

Piller says that the problems with the episode had largely to do with budget. He notes that it was initially a very ambitious show that had to be cut down in size due to its expense. "Originally," he explains, "we had planned to make two towns, one before the explosion and one after the explosion, and we couldn't afford that. So essentially the second version of the town was a much darker, smokier, less distinct place. We had people occupying the same place at the same time, and you needed some touchstones, some anchors, to say where we were, and I'm not sure we had those."

The scenes at the gates of the alien world's reactor, which is the source of the planet's Armageddon, were filmed at the Tillman Water Reclamation Plant, previously used by *TNG* as both the Edo planet in "Justice" and Starfleet Academy in "The First Duty."

Episode #4
"Phage"
Original Airdate: 2/6/95
Teleplay by Skye Dent and Brannon Braga
Story by Tim DeHaas
Directed by Winrich Kolbe
Guest Starring: Cully Fredericksen (Alien #1), Martha Hackett (Seska), Stephen Rappaport (Alien #2)

As the crew searches for *Voyager* power sources, it comes across a planet that seems to be filled with dilithium crystals. Upon further investigation, they learn that the planet is really a base for an alien race that must steal body organs to fight "the Phage," a disease that eats away at their bodies and destroys their organs. The aliens, the Vidiians, steal the lungs of Neelix, who is kept alive via holographic lungs supplied in sick bay. The drawback is that he can never move or those lungs will "malfunction." Ultimately, he is saved by the donation of one of Kes's lungs.

By episode's end, Janeway con-

••••

fronts the leader of the Vidiians, both horrified by what they do to other living creatures and sympathetic to their plight. Nonetheless, she delivers a warning to the aliens that any such attack on her people in the future will be met with the deadliest of force.

••••

The original pitch of "Phage" was that Paris had had his heart blown out by something and the ship's doctor equipped him with a holographic replacement. "It's a great idea," says Brannon Braga, "although the drawback is you can't leave sick bay. Around that time, Jeri, Michael and I had been batting around the idea of an alien race that gathers organs. We said, 'Well, what better thing than this?' and we put those ideas together to see what we'd come up with. Ultimately, I ended up changing the heart to lungs and Paris to Neelix. It was the first time everything came together: the directing, the music, the actors, and you saw Voyager hitting its mark. Some really nice character work there — you can see the characters blossoming. One of my better efforts."

Kenneth Biller agrees. "This is a great Star Trek episode. The aliens that Brannon created were so interesting and so different from anything we had seen. It's also an episode where you started to get to know the doctor, and the character work that went on between him and Neelix was fantastic."

The Phage aliens, points out Jeri Taylor, work well because in their own way they epitomize the Star Trek philosophy. "The idea of a race that does really unspeakably horrible things but does them simply because they're trying to survive, we thought was a very complex kind of agenda," she says. "We love it when our adversaries are not one-dimensional villains but have attitudes and textures and layers to explore. I think the Phage people have really given us those. Michael Westmore did an outstanding makeup job on them. They are truly grisly-looking people without looking like horror-monster-movie stuff. We were real pleased with that."

Director Winrich Kolbe says that "Phage" is one of his favorite episodes of any Star Trek series he has directed because it "takes aliens off that pedestal of being weird and gives them some humanity. We are dealing with a very grotesque

exterior but a very human emotion. These are a people who are basically dying and are trying desperately to save their species. It's something we're very aware of, given organ transplants these days."

"Someone compared it to [Star Trek's] 'Spock's Brain' or something like that," says Michael Piller. "I don't know about that, but I can tell you that I liked the idea of an alien culture who are a civilized people who are forced to do uncivilized things in order to survive. It's a very interesting look at how the human race could devolve if things don't go right.

"Adversaries shouldn't be pure evil," he adds. "[The Vidiians] are a race of people with their own set of values which are different from ours and driven by different agendas. Even though they're ultimately doing something hideous and terribly wrong as far as our conduct is concerned, from their point of view they're doing it to survive and that makes it OK."

"We sat around a number of days talking about new adversaries," recalls Taylor. "Who's interesting? What's interesting? What's an agenda we find interesting? En route we came to these people who harvested organs. We'd gone through cannibalism and a lot more bizarre things and then we finally hit on the idea of a culture that was dying of an incurable virus that would go to any lengths to make themselves and their species stay alive. I think they are creepy and scary and they would do anything to pursue their end, but if you start with a premise like that, it's impossible to make them completely evil because their motivation is completely understandable. If anything, it's more scary if you realize that underneath that grotesque, deformed body there's someone who was once young, strong and beautiful."

For writer Skye Dent, a former journalist who was asked to develop the premise after pitching several other ideas to producer Brannon Braga, the idea of the Vidiian harvesters was provocative. "I thought about a time when I first moved to California when I was learning how to parachute," recalls Dent. "It always seemed to me a lot of fun, and I was never really worried about it because I just figured if anything went wrong with the parachute that I would just die. And then I start hearing these stories or running into people who had actually lived — but they lived

to be paraplegics. And that's part of what this story is about. Because death isn't that scary to me — having to live as a paraplegic would be even scarier to most human beings. And that's how Neelix feels."

However, Dent has reservations with the way the aliens were portrayed in the show's coda. "Things definitely changed from the time I handed in my script, because when I saw it on the screen, the villains at the end just seemed very wimpy to me," she says. "Even though they were saying the same dialogue I had written, I had envisioned them as being very arrogant people. And even though they knew what they were doing was wrong in terms of the actual action, they were very confident that because they were culturally superior, they were totally justified in killing people and taking their organs."

The writer admits to immediately gravitating toward Neelix as the center of the story because of his relationship with Kes. "They were the only two on board that have any sort of defined relationship," she says. "I wanted to do a script that would affect one person and that would tear at the emotions of another so that you would see how it would affect her. I didn't want Janeway or Chakotay or any of the others to be injured because at that point nobody cared about them as much. We cared about Neelix and Kes immediately because we could see how much they cared about each other."

Ethan Phillips, who plays Neelix, notes, "It gave me a chance to display a lot of vulnerability in the guy and show the relationship with Kes progressing as he gets more into what he does on the ship as a chef and a guide."

A true highlight of the episode was the scene when Janeway realizes what the aliens are doing and she is both repulsed by and sympathetic to their actions. "We thought Janeway was put in a true dilemma when she realized what she was dealing with," says Taylor. "In fact, Kate Mulgrew was herself fighting tears when that scene was being shot, when she heard the story of those people. She, as a person, was so genuinely affected that she was really fighting not to break down. I think that comes across in the portrayal of a woman who is torn and struggling and has great sympathy for these aliens, yet

••••

Kate Mulgrew served on a silver platter (copyright © 1995 by Albert Ortega).

she must say, 'If you ever come near my people again, I'm going to wipe you all out.' That was an episode that, for me, delivered on all counts."

Episode #5
"The Cloud"
Original Airdate: 2/13/95
Teleplay by Michael Piller
Story by Brannon Braga
Directed by David Livingston
Guest Starring: Larry Hankin (Gaunt Gary), Angela Dohrmann (Ricky), Judy Geeson (Sandrine), Luigi Amodeo (The Gigolo)

Janeway decides to have the *Voyager* investigate a nebula they discover, but not until they pass through it do they realize that this so-called nebula is actually a life-form that they have injured by entering. Now the crew must heal this creature before escaping.

• • • •

"A troubled script from day one," proclaims Michael Piller. "When scripts are in trouble, I'm frequently the one who gets them because nobody wants them and nobody knows what to do with them. So I sat down at the typewriter knowing we had the cloud part of the story. It was an interesting special-effects show in that regard, but it was such an expensive optical that we couldn't spend a great deal of

time on it, so we had to come up with other material. Fundamentally, what we had a chance to do was take a look at the characters in further detail. I also like the continuing relationship that we were able to develop between Paris and Kim, and Chakotay and Janeway. I think we were able to turn the corner on the depression that comes with being lost."

Adds Brannon Braga, "One thing the story was always about was our injuring this creature and having to help it. What Michael did with the teleplay was make it all work. Michael loves *Pulp Fiction,* and I think there's a little bit of that in the way the characters talk to each other, going off on tangents. It worked really well."

Jeri Taylor is defensive of the teleplay's mystic side, in which the captain joins Chakotay on a vision quest. "I think one of the reasons we didn't develop Chakotay as much as we should have was because we learned early that it's really easy to slip into the stereotypes and clichés of his Indian background," she says. "People are always pitching Chakotay vision-quest stories, and we wanted to go toward the direction of underdoing it rather than overdoing it. 'The Cloud' is the only reference that is talked about, but we do not actually experience it in the first season. It has been extremely controversial, which I love. I'm delighted to stir up controversy. We are positing that maybe American Indians in the twenty-fourth century have a technology that allows them to tap into their subconscious in a safe way so that they no longer have to take drugs, fast or go to sweat lodges. Consequently, they navigate their unconscious frequently and are very much more comfortable with it than most of us. I see nothing supernatural about that. This is a man going through his own unconscious, tapping into whatever is inside him that can help him navigate through his life."

Piller, who rewrote the episode, conferred with the show's Native American consultant and used a piece of his own personal backstory in writing the scene. "It was an experience that I had personally in a pain-control clinic when I was having dreadful problems with my back. The teacher basically led us on a visual exercise, and I found myself on a beach. I looked and saw a small lizard, so

that moment in the episode is a testimony to my own back problems. My inner adviser is a lizard."

For director David Livingston, the opportunity to create a miniature beach set on Stage Sixteen incorporating a shot of the ocean taken by visual effects coordinator Ronald B. Moore was particularly appealing. "It was kind of a weird sequence," Livingston recalls. "Piller wanted us to shoot it in Janeway's office, but I wanted to go to the beach. I didn't want to use a lizard, but it was from his own life, and he wanted a big, kind of cruel-looking animal. We shot what felt like a thousand feet of film trying to get the lizard to move. He just sat there for ten minutes. We had a hair dryer on it, trying to get it to move around without hurting it. The thing was so lethargic it would just sit there. We shot it second unit because there was no time to do first-unit lizard work."

Chakotay's exposing Janeway to his mystical Indian beliefs was only a small part of what Piller considers one of the most successful shows of the season. "The least interesting part about writing it for me was the technobabble that was necessary to create the story of this creature," he explains. "I don't think we've ever done a show quite like this, where the premise essentially was that the *Voyager* had to act as a pacemaker for an alien creature. Certainly we've done other alien creatures that we couldn't recognize were life-forms, but this is the first time we'd ever done anything quite like that. Only I knew that from a production standpoint and from a writing standpoint, that would take up about twenty pages and leave me forty or thirty-five more that I had to fill with something else. I just started saying, 'OK, what can I do with this character, what can I do with that character?' and I wrote a variety of relationships into the show and did it with enough humor that it was just fun. That's what it really came to."

"One of the things that we always look for is the 'Wow,' a science-fiction hook," says Taylor. "We think the audience wants to have some kind of mind-bending thing like the big cloud is living and, with great expertise, we're able to integrate with character arcs. 'The Cloud' did that in a nice way that was not really planned. Michael took it over, and it was just sort of a big glumpy story of this damaged creature that we feel we have to repair, with opticals that were horrendously expensive, and Michael scaled that part of it way back and then launched into all the various character scenes, which I thought were warm and delightful."

David Livingston, who had already stepped behind the camera for a number of episodes of *TNG* and *DS9*, was given his first opportunity to shoot *Voyager* with "The Cloud." "I was disappointed when I read the script because I thought it was just another space-creature thing," concedes Livingston. "We had visited that territory before and in fact we did it a couple times on *Voyager*. But this script was deceptive because the most interesting part of that show was all the B stories with the pool room and stuff. The B stories on board the ship made the A story OK for me."

Livingston took particular relish in shooting the holodeck pool-room scene, which involved a number of extras in an area that has become one of *Voyager's* standing sets. "It was fun to work with Judy Geeson from *To Sir With Love*. It's fun when you do all of that stuff because you're not just shooting people on the bridge. It's more of a challenge."

Episode #6
"Eye of the Needle"
Original Airdate: 2/20/95
Teleplay by Jeri Taylor
Story by Hilary J. Bader
Directed by Winrich Kolbe
Guest Starring: Michael Cumpsty (Lord Burleigh), Carolyn Seymour (Mrs. Templeton), Vaughn Armstrong (Telek), Tom Virtue (Baxter)

The crew members of the *Voyager* become hopeful that they may have found the possibility of getting home when their subspace communications through a wormhole are actually responded to by someone in the Alpha Quadrant. Eventually they discover that the recipient of their signal is a Romulan named Telek, who is at first distrustful of Janeway's story but eventually comes to believe her and tentatively agrees to allow crew members to beam through the wormhole to his ship.

However, in a twist at episode's end that would do Rod Serling proud, their hopes of getting home are dashed upon learning that Telek exists fifty years in their past.

••••

Michael Piller has high praise for the script, feeling that Jeri Taylor did a terrific job in realizing its full potential. "It's a neat story that's a surprise all the way to the end," he says. "A very claustrophobic, interior show, but the mysterious voice on the other end of the telephone line is always a great hook. A real good story with personal stakes."

Adds Kenneth Biller, "That feeling of having the brass ring in your hand and then losing it is really moving. One of the things we've done is we haven't shied away from showing the darker, sadder side of the predicament these people are in."

Writer Hilary Bader, a former *TNG* intern, had pitched the concept for the episode, which is one the staff immediately wanted. According to Jeri Taylor, who wrote the teleplay, the notion of the wormhole, of making contact with someone on the other side with the prospect of getting home, probably would have been enough to sustain an episode. "But the wrinkle that the Romulan was actually from fifty years in the past was wholly unexpected," she offers. "I don't think people saw that coming, and that made it very special. I love writing people shows and the building of this arc between Janeway and this Romulan commander — which began with his complete doubt, skepticism and weariness, all those Romulan things — in a sense, by long distance, that built into a relationship and closeness and almost a friendship. The idea that by the end he was almost our champion was a lot of fun.

"We did not want to see too many faces from the Alpha Quadrant," she adds. "We felt we needed to have people out there and alone and sell the idea that we're far away, but just occasionally sprinkle in the presence of someone like the Romulans as long as it works with the story and isn't gratuitous."

One decision Taylor made was not to show members of the crew composing the communiqués that the Romulan had promised to convey to their families. "It was certainly something we talked about," says Taylor of the crew's interstellar missives. "But we decided that to leave it unspoken might be more powerful. We do have a premise floating around that I think is going to be even stronger in which we retrieve subspace mail that was scrambled when it was sent to us and we stumble on these messages sent to the ship from various people that were supposed to arrive with us before we went into the Badlands and now, a year later, we are getting messages from mothers and Janeway's boyfriend back home."

"I think it was one of the first shows that genuinely dealt in a complete way with the plight of being in outer space," she continues. "I think it was when the audience began to identify with the characters and realized they are up there and having a hard time. This spoke right to the franchise of the show, and it was wonderfully directed."

"It was Jeri's first script, and I think she did a wonderful job," says Piller. "It turned out to be a great show with a very original premise that you could not do on any other show, where you are on the other side of the universe communicating with somebody through a wormhole. The irony is that we are not just separated by space but time. I think it's very neat."

Piller, who has expressed reservations with the way the Romulans were developed on *TNG*, was pleased with their portrayal in this installment. "It worked very well for this show," he says. "We've always sort of used the Romulans as stock villains in a World War II way. I always felt the Romulans were the Germans and the Klingons, the Japanese. This was much more multidimensional."

Episode #7
"Ex Post Facto"
Original Airdate: 2/27/95
Teleplay by Evan Carlos Somers and Michael Piller
Story by Evan Carlos Somers
Directed by LeVar Burton
Guest Starring: Robin McKee (Lidell), Francis Guinan (Minister Kray), Aaron Lustig (Doctor), Ray Reinhardt (Tolen Ren), Henry Brown (Numiri Captain)

While visiting a world that is engaged in war with a neighboring planet, Tom Paris is accused of a murder he didn't commit. As punishment, his brain is implanted with a device that forces him to

••••

relive the victim's death every fourteen hours for the rest of his life. Tuvok takes it upon himself to prove Paris's innocence and is ultimately forced to use the Vulcan mind-meld to restore Paris to normal before he loses his mind.

••••

The show stirred different feelings among both the cast and creative team, all of them equally passionate.

"This to me was absolutely the least successful story that we did," says Jeri Taylor. "Michael [Piller] feels that it was one of the best that we did. We are at odds over this, as we are occasionally. The premise was a great sci-fi premise, the idea of punishment being that the perpetrator experiences his victim's death. That's what we bought. That was sensational. What I did not care for, and Michael Piller and I are at odds about this, is that he rewrote the episode, took it in the direction it went, and he was extremely pleased with it. I thought it was a mistake in an early episode of a franchise which says we're in a new, different, unexplored part of space that's unfamiliar to us, to do an homage to an 1940s American film style. He wanted to do film noir. To me, that was not the way to go."

She also felt that the episode "damaged" the character of Tom Paris. Even though what he had done in real life was different from what the implanted memory device suggested, the show nonetheless gave the impression that he came to this planet and began hitting on the wife of one of its people. "It was a very unattractive posturing for him," Taylor points out. "That's the kind of cliché the character could easily fall into. By that point, I was really fed up with it and after episode six, I didn't allow any more smarmy womanizing references to go through, because that's all we were saying about his character. It was very one dimensional, very unattractive. Unfortunately, we didn't replace it with anything else, so Tom Paris didn't do much of anything. That's why we needed to develop him in the second season into something more heroic."

For his part, Piller defends the script, rejecting the notion that it is a remake of the *Next Generation* episode "A Matter of Perspective." "A lot of people had questions about it and they thought we made Paris and his approach to women unattractive," he says. "I thought it had all the elements of *Star Trek* and science fiction working for it. It had a really strong mystery, a very strong style; it had space battles; it had investigations with Tuvok at the core of it, so we could see what he does for a living; it had sex and romance and terrific performances."

He also defends the episode's noir elements. "I was working on this episode and I think it had a lot of original science-fiction ideas," Piller says. "The idea of punishing somebody by making them relive the last few minutes of their victim's life is terrific, as is the idea that somebody would use someone's brain to smuggle information to an enemy. Taking these elements and weaving them into a story that was affecting and intriguing was difficult, and I had a great deal of fun getting into my trench coat and going to the word processor and doing it."

"Piller wanted to do film noir and he wanted to shoot it in black and white," notes David Livingston. "And then he wrote all this noir dialogue, literally. It was questioned why they were speaking American 1940s dialogue. It was a little bit on the nose in that regard. Then I suggested a peekaboo haircut for the woman so that she looked like Veronica Lake. I figured if you're gonna do it, go all the way. But the opening sequence was effective and interesting. It was Michael's homage to film noir. Michael was really into *Pulp Fiction* at the time and he said, 'Everything should be like *Pulp Fiction*.' I think this was his *Pulp Fiction*."

Tuvok had always been envisioned by Piller as a Hercule Poirot–like character, although initial plans to cast an older black actor were scuttled when Tim Russ read for the role. In any case, problems in writing the character remained. "Unlike Spock, who was half human, Tuvok has no such inner conflict, so of the characters he has been one of the hardest to get to. And Tim has got very strong feelings about where he'd like to see this character go."

Russ shares Piller's enthusiasm for the episode, which was the first since the pilot to focus on the Vulcan. "I really enjoyed it," he says. "I thought LeVar Burton did a great job of directing the stylized film noir. I love the fact that we get to see the mind-meld from the inside out and got a chance to actually go inside [Tuvok's] mind and see the meld from his point of view, which has never been done. I thought it was just great."

Episode #8
"Emanations"
Original Airdate: 3/13/95
Written by Brannon Braga
Directed by David Livingston
Guest Starring: Jeffrey Alan Chandler (Hatil), Jerry Hardin (Dr. Neria John), Cirigliano (Alien #1), Martha Hackett (Seska), Robin Groves (Hatil's Wife), Cecile Callan (Ptera)

While exploring a strange new world, the crew accidentally discovers the burial ground of the Uhnori, which leads to Harry Kim's being caught in a subspace vacuole and transported to the alien culture's homeworld. His arrival has serious ramifications for the Uhnori, who immediately begin to doubt their traditional belief in the afterlife. Harry eventually realizes that his only hope of returning is to die so he can travel back to the burial site through the Uhnori "death station." Then it is up to *Voyager*'s holographic doctor to bring him back to life.

••••

"I wrote a first draft that I thought was one of my best scripts, and it is cer-

Robert Duncan McNeill as Lieutenant Tom Paris (copyright © 1995 by Albert Ortega).

••••

tainly one of my best concepts," says Brannon Braga. "Our reality being somebody else's afterlife and one of our people coming back from the dead in return for an alien was a good idea, solid sci fi, and an issue explored. My shows don't always deal with issues, but this one deals with issues of euthanasia. I got a lot of notes and did rewrites I wasn't happy to do, but in the end they were right and I was wrong."

Says Kenneth Biller, "A great notion and a notion that delivered on the promise of the series, which is weird stuff in a weird place far away from home. Just the whole notion of somebody waking up in the middle of an alien funeral, realizing that we come from some other culture's afterlife, is really fascinating, and it was a great personal story for Kim. It's about death and it's about a guy who has to be willing to take the plunge — be willing to die — to live again. Wonderful stuff."

Jeri Taylor believes that Braga poured his heart and soul into the teleplay. "Ultimately, it was an episode about something," she says, "and it was thought-provoking. I got a great deal of response from people who appreciated the effort to explore a subject of that magnitude. I do have some quibbles about some of the production elements of it. I think some of the aliens on the other side were a little hokey."

"I always felt that it was more philosophical than dramatic," adds Michael Piller. "I don't think it quite realized its potential. I think the actor that played the doomed alien on the other side was terrific. The show had a great deal of potential and was philosophically fascinating, but there's just too much conversation about philosophy, and it didn't have a strong enough character arc for my tastes."

"I said to Jeri Taylor that I had to do something different and the only thing I could come up with was to dutch the camera," admits Livingston of directing the show and presenting its alien afterlife milieu on a skewed camera angle. "They all threw up their hands because I did that in [DS9's] 'Crossover' and took a lot of shit for it. I said it was the only thing I could think of to do visually that would make it different. Rick [Berman] didn't want me to do it, and Jeri finally agreed, and eventually Rick did too, but they didn't want me

to go too far overboard with it. I didn't do it as much as I wanted, but I did it enough so that you have a sense that things look slightly unbalanced and skewed."

Livingston, who was suffering with the flu while shooting, adds, "I wanted the mood of the Other Side to be much darker and the sets to be weirder and stuff, but time and everything conspire against you. I initially wanted everything bright in the emanation room where they're waiting to die, and it was a mistake on my part. It should have been much moodier and darker and weirder. If I have any regrets, it's that."

" 'Emanations' was particularly trying on me," says Garrett Wang, who, as Harry Kim, passes from one universe to the next and back in the course of the show. "The seven or eight days of shooting were tough because as actors, we play parts where a character is dying but not where a character dies and comes back to life, which is very difficult because there's no precedent to that in one's life experience. When I was pretending to be dead, I concentrated on trying to slow my heartbeat down and on physical things and manifestations. When I was young and on my martial-arts kick, I would read about ninjas who are going to attack and people won't know it because they've sucked in their aura. That's what I tried to do. It was interesting because David left up to me when I actually came back to life after I was injected with the hypospray. He said, 'Choose when is the time that it will affect you and jump-start you back.' And so when I did come back I took in this big breath and had goose bumps all over me."

Working with Livingston on "Emanations" was a joy for Wang. "David affords the actors the time they need," he says. "The pace is so quick that some directors will be satisfied with something because the camera angle and the lighting were perfect and the acting was sufficient for them, whereas if I feel bad about a certain take acting-wise with David, I can do it again — which is really a nice luxury in TV."

Budget exigencies contributed to the lack of scope evidenced in the show. "It was a very tricky episode to do," says Taylor. "It was one that Brannon really felt strongly about and he, being consumed with dark things, wrote the script. It was

very tricky in the beginning. He got so involved with the political debate that the story and the people sort of got lost, but I thought he addressed that very nicely. I think that maybe some of what we saw of the other life was somewhat disappointing. The concept that our life is their afterlife was a very high-concept sci-fi notion, which I think is part of the best things that Star Trek does."

Episode #9
"Prime Factors"
Original Airdate: 3/20/95
Teleplay by Michael Perricone, Greg Elliot and Jeri Taylor
Story by David R. George III, Eric Stillwell, Michael Perricone and Greg Elliot
Directed by Les Landau
Guest Starring: Martha Hackett (Seska), Josh Clark (Lieutenant Carey), Andrew Hill Newman (Jaret), Ronald Guttman (Gath), Yvonne Suhor (Eudana)

Once again, Voyager's hopes of getting home are renewed when they encounter the Sikarians, a race devoted completely to the pursuit of pleasure with the ability to travel more than forty thousand light years in an instant. Unfortunately, Janeway discovers that these aliens, who claim that they will help Voyager, have no plans to do so and are merely using the crew for their own amusement.

Janeway has the opportunity to basically steal the technology that might allow Voyager to traverse a huge distance, but ethically can't bring herself to do it. Using logic to rationalize his decision, Tuvok leads a team to steal the device and install it in Voyager's engine room, only to have it nearly destroy the starship once it is engaged. It all comes to a head when Janeway and Tuvok are alone together, with Janeway feeling utterly betrayed.

••••

The episode was filled with conflict, some of which filtered off stage as well.

"The problem we had was Tim Russ had a lot of trouble with it," says Jeri Taylor of actor Russ's reservations about Tuvok's betrayal of Captain Janeway. "Tim has a very protective feeling about Tuvok. I suspect Tim is actually a Vulcan. He thinks like Tuvok and he knows the original series very well. He knows Vulcans, he knows Spock, he knows his *Star Trek* role and he knows every tiny facet of anything Vulcan. He was very afraid that this was something a Vulcan would never do. I disagreed; Michael disagreed. We saw it as a noble, heroic act that he would do to spare his captain her personal ethical dilemma and that he would find the logical way to rationalize that. I told Tim that if he is never gong to have flaws or make a mistake or take a step that's beyond the Vulcan limit, what are we going to do with him? It's a death signature to a character that he cannot push the envelope and that his reach does not exceed his grasp at some time. We made some minor modifications that made it possible for Tim to integrate that action into his conception of his character and we shot the film. To my mind, it's one of the best that we did first season."

Michael Piller agrees, likening the debate to that about *TNG*'s "The Enemy," another episode in which an actor vehemently opposed an unpleasant choice made by his character (in that case Michael Dorn was opposed to allowing an ailing Romulan to die when Worf withholds a critical blood transfusion). "Tim was adamant that he would never, as a Vulcan, violate the trust of his captain. We felt very strongly the opposite way. Someone who thinks logic is the answer to all questions should think again. Logic can lead you the wrong way too."

"We had a good deal of debate about how far we were going to take that particular move from this character," says Russ of Tuvok's violating the captain's orders in the show. "I think that the only thing we didn't have enough time for was to get more clarification on the reasons for his motivation. I think there was a basic difference between what I thought and the producers thought in terms of why he did what he did. We could have clarified those reasons more than we did, but there just wasn't enough time to go back and forth on it since we were shooting in a few days. We changed about thirty percent of the script just from my input alone. I would have liked to have changed about another twenty-five percent. The main thing that they wanted was for Tuvok to use logic as to why he did it. Now, that's not a reason why you do anything. That is just a method by which you do things. It's

a method of execution. It's a way of thinking and a way of doing things, *not* a reason for action. There are Vulcans who are capable of choosing whatever road they wish to choose. Look at the feature *Star Trek VI: The Undiscovered Country;* there's a Vulcan character who's a saboteur. Now why has she chosen this particular path? She believes in whatever philosophical doctrine it is that she believes in and she chooses a methodical, logical way of executing it. She does her part. They never explored those reasons, but she was Vulcan. She wasn't another race, and so you know you could question from now till doomsday why she, as a Vulcan, joined in a conspiracy, and Tuvok also sacrificed his commission and risked court-martial in order to help the captain achieve her goal. He did this because he had a special relationship with her and he knew he was going to be court-martialed. It's a sacrifice. It's kind of a choice. There's nothing logical or illogical about it, it's just his choice.

"The second thing about it that I wanted to point out was the fact that Janeway says, 'How can I tell the crew I can't get involved because of my principles,' and, in my position as tactical security officer, I also wanted to make a point that if she did not do that she might be risking mutiny," he elaborates. "Lieutenant Carey, who was a regular Starfleet officer, was involved in the conspiracy. He was not a Maquis. He was involved in getting that thing to work as well. He wanted to get home. How many others wanted to do that, and how many others in a situation like that would be willing to take over the ship? You're walking a very precarious balance when you're that far away from home. The base of authority is nowhere near you. It's almost the same as a pirate ship. If you don't give the pirates enough gold, you as captain aren't going to be captain anymore. If you are in a situation in a society where everything breaks down, it's every man for himself when there's no authority to back up the law. Take away the police — you saw what happened in L.A. — and you have riots. OK, so without the authority, people are going to do what they want to do, and I think that Janeway is walking a very fine line in making a decision based on her standards and principles when all they're talking about is a trade, not a direct viola-

tion of the Prime Directive by taking the technology. They offered to trade it with someone who was on the planet for something that they had as a commodity. It was a very technical reason why she did not want to do it. And that I don't think would've been seen the same way by a lot of crew. I think there would've been a lot more tension and a lot more trouble."

For Michael Piller, Janeway's dilemma had great resonance, although the hedonistic alien culture was less effective. "I just felt nothing seemed to work with the aliens. They looked like they should be on that commercial with the director for HBO where they go to a party and everybody mistakes this guy for an HBO movie director. What was tricky about it was to flesh out those pleasure seekers so that they were something other than people walking around always talking about pleasure. I don't think people act like that, so I looked for other things, including the idea that stories were very important to them. We felt really good about the script when it was done. I think it was one that everybody thought was working. We got a little concerned with the dailies because the stuff that was happening on the planet, in spite of all our efforts, was tending to look a little too much like that hedonistic Roddenberry-esque society. I was worried that it was going to be sort of off-putting and that people would not get involved with what the real story was, which had to do with our people and the moral dilemma that was happening around the ship. But when it was done, I thought it was marvelously produced and that part of the story you kind of moved through really quickly. When you got onto the ship with the dilemmas and decisions, that's when the story grabbed hold."

Episode #10
"State of Flux"
Original Airdate: 4/10/95
Teleplay by Chris Abbott
Story by Paul Coyle
Directed by Robert Scheerer
Guest Starring: Martha Hackett (Seska),
Josh Clark (Lieutenant Carey)

As it continues home, *Voyager* intercepts a distress signal from a Kazon vessel that seems to have been damaged by Federation technology. This results in

• • • •

the realization that there is a traitor aboard the starship who has given technology to the Kazon. That traitor turns out to be Seska, who is also revealed to be a surgically altered Cardassian.

••••

Doesn't anyone remember the lessons of *TNG*'s McCarthyesque "The Drumhead"?

"It was different in the sense that it was a mystery," remarks director Robert Scheerer, a veteran of *TNG* and *DS9*. "It was something that is hard to categorize very easily, but it was a rare episode in that regard. It was something that was fun to do because of that — to take the scenes like the ones with the young man [Lieutenant Carey] who was also suspected and try and turn that into as much of a diversion as possible so that it wasn't clear who it was that was causing all the problems. And even though it was clear very early on who it possibly was, I tried very hard to prevent it from being obvious until the last possible moment that it was revealed to be Seska. I approached it on the basis of a mystery, which is something you don't get a chance to do very often with *Voyager.*"

"Originally," he adds, "they called the episode 'Seska,' which obviously gave away everything. They changed that before we shot. I kind of liked the fact that it was not someone who was very well known among the crew. She'd done three or four of the shows beforehand, and I suspect she may be back later on. We worked very hard on that. The girl [Martha Hackett] was a very good actress and we particularly took care that her relationship with Robert [Beltran] was a genuinely loving, warm relationship and that her caring for him had nothing to do with the fact that she was a spy who was trying to get home."

The story was set up early in the season with the introduction of Seska, a disgruntled Maquis officer in "Parallax." "Seska came about in a not very planned way," Jeri Taylor says. "['State of Flux'] was one of the first [stories] that we bought, and we realized it would probably be a good idea — since all of these people are new — if we did some stories in which we established this character before we did a whole episode about her. It would have more emotional resonance for the audience, and so we started doing that.

Then we found her character to be very useful because she could be the voice that wanted to take the technology and go home in 'Prime Factors,' and that's a very good thing to have. You don't always have rumbling in the lower decks or mutinous people on purely Starfleet ships. Seska gave us conflict and bite, and we actually pushed ["State of Flux"] further down the line so we could use Seska. She was very well established by the time we got to it."

"This is a show that I worked on quite a bit," says Piller. "It has a good payoff. I felt the most important challenge was to keep the audience guessing until the very end. It's a very tricky, complex mystery story which is so intricately woven that the audience might believe she's innocent of the crime until the very last moment, and then, of course, the revelation comes. I thought it was a very rewarding story."

Taylor disagrees. "The show was OK," she says. "It worked better than it might have simply because we had Seska in the earlier shows. People had a sense of who she was. Michael did an interesting thing when he gave Chakotay and Seska the backstory that they had been romantically involved, which had not been in any other versions. I think that made Chakotay's struggle all the more poignant. You really saw what the stakes were for him because of that, and ultimately he did the right thing and what his duty compelled him to do. Those are always good stories."

Creating the Kazon melted into the machinery of their ship was one of the most difficult production tasks of the episode, and the art department hired an outside special-effects lab to create the elements for the shot. "The art department was concerned that it would be hard to kind of meld a body-form around a desk and make it look realistic, but it was so dark in there I don't know if the audience got the full impact of it," says David Livingston. "It was the old *Star Wars* deal where Harrison Ford is frozen in carbonite in the wall of Jabba the Hutt's palace."

Episode #11
"Heroes and Demons"
Original Airdate: 4/24/95
Written by Naren Shankar
Directed by Les Landau

Guest Starring: Marjorie Monaghan (Freya), Christopher Neame (Unferth), Michael Keenan (Hrothgar)

When the *Voyager*'s holodeck is taken over by an alien being that strikes out by transforming living creatures into pure energy, the ship's holographic doctor must overcome his system limitations and enter the holodeck's computer to do battle with the alien and restore everyone to normal.

••••

"A delightful show," proclaims Jeri Taylor. "It was one of these uniquely original ideas of putting the doctor on the holodeck in *Beowulf*. It's what makes *Star Trek* such a delight to work on, because where else could you do a story like that? It just opens it up to all kinds of really terrific, tantalizing ideas. It was also the first time the doctor got out of sick bay, which was a lot of fun. People adored this episode, and Robert Picardo was wonderful."

"Naren Shankar, who is not on staff anymore, came back and wrote this episode and did a wonderful job creating the holodeck environment for *Beowulf*," says Piller of the former *TNG* story editor and science adviser's script for the show. "It was very well produced and was just

Robert Picardo, Coach Cutlip on **The Wonder Years**, *is* **Voyager**'s *holographic doctor (copyright © 1995 by Albert Ortega).*

••••

wonderful. Picardo is a wonderful actor. I see him as the fish out of water."

Taylor is quick to dismiss those who would peg this show as just another holodeck adventure. "It was one of those irresistible ideas, and the holodeck is a lot of fun. We put people in the holodeck and get them into trouble, but you get to see things you haven't seen before on *Star Trek*. And isn't getting there half the fun of it? Show me the person that doesn't think that's a lot of fun and says, 'I've seen this before,' and I will show you a really dull person. I thought it was delightful. It was also different in that it was the doctor's first away mission. So it was a great way to break him out of sick bay. I think it transcended the idea of 'Oh, we're in trouble on the holodeck.'"

For the episode, a forest set was constructed on one of the show's swing stages. Greenery and backdrops were brought in along with the construction of the Great Hall. In addition, director Les Landau was able to make use of a crane for his establishing shots of the holodeck environs. "Les used a lot of close-focus lenses to get this tremendous sense of depth, and you get a lot of big, wide shots," says David Livingston. "We had a lot of really cool-looking extras, and the art department really had a lot of fun putting together all these elements. It was fun from a visual standpoint because we got to do stuff that we don't normally get to do. It was something grounded in reality here on Earth, so we could kind of go for it since we had a template and didn't have to create something out of whole cloth. Everything there was in mythology and in historical record, so all the departments could go back to them and then kind of expand upon them, and that's why I think it was very successful."

Even though Garrett Wang only appeared briefly in the episode, he numbers it among his favorites. "I had chain mail on me, which was great. As an Asian American actor, I'm not really afforded the chance to play period pieces. I could never get a role in *Braveheart* or *Rob Roy,* so it was a blast."

The show also further established Robert Picardo's doctor as one of the show's most beloved characters. "The writers know exactly what they want to

do, but I think that as the show progresses, I've managed to incorporate certain of my own personal quirks as an actor into what is the doctor," he says.

Brannon Braga notes, "Ironically, when we first set out to map out what the characters would do and what they would be like, we didn't know what to do with the doctor. Surprisingly, he's one of the most popular characters. You can see that he's the funniest character and certainly the one most akin to [*TNG's*] Data."

"An episode where you got to see the doctor really grow and take on challenges you never thought he would have to face," says Kenneth Biller. "It's tough to do these holodeck episodes. After Rene Echevarria did the *Next Generation* episode 'Ship in a Bottle,' it becomes hard to top that in terms of holodeck stories. Not that this topped that, but it was very successful and a lot of fun, giving Bobby [Picardo] a chance to shine."

Episode #12
"Cathexis"
Original Airdate: 5/1/95
Teleplay by Brannon Braga
Story by Brannon Braga and Joe Menosky
Directed by Kim Friedman
Guest Starring: Brian Markinson (Durst), Michael Cumpsty (Lord Burleigh), Carolyn Seymour (Mrs. Templeton)

Returning from the exploration of a black nebula, Tuvok and Chakotay have been injured, the Vulcan only slightly, while Chakotay's neural energy has been drained. What follows is a study in paranoia as an alien presence seems to leap from crew member to crew member attempting to manipulate the ship. It turns out that this "alien" is actually Chakotay's subconscious mind trying to save the *Voyager* from the nebula, not destroy it.

••••

"I thought it was going to be horrible," says Brannon Braga of the episode. "I didn't have a good time writing it. Basically a twist on the alien-invasion story in that the alien is actually Chakotay's subconscious mind. In the end, though, it's really not about anything. Not my greatest shining moment. It's got tension and action at a point when we needed an infusion of that, but that's about it."

Concurs Jeri Taylor, "A show that sounded better in concept than it turned out to be. Some people liked it, but I wasn't sure it was entirely successful. I thought it was a little confusing and so is the twist. It was talky and not as compelling as it should have been."

Kenneth Biller, on the other hand, really enjoyed the episode. "I love the twist," he says. "I think it represented an interesting game of cat and mouse during a period when we were stuck doing a whole bunch of bottle shows."

"There were logic problems," admits Michael Piller. "I was not comfortable with the logic of a lot of the things going on. And I thought that once the possessions became known, Janeway was acting like the alien through the whole thing. It just seemed like it was very eerie and moody, but there's not a lot of logic to the way people were acting in the show. The idea of doing *Ten Little Indians* with the murderer changing places was a fascinating idea, but it got very complex and dry and was a hard premise to solve. It's one of my least favorite."

David Livingston's reservations revolve around the use of Chakotay's medicine wheel, which became a key plot point. "I wanted to actually paint it onto the set because it's what B'Elanna would have done," he says. "She doesn't care if she's defacing anything. She's going to come in and take care of her friend. They resisted it, and instead we had this piece of skin with a design on it hung in there. I think it would have been more fun if she had painted it onto the wall of the set regardless of the consequences."

Tim Russ expresses concern over another plot point he feels was inappropriate for his character as well. "The whole bridge scene with the phaser battle and stuff was different originally. It didn't make any sense. It wasn't consistent with Vulcan attributes, and we had to change it. I said to Jeri, 'You cannot execute this kind of thing in the story because it makes no sense. It's not consistent. It's a physical fact.' In the script, they had Tuvok blinded by the flash, but Vulcans have a secondary eyelid to protect them, and that's been established. Amazingly, the director brought those points up in a story meeting because she had problems with the scene because it didn't make any sense in terms of filming and blocking. We both were sort of in league for different reasons, but she brought it up in a story meeting, and they just basically dismissed her. What we run into, even in *Star Trek,* is that in most television there is a certain degree of mediocrity. Hell, you can see mediocrity in a hundred-fifty-million-dollar film where they completely forgot what the story was about. In television, what I see these days is that people just want to get from point A to point B, and they've got a great plot twist and it butchers all the character development, but 'Gee, it's a great surprise.' Well, it's not justified, and to me it's not justifiable to jeopardize the integrity of the character in order to get a rise out of somebody because then you've just made the thing inconsistent."

Russ admits he is also disturbed by the show's pervasive use of technobabble. "It's one of the reasons I never really got warmed up to *The Next Generation,*" he says. "How can you warm up to something that you're not really understanding entirely? Half of that stuff is made up. I think they're hurting the broad base of their audience by doing that. It bothers me a great deal. I think they should use technobabble much more sparingly. It takes the same amount of time to say the same thing, but in a way that makes sense: 'Sensors indicate there's something out there. It's approaching at such and such miles an hour.' That's not complicated."

The *Jane Eyre* story line on the holodeck is a continuing story arc created by Jeri Taylor that replaced initial plans for Janeway to indulge in a pioneer-woman holodeck program. "It's a story line that Jeri came up with and it's continuing," says writer Ron Wilkerson, who saw the story continued in his script for "Learning Curve." "I'm not sure where it is going, but I really trust her because she's got such great instincts. It's in Jeri's head so far, and I can't wait to see more."

Episode #13
"Faces"
Original Airdate: 5/8/95
Teleplay by Kenneth Biller
Story by Jonathan Glassner and Adam Grossman
Directed by Winrich Kolbe

Guest Starring: Brian Markinson (Sulan and Durst), Rob LaBelle (Talaxian Prisoner), Barton Tinapp (Guard #1)

Torres and Paris are abducted by the Vidiian Phage aliens and taken to a bizarre prison where scientific experiments are being conducted. During one of these experiments, an alien scientist named Sulan splits B'Elanna into two separate beings, one completely human and the other Klingon. Both sides of her nature must work together to escape the laboratory and rescue Paris.

At episode's end, the Klingon half is killed by an energy blast, while the human B'Elanna, who feels she needs to get used to her new body and personality, is told by *Voyager*'s doctor that her Klingon DNA will eventually reemerge and she will return to normal.

• • • •

Ever since the original *Star Trek* split Captain Kirk in two (remember the *evil* Captain Kirk in "The Enemy Within"?), every sci-fi series from *Logan's Run* to *V* to *Knight Rider* to *Star Trek: The Next Generation* has split one of its leads into two components. *Voyager* was no exception.

"I was not even in favor of buying this idea originally," admits Jeri Taylor. "I thought it was a tired idea, and it was too on the nose for B'Elanna. Ultimately it turned out far better than we had any right to expect. Ken Biller came up with marrying that idea with the Phage aliens, and that's what I think ultimately made it work and made it credible. I thought Roxann did a wonderful job of playing two completely different characters."

Agrees Brannon Braga, "Usually when a show does the evil twin, it's on its last legs and they're desperate. We figured, 'Hey, why not get it out of the way right now?' I always felt that splitting her was a mistake, like making Data human. Why do it? Why see it? Why resolve any of her feelings? None of us believed it could be pulled off, but Ken did it with the Phage aliens. If anyone has the technology to do this, they do. In the end, it was an effective episode."

As Kenneth Biller explains it, prior to his joining the *Voyager* staff, a story idea had been purchased by writer Jonathan Glassner (*Island City, The New Outer Limits*). In that story, B'Elanna walked

into a machine and came out the other side having been split into human and Klingon versions of herself. The aliens responsible are experimenting on purification within a species. Although Biller didn't like the specifics, he was nonetheless attracted to the idea of exploring the human-Klingon hybrid.

"I have a younger adopted brother who's biracial, and it's very interesting to see how he has had to deal with his identity," says Biller. "So this story idea, thematically, is very interesting to me. The original idea was very melodramatic and hokey. I admit my version was melodramatic too, but I think melodramatic in the tradition of *Star Trek.* It suddenly occurred to me that Brannon had created these aliens in 'Phage' who, we have already established, have this incredibly sophisticated medical technology and have been searching for a cure to this disease. Then I realized that the Klingons have these systems that allow them to fight off disease and injury much more effectively than other races, and they're so virile. Maybe they would be resistant to this thing. If I were this scientist with this incredible technology and I encountered a species I'd never seen before and it seemed that there was some promise she might hold the secret to a cure to this disease, I would do exactly what he did. I hit upon what I thought was a very organic way of doing something that might otherwise be really hokey."

Biller goes on to explain that "Faces" provided him with the opportunity to explore some interesting themes about identity and appearance, and to explore the ways in which we perceive ourselves. "I love the moment when B'Elanna finds herself human, touches her forehead and realizes she doesn't have these ridges anymore, and it causes this memory of being a little girl with these Klingon ridges on her forehead in a place where nobody else looked like her," he reflects. "Then there's the irony that she suddenly looks the way she wanted to as a little girl, yet she's stuck in this prison camp, dying."

A bizarre relationship between the Klingon B'Elanna and the Vidiian scientist Sulan develops, as a result of which the latter actually kills crew member Durst and grafts the man's face onto his own,

• • • •

145

ruined by disease. "I love the beauty-and-the-beast aspect of their relationship," Biller says. "When he cut that guy's face off . . . that's my classic moment in *Voyager* first season. They're great aliens in the tradition of *Star Trek* because they're ruthless, scary, formidable, but they have pathos. That moment in particular sort of personifies that. This guy does this horrifying thing, yet he did it because he was falling in love with this woman who, in her physical prowess, is his ideal of beauty. Because he is humiliated and embarrassed about the way he looks, in his mind this is the way to make her feel better and more comfortable. She says, 'You killed him,' but his rationale is 'Yes, but his organs will save more than a dozen lives.' While I certainly don't embrace his point of view, it is hopefully an interesting and complex one that makes it more than just a horrific moment. It's a horrific moment that has another kind of resonance."

According to Jeri Taylor, the climax of that episode generated quite a bit of negative mail to the production office. "I got a number of really nasty letters," she says, "largely about a couple of things. One, that our people got out of there and left the rest of the poor devils behind in that awful prison. And two, that nobody seems terribly sympathetic with B'Elanna at the end. That wasn't our intent. What was written in the action line as Chakotay's attitude toward her, which is certainly comforting and all of that, made it look like he was simply not responsive. People said, 'Couldn't he put his arm around her and show some warmth?' In retrospect, they're probably right."

"It was great," says Biggs-Dawson of the show in which she played two roles. "It actually was just this wonderful learning experience [in] that I was able to delineate these two sides that up until then were just sort of metaphors. I was able to personify two aspects of this character, and it was very revealing to me and it taught me a lot. It was really a lot of fun.

"They were very careful in scheduling and tried not to have me split a day where I was in one character and then the other, not only for me but because the makeup was so long and difficult," she adds. "They only concentrated on one character for the most part one day and then switched to the next character the next day. It was sort of like doing repertory theater."

Director Winrich Kolbe was also able to avoid relying exclusively on split screen thanks to the casting of an exceptionally realistic photo double for Biggs-Dawson. "She was very intuitive and very much able to almost mimic me," Biggs-Dawson says. "I was able to tell her what I was going to be doing so she could give me the beats that I could react to properly. She was very good and supportive, and I was able to act off of a real person, which was helpful."

"This was a story that a lot of people had trouble with, and it was almost abandoned at one point in time," says Michael Piller. "We knew we could not do the evil-versus-good story that the original *Star Trek* had done, but it seemed that the half-human, half-Klingon conflict between B'Elanna as a woman divided would be really interesting to see. In the first draft of the story we did, it was somebody's idea that this could be the result of a hideous concentration-camp kind of experiment, that is, genetic demonstration of some sort. But it wasn't until Ken Biller got the rewrite that he solved every problem overnight. I was very impressed because I hadn't figured it out, and Ken did a lovely job on it. I think the show turned out quite well."

Also pleased was Skye Dent, who created the Vidiians in "Phage." "I thought they did a great job," she says. "It was better than mine, actually. It was just so dramatic."

Episode #14
"Jetrel"
Original Airdate: 5/15/95
Teleplay by Jack Klein, Karen Klein and Kenneth Biller
Story by Scott Nimerfro and Jim Thornton
Directed by Kim Friedman
Guest Starring: James Sloyan (Ma'bor Jetrel), Larry Hankin (Gaunt Gary)

Neelix encounters a Haakonian scientist named Ma'bor Jetrel who created the Metreon Cascade, a weapon used to destroy much of the Talaxian race, including Neelix's family. The man is allowed to board *Voyager* when he claims that Neelix will fall ill from long-term effects of the device that he can treat.

Neelix doesn't trust him, and this feeling proves to be accurate when it turns out that Jetrel is the one suffering from the illness and he is hoping that something in Neelix's physiology will result in a cure.

••••

"It's pretty clear that it was a Hiroshima metaphor, but it also gave us the opportunity to show a completely other side of Neelix," says Jeri Taylor. "I thought that Ethan Phillips was masterful in the way he plays something heavy and serious as well as he plays some of the lighter stuff. A thought-provoking episode, it had substance, was really about something, and those are the things that I think work very well for *Star Trek*."

Concurs Brannon Braga, "It removed Neelix from being just comic relief, which I think is important. You don't want him to become the joke of the ship."

Kenneth Biller admits that writing the script was extremely depressing for him. "I did all of this research about Hiroshima," he says, "yet it was a fascinating idea to say, 'What if Oppenheimer was confronted by a survivor?' and then make that person see how he would respond. I thought Ethan was great and James Sloyan did a great job. They were wonderful together, and it was great to sink my teeth into something serious."

Ethan Phillips, who portrays Neelix, sans makeup (copyright © 1995 by Albert Ortega).

••••

"I was very impressed with that show," offers Michael Piller. "It was a very complex show to make work, and we had a lot of trouble making the story interesting enough. Fortunately, the two actors [Phillips and Sloyan] working together was just terrific. And I found it extremely moving."

Piller, however, rejects the idea that Jetrel's cascade weapon was a metaphor for the atomic bomb. "You can't say that every show is making a comment. It's not. Basically, we're using the Oppenheimer character as an inspiration to tell something about one of our guys. So is it unsympathetic? I don't know. I look at that show and I find the Jetrel character tortured. And I think Oppenheimer was. He's trying to correct a grievous wrong. I think that the character is not an unsympathetic one."

The episode also further developed the relationship between Neelix and Kes. "They work very well together," says Piller. "Jennifer [Lien] is just terrific. There's something about an actor who gives you honesty that you can't buy or teach. It just comes from inside. She's twenty-one years old, and there's a depth in her eyes that just comes through every time she's on camera."

Ethan Phillips admits the long hours in makeup can take a toll on him. "If the episode features my character it can get hard," he says. "I can be there for a long, long time, and my face takes a beating because of the makeup. I think it's surgical glue they use, and they remove it with a pretty intense thing too, but my makeup guy is so good. But still, after five days of that I get very raw and very sleepy. It takes about two and a half hours to get on, an hour and a half to get off and probably another hour and a half during the day to maintain it. The longer the day lasts, the harder it is to keep it all together. You pass a threshold after ten hours' work where you want to rip it off. If I did, all I would have underneath is a skull. Rene [Auberjonois] and Armin [Shimerman] both told me about some tricks with the makeup and acting behind the mask and face care that were very helpful."

Writers Ron Wilkerson and Jean Matthias had a script in the running for Neelix that was tabled so that "Jetrel," a bottle show (and therefore cheaper), could

be done. "I was really disappointed that we didn't get to do that episode because it would have established Neelix as a much more substantial character," says Wilkerson. "The story was essentially like *Carlito's Way* in the sense that this guy comes on the ship and Neelix pretends he doesn't know him, but in fact they were in jail together and he helped Neelix escape and they split up afterward, and now he's looking to get Neelix to do something for him or he'll reveal his past to everyone. I thought it was a nice episode because you saw another side to Neelix rather than just the comic foil character that you've seen."

Adds Wilkerson, "Once we got word that the story had been put on the back burner, we started coming in with new ideas. It was actually the next pitch that we sold Jeri Taylor that was the B story to another concept we had that became 'Learning Curve,' in which Tuvok became involved in teaching some Maquis cadets, and we realized that it was not a B story but an A story and we sold it."

Trek veteran (and Lexus car pitchman) James Sloyan is turning out to be the Mark Lenard of modern *Trek*, having starred in episodes of *TNG* ("The Defector"), *DS9* ("The Alternate") and now *Voyager*.

Episode #15
"Learning Curve"
Original Airdate: 5/22/95
Written by Ronald Wilkerson, Jean Louise Matthias and Jeri Taylor
Directed by David Livingston
Guest Starring: Armand Schultz (Dalby), Derek McGrath (Chell), Kenny Morrison (Geron), Catherine MacNeal (Henley Thomas), Alexander Dekker (Henry), Lindsey Haun (Beatrice)

When there is a rise in Maquis activities that go against Federation rules, Tuvok is assigned to train four Maquis members in Starfleet protocol and discipline.

At the same time, a virus has entered the ship's bineural circuitry, which threatens the lives of everyone aboard. By episode's end, both plot lines converge as Tuvok's trainees have to pull together heroically to help save the ship.

••••

The episode inadvertently proved to be the first-season finale. "It wasn't our

intention," says Michael Piller, noting that the final four episodes produced for the first season were held to kick off the second year of episodes. "It's an old story device, but it was a natural for us and it allowed us to exploit the franchise within the show. It took the Maquis background, established the problem, put Tuvok in charge, and we see how he guides them and how he learns something about himself. In that regard, I thought it worked nicely."

Brannon Braga feels that "Learning Curve" was an effective bottle show. "It's a good idea for an episode, actually," he notes. "Tuvok becoming the drill instructor is charming. I am somewhat bothered that it was our final episode because it's a soft episode. It didn't have big action set pieces or the grandiose themes that we like our finales to have. In its own right, though, I thought it was fun."

"A solid episode," agrees Kenneth Biller.

The episode's worst offense is a tech catalyst that can easily be called totally cheesy. "I came up with the gag that Neelix's cheese was causing the problem," says Biller. "I thought it was hilarious, but I don't think people got it that there was some tongue-in-cheek element."

"We liked that," says writer Ron Wilkerson of the plot device. "We liked the aspect that something very mundane can bring down something great and mighty. And why not? What's wrong with that concept? We've seen lots of wrenches in the works in almost any kind of mechanism that you can imagine, and cheese was something somebody came up with during the story break as being the most innocuous kind of goofy thing. It was a little bit of humor in the midst of this chaos that was going on. We liked that idea. After all, a tiny grommet knocked out the power generators in Niagara Falls that blacked out New York City for an entire evening twenty years ago, and a little break in an O-ring knocked out the *Challenger*. So if tiny, stupid little things bring down the mighty, why not cheese?"

"It might not be a season finale, but it's a good, solid show," says Piller. "I thought it was entertaining. It was a show that we had never done before that we could do here for the first time."

For writers Wilkerson and Matthias,

the opportunity to develop Tuvok was irresistible after having previously introduced a Vulcan character in their script for *TNG*'s "Lower Decks." "As freelancers, one of the things we do is look to see who is the character that is underused and then try to develop some new stories. We are looking at Kes right now because she is underused."

For director David Livingston, making the bottle show visually interesting was of foremost importance. In the case of Tuvok's mandatory run through the ship's corridors, Livingston made creative use of the Jeffries tube. "I was told I had to shoot the show on schedule," says Livingston. "I put the camera in one place in the Jeffries tube, and all of the Jeffries tube scenes were shot from the same camera position. All the stuff of climbing up and down and coming through a tube was literally shot through a ladder, and all we did was vary the action and vary the camera angle, but basically the camera never moved when they were in the Jeffries

tube. When it's all cut together, the audience doesn't know. They think they've been in all these different places throughout the ship, but they haven't."

For the corridors, Livingston used the hallways on Stage Nine, reversing his camera angle and changing lenses for the various decks of the ship. "When you turn the camera around, the audience thinks you're in another place, and that does give a sense of opening it up and making it seem bigger," he explains. "It was a nice show for me to be able to do, and I had a lot of fun with it. I got to add a lot of bits into it that weren't necessarily in the original script. There's a three-shot of the three Maquis, and you think that's all the people that Tuvok's talking to and then, all of a sudden, this blue guy's head comes into the shot and you realize he's talking to this fourth guy as well. Rick [Berman] thought it was hokey, which I get accused of sometimes, but I liked it."

In the episode's original coda, Neelix and Tuvok have a conversation in

which Tuvok realizes he has had an effect on his Maquis charges. "It was done physically with a trick that Tuvok had been trying to teach the students, a Zen kind of thing which involved holding a rod a certain way," says Wilkerson. "None of them could do it properly, and ultimately Neelix showed Tuvok that he could do it, implying that he had learned it from Maquis, so Tuvok had gotten through to them. It was a cute moment and, unfortunately, it didn't make it into the cut."

Jeri Taylor found the episode appealing because it allowed the Tuvok character to stumble a bit. "The story put him in a place where he could really get fractured," she says, "and that was a lot of fun. I think, again, it was allowing Tuvok to make mistakes and realize that he couldn't handle this group of unruly Maquis the way he had handled Starfleet Academy cadets. He had to learn to grow and adjust and make some movement. I think to do that for a character is wonderful."

••••
CHAPTER TWELVE

Voyager: Season Two

As it entered its second season, *Star Trek: Voyager* had proven that even without the *Enterprise, Star Trek* could continue to boldly go where no one had gone before. As the flagship of the United Paramount Network, the series, while not reaching the stellar highs of *The Next Generation*'s ratings, continued to perform respectably in the weekly Nielsen numbers.

There's no denying that the second season received a mixed reaction from fans and critics alike. Indeed, there are even staff members who aren't entirely pleased with the direction the show traveled during its sophomore year.

While feeling positive about many of the stories they developed, Jeri Taylor admits, "I sense that we have lost something that we started out with. We started with a premise that promised to take us back a little closer in spirit to the original series, the idea that we were out where people had not been before, that there were new and glorious adventures to be had, that we had a crew of very interesting people mixed together and finding out about them would be as much fun as their adventures with aliens. I think for whatever reason we've lost a spirit of fun; our people have begun taking themselves *very* seriously. The first two *Enterprise*s were places where people wanted to be. They kind of said 'Yeah, it would be great to be along with these people.' I'm not so sure that the *[Voyager]* ride is that much fun anymore. They're a real good crew, they do things well, but I don't think they've jelled as a family. I don't think we are getting into those kind of interpersonal relationships that would happen with people in this situation. They don't laugh together; they don't joke together. They don't have fun. All they do is have these serious, dire adventures. I think the story-telling was a little dour in many instances. Gene's original vision of the twenty-fourth century was that it was a good place to be, that mankind had evolved to this higher

level. People cared about each other; they were better, more decent people than we are now. I'm not sure that we're living up to that. I think our people may bicker more than I'm comfortable with. I also want to leave Kazon space behind. I think that by repeating the same aliens over and over and over again, we're creating this curious impression that we're stuck and going in circles.

"In any case," she offers sincerely, "we've given the show's problems a lot of thought and we'll be making changes in year three."

Michael Piller, in an exclusive, no-holds-barred interview with journalist Kevin Stevens for *Sci-Fi Universe* magazine, seemed considerably more enthusiastic. "As it turned out, for me this was one of the most rewarding creative years of my professional experience," said Piller. "From my perspective, I remembered this season why I fell in love with the franchise in the first place. I remembered what made me so happy writing *Star Trek:* the ability to write about the human condition, to write television that is making a difference, that really has something to say and gives people something to talk about at breakfast the next morning. I rediscovered a passion that I haven't had for a while, so for me it started from a beginning of grim depression to feeling like, 'Wow, we did it again. There is life left yet in the franchise.' "

One problem certainly was that too many episodes seemed to rely on the crew's needing to stop at a planet, being forced to crash-land or even land the ship because of some weird atmospheric problem. In addition, the crew often seemed to become involved with situations on alien worlds in order to propel the plot rather than service story logic. In one episode, Neelix comments, "You don't have to impress me with your technobabble." It's a sentiment shared by many viewers.

But for all the problems, *Voyager* also managed to entertain, enlighten and even educate over the course of its twenty-six second-season episodes, providing some memorably moving character drama and pathos in episodes like "Innocence," "Resolutions" and "Lifesigns," while supplying ample doses of action and space opera in shows like "Maneuvers," "Basics" and "Investigations." And

the characters the writers had bemoaned as being underserviced a season earlier finally got their due, with Tom Paris featured in a nearly season-long arc involving possible transgressions in his loyalty, and Chakotay at center stage in such shows as "Initiations" and "Tattoo," which delved into his background and Indian heritage.

"To me, we took what looked to be, in my opinion, the weakest start to any *Star Trek* season that I have been involved with and turned it into the best, or certainly the best season of quality story-telling, that I have been involved with," Piller added in his *Sci-Fi Universe* interview.

Piller, who rejoined the staff on a full-time basis after being sidelined by his experience creating a short-lived TV Western, *Legend,* for UPN, was virtually absent from the second half of *Voyager*'s first season. "I fully expected that Michael would not come back this last year, and in fact he came very close to not coming back," says Taylor. "I had known for a long time that he wants to go into development and was really burned out on *Star Trek* and ready to make a shift in his career, so I was really thinking along those lines all along."

Then *Legend* was canceled by UPN, and Piller had a decision to make. "In June of ninety-five, he came to me and said he had decided to stay with it for one more year, and I was completely taken aback but delighted," says Taylor. "Michael is a wonderful writer and has a great vision, and he takes a huge burden off. Having him here as a full-time writing entity is the best of all worlds."

"When we created *Voyager*, I really wanted the freedom to be able to go off and do other things," recalled Piller. "When I left to do *Legend,* I continued to be in the story breaks. Giving notes on all stories. Killed a few. And I went over scripts and gave copious notes. I did all the things executive producers do except write. Jeri really carried the ball, and that's the fundamental reason I insisted we bring Jeri into our group [in creating the show]. She did exactly what I hoped would happen and is doing a wonderful job. I'm still very passionate about *Voyager*. And passion comes from character for me, and if you fall in love with your characters. The reason *Legend* had a particular place in

••••

my heart is because it came out of my mind and it wasn't a derivative of Gene Roddenberry.

"I have never had a better job of working with better people than I have on *Star Trek*. The only problem for me is to stay fresh. And by doing *Legend* I was able to really flex muscles and do things that I hadn't been able to do in seven years. And that makes my life exciting creatively. It was also agonizing just trying to find the hours in the day to do justice to the show. Ira [Behr] was doing a terrific job on *Deep Space Nine*, so I didn't spend much time with them. At the beginning of the first year of *Voyager,* I told Jeri, 'The last couple of years were too easy for me. I'm going to see how far I can push myself this year.' And I told her all the things I was doing. I was thinking back to the third season of [*TNG*] — and there was no year that was worse in my life, because it was constantly a minute-to-minute crisis. And to write your way out of that, you sort of said to yourself nothing can harm you. And then we built on that, but the more success and the more talented people you develop, the easier it became for me.

"So I wanted to push myself again and I pushed myself a little too far. Actually, what was meant to happen was *Legend* was supposed to be next year in

my mind, and it got picked up a little too quickly since they wanted it on in January, the same time *Voyager* debuted. But I knew that was asking for a death wish, so [actor] Richard Dean [Anderson] and I insisted it debut in April, and I was able to spend the first half of the season dedicated almost exclusively to *Legend.*"

When *Legend* was canceled despite Piller's best efforts to prevail on the network to renew the critically acclaimed but low-rated series, he decided to go back to the future. Reflecting in *Sci-Fi Universe* on his return to *Voyager,* Piller noted, "At the beginning of the season, it was quite clear that *Legend* wasn't coming back, and I had to make a decision about what my involvement was going to be on *Voyager.* I was obviously kind of depressed about the failure of *Legend* and I had talked to myself about moving on from *Star Trek* for a couple years, so it was not easy to come back. But at the same time, I felt I owed this show something. I had spent the first ten episodes of the first season heavily involved and then had to move into *Legend* almost full-time. I gave the last half of the first season of *Voyager* extremely limited attention. I was involved in the story breaks and I was involved in giving notes, but I did no writing. I realized that I had an obligation.

"I had left them terribly shorthanded, and the results of that were very clear to me when I took a hard look at the beginning of the [second] season. We had almost no development. It reminded me a great deal, the season as a whole, of the third season of *Next Generation*. This staff looked at our development at the beginning of the season, and we had nothing on it, and we were about to start production. I had taken a long vacation to think things out after *Legend* went down. I needed the time. I was just exhausted. And I came back and looked at the development board and said, 'We have a real problem here,' and I basically said, 'I'm just going to roll my sleeves up and throw myself body and soul into this season of *Voyager,* because it really needs me.'

"Perhaps I needed it as well."

But with the second season over, Piller has finally decided to do what he had long thought about, leave the series permanently. "For me, it's a great time to go — when you're feeling completely ful-

filled by your own creative endeavors. So I have decided to move on this season, into a development deal with Paramount. I will continue as a consultant, but that means they don't have to listen to me anymore."

In reflecting on the season, Piller admitted that "there are a lot of people who don't consider a lot of these stories [this season] science fiction. But certainly you can make a case that facing the Kazon in battle is futurist storytelling. My definition of science fiction states that the stories should be about something. If I asked you what a story is about — and I'm not talking the plot, I'm talking the theme — and you can't tell me what it's really about, it has failed on a fundamental level, probably on a fundamental level for storytelling in any medium, but particularly so in the *Star Trek* genre.

"I think what makes *Star Trek* is that it's always trying to be about something. I like metaphysical stories a lot, and I like them as part of a mix, but this franchise has gotten very metaphysical over the last seven years, and sometimes I thought we were almost getting weird for the sake of weird, complex for the sake of complex, and I really wanted there to be a fundamental narrative line that the audience can identify with and understand and empathize with."

One of the problems was that the new season of *Voyager* had been saddled with the leftovers from the previous year, which the network had held back to launch the second season in August to get the jump on the other networks. Unfortunately, those shows were some of the weaker installments filmed. "What I found when I came back were the first shows that we were forced to begin this season with, left over from last season, when we were tired and our budgets were empty. I had problems with them," Piller explained. "They all had real good premises, but I had a serious problem. I thought they were all average episodes. You don't want to start the season out with average episodes. Even the episode with Amelia Earhart ["The 37's"], while it had a wonderful premise, I just felt that it never added up to anything after the first one or two acts. I just never felt a payoff to it.

"So you had four shows that the network had committed to put on the air

TV GUIDE

Feb 17-23   99¢

SEINFELD's JULIA LOUIS-DREYFUS Sexy. Funny. Revealing.

A *Voyager* First

When **Star Trek** Worlds Collide

John de Lancie and Kate Mulgrew

It's a cosmic war of wills as *Next Generation's* Q squares off with Captain Janeway

BY MICHAEL LOGAN

• • • •

first because they wanted to start the season early. But then I read the first three scripts, and they were problematic as well," added Piller. "These were three additional shows that were not working very well, and I said to myself, 'We have seven shows here that are going to start the season off, and I don't have a lot of faith in any of them. So I came back, and we started getting together as a staff. Rick [Berman] came in with us, and we had some emergency development meetings, daylong things, something we hadn't had to do since the third season of Next Generation. We just started scrambling to come up with the most story ideas we could."

One thing Piller had realized during his tenure on Legend was that the television environment had changed dramatically since he had joined the staff of The Next Generation nearly ten years before. "When I went out into the cold, real world with Legend and saw what was going on, I found the network was constantly on my case. I wasn't doing anything different than I had been doing on Star Trek, but they were on my case to write shorter scenes and pick up the pace of the scripts. I used to write three- and four-page comedy scenes on Legend that I thought were great, and they'd say, 'We don't want three- and four-page comedy scenes. Get to the murder!' They'd say, 'Make it more like ER, Mike.'

"I took a look in a cold, analytical way at the television scene, and frankly it has changed remarkably in seven years," said Piller. "ER, Law & Order, NYPD Blue and other hour shows tell stories in very different ways than we do. I realized that some of these television shows were writing twenty-second scenes, and it was less a combination of traditional three- or four-page character scenes and more like a scrapbook, telling stories with a mosaic of images. So I came back and I looked at those four shows of ours, and I read the three other scripts that were completed and I said, 'This is just not nineties television.' I came in and sat down with the group and I said, 'Guys, I don't think we can get away with this anymore. The pace of these shows is languid. Yes, we have a loyal audience, but I think we have to look at ways of telling stories in a much more vigorous, energetic fashion.'

"Well, people started looking at each other, like, 'Wow, he's just going to change Star Trek. He's going to come in here and he's going to change it completely.'

"It was an interesting place I found myself, because I'd been spoiled by the luxury of Star Trek. Rick, Jeri and I would always talk in terms of next year, should we make a three-year deal with this guy or something, and most people in this business talk about the next set of ratings."

With the blessing of Jeri Taylor and Rick Berman, Piller was able to implement many of the changes he envisioned, experimenting more dramatically with the show's formula than any previous Trek had. Among the ideas Piller introduced to the show were a season-long arc that involved the Kazon's attempting to seize the Voyager for their own nefarious ends and an espionage story involving a spy aboard the ship who needed to be ferreted out, prompting Tom Paris's increasingly insubordinate behavior toward his commanding officers.

"I didn't want to rely on the accepted methods of storytelling that we've become comfortable with on Star Trek," Piller explained. "I wanted to see if we could extend the craft of storytelling on Star Trek, and I think it's been successful."

That assessment isn't shared, however, by everyone. Among those who felt the plot threads were less effective was Jeri Taylor. "The Kazon was Michael's push," she says. "It was not anything that I thought worked very well, and I can tell you that we are going to be letting go of the Kazon in the future. I don't find them particularly interesting adversaries." Taylor plans to abandon story arcs in the third season and concentrate on the standalone, more anthological stories championed by Brannon Braga.

"I feel that Voyager should be the X-Files of Star Trek," says Braga. "The Delta Quadrant should be the strangest place we've ever seen. Instead, the aliens look a little too familiar, and we're not delivering enough high-concept science fiction. Don't get me wrong: We've had many excellent episodes, but I want to do more brain-twisting, challenging stories. We just want to make sure we keep telling the best science-fiction stories we can.

That's the Star Trek tradition, and that's what Star Trek fans have come to expect. I don't mean to sound negative. I'm very proud of the show. We all are, but when you're a writer working on a franchise that's done over three hundred episodes, you have to give your stories a great deal of scrutiny to keep it fresh."

"I don't know in retrospect if it [the introduction of story arcs] was a good idea or not. I did not want us to be guilty of simply doing stories the same old way because that's the way it's always been done," admits Taylor. "A lot of series now are having story lines that thread through multiple episodes, and we just thought we'd give it a try, never having done it on Star Trek. There are some ways in which I think it was successful and other ways in which I don't. I think there were some episodes this year that might have been little classics but that will be forever tainted by a strange couple of scenes that will have no meaning in the future. People will say, 'What's that doing in there?' "

Aside from the Kazon, however, recurring villains will continue to appear. The Vidiians, who were also introduced the first season and exploited in several episodes in the second, proved more palatable to many of the show's writers, including Taylor. "We felt with the Kazon we needed to address the tenor of our times and what it was happening in our cities and recognizing a source of danger and social unrest," she says. "We wanted to do that metaphorically, but it was sort of a difficult kind of structure. The Vidiians are a creepy group of people, however, that go around stealing body organs because they have been decimated by a flesh-eating virus. In order to survive, they have become these harvesters of body parts, and working with [makeup supervisor] Michael Westmore, we made sure they looked different from what we had seen on Star Trek and Deep Space Nine before."

Among those glad to see the Kazon gone is Tim Russ. "The only thing about it is that we are presumably in motion toward home, and I don't know what the Kazon's realm covers," says the actor. "You know, how expansive is it? They can only be with us for so long, you know, from what I can gather, unless they reestablish. They are nomadic. They have to be nomadic to the point where they're always roaming and that you could stretch out for a while, but you can't stretch out a territorial dispute, because we're no longer in the territory. We're out of the range of a lot of things because we were on the move, and that's something the writers just built right flat into the story. Three years from now you can't be talking about the Kazon."

Proving a valuable addition to the show in its second year was Lisa Klink, a writing intern who sold a story to *Deep Space Nine*, "Hippocratic Oath," and then was invited to join the writing staff of *Voyager*, contributing some of the season's best episodes. And for the show's third year, former *Next Generation* staffer Joe Menosky will join Ken Biller, Braga, Tay-lor and Klink. "He is a wonderful writer and a creative person and a lovely human being," says Taylor. "If we have him, I think we will be very well staffed with five people."

For his part, Michael Piller believes that *Voyager* will be well served by the staff he leaves behind now. "I take great pride in the growth that the staff has shown," he stated. "My challenge to the staff has been, from the beginning of the season, that we get back to the basics. The title of the cliff-hanger I wrote, my final episode for the show, is 'Basics.' The title was not chosen casually. Basics. It's my last will and testament. I'm going on with my career. As far as I'm concerned, the *Star Trek* experience has been wonderful. I would never have gotten the opportunity to do *Legend* without it and I'm in a wonderful place."

With Piller gone, does Taylor plan to be the steward of further *Star Trek* series? "I can't see myself doing it, because I plan to retire long, long before that. My husband has retired, and we have bought a home in Northern California. He is in the process of remodeling it now, and by the time he finishes that, which will be some years to come, I would like to go and join him there. So I think that this will be my last involvement."

Even without two of the most prominent great birds of *Star Trek*'s nineties galaxy, at this point there can be little doubt that the science-fiction franchise to end all franchises will continue to live long and prosper.

• • • •

CHAPTER THIRTEEN

Voyager: Season Two Episode Guide

"The 37's"

"Initiations"

"Projections"

"Elogium"

"Non Sequitur"

"Twisted"

"Parturition"

"Persistence of Vision"

"Tattoo"

"Cold Fire"

"Maneuvers"

"Resistance"

"Prototype"

"Alliances"

"Threshold"

"Meld"

"Dreadnought"

"Death Wish"

"Lifesigns"

"Investigations"

"Deadlock"

"Innocence"

"The Thaw"

"Tuvix"

"Resolutions"

"Basics, Part I"

• • • •

Episode #16
"The 37's"
Original Airdate: 8/28/95
Written by Jeri Taylor and Brannon Braga
Directed by James L. Conway
Guest Starring: Sharon Lawrence (Amelia Earhart), David Graf (Fred Noonan), James Saito (Japanese Soldier), Mel Winkler (Jack Hayes), John Rubinstein (John Evansville)

The *Voyager* encounters an ancient Earth truck floating in space. When they beam it aboard and examine its fuel, which is perfectly preserved, this bizarre discovery leads them to a planet where they find several human bodies preserved in perfect cryo-stasis. Among those freed from their incarceration is Amelia Earhart, who, it is learned, was abducted in 1937 from Earth along with several other people, including a Japanese soldier, by extraterrestrials. On this same planet exists a utopian human civilization that Janeway fears may lead many of her crew members to abandon their duty and remain behind.

••••

The episode was actually intended as the finale for the first season until UPN held back the final four episodes of the show to launch the second season earlier than other networks would unveil their programming.

"I think it worked better as a season ender than as an opener, but so be it," says Jeri Taylor. "It was a franchise-oriented show, and having the season close with that sort of brave feeling that we've banded together, we're not going to stay on some planet, we're committed to each other and let's head home would have been a nice way to conclude the first season."

"Amelia Earhart being the victim of an alien abduction along with several other people is major hokey," says Michael Piller. "It's very old *Star Trek*. But we did get to land the ship, and that's pretty amazing."

"I'd like to see more of what this episode was like," says Tim Russ. "More wild and fantastic discoveries and things. I don't mean just spatial anomalies. I mean cultures and races and beings and ideas that are a challenge, which has always been the case for the science-fiction fanatic. I really like that kind of thing. Stories and things that are bizarre and unusual, things that you've never seen before or never thought about before in certain terms."

Opines Brannon Braga, "I think it's just the kind of show we should be doing: far-out, high-concept shows. It was a hit-and-miss kind of episode. There was some fun stuff, but in the end it really wasn't about much. I thought it was fun. I really enjoyed the meeting of Amelia Earhart and Janeway, the first woman of flight and the ultimate woman of flight. There was some very cool stuff in there. I think where we got into trouble was with the humans who had evolved differently and the big cities that we never see. That's where you groan. Up until that point, I thought it was intriguing."

NYPD Blue's Sharon Lawrence, who guest starred as Earhart, was thrilled to have the opportunity to play the famous aviatrix. "It was just a great experience," she comments. "I've always been fascinated by Amelia Earhart and to get the chance to play this kind of character is something I just couldn't pass up."

Episode #17
"Initiations"
Original Airdate: 9/4/95
Written by Kenneth Biller
Directed by Winrich Kolbe
Guest Starring: Aron Eisenberg (Kar), Patrick Kilpatrick (Razik), Tim de Zarn (Haliz)

Chakotay borrows a shuttlecraft to perform the Pakra, a solitary Indian ritual to commemorate his father's death. He inadvertently drifts into Kazon-Ogla territory and is attacked by a young Ogla warrior, Kar, whose ship he disables and whom he transports aboard his shuttlecraft. When the two are seized by the Kazon, Chakotay is taken prisoner and Kar is disowned by the Kazon for failing in his mission. Meanwhile, the *Voyager* goes in search of Chakotay, who escapes only to crash-land on a Kazon staging planet with Kar still intent on killing him.

••••

"I thought it was reasonably successful," says Jeri Taylor of the episode. "We gave ourselves a very difficult task by writing a part for a fourteen-year-old young man. We ended up casting Aron Eisenberg, who plays Nog on *Deep Space Nine*, and more people were aware of that than I would have thought. He didn't look anything the same, but he has a very distinctive voice. It broke the suspension of disbelief and made people say not, 'Oh, there's a young man in pain,' but, 'Oh, it's Nog from *Deep Space Nine*.' As soon as the mind is doing that, it's not involved in the story. Aron is a wonderful actor, and we cast him because the boys that we read were simply not able to bring to it the richness and the depth that we wanted. We got the good actor, but we got a recognizable one."

Episode #18
"Projections"
Original Airdate: 9/11/95
Written by Brannon Braga
Directed by Jonathan Frakes
Guest Starring: Dwight Schultz (Lieutenant Barclay)

The doctor discovers that *Voyager* has been attacked by the Kazon and that most of the crew has abandoned ship. He learns from a holographic Lieutenant Barclay (from *TNG*) that he is actually Dr. Lewis Zimmerman, the holoengineer who created his programming, and that unless he destroys the *Voyager,* he will die and be unable to leave his holodeck illusion.

••••

Says Michael Piller, "This is a wonderful show. He basically finds himself trying to find out what reality is. Is he really a hologram or is he the only real person on board? It's a fascinating episode."

"I'm very proud of that one," offers Brannon Braga. "I just wanted to do a doctor show, and basically a one-liner just popped into my head one day: What if the doctor discovers that *Voyager* is a hologram and he is real? Then I got into the argument 'I think, therefore I am'; what does being real mean? I just thought it was an opportunity to do a real mind-bending kind of story. Then we came up with the idea of putting Geordi LaForge in there, but then I thought it would be much more fun to have Barclay and the doctor, and those two were so good together they should have a spin-off series."

Although the doctor continues to remain nameless, the naming of his creator, Dr. Zimmerman, finally realized the dream to use production designer Herman Zimmerman's name as inspiration. "I

••••

think Paramount has been waiting for the right licensing agreement to be struck," actor Robert Picardo says of the doctor's name. "I believe they've finally decided my name will be Dr. Scholl. The other names that were considered and rejected were Dr. Pepper, Dr. Ruth and Dr. Kevorkian. I think the whole notion of an indecisive computer program is funny for the producers, and I think I will continue to be named by various beautiful women guest stars, and then when they're out of my life, I'll simply change my name to the one that the next beautiful woman guest star chooses, and that kind of works for me."

Of course, leaving the character nameless creates yet one other piece of *Trek* lore that can continue to be addressed. "I think that some of the most interesting things about the character are his limitations, and if we solve them all too quickly, well, then I'll have nothing left to do," muses Picardo.

Of Picardo's remarkable performance as the doctor, Piller comments, "I never had a doubt in my mind that the doctor would be developed into the most popular character. And I knew that because I was having a hard time communicating what I had in my mind to people, I really had to write the doctor's voice for about five episodes before people started catching on. The character of the doctor is a servant, but in a defensive way which shows vulnerability. It's very hard to communicate that, and there must have been a hundred actors who came in the room who couldn't figure out what to do. I knew it would be hard. You have a character who is not human, who has basically been forced into existence and he's just trying to adjust to a new kind of life. He's self-aware, he's definitely got an inferiority complex, and so he's trying to measure himself as to where he is going to fit into this world.

"Those are the qualities that a character like Data had, who looks on the human race and gives us a mirror image of ourselves through an objective, nonhuman point of view. To be able to come up with another one of those characters and do it in a fresh way is quite an achievement."

Jeri Taylor shares Piller's enthusiasm for both the performance and the character. "We wanted the kind of brusque curmudgeonly attitude from him that has to be grounded in truth, in something real. Why is he like that? How would he behave in a given situation? What would be the response of this person to this intrusion or this problem? Then, once we have that, how would he express it? So it's more a fundamental problem than just dialogue, and we're still kind of working our way through it. We're continuing a very nice arc with him in which he begins to think of himself not as just the emergency medical hologram, the E.R. doctor who comes in, patches and leaves, which is how he arrived, but it's made clear to him that he's a member of the crew. He has to deal with people on a continuing basis and he's the only doctor there is. He can't just patch and go. He's having to do things that he never contemplated doing and he begins to have a sense that, you know, by God, he deserves a little more respect than he's been getting; so that whole thing is he never had a name and then eventually he says, 'Damn it, you know, I deserve a name.' So it's proving fascinating but taking a lot of care in establishing."

Episode #19
"Elogium"
Original Airdate: 9/18/95
Teleplay by Kenneth Biller and Jeri Taylor
Story by Jimmy Diggs and Steve J. Kay
Directed by Winrich Kolbe
Guest Starring: Nancy Hower (Ensign Clarke), Gary O'Brien (Crew Member), Terry Correll (Crew Member)

Strange alien life-forms attach themselves to the starship and create an electrophoretic field that increases Kes's metabolic activity and accelerates her reproductive process, causing her to enter the elogium, the time of life when Ocampa become fertile. Kes's dilemma arises because Ocampa can only experience the elogium once, and so she must decide with Neelix whether or not to go ahead and have a child.

••••

"This episode dealt with puberty," says Tim Russ, "and that reflects a nice range in stories. I'd like to see more challenges to our concepts and ideas and attitudes and traditions, as they've done

Although you won't recognize it from this photo, Jennifer Lien portrays the alien Kes (copyright © 1995 by Albert Ortega).

with a couple of shows. 'Emanations' was one of them; the other is 'Elogium.' All this stuff is dealing with things that people go through and that is the essence of what Roddenberry was putting together in having the science fiction of this show capture or deal with questioning our values and our concepts and what our traditions should be. That, I think, is the most important part of *Star Trek.*"

If nothing else, "Elogium" finally let viewers know that Neelix and Kes weren't sharing quarters. The two lovebirds may have been inseparable, but when it came time to turn off the lights, they did it in separate bedrooms. "Here's our thinking on that," says Jeri Taylor of the *Trek* equivalent of the Hays Code. "Yes, they are a couple. They are devoted and committed to one another. It is probably sexual, although that's not something that we really want to emphasize. A great deal of our audience is quite young and watches this show with families, and there are some questions which we don't think should be asked. Kids shouldn't be turning to Mommy and Daddy and asking, 'What's that?' or 'What does that mean? Are they married?' I just think we have a responsibility. We made a decision not to have them already married. Although that's a particularly earthbound custom that may not exist elsewhere in the galaxy, there may be the occasion to do some kind of ritual which would cement them and move them in together. But this is the nineties. It's an era where we think that sexual responsibility is a much better message, and we didn't want to be in a position of saying it's fine for them to live together and do whatever they want and not be married. Our audience is still an Earth audience, and a lot of people have values that are very strongly against that."

A far cry from the original *Star Trek,* in which Kirk was bedding down a voluptuous interstellar vixen on a weekly basis. "In the sixties, *Star Trek* was a much racier sort of show," admits Taylor. "Gene [Roddenberry] felt very strongly that sexual freedom was important. In the nineties, we think that sexual responsibility is a better message. If we're going to err on one side or the other, I would frankly rather it be on the side of responsibility, and be too cautious rather than too bold."

Comments Michael Piller, "Neelix had the best part of all in the pilot, and that's why I think people tried to make him the new Spock, but the bottom line is that he and Kes were always meant to be a couple and they were supposed to have, for the first time, a romance aboard a ship. To see what life is like for somebody who is involved with a relationship on a spaceship is interesting. In a sense, Neelix is sort of the flip side of Quark. You know, he's helpful, but he's got information about the terrain we're in and people come to his restaurant to chat with him about things. But I think we could definitely develop Neelix more."

Taylor is quick to draw a distinction between the wacky Talaxian and Quark, the feckless Ferengi with whom he is often compared. "They're very different, and in the same way we don't want the doctor to be Data, we don't want Neelix to be Quark. Neelix is not a con man. Neelix is grasping and inquisitive. Neelix is an extremely bright person and he is a survivor who has been forced into reduced circumstances at times in his life just to make it. But he has always made it, and his guiding kind of motivation now is to be helpful to people, and he genuinely wants to prove that he is worth being on this wonderful ship, where he's now living

in luxury more than he could ever have dreamed with the woman that he absolutely adores. So it is a golden gift, and he is really in there pitching with all hands to justify himself and to make himself seem worthy of all of this. So it's a very, very different coloration from Quark."

Episode #20
"Non Sequitur"
Original Airdate: 9/25/95
Written by Brannon Braga
Directed by David Livingston
Guest Starring: Louis Giambalvo (Cosimo), Jennifer Gatti (Libby), Jack Shearer (Admiral Strickler), Mark Kiely (Lieutenant Lasca)

Harry Kim is shocked to awaken on Earth in twenty-fourth-century San Francisco, where he works as a design specialist in Starfleet Engineering. Reunited with his fiancée, Libby, he accesses his service records and learns that he was never a crew member aboard the *Voyager.* Rejecting the desire to stay, Kim is approached by Cosimo, an alien being who takes the shape of a local store owner and explains that a temporal anomaly in the space continuum has led him here. If Kim doesn't set things right, Tom Paris will be condemned to life as a convicted traitor who lives as a paranoid, paroled drunk in Marseilles. Unfortunately, this leads Starfleet to believe Kim may actually be a spy for the Maquis.

••••

"I felt that this was a great premise that didn't live up to its potential," Michael Piller told *Sci-Fi Universe.* "I felt productionwise it was quite good, and I felt there were some good scenes in it. I had always envisioned a Hitchcockian, *Vertigo* type of tension in this show that I don't think we ever achieved. There were long, languid scenes that cut the tension, and I felt the resolution was too easy. I didn't know personally how to recommend a solution, but having the alien sit down and say basically everything you needed to know about this show and more in one scene, and here's what you do to get out, didn't work. It just felt like we didn't earn our way out of it."

Brannon Braga admits he was disappointed with the episode. "If you're going to do alternate reality, make sure it's

just a very good story, and this one just didn't turn out very well. I didn't think the chemistry between Kim and his girlfriend was very good. There's always some cool stuff, but it didn't work as an episode. I had actually written Counselor Troi into a big scene where Kim is being interrogated. It's the admiral now, but it was Troi working for Starfleet, where she really grills Kim. But we couldn't work it out with Marina [Sirtis], so I rewrote it."

The episode guest starred Jennifer Gatti as Libby, Kim's fiancée. Gatti had previously played a Klingon, Ba'El, in the two-part *Next Generation* episode "Birthright." Gatti admits that both she and Garrett Wang had concerns about the character's desire to find a way back when he was clearly so homesick on *Voyager.* "Garrett and I had a lot of discussions about that, actually," says the actress. "I guess it's because Paris's life had been affected by whatever it was that happened. Frankly, I still don't know what happened, but he wouldn't be able to live with the guilt. And I think that he has a certain confidence that they are going to get home."

That wasn't the only aspect of the episode that confused Gatti. "Actually, I can't figure out: Is Libby still waiting for him, or, if there are two Libbys, is one of them now wondering where he went while the other one believes he's on *Voyager*? That episode fascinates me because I still think about it and I'm not sure what happened. I don't think it was another reality. I think it was the present. He changed the past and he changed the future in terms of the present. When he went to San Francisco, he completely changed everything that happened in the present. I'm figuring this out as I talk to you. So I guess Libby went back to believing that Harry was on *Voyager.* Garrett and I talked about how to bring Libby back, and the only thing we could think of is a holodeck fantasy. When he's lonely, he goes and talks to Libby."

Adds Gatti, "The interesting thing about *Star Trek* is that I went in and did *Next Generation,* and then they were casting *Voyager* and I went in to read for the part of Kes, and it came down to me and Jennifer [Lien], and she got the role, but they knew me and they knew my work. When the part of Libby came up, they still made me work for it. I went in about four times. I read for the same people four times. They're very particular about what they want. They're very thorough."

Gatti can't help but laugh, though, that she seems to have become a *Star Trek* symbol, since in both of her episodes she needed to perform scantily clad. "I always seem to have my clothes off." She laughs. "I guess now I'm a *Star Trek* babe, huh? Ba'El was kind of a Klingon babe. Actually, when I got the part and they were shaping the forehead and the nose, they told me they were very particular, because Ba'El was the first beautiful Klingon woman. When I did the bathing scene [in "Birthright"] I was pretty much naked except for the paint and the hair. My first day on the set I had to go on in with pasties and a G-string and bathe in the water. I was the first naked Klingon girl — and they couldn't show too much, because no one's quite sure what a Klingon looks like naked, technically.

"Then I get Libby and I realized: I'm never dressed till the very end. I'm in a pajama top and I'm in a towel, and I'm like, 'There's a pattern going on here.' I have to feel a little complimented, after all, because apparently somebody likes me without my clothes on."

Garrett Wang, like his on-screen alter ego, is one of the show's most enthusiastic cast members, although he'd still like to see his character more involved on a weekly basis. "I think Harry Kim needs to be fleshed out more," he says. "There needs to be some more color with the characters. Some more background stuff touched upon which will be. I've talked to the writers about that. In 'Non Sequitur' he gets some more color and more confidence, which is great. Obviously, as the youngest, he's going to be the one who they're going to point to in terms of getting caught or captured or mistakes happening. It's easier to write Kim as the person who initiates that as opposed to somebody like the captain having all the mistakes, but I like to see the character develop more experience and develop into a person who has background and beliefs. I'd also like to see more of Kim's cynical sense of humor come through, which he had in the pilot. Especially in the scene with B'Elanna in the prison cell; she

asks if I was involved in capturing her, and I say, 'Yeah, I got a phaser right here in my hospital gown.' That kind of sarcasm adds more color."

Episode #21
"Twisted"
Original Airdate: 10/2/95
Teleplay by Kenneth Biller
Story by Arnold Rudnick and Rick Hosek
Directed by Kim Friedman
Guest Starring: Judy Geeson (Sandrine), Larry Hankin (Gaunt Gary), Tom Virtue (Baxter), Terry Correll (The Crewman)

A spatial distortion results in the transformation of the structural layout of *Voyager.* As the ship is compressed and twisted, the crew must work frantically to stop it before the ship is destroyed. During their attempts to reverse the distortion, Janeway is disabled by the strange force, Neelix is trapped and the rest of the crew is isolated in the labyrinthine maze of the ever-changing ship. With time running out, the remaining officers hole up in the holodeck bar as the ship begins to close in on them.

•• • •

"Twisted" was the last of the four "holdover" shows that had originally been filmed for the first season. Considered the worst of the four episodes, "Twisted" was held back, airing after "Non Sequitur," a second-season episode.

In the *Sci-Fi Universe* interview, Michael Piller admitted he was anxious to move the season in a new direction after exhausting the string of middling first-season episodes. Piller felt that "Twisted" in particular did some character damage that he would attempt to repair in the next episode, "Parturition." "After 'Twisted,' I was terribly concerned about Neelix. I was afraid we were going to destroy this character if we made him the buffoon of the ship. If all he is is comic relief, we're in trouble. The jealousy he was showing toward Kes was becoming irritating, so we wanted to put that to bed quickly."

In the episode we also see a more understanding side of Tuvok when he bends the rules to allow Harry Kim to go to Kes's birthday party in the holodeck despite being on his duty shift. "I think it's going to be inevitable that [Tuvok is] going to develop more relationships with the

Tim Russ (Tuvok) strikes a decidedly Vulcan pose (copyright © 1995 by Albert Ortega).

crew," offers Tim Russ. "Apart from the captain, whom he already has a relationship with, you're going to see more relationships developed because he's isolated out there with everyone else. It's just like being in the trenches of war; it does draw people together. It's much stronger as opposed to when you're in Federation space and basically just doing a job. Now you've got more than a job; there's more at stake. You know every day could be your last day; you've got nobody to help you out there. So it's much more of a bond that's got to be created. You're forced into that, and I think what you're going to see is [that] his understanding of the way human beings are is going to be more profound as well as his effort to be more understanding. He'll make gestures to try and communicate, like when he lets Kim go to the birthday party by telling him, 'Well, I imagine you could inspect the conduits in the holodeck,' without saying 'You're allowed to go.' We know what he means, and that's the kind of thing that I'm talking about. He understands that this means a great deal to this person, even though Tuvok could care less about it. But he understands that this is something important to Kim and he's trying to communicate and work with them on a level other than that of being military."

•• • •

157

Roxann Biggs-Dawson has enjoyed playing a Klingon with a divided emotional nature, which has presented some interesting interpersonal dynamics with the logical Tuvok. "In 'Twisted,' she's really at odds with Tuvok and his rational ways of thinking. It's a good challenge for her," she says.

Unfortunately, one problem it seems the cast will always have is with the ever-present technobabble. "I know my constraints now," says Garrett Wang. "I know that I have to really bear down and close everything off and just focus on what I'm trying to say. If you try to memorize just by rote, it gets a little tough. You have to kind of realize what is being said. What is the message, what is your objective in that scene or that dialogue?"

Episode #22
"Parturition"
Original Airdate: 10/9/95
Written by Tom Szollosi
Directed by Jonathan Frakes

Tom Paris begins to develop an interest in Kes, which stirs violent jealousy in Neelix, who instigates a mess-hall fight with the cocky pilot. Afterward, Captain Janeway sends the two on a shuttle mission to a planet where they hope to find food supplies for the ship. When the ship is forced down in a storm onto the surface of the treacherous planet, they crash-land and take shelter in a cave, where they find an embryonic pod that produces a baby hatchling. They agree to care for the baby until its parent arrives to take it home.

••••

"I think Kes and Neelix still need to explore some issues of trust," says Jennifer Lien. "I think Neelix's jealousy is getting to be minimal because the character is learning. They've grown in this relationship. When it becomes too obsessive, it becomes scary, and I don't think that's what the character of Neelix is all about."

Directing the episode was Jonathan Frakes, whose directorial work, along with that of his *Next Generation* castmate LeVar Burton, has spanned three *Trek* series: *The Next Generation, Deep Space Nine* and *Voyager*. For the cast of this latest *Trek* incarnation, having experienced helmsmen on board can often be a blessing. "It makes a tremendous difference," says Tim Russ. "Jonathan and LeVar

are much more efficient and more fun to work with. They're easier-going. On one episode, I had three hours of sleep, maybe less, I had a cold that was killing me and it was a heavy dialogue scene, and LeVar was directing and it all came off very nicely, I think, because of the way that LeVar put it together. It wasn't mindless take after take. With some other directors, all they do is look at the monitor to make sure everybody's head is in the right place. They're more concerned with that than they are about what's going on, and, consequently, it gets rather tedious. Whereas LeVar and Jonathan Frakes not only know what it's like from the reaction perspective, but you can't pull anything over on them because not only do they know when something is right, they also know when you didn't get that line right or that you bluffed your way through that thing or whatever. They know that you didn't deliver your line like it's supposed to be delivered and they catch it every time because they've been there.

"They also know *Star Trek*," he continues, "and they know what they're going to use. They know what Rick Berman's going to use, what he's not going to use; they know what's going to get cut and what's not going to be cut. They know that already, so they're not going to shoot all this extra footage they don't need. It's not endless coverage. You'll get the coverage, but you'll hear 'Cut and print,' and those are the words you want to hear, 'Let's print and move on.' They also know it's television and it's going to look a certain way whether you do it in two takes or you do it in twenty."

Ironically, "Parturition" was very similar to the penultimate episode of *Space: Above & Beyond*, the short-lived Fox series. In that show, the landing party discovers alien hatchlings on a planet and decides to care for them, not realizing they are baby Chigs, the alien race with whom Earth is at war.

Episode #23
"Persistence of Vision"
Original Airdate: 10/16/95
Written by Jeri Taylor
Directed by James L. Conway
Guest Starring: Michael Cumpsty (Lord Burleigh), Carolyn Seymour (Mrs. Templeton), Stan Ivar (Mark), Warren Mun-

son (Admiral Paris), Lindsey Haun (Beatrice), Thomas Alexander Dekker (Henry), Patrick Kerr (The Bothan), Marva Hicks (T'Pel), Kennedy (Crew Member)

As they ready for a first encounter with the Bothan species, a strange psionic field causes the *Voyager* crew members to succumb to a delusional state and brings their most deeply buried thoughts to the surface. During the ordeal, characters in Janeway's Victorian holonovel program become real, and her beloved Mark, the man she left behind on Earth, appears to her. Paris faces off with his disparaging father; Tuvok is reunited with his wife, T'Pel; and Torres is seduced by Chakotay. The ship is effectively disabled, so it's up to an unaffected Kes and the doctor to block the mysterious field.

••••

Says Jeri Taylor, "It was a show that I had wanted to do since last year. I got a great deal of opposition from the studio, in both story and script form. They thought it was a very soft story and they just didn't get it. They want more fights and more aliens. They weren't high on this at all and didn't want it to appear as early in the year as it did. Then it got made and everybody loved it. Then we got all the phone calls that said, 'Wow, that turned out well.'

"I knew it was going to work," adds Taylor. "I may be wrong about this, but it was the first show of the season that got a little buzz coming from the audience."

Originally Taylor had planned to make Janeway's holodeck novels a pioneer adventure, but perhaps because of the easy comparisons that could be made to *Dr. Quinn, Medicine Woman,* she adopted the *Jane Eyre*–tinged story line. "The holonovels are something that she does like I read adventure novels and thrillers — as a stress reliever," says the writer. "So these are like reading in the twenty-fourth century. You go and you actually play one of the characters. So it's the only place where she can forget about being a captain for a couple of hours and get into a completely different situation, where she has a husband and she has children and she lives a life utterly unlike the one that she lives. It's more that kind of motivation than an intellectual curiosity

••••

about a period of history. In my heart I would like to see her sort of finish this novel and start another one next season. Whether that will happen, I cannot say. We may return to a different novel for her, but that was one of those things that we were not getting the feedback from the fans that seemed to justify its continuing. A lot of people had problems with Janeway being in what would be considered a servile position. A lot of people just aren't fans, as I am, of Gothic novels and just sort of didn't get it. I thought it was great fun, but I'm never afraid to cut our losses if something isn't working."

As a result, fans who were following Janeway's Victorian adventure never found out how the story ended. "We wrote a conclusion in which everything got knitted up," says Taylor, "because I thought it was a shame to just leave it." As of yet, however, that ending hasn't been filmed.

In the episode, Janeway is reunited with a man she thinks is her boyfriend, Mark. Originally Taylor had hoped to make Mark Janeway's husband. "It was just something I really felt strongly about and I argued to have them absolutely married," recalls Taylor. "They certainly are a couple that's devoted to each other. It looks like marriage is a dying institution in the twenty-fourth century. It's not a good message. I don't like that. I think that we will struggle with what happens with Janeway, and she will struggle with exactly what she is to do. At the moment, she is determined they're going to get back quickly, and so we're going to go with that kind of inertia for a while. We are really letting the characters develop and seeing where they take us."

Episode #24
"Tattoo"
Original Airdate: 11/6/95
Teleplay by Michael Piller
Story by Larry Brody
Directed by Alexander Singer
Guest Starring: Henry Darrow (Kolopak), Richard Fancy (Alien), Douglas Spain (Young Chakotay), Nancy Hower (Ensign Wildman), Richard Chaves (Chief)

When Chakotay leads an Away Team to drill for minerals on a moon's surface, they accidentally disturb a village and encounter its defensive inhabitants, a group with Indian origins. A regretful Chakotay then experiences flashbacks of himself as a bratty fifteen-year-old who disappoints his father by not embracing the traditions of his tribe. Using advanced technology, the natives disable *Voyager* and the endangered Away Team must transport out, leaving Chakotay alone on the planet after he is hit by a tree. When he's confronted by the aliens, they respond to his familiar tattoo marking and Chakotay recognizes the tones of their language as those of his own people. Applying what he recalls from his father's teachings on their heritage, Chakotay assures the natives of *Voyager's* peaceful intentions and his sympathetic perspective.

Meanwhile, while tending to the pregnant Ensign Wildman, the doctor is challenged by Kes to show more compassion for his patients. So he programs himself with a simulated flu virus to experience the discomforts living beings can feel.

••••

"Up until that point, the shows really weren't about anything," Michael Piller admitted to journalist Kevin Stevens. "Here was an episode that really went back to basics. It was 'Let's try to make this show not just about a man finding Indians in space, let's make it about Chakotay. Let's talk about character. Here's a man who has lost his faith, and he gets it back through this journey. That's a very interesting thing to write."

The teleplay ended up being the first one to receive the Piller imprimatur after the cancellation of *Legend,* when Piller found himself hard at work injecting life into the sputtering second season of shows. "This is the first story that came out of the emergency development meetings that we had," he recalled. "It was a show that had been virtually abandoned from last season, a story that had been pitched and we bought but which didn't turn out right. Nobody could figure out how to make it work, yet I'd always been attracted to the idea of the pitch, which was that Indians have these myths about sky spirits, and a natural extension of that myth was that these could have been travelers from space. For Chakotay to find evidence of these sky spirits seemed to be the beginning of a terrific personal journey.

"I looked at this as an opportu-nity to really delve into his character. I had the idea of doing flashbacks at this development meeting and I said, 'Let me take a crack at it. I think I can do something about his relationship with his tribe and his father and cut back and forth and maybe go back to the original sky spirits,' he said. "This was a beginning for me of rediscovering what was so neat about writing *Star Trek.* Suddenly I was writing a story about a man who is, during the course of investigating a mystery, reconciling his conflicts with his father, learning to embrace his cultural heritage, learning about Indian lore and even anthropology. So many different elements were working together in the script, it was very, very satisfying."

Piller was not without his criticisms of the finished episode, however. "There was a certain intensity, a certain dark, brooding quality that we wanted to get out of Chakotay that I think we didn't get to. The location work was quite disappointing, and I felt that the show was named 'Tattoo,' but you could barely see the tattoos on anybody. But in general I thought it was a show that led the way in terms of being about something."

Episode #25
"Cold Fire"
Original Airdate: 11/13/95
Teleplay by Brannon Braga
Story by Anthony Williams
Directed by Cliff Bole
Guest Starring: Gary Graham (Tanis), Lindsay Ridgeway (Girl), Norman Large (Ocampa Man)

The crew discovers an array identical to the one manned by the Caretaker in the pilot with Ocampa colonists nearby, which they believe can lead them to the Caretaker's mate and, in turn, possibly home. Meanwhile, the Ocampa leader, Tanis, assists Kes in honing her rapidly maturing mental abilities, which Tuvok has been helping her master. As hope builds that the female Caretaker, Suspira, can take them home, they realize that she has a secret agenda to destroy them, believing that the crew of the *Voyager* is responsible for destroying her mate.

••••

"Kes is someone that's sort of emerging and flowering," says Jeri Taylor.

••••

"In a sense, the most interesting thing about her is that she has such a short life span, but what do you do with that? So we also made her this incredibly bright, inquisitive, curious person who was unafraid to stand up and challenge the most sacredly held precepts of her society because she wanted to know more and be more, and she will continue on this quest, and we are gradually endowing her with specific capabilities of the mind, things that her ancestors had and which atrophied because the Ocampa have been taken care of for so long that there was no need for them to do a lot of things and they just kind of withered and became lazy. She wants to get back to what the Ocampa really are, and that will involve some paranormal kinds of sensibilities and telepathic abilities that she's going to be discovering even as the audience is."

Clearly a concern of Michael Piller's was writer Brannon Braga's involvement with the writing of the latest *Trek* feature, *First Contact,* which often took priority over his *Voyager* chores, something that Piller was intent on putting an end to. "I can tell you that we've had long discussions about that, because I was of the opinion, and I was not the only one, that Ron [Moore] and Brannon's involvement in writing the first movie severely hurt the quality of the seventh season of *Next Generation.* And as the creator of *Deep Space Nine* and *Voyager,* I felt that I had to express my own concern that if they were to do this again, they were not to sacrifice any participation in the series, either series, in order to do it. If they wanted to go to the extreme effort and hard work to do it in their spare time, that was their business. But they're not to miss meetings, they're not to miss assignments, they're to hold up their end of the bargain. And they agreed to do that."

Guest star Gary Graham, perhaps best known for his role as Detective Matthew Sikes in the *Alien Nation* TV series and movies, reflects on the episode, "They're *very* tightly wound over there. That's not to say it wasn't a rewarding experience, but it was about as fun as taking a midterm when you really, really have to make a good grade. I'm used to working with the cast and the script and having a lot of open communication, but I wanted to change two words at *Star Trek* and it took thirty minutes to get script approval on that back from the Ivory Tower."

Episode #26
"Maneuvers"
Original Airdate: 11/20/95
Written by Kenneth Biller
Directed by David Livingston
Guest Starring: Martha Hackett (Seska), Anthony DeLongis (Magh Culluh), Terry Lester (Haron), John Gegenhuber (Kelat)

Kazons invade the ship and steal a transporter control module that will enable their leader, Culluh, to master Federation technology. The *Voyager* crew soon learns that the scheme was masterminded by Seska, the Cardassian traitor from last season's "State of Flux." When Janeway insists on retrieving the technology for fear of changing the balance of power in the quadrant, Chakotay sets out alone in a shuttlecraft, disobeying orders, and is captured by the Kazon while the *Voyager* braces for a showdown in space against the massing Kazon fleet.

••••

"This is another one of those shows where I don't think we spent the money to execute the premise well enough," said Michael Piller in *Sci-Fi Universe.* "This particularly was a show in which I was afraid the audience wouldn't have a clue what was going on because they never saw a lot of crucial stuff. *The Enemy Below* sequence in the third act had the potential to be a really terrific sequence, yet optically I felt a little shortchanged by it. Basically, we had to thread a needle without the visual, optical support for that. I just think it was very confusing.

"We had a real opportunity to do some nice work here with Chakotay," Piller added, "and I think if you look at this season, both Chakotay and Tuvok have shown the most growth, with Paris immediately behind. I think that there's a personal drive that Chakotay had in this show that's very dramatic."

Episode #27
"Resistance"
Original Airdate: 11/27/95
Teleplay by Lisa Klink
Story by Kevin Ryan and Michael J. Friedman
Directed by Winrich Kolbe
Guest Starring: Alan Scarfe (Augris), Tom Todoroff (Darod), Glenn Morshower (Guard #1), Joel Grey (Caylem)

Trying to obtain tellurium, which is needed to power the ship's warp engines, Janeway, Tuvok, Torres and Neelix transport to an Alsaurian city that is occupied by the fascist Mokra. During negotiations for the tellurium, Mokra soldiers open fire in the town square and capture Tuvok and Torres. Janeway is helped to safety by Caylem, an eccentric local who believes that she is his long lost daughter. Neelix escapes and tells Chakotay that the Away Team has been incarcerated. While the *Voyager* crew attempts to convince the Mokra that its intentions are peaceful, Janeway, with the aid of Caylem, infiltrates the prison to free Tuvok and Torres.

••••

The episode starred legendary stage actor Joel Grey, who gives a moving performance as Caylem, a man of broken spirit who has lost his wife and daughter to the evil Mokra. Playing the imposing Augris, the Mokra leader, is Alan Scarfe, a *Next Generation* veteran who appeared in several episodes of that series, including "The Defector."

"Getting Janeway into a completely different milieu, where she's not on the bridge, she's not being captain, was all wonderful for the character," says story editor Lisa Klink. "One of the best things you can do for a character is get them out of their normal situation."

Klink, who had just been invited to join the staff after selling "Hippocratic Oath" to *Deep Space Nine* and doing an internship on the series, received a baptism by fire. "I kind of thought they would get me started a little more slowly, maybe doing some rewrites, maybe doing some story work, but 'Resistance' was the first thing they hit me with," says Klink. "They had bought this story document from freelancers, and it had kind of been shelved temporarily. The story was very problematic. First, because it's about the old guy. How do you make it about Janeway? The second problem was [that] the story's episodic. They go here; they go there. We needed an overall arc to the story, and Janeway needed to be driving it. Budget was also a problem, because we generally build two new sets, and this whole thing

••••

takes place on an alien planet. They have to start out on this journey from some-place and end up someplace, and that's our two sets. Do they go anyplace in be-tween? We have to build that too, then. It was an arduous [story] break. It went on a couple days. We ended up building three sets — a town square, the prison, and [Caylem's] cabin. We tried really hard to set in the cave set, which is a standing set, but just couldn't do it. It was a horren-dously expensive episode."

Episode #28
"Prototype"
Original Airdate: 1/15/96
Written by Nicolas Corea and Kenneth Biller
Directed by Jonathan Frakes
Guest Starring: Rick Worthy (3947), Hugh Hodgin (6263)

The crew discovers a deacti-vated robot floating through space and beams it on board. Torres takes it upon herself to repair the mysterious mechani-cal being, and when it is reactivated, they discover that the unit, a sentient artificial life-form, is called Automated Unit 3947 and that its race is facing extinction. The robot asks the chief engineer to build a prototype so that more units can be con-structed, but she must refuse because the Prime Directive bars her from interfering with alien cultures. However, when the unit's home-ship appears, he abducts her and threatens to destroy *Voyager* unless she creates a new prototype.

••••

"Another one of my orphans," Michael Piller noted in the *Sci-Fi Universe* interview. "Nick Corea came in and pitched a story that had us wandering into a war between robots, which seemed to be a pretty corny idea, but I liked it be-cause it gave us a new adversary that was not humanoid. I just think it's terribly im-portant for us to challenge ourselves to come up with new kinds of aliens, and we had never done a robot like this. Frankly, Jeri was not enamored with this story, and both she and Rick [Berman] were very concerned that we were not going to be able to pull off a robot, so I ended up as the one saying, 'Guys, this is *Star Trek*! You're going to tell me we can't do robots? They can do robots on *Outer Limits*, but the top science-fiction franchise on televi-

sion can't do robots?' So finally they sort of grumbled and went along with me on this."

Episode #29
"Alliances"
Original Airdate: 1/22/96
Written by Jeri Taylor
Directed by Les Landau
Guest Starring: Charles Lucia (Mabus), Anthony DeLongis (Magh Culluh), Martha Hackett (Seska), Raphael Sbarge (Michael Jonas), Larry Cedar (Jal Tersa), John Gegenhuber (Kelat), Simon Billig (Hogan), Mirran E. Willis (Rettik)

The *Voyager* sustains an attack by the Kazon that results in the death of a crew member, which prompts Chakotay to ask Janeway to begin thinking more like a Maquis. Realizing that they must strengthen their position in the quadrant if they are to survive, Janeway agrees to ini-tiate plans to create a strategic alliance with leaders of several Kazon factions. Acting as an intermediary with the Kazon, Neelix takes a shuttlecraft to the planet Sobras, which houses a Kazon settlement. There he contacts an old acquaintance, Jal Tersa of the Kazon sect Pommar. While Janeway's meeting with Culluh and Seska is unsuccessful, Neelix is able to befriend Mabus, the governor of the Trabe, an ex-iled sect that is bitter enemies with the other Kazon. Believing that the Trabe only desire peaceful coexistence, Janeway forms an alliance with them, only to dis-cover that she couldn't be more wrong.

••••

"I liked the dilemma that Janeway was put in; I thought that was in-teresting," says Jeri Taylor. "I regret the fi-nal speech I put in her mouth, because it came across as exactly that, one of these preachy, Picard-like moments where she has to lecture people about the impor-tance of something. It seemed like a good idea at the time."

The Kazon proved a source of much contention on staff throughout the year, with Michael Piller championing their inclusion in the seasonal arc despite the fact that most of the staff found they were not working as adversaries. "They're just sort of big, loutish characters that cause our people to overact," acknowl-edges Jeri Taylor. "For some reason, they all turn into mustache-twirling villains as

soon as they get that makeup on. They had a cartoonlike quality that I think was not our finest hour."

Michael Piller observed in *Sci-Fi Universe,* "I'll be curious to know what the audience's perception is, if our invest-ing in the Kazon this season worked. I've been very satisfied with the impact of the arc. The stories have taken us from a be-ginning to a satisfying end. I think they've helped define what our life is like in this quadrant."

In Piller's scenario, the Delta Quadrant was supposed to be not unlike contemporary East Los Angeles. The Ka-zon were meant to be a metaphor for to-day's street gangs. "Our intention was to create a sort of disorganized anarchy, them-against-them as much as them-against-us," he said. "The wish that I had, which was not fulfilled, was that we would only cast people between eighteen and twenty-five-ish so that these would be young, angry people who never lived to be old enough to have the kind of experi-ence and perspective on the world that, say, the Klingons and the Romulans might have. They were much more emotional, short fused, and therefore had fewer ex-pectations, which I think is indicative of street gangs today."

However, casting so many piv-otal roles with such young actors proved too difficult. "Older actors gave more pol-ished performances," offered Piller, "and as the season progressed, I think they got older and older still, and as a result, I think we didn't fulfill the full potential of the Ka-zon, even though I think they were written pretty well. I think they ultimately came out being sort of Klingon-ish and I regret that we didn't stick to our original vision of keeping them young."

In order to better understand the Kazon, Ken Biller created an elaborate so-ciological backstory about the Kazon, ex-plaining their history and customs. "It was quite thoughtful and very well worked out, and they looked quite interesting in that paper," notes Taylor. The backstory created by Biller explaining the Kazon's history with the Trabe was used in "Al-liances" as well as in "Initiations," in which Kazon customs were dealt with.

"That document came out of the research that Ken did for 'Initiations,'" re-marked Piller. "He felt it would be valu-

••••

able — because we were going to invest a whole season into these guys — to provide writers with a clear backstory so everybody would be working from the same page. I think it influenced the season greatly. It was an enormous contribution."

Episode #30
"Threshold"
Original Airdate: 1/29/96
Teleplay by Brannon Braga
Story by Michael DeLuca
Directed by Alexander Singer
Guest Starring: Raphael Sbarge (Michael Jonas), Mirran E. Willis (Rettik)

Lieutenant Paris takes on the responsibility of breaking the warp barrier, becoming the first person in modern *Star Trek* to make a transwarp flight. But soon after his shuttle returns from warp ten, Paris begins undergoing a startling metamorphosis. As his cell membranes begin to degrade, he dies. Then, hours after he is pronounced dead by the doctor, Paris is discovered breathing, and his body begins to mutate, transforming into a half-human/half-amphibian that is intent on mating with Captain Janeway.

• • • •

"We're taking a lot of flak for that," admits Jeri Taylor. "There's been a real lashing out. I recognize that people who are on the Internet and who write us letters are a tiny portion of our audience, but when it is as overwhelming as it was on this episode, you begin to take notice. Some of this anger was misplaced, I thought. A lot of the ire seemed to be caused by the fact that we stated that no one had ever gone warp ten before, and people flooded us with letters saying, 'That's not true, in the original series they went warp twelve and warp thirteen.' We should have had a crawl before the episode explaining all this, but it really was a recalibration of warp speed. Gene made the determination at the beginning of *Next Gen* that warp ten would be the limit, and at that point you would occupy all portions of the universe simultaneously, which always seemed like a wonderfully provocative notion. Then the question is 'What happens if you do go to warp ten, how does that affect you?'

"So we all sat in a room and kicked it around and came up with this idea of evolution and thought that it

would be far more interesting and less expected that instead of it being the large-brained, glowing person, it would be full circle, back to our origins in the water. Not saying that we have become less than we are, because those creatures may experience consciousness on such an advanced plane that we couldn't conceive of it. It just seemed like a more interesting image, but it is not one that took with the audience. The fact that we were turning people into salamanders was offensive to a lot of people and just plain stupid to others."

Brannon Braga believes that "Threshold" was a great story that suffered somewhat as a teleplay. "It's very much a classic *Star Trek* story, but in the rewrite process I took out the explanation, the idea behind the ending, that we evolve into these little lizards because maybe evolution is not always progressive. Maybe it's a cycle where we revert to something more rudimentary. That whole conversation was taken out for various reasons, and that was a disaster because without it the episode doesn't even have a point. I think it suffered greatly. I got the note that it wasn't necessary, but in fact it really had a lot to do with what the episode was about. Big mistake taking it out."

One of the elements of the story that many fans found off-putting was the abundant technobabble in the script. It's an element that bothers not only fans but cast members like Tim Russ as well. "As a matter of fact, it's one of the reasons that I never really got warmed up to *Next Generation*," says the actor, a fan of the original *Trek*. "I mean, how can you warm up to something that doesn't make sense? Half of that stuff is made up. It's based very loosely on real physics theory, but most of the stuff is made up. There are people who really live in that world and really dig that kind of dialogue. I think they really like it, but it doesn't make any sense to me. I think it's a waste of time in terms of explaining something. I think that they're hurting the broad base of their audience by doing that. I think that you have a broader base of audience appeal if you have a story where the audience doesn't have to think so much about the physics and try and interpret what was said in an entire page of dialogue. A whole minute and a half goes by, and all they hear is a

bunch of gibberish instead of knowing what a device does or how it jeopardizes or helps the situation. It bothered me about *TNG* and it bothers me about *Voyager*. This show is checkered with it. You know, we have a scene about people and you have a scene about technobabble and you have a scene about people and then you get technobabble — back and forth, back and forth. I've heard explanations of gravity, of how gravity works in time and space, which is very simple. The guy said imagine you've got a mattress in front of you. You poke your finger into the mattress and then you put a ball on the mattress and the ball goes toward your finger because everything dips toward your finger. That's gravity. That's how gravity works in space. It's the same thing with a planet. It bends space to the point where it attracts things around it. You know, it's a very simple explanation. Occasionally you can use it, but I think they should use it a lot more sparingly. It takes the same amount of time to say the same thing but say it in a way that makes sense."

The pitch for "Threshold" didn't come from your ordinary spec script writer but rather the president of New Line Cinema, Michael DeLuca. A lifelong sci-fi fan, DeLuca has not only championed genre projects as one of the youngest and most powerful studio executives but also as the writer of John Carpenter's *In the Mouth of Madness*, an homage to the works of H. P. Lovecraft that despite a tepid box-office response has gained a cult following among horror fans.

Episode #31
"Meld"
Original Airdate: 2/5/96
Teleplay by Michael Piller
Story by Michael Sussman
Directed by Cliff Bole
Guest Starring: Brad Dourif (Ensign Suder), Angela Dohrmann (Ricky), Simon Billig (Hogan)

When a crew member is murdered, Tuvok's investigation leads him to suspect that Ensign Suder is the perpetrator of this heinous crime. When Suder admits to the crime, Tuvok is bedeviled trying to find a logical motive for the act, so he attempts to understand Suder by mind-melding with him, which leads to a growing insanity in the Vulcan. In order to

• • • •

162

cure him, the doctor initiates a treatment that removes Tuvok's emotional suppression abilities.

••••

" 'Meld' was an important show for me," said Michael Piller in his exclusive interview with Kevin Stevens. "I had been after freelancers for a year or so to give me a story about Tuvok and random violence, because I felt that the ultimate nightmare for Tuvok, for a Vulcan, would be to bring some logic to the kind of random violence that you see on *Headline News*. As a fairly intelligent human being, *I* don't understand how it occurs and I can't explain it. Imagine what it must be for a Vulcan, who *must* explain it in order for it to exist within his own personal set of values. I knew there was a story there. One of the interns, Michael Sussman, somebody who I think has a great deal of promise, listened to me tell that to a freelancer one day, and the freelancer didn't get it, but Michael came in and pitched me a story. Even though it wasn't exactly what we wound up doing, it was close enough that we said, 'Let's pursue it.'

"We felt that Mike didn't have the experience yet to write the script," added Piller, "and we were under a great time crunch. You have to understand that during this section of the season we were writing shows as quickly as we could to get them up on their feet, because we weren't sure what the next show was going to be. I decided to just take this one on myself. It turned out to be a very interesting, disturbing experience. I hired a consultant, a psychiatrist with great credentials, and I showed him the story, the beat sheet [outlining the plot] and the script. We talked about language and exactly what we were dealing with in this story, and I began to understand the pull of violence, the seductiveness of violence. The interesting thing about the show was that the plot is entirely predictable. What makes it rise above is the ability to make that story talk about something, to talk about violence and to see the different facets of it. The thing that *really* made it work was Tim Russ's performance, which was just remarkable.

"I had a very difficult time with act five, where Tuvok goes berserk and tries to get out of the force-field. It was because by the time I got there, I couldn't remember what the hell I was writing about," said Piller. "It just seemed dark and grim and mean, and I couldn't figure out for what purpose. What's the point of all this? It was Rick [Berman] and Jeri [Taylor] who really steered me back by taking something that was already mentioned earlier in the script and saying, 'That's interesting, you should explore that more,' which was the capital punishment issue. By making capital punishment what is driving Tuvok to commit violence in the fifth act, it becomes a much more universal show, because everybody then has to say, 'Well, is it my violent instinct that is driving my need for capital punishment to punish the violent?' I think that really made the show work."

Brannon Braga believes that "Meld" is his favorite episode of the season. "Superb," he says. "It doesn't get any better than this: melding with a psychopath, and the psychopath starts to take on the Vulcan tendencies and vice versa. An exploration of murderous tendencies and evil. Just absolutely fascinating, and I think Tim Russ made himself known as one of the best actors on the show. Tuvok really broke out in that episode."

Russ has enjoyed not only the chance to stretch his own range but the established boundaries of the Vulcan race as well, being a devoted fan of the original *Star Trek* and Leonard Nimoy's portrayal of Spock. "I was more than fortunate enough to get this particular gig," he says. "I do look at it as a transitory thing that's going to be over at some point in time, but I was fortunate enough to be able to land this particular role and I think it is, more than anything else, just a question of destiny for me particularly. Somebody else could've gotten it and not known anything about the past shows or cared in one way or the other about *Star Trek*. They would've tried to carry on and do what they had to do, but it just happened that I happen to have that sort of knowledge which contributed to my getting the role in the first place. It comes out of, I think in part, a very large part of luck and somewhat of destiny to be in this thing. I worked with Leonard Nimoy when I was in college. When I was an undergraduate in college I worked with him in a play, and here I am playing a character that he, for all intents and purposes, created. He's an icon within science fiction. We are carrying the torch for that character. The whole thing goes full circle."

Episode #32
"Dreadnought"
Original Airdate: 2/12/96
Written by Gary Holland
Directed by LeVar Burton
Guest Starring: Raphael Sbarge (Michael Jonas), Nancy Hower (Ensign Wildman), Michael Spound (Lorrum), Dan Kern (Kellan)

The *Voyager* detects a Cardassian-designed missile from the Alpha Quadrant that is traveling toward Rakosan, a heavily populated planet in the Delta Quadrant. Lieutenant Torres reveals that the missile, created by the Cardassians, was stopped and reprogrammed by the Maquis to attack the Cardassians but became lost in the Badlands. As the Maquis responsible for reprogramming the missile, Torres beams over to the missile in an attempt to disarm it. When she is there it misleads her, believing she's been co-opted by the Cardassians, and attempts to fulfill its mission by destroying the planet it is approaching.

••••

"Roxann, in some amazing way, is able to find all of the gray in between Torres, and she's very, very rich," says Jeri Taylor. "This is a character with a lot of sort of self exploration to do. She is the character that many people might identify with. She has some aspects of herself she wishes she didn't have. It's like, 'I know I wish I didn't keep losing my temper. Why do I do that? Why do I always make that same mistake?' And what she will come to wrestle, as all of us like that must do, is to accept herself for what she is and go on rather than wishing she could purge herself of something that she just doesn't find comfortable. There's a lot of passion there, a lot of good juice for a writer. She's really sort of eclectic. She's human and Klingon, and the human part of her is Latino, so she's got all this wonderful kind of ethnicity rolling around in there."

For Biggs-Dawson, the continuing exploration of her character has provided some wonderful acting challenges, including "Dreadnought," in which she faces off against a weapon that she has not only programmed but given her own voice to. "I figured, well, I'll just learn as I go along," she says. "It's been a great learning experience because gradually I can peel away the layers of this character. I just learn more every week about her, and it's been really fine."

"Dreadnought" was a chance to feature the actress, who hadn't been showcased in several episodes, though Roxann has no complaints. "Even when I'm not featured in a particular episode, I feel that the writing has been so strong that each episode has something to reveal to me about who [Torres] is and helps me fit more of the puzzle together," she says. "Also, I think if I wear this makeup any more than I am, I'd never have another job in my life because my skin would be completely ruined. I'm at my tolerance level as it is, absolutely."

Unlike Worf, who literally wrestled with demons, Biggs-Dawson's Klingon character is vexed by internal demons. "I think with Worf it was more of an external Klingon struggle and with B'Elanna it's more internal," she comments. "In that way, it's very contemporary. I just think we're living in a society now where there's a lot of internal struggle as everyone tries to figure out where they belong. The world has gotten so populated and so huge, and there are so many moral and ethical issues just trying to figure out where you belong in the whole human thing that the internal struggle is very much a part of the here and now and how we face the world we are living in."

Episode #33
"Death Wish"
Original Airdate: 2/19/96
Teleplay by Michael Piller
Story by Shawn Piller
Directed by James L. Conway
Guest Starring: John de Lancie (Q), Gerrit Graham (Q2), Jonathan Frakes (Commander Riker)

The *Voyager* encounters a renegade Q who has escaped his inprisonment within a comet and demands asylum from the Q Continuum aboard the ship. Shortly thereafter, Q arrives to force Q2 to rejoin the Continuum. However, Q2 wants nothing more than to be granted sanctuary so that he can commit suicide after having lived an extraordinary immortal existence. Paying heed to Starfleet regulations,

Janeway convenes a hearing to consider the request, with Tuvok acting as counsel to Q2. Behind the scenes, Q attempts to come to a secret deal with Janeway by offering to bring the ship home in return for a favorable verdict.

••••

Although bringing Q to the Delta Quadrant may seem like the ultimate sweeps stunt, many were surprised with how well the episode actually turned out, none more than John de Lancie himself, who plays the often mischievous and dangerous Q.

"When the script is as meaty as 'Death Wish' you don't need all the banter and the stuff Patrick [Stewart] and I had to add on some of the weaker Q episodes of *Next Generation,*" says de Lancie. "We didn't need any tricks. I've played Q nine times and my feeling is that I want to be able to bring a different facet to it each time. And the writers, I think, want to do the same thing. This one was interesting because the element that has made this character so popular, that kind of 'in your face, fuck you' quality again was overshadowed by how well the script was written and what the story was about. I thought, rather than play that, maybe it

John de Lancie reprised his infamous Next Generation *role as Q in the second-season* Voyager *episode "Death Wish" (copyright © 1995 by Albert Ortega).*

was time to play this one much more introspectively."

De Lancie admits that he continues to be amazed by his place in the *Star Trek* mythos, never having anticipated that nearly a decade after stepping on the stage to shoot "Encounter at Farpoint," the *Next Generation* pilot, he'd still be portraying this intriguing character. "The fans are always terrific," he says. "And the alternative to being known and popular is not so hot: being not known and not popular. So I don't have any problems with it. I guess I don't like traveling and sometimes that's an issue, but it has afforded me a great lifestyle and opportunities that I never would have dreamed of having. As Gene Roddenberry said to me on the third day of shooting 'Farpoint,' he said, 'Oh, John, we really like what you're doing, and I think we're going to be using you quite a bit.' And I said, 'Oh, great.' A few days later, he came back to me and said, 'Oh, John, you have no idea what you've gotten yourself into.' And I said, 'What do you mean?' and he said, 'Oh, you'll see. You'll see.'

"But I'm still kind of a peripheral character in all this. You know, nine episodes does not a career make. So I've been fortunate in being able to work on a lot of other things, and when *Star Trek* for me started, which was with the pilot about nine or ten years ago, I found myself working a lot anyway. *Star Trek* has become like this icing on the cake."

"Death Wish," which examines the issue of assisted suicide, has its genesis in a "pitch" from Michael Piller's son, Shawn, who originally mentioned the idea to his father. Piller recalled that "my son heard me chatting away at the dinner table and he came in and started pitching and he gave me this basic idea and I had him come in and pitch with everyone in the room. Everybody knows Shawn and would like to help him. But we're not just going to hand him an assignment because he's my son. I'm pretty tough that way, but he came up with this thing himself and he wrote the story himself. He would have loved to have written the script, but as I said, there are no favors here. He had never written a teleplay, and I wasn't going to pay him to practice on us."

Piller admitted, "I was never happy with the Q show we did on *Deep*

Space Nine. It just felt like a stunt, and I have never been happy doing something strictly for stunt. I don't mind doing something that's promotable, but I want to start out with a story that's worth telling, and this show was about a genuine human concern in that Q2, who can live forever, doesn't want to. What a twist on the normal wish that humans seem to have to live forever."

Episode #34
"Lifesigns"
Original Airdate: 2/26/96
Written by Kenneth Biller
Directed by Cliff Bole
Guest Starring: Susan Diol (Dr. Danara Pel), Raphael Sbarge (Michael Jonas), Martha Hackett (Seska), Michael Spound (Lorum), Rick Gianasi (Gigolo)

The ship detects a distress call from a life-form, which they realize is a dying Vidiian female, aboard an approaching spacecraft. The doctor, in treating her for advanced stages of the Phage, creates a holographic body for the woman, a hematologist named Danara Pel. During their work together, there is a growing attraction between the two, prompting the doctor to ask Pel on a date in the holodeck, where he recreates Mars and a fifty-seven Chevy. Meanwhile, Lieutenant Paris continues to be insubordinate to Chakotay, and tension grows as Seska recruits the spy Jonas to plan an accident that will damage *Voyager*'s warp coils.

• • • •

"That's the one that would have been classic if it didn't have that stupid scene with Paris in it," offers Jeri Taylor, who was deeply concerned about the recurring plot thread of a traitor on board the *Voyager*. "It would have been one of those little jewels, but it will be forever tainted.

"There was an enormous amount of contention about that script," she continues. "Everybody had a different idea about what to do with it. Ken [Biller] wrote one draft that he felt very strongly about, and Michael and I really felt it should go a different way, and he rewrote it and ultimately felt much better about it. The ending was changed I don't know how many times. We were trying to find something that felt dramatically satisfying yet sent out the kind of message that we

wanted to be sending, that would be honest and yet not depressing. If you get into people dying, it's a very, very tricky area. There was an ending in which she opted to stay as a holographic character and die within days because she'd rather have lived like that, whole and beautiful, and only have a few more days, than go back to her diseased body. But we really felt that would be an irresponsible message to send. Ultimately, I think the message we were sending was that even people who are ill deserve to be loved and not to be judged on the basis of their illness."

Episode #35
"Investigations"
Original Airdate: 3/13/96
Teleplay by Jeri Taylor
Story by Jeff Schnaufer and Ed Bond
Directed by Les Landau
Guest Starring: Raphael Sbarge (Michael Jonas), Jerry Sroka (Laxeth), Simon Billig (Hogan)

Neelix launches an intraship news show and learns that Tom Paris plans to leave the ship to become a pilot with the Talaxians. After Paris's exit, Neelix is shocked to learn that the former *Voyager* lieutenant has been kidnapped by the Kazon-Nistrim and the scheming Seska, who intends to seize the *Voyager* for her own nefarious ends. Neelix confides to Tuvok that he has found illegal transmissions made to the Kazon from the ship and suspects Paris. He is soon clued in that Paris's insubordinate behavior was all part of a sting operation to uncover the real traitor aboard the ship, which leads them to Michael Jonas.

• • • •

The exploration of the Paris arc utilizing Seska as a villainous foil for the crew was primarily the idea of Michael Piller, who had championed the ongoing story. "I thought we had an interesting sort of villain with Seska, and she allowed us to go behind the scenes with the Kazon," he said. "Creating villains for *Star Trek* is a very difficult matter. Seska helped define the Kazon for us, and I was very, very satisfied with the character arc that Seska took us on. I enjoyed the whole thing with the baby and Chakotay and the spy stuff. I know that Rick and Jeri were not very comfortable with that character and I think that Jeri was unhappy in general

with the Kazon, but I think it was important and valuable to create this adversary, and to me it really created a wonderful framework for all the other stories to appear within."

Jeri Taylor adamantly disagrees. "Given our franchise, which is we're way over here and we're trying to get way over there, to have the same people cropping up episode after episode gave the curious impression that we were standing still in space instead of going somewhere else. People began to ask, 'When do you get out of Kazon space? Surely they don't occupy the whole quadrant?' I also thought that we played the same story over and over again: Seska sets a trap and we walk into it and we get out. I just felt that it got repetitive and ultimately was not very interesting."

By "Investigations," Taylor was happy to jettison the plot thread that she felt had become an albatross. "By this time, I was just frankly turned off to the whole idea of the Paris arc. I really thought that it wasn't working, and so bringing it to a conclusion felt obligatory rather than challenging. I was much more interested in Neelix's newspaper, which I thought was fun.

"Michael wanted to use the electronic newspaper as a stylistic device in order to tell the story in a different way. That meant that we would only experience the story from Neelix's point of view," adds Taylor. "It meant we would not see Tom Paris on the Kazon ship and we would not be redeeming him by showing him as a hero. We were actually into the shooting of that episode when the studio read it and quite rightly — I was happy for their intercession at this point — said, 'You can't do this. We've got to have the action. We've got to see Tom be a hero.' So we went back and shot the scenes of Tom on the Kazon ship and his escape and all that derring-do, and I think it was an absolutely essential component of the show."

Episode #36
"Deadlock"
Original Airdate: 3/18/96
Written by Brannon Braga
Directed by David Livingston
Guest Starring: Nancy Hower (Ensign Wildman), Simon Billig (Hogan), Bob

• • • •

Clendenin (Vidiian Surgeon), Ray Proscia (Vidiian Commander), Keythe Farley (Vidiian), Christopher Johnston (Vidiian)

Attempting to evade the Vidiians, the *Voyager* enters a plasma cloud that causes the warp engines to stall. Proton bursts explode within the ship causing heavy casualties and a breach in the structural integrity of the hull. When Ensign Kim and Kes are sucked out into space, Captain Janeway is shocked to find a duplicate *Voyager* with an identical crew existing in a parallel universe. As the crew attempts to deal with the disaster, the doctor struggles to keep Ensign Wildman's newly born baby alive and Janeway discovers that a divergence field has caused all sensor readings to double and that with all the particles duplicating, there is not enough antimatter to sustain both vessels. As the Vidiians press their attack, the two Janeways must meet to determine a solution in which only one ship will survive.

••••

Brannon Braga explains, "Sometimes I get ideas for dramatic structures in playing with time and space and the ways in which we can tell stories. I just thought it would be really bizarre if you told a story for an act or two and suddenly you found yourself in the middle of a different story on a different *Voyager,* but they're occupying the same point of time and space. My favorite scene is the moment when you're on the *Voyager* that's coming apart at the seams, Kim is sucked into space, etcetera., and then you cut to a pristine, calm *Voyager,* but you get this glimpse of the other *Voyager* and then you pick up *that* story. It was extremely tough to shoot, but we needed a show that was pure action and pure high-concept sci-fi. I thought it turned out well."

"We have done a number of double stories in the history of *Star Trek,*" says Jeri Taylor. "We even had in development a story of two *Enterprises* in *Next Gen,* but it just was not working. It's a very difficult thing to bring off. We were trying to double every character and do an arc with each character and the double. For example, what would Troi say to herself? It just got very muddied and garbled and we abandoned it.

"So it was with some trepidation that we approached this idea, but I think that by limiting it, it worked. Kim

was dead, so you only had the other Kim. Kes was doubled, but she was unconscious most of the time so the focus was on the two Janeways, the two captains trying to work their way out of their dilemma. It gave it a focus and a limitation that I think helped the storytelling. The show came out enormously short, however. It was like eight or nine minutes short, and we kept writing scenes, and they just kept getting gobbled up on those stages. It's much better to be long than to be short. There's never any accounting for it. Why is one seventy-page script eight minutes long and with this one, with the same director, we had seventy-five pages and had to shoot two extra days to get enough material to make it long enough? It was not an inexpensive show as a result, but what I was so pleased about was I would defy anybody to know what the added material is. It is seamless. Some of the added scenes are some of the better scenes. They do not stand out as fill at all."

It was also an episode that could easily be described by the *Trek* adjective Braga-esque. Clearly, few writers in the history of *Trek* have developed such a distinguishable imprimatur as the veteran scribe. "It was one of those intricate little puzzles that Brannon loves to do," says Taylor. "I think it came out very well. David Livingston did an outstanding job with the direction, and it just didn't stop from beginning to end."

Episode #37
"Innocence"
Original Airdate: 3/8/96
Teleplay by Lisa Klink
Story by Anthony Williams
Directed by James Conway
Guest Starring: Marnie McPhail (Alicia), Tiffany Taubman (Tressa), Sarah Rayne (Elani), Tahj D. Mowry (Corin), Richard Garon (Lieutenant Bennet)

Tuvok and Lieutenant Bennet's shuttle crash-lands on a world that they learn is sacred to the Drayans, a race that has avoided contact with others for decades. As Bennet lies dying from his injuries, three frightened Drayan children come out from their hiding place, telling Tuvok that they have been abandoned by their people, who have left them on the planet to die, warning that the "Morrok,"

the messenger of death, will soon be arriving. While Tuvok tries to allay their fears, Janeway makes contact with the Drayans' first prelate, Alicia, leading to a startling revelation: The Drayans age backward, and these "children" are actually at the end of their life spans.

••••

"I was not all that excited with the premise," says Lisa Klink. "It sounded like a sitcom episode. But what ultimately caught my attention was the idea of Tuvok as a father. What are Vulcan fathers like? Are their kids born logical? Probably not."

Klink's problem, however, was finding a science-fiction spin for the traditional storytelling motif. "The rest of the staff came to my rescue there," says Klink, "because I had nothing to do with that concept. The freelancer Anthony Williams had pitched us an idea where these kids were in trouble and they were disappearing one by one into this cave. We didn't end up going with his sci-fi premise, but the idea that something mysterious was happening to them kind of stayed with it, and it ended up being the reverse-aging thing. Actually, once the whole death thing came up, it helped a lot, because it took the cutesy edge off it. It added a layer of darkness over the whole thing. We even started off the episode with a crewman dying. Michael Piller was nice enough to call me and tell me I should submit it for a Humanitas Award."

"Our challenge with Tuvok is to put this character in situations which will press him and give him some kind of emotional arc, although he can't express those emotions," says Jeri Taylor. "There aren't many situations that allow that kind of thing to happen, but 'Innocence' was one that I thought worked like gangbusters."

The episode was a great chance for Tim Russ to shine in the spotlight, although the actor is admittedly happy to be part of a large ensemble. "Throughout the pilot and subsequent episodes I was there as part of the ensemble. I think some of the other actors on occasion felt that they might've been left out for a while and didn't have a feature story, but I knew that I was going to get a feature story sooner or later. I knew that because they told me and also because I knew the difference between the original series and this one is

••••

you've got a whole bunch of people now. You've got nine people in this cast, which is bigger than the other two shows that came out previously. What it does, on the plus side, is it gives you an opportunity to rest on occasion. Whenever we did a heavy story, it guaranteed the next story was going to be light. It was going to be a day or two of work at the most, or not that much dialogue, so you had a break. And then you'd build back up again, and then they give you another big story.

"The downside of it is that there are so many characters involved that the relationships have become like a bunch of small groups as opposed to one whole. You have pairings of different people and story lines and relationships built in that sense, as opposed to the original charter's path, which is basically the three of them [Kirk, Spock and McCoy] involved in all the stories in one way or another. Now it's like we can split the Away Team up in any number of directions and leave somebody else on the bridge, and you can develop the story line for Kes or Neelix or someone else. Also, I knew my character. Everyone else was trying to discover all these things about their characters, but I've already got a foundation and all I have to do is build on that foundation."

Garrett Wang recalls that when Russ got to meet Leonard Nimoy for the first time since scoring the role of Voyager's Vulcan tactical officer, it was a historic moment. "It was really funny because right after we finished shooting we went to New York when UPN flew us out there to do presentations for the advertisers for the fall schedules. Leonard Nimoy was there because he was producing a show at the time [Deadly Games]. And he was there and he was in the green room waiting to go on, and I went to Tim, 'Leonard's here.' And he was like a little kid. This big old smile came across his face and he got so nervous. He was like 'Spock's here,' you know? It was just a joy to watch. Everybody's used to Tuvok being a very serious Vulcan and then Tim Russ gets all excited over meeting Spock. It was just a trip."

Episode #38
"The Thaw"
Original Airdate: 4/29/96
Teleplay by Joe Menosky

Story by Richard Gadas and Michael Piller
Directed by Marvin Rush
Guest Starring: Michael McKean (The Clown), Thomas Kopache (Viorsa), Carel Struycken (Spectre), Patty Maloney (Little Woman), Tony Carlin (Physician), Shannon O'Hurley (The Programmer)

The Voyager encounters automated messages from a Kohl settlement that survived an environmental calamity by going into artificial hibernation. Bringing the cryo-chambers aboard, the crew finds the humanoids have been perfectly preserved. In an attempt to free the Kohl from their stasis, Torres and Kim enter the chambers themselves and encounter a virtual environment created by the computer controlling the Kohl pods. There they are confronted by an evil clown, who epitomizes fear, holding all the Kohl survivors hostage. He warns that Torres and Kim will never be able to leave this virtual prison.

••••

"A wild episode," says Jeri Taylor of a show that featured veteran funnyman Michael McKean as the clown. "It looked unlike anything we've ever done on Star Trek. It takes place in a virtual reality, and it's a pleasant place gone demonically bad. We hired background performers from Cirque du Soleil to provide a very strange, sort of carnival-like atmosphere. Our director of photography, Marvin Rush, directed it, and he was probably just the right person, with his visual eye, to do this show."

The episode also provided another chance for Rush, veteran DP for The Next Generation and Deep Space Nine, to step behind the camera as director. "I came close on one other show before doing 'The Host' on Next Generation," says Rush. "I was doing Frank's Place, and if it had gone another season, I would have had the chance to direct. So when I came over to Next Generation, I didn't mention much about it the first season, but I sort of alluded to it."

Comparing his responsibilities as DP and director, Rush notes, "The biggest difference for me was that although I was working during the [directing] prep, the intensity of work on the set is very different. Prep is a chance to sit and think and ponder, and I have very little pondering

time when I'm lighting a set. It's mostly make a quick decision and execute and then move on to the next quick decision and execute that. There's a certain amount of planning, but with the nature and speed of production there's an awful lot of just go with your first mind. With the director, he has seven days, and with the weekends, you ought to be able to come up with something. Have a good plan, talk to people, get some things.

"The cameraman is a collaborator, and it has a lot to do with how much the director wants from the cameraman. If he has a question, I hope that I have the answer. If he wants me to suggest something, then I wait for a little bit of a lead from him and I do. If he doesn't want help, and some directors don't want help, then I don't give it. I'm not trying to hold back, but if by helping or putting in my two cents, it gets in the way, it's better that I don't. My motto is always to give the director as much help as he wants and he needs. It's a judgment call on my part."

Episode #39
"Tuvix"
Original Airdate: 5/6/96
Teleplay by Kenneth Biller
Story by Andrew Price and Mark Gaberman
Directed by Cliff Bole
Guest Starring: Tom Wright (Tuvix), Simon Billig (Hogan), Bahni Turpin (Swinn)

While beaming back from taking vegetable samples on an unexplored planet, Neelix and Tuvok are combined into one person. Dubbing himself Tuvix, he still finds himself emotionally drawn to Kes, who doesn't reciprocate his feelings. Quickly becoming a valued member of the team, Mr. Tuvix forces the crew members to confront an unwanted dilemma when they find a way to separate Tuvix back to Tuvok and Neelix, and Mr. Tuvix tells them he does not want to be separated.

••••

Says Jeri Taylor, "The remarkable thing is that we found an actor who lets you actually buy this wacky premise because you can believe this actor as Tuvok and you can buy him as Neelix. It's also what happens when the crew no longer has Tuvok and no longer has Neelix but has this new entity, and the pressure that is brought to bear on Janeway as a result."

The character most disconcerted by Tuvix is Kes, with whom Tuvix wishes to continue a romantic relationship. Jennifer Lien admits that over the first two seasons she's had the opportunity to play a wonderful character. "I like Kes," admits the actress. "She's strong and curious and intelligent. We've developed the character and these traits over the past two seasons, but she's still a child in a way, with the same fears and inhibitions and worries that we all have. This kind of diversity in a character is challenging, and that's good."

Like many episodes that came before it, "Tuvix" (originally entitled "Symbiogenesis") was considered by some to be derivative of other *Trek* stories, including the granddaddy of all transporter accident stories, the original *Trek's* "The Enemy Within," in which Kirk is separated into both a good and an evil character. "Magazines come out and basically say that we're copying some other *Star Trek* episode from the original series or *Next Generation*," said Piller. "It says more about *Time* magazine I think than it does about *Star Trek*. . . . You've got to do the best you can with what you have to work with and, as you've heard me say over and over again, you've got to keep new people coming in and pitching because otherwise you're going to be retreading on old ground. And it's healthy to keep people coming in the door, even if it's one out of fifty or a hundred with an original idea."

Episode #40
"Resolutions"
Original Airdate: 5/12/96
Written by Jeri Taylor
Directed by Alexander Singer
Guest Starring: Susan Diol (Dr. Danara Pel), Simon Billig (Hogan), Bahni Turpin (Swinn)

When Chakotay and Janeway contract a deadly virus from an insect bite on an alien planet, they are forced to remain behind, leaving Tuvok in command. As the ship leaves communication range, Janeway tells Tuvok that he is not to contact the Vidiians despite the fact that their sophisticated medical technology may be able to assist them in finding a cure for the virus. On the planet, Janeway and Chako-

tay, realizing they may be stranded together for the rest of their lives, explore their feelings for each other.

••••

" 'Resolutions' is the episode I had the most fun with all year," says Jeri Taylor. "We have Janeway and Chakotay with their story, but the other side of it is interesting too, because it's dealing with the crew's loss of their leaders and the various ways in which they handle that and ultimately what they decide to do with it. Very often we have several characters isolated and there's a very interesting story going on there, but you've got to cut back to the ship at some point, and too often it's a story of the ship looking for those people, and you go through some very uncompelling things. But here was an instance where I felt the ship side of it was working as well as what was going on on the planet, which was itself extremely interesting.

"I like our characters to grow as people do," she continues, "which is a day at a time. You never know what life is going to throw at you. You never know the person you're going to be ten years from now. There's no way to anticipate that, and I think we evolve into better storytelling and more honest character development if we let the characters grow in a slow process. I think it broadens the canvas. Things may occur to us that would never have occurred to us if we

were on the track to a specific goal with a character."

Taylor admits that it was important to maintain Janeway's authority even in a potentially romantic situation. "We acknowledge that we are walking a very dangerous sort of tightrope with a female captain. She is judged by different standards. If she shows any weakness, if she shows too much emotion in a situation of stress, it damages her in the eyes of the audience," Taylor says. "So we have to be careful that in professional situations, in leadership situations on the bridge, at all times she is completely in control. But to do only that with her would be to do a great disservice to the character and to the actress, who is capable of a broad range of things. I think that we have given her more emotional stories this season and as a result, we have deepened her character. I would hope to do much more of that in the future."

Less interesting for some fans may be the involvement of Janeway and Chakotay, which was a far cry from *The Blue Lagoon*. Says Robert Beltran, "It's *Star Trek* romance, which means we touch hands and it's supposed to be *thrilling*."

Episode #41
"Basics, Part I"
Original Airdate: 5/20/96
Written by Michael Piller
Directed by Winrich Kolbe
Guest Starring: Brad Dourif (Ensign Suder), Anthony DeLongis (Magh Culluh), John Gegenhuber (Teirna), Martha Hackett (Seska), Henry Darrow (Kolopak)

The *Voyager* receives an emergency message from Seska, who reveals that the newly born son of Chakotay and Seska is going to be banished by Kazon leader Culluh to a servant colony. Soon afterward, an injured former aide to Seska, Teirna, arrives in a shuttlecraft and is beamed aboard for emergency medical treatment. He offers to help them navigate Kazon territory to rescue Chakotay's son. Unfortunately, the crew realizes it's all part of a trap when the *Voyager* is barraged by Kazon ships. Looking to recruit allies, Paris escapes in a shuttlecraft as the Kazon-Nistrim take over the ship. Cullah and an alive and well Seska enter the bridge triumphantly and banish the *Voy-*

ager crew to the surface of Hanon Four, a primitive planet on which dinosaurs still roam. As the episode ends, the crew watches helplessly as the *Voyager* departs, now manned by a Kazon crew with only the psychotic Ensign Suder and the doctor still hidden aboard.

• • • •

Departing *Voyager* executive producer Michael Piller was intent on providing the season with a coda that would incite the excitement of his acclaimed *Next Generation* cliff-hanger "The Best of Both Worlds." In his discussions with Kevin Stevens about the season, he explained, "This episode is the biggest two-hour story in the history of the franchise. It's very ambitious, and I think it's a lot of fun. When we were going in, there was a real question of whether it was going to be a new alien group who steals the ship or the Kazon. I was the one who really drove the unit toward the Kazon, because I felt we had built up this arc with them and it was a natural conclusion. The issue of [Seska's] baby was still unresolved, and I just felt it was a natural way to go.

"There was some concern about the violence in the second part, which we have toned down. This story had Seska ex-

periencing the ultimate culmination of all her evil. I had the opinion that she needed to lose something very dear to her to pay for her crimes, so it was my opinion from the beginning that the baby should die, that her loss should be what she loves most, her child. Rick [Berman] and Jeri [Taylor] felt that it was in extremely bad taste and too violent. Although the studio liked the ending that I wrote, Rick and Jeri felt that they could not live with it, so we started exploring other endings. These included having Seska grab the baby and having Culluh die, which was certainly doable — if you believed that Seska really loved Culluh and moaned about losing him, but I don't think anybody would buy that. I didn't think that was satisfying enough, that she didn't get her just reward.

"The next alternative was to kill Seska, which certainly would be a dramatic reward, but that left us with Chakotay's baby on the ship," said Piller. "Chakotay would not just let anybody take that baby off the ship. Jeri wanted no part of a baby being left on board, so she vetoed that one. Well, the only other solution I could think of, somewhat contrived, I will admit, is that it turns out it's not

Chakotay's baby after all. She thinks it is, but it's not."

Among those expiring in the conclusion of "Basics" is Ensign Suder, whom Piller created for 'Meld' earlier in the season. "It's a real wipeout," Piller commented. "Jeri never cared for Suder and had no interest in developing him any further, so there was no point in keeping him alive. And a dramatic arc is fully realized by having his death occur at the end of part two. He heroically sacrifices himself for the ship."

Surprisingly, "Basics, Part II" was *not* filmed back-to-back with part I. "It doesn't matter, because we have so much time in postproduction, we can film the last four in any order we want," says Taylor. "We waited because the second half of the cliff-hanger is a heavy location show and with daylight saving time and longer daylight hours, we simply got longer days in which to film outdoors."

The extensive location shooting took place in Lone Pine, California, which required the cast to spend extensive time off the lot, as did the visual effects team in order to provide the episode's dinosaur-like creatures as well as the *Voyager*'s ascent into space after stranding the crew.

• • • •

CHAPTER FOURTEEN

Making Contact: Behind the scenes of *Star Trek VIII*

While the box-office success of 1994's *Star Trek: Generations* — which pulled in approximately $130 million — must have been reassuring to Paramount Pictures, it nonetheless left a few questions unanswered. Primary among them was whether the film was actually a successful transition of the television hit *Star Trek: The Next Generation* from the small screen to the large, or if the audience was coming first and foremost to see William Shatner play the death scene of Captain James T. Kirk. Whichever it was, the answer was elusive.

It is undoubtedly for this reason that Shatner thought he had a reasonable shot at convincing the studio to go with his scenario for a sequel that would allow the two captains — Kirk and Jean-Luc Picard — to interact one last time. Eventually issued as a novel titled *The Return*, Shatner's tale had the Romulans and the Borg using advanced technology to resurrect the dead Kirk as an instrument that would serve a twofold purpose. First, it would provide the Romulan Empire retribution for a perceived act of war committed by Kirk during the original series. At the same time, it would allow the brainwashed captain to kill Picard, thus eliminating the one potential threat facing the cybernetic Borg, a hive-consciousness that Picard had briefly been made a part of during the course of *TNG*. By the end, Kirk is reunited with the elderly Spock and McCoy (who are still alive in the *Next Generation* era) and, together with Picard and his crew, they all travel to the Borg homeworld, where Kirk — in a far more effective and heroic moment than the one afforded the character in *Generations* — sacrifices himself to end the Borg threat, hopefully forever.

"I thought that the studio would jump at the chance of seeing Kirk and Picard together again," says Shatner. "And thusly I created a story that I thought they might like. I gave the synopsis to Paramount and Rick Berman, and they both loved it. I thought, 'Well, my fantasy is coming true.' But then I read in *Variety* that the next film would be a *Next Generation* film completely with no members of any other crew in it. So [Paramount president] Sherry Lansing and Rick Berman had both said that they loved the synopsis, then I read they're going another way. That's how I learned about their plans. It wasn't a change of plans on their part, because they never said they wanted to do it."

Executive producer Rick Berman acknowledges that he did indeed read Shatner's story premise. "The feeling," he explains, "is that although it was an interesting idea, it was really not the direction we wanted to go at that point. We wanted to do a film that was pretty much isolated to the *Next Generation* characters."

Cowriter Brannon Braga, who never read the idea, rejects the notion of reviving Kirk. "I think it would have been disastrous to kill Kirk in the first movie and then bring him back in the second," he offers. "It would just feel chintzy and would take away any kind of credibility we've tried to establish. I just don't think that film would have done very well."

Once it was finalized that the new film, first titled *Star Trek: Resurrection* but eventually changed to *Star Trek: First Contact*, would be a *Next Generation* film, Berman and cowriters Braga and Ron Moore began to develop a story line that would make the franchise even more inviting for the moviegoing audience than the last one.

"We held back in certain action sequences in [*Generations*] that we should have fought a little harder to get," Berman admits. "More important than that, we did a story that was a little too dour. We did a story about a very serious Picard who was mourning the loss of his brother and nephew, and was quite ponderous and sad. It was time now to move to something that was a little bit more action/adventure, something that the fans could have a little bit more fun with. That was one of our major goals. This was going to be a reelin' and rockin' adventure movie with a lot of fun to it and a lot of great action sequences that turned Picard into kind of an action hero rather than a brooding intellectual. These are things that I don't regret having done in the first film, but once we did them it was good to go a new route now."

Patrick Stewart, who has taken on a variety of truly diverse roles since last portraying Picard, is pleased with the direction that the *First Contact* script has taken in terms of the entire ensemble and in particular his on-screen alter ego. "There were aspects of the previous movie that had left me feeling a little uncomfortable when we'd finished," says Stewart. "It was interesting to have that thread in there of the brother and nephew's death, but it added a slight shadow to Picard over the whole movie. If you're going to satisfy the function of a character like this, essentially what he has to be first and foremost is heroic. And so that was in everybody's mind when this script was in development. You've got to put Picard back on the bridge of the *Enterprise* and have him leading the troops, and not [make him] somebody having to deal with all kinds of psychological issues. But then it became a Borg story, and the demons were immediately present."

Ira Steven Behr about to be assimilated by the Borg (copyright © 1994 by Albert Ortega).

The idea of using the Borg, says Berman, was pretty much a given due to their enormous popularity on the television series. "I think their appeal is their hivelike quality, the fact that they are not an individual culture but a culture made up of countless drones all with one voice and one mind," he explains. "That makes them very curious, mysterious, and thus very frightening to people. We've used them sparingly on the series, and it was time to come up with a way to use them in a feature film. We also had the money to develop the way they looked, the way they were made up, the way their costumes worked in a manner that we couldn't afford in episodic [television]."

Production designer Herman Zimmerman has his own theories as to why the Borg are so popular, comparing and contrasting them with the deadly extraterrestrials in the *Alien* film series. "*Alien* certainly featured the quintessential monster," he explains. "What I think is different about the Borg as antagonists is that they once were human or humanoid organisms, and the monster from *Alien* was always a creature of an entirely different species with no concern about human values of any kind. The Borg have had hu-

Star Trek: First Contact *casts James Cromwell as scientist Zefram Cochrane, creator of the warp drive, who plays an integral role in* **Star Trek** *history (copyright © 1996 by Albert Ortega).*

manity or humanoid origins and are now assimilated into this machine culture. In a way they are more scary than something that tears you apart, because they *don't* tear you apart. They make you over into something you don't want to be. To me, that's much scarier than just being killed. That's the kind of nightmarish bad guys we're creating."

Beyond utilizing the Borg, Berman wanted the new film to involve some aspect of time travel. In the end it was decided to graft both ideas. "It just became a question of what time period we would go to," says Ron Moore. "We went through a lot of different time periods in the development, from the Italian Renaissance to the present to the Civil War. Nothing really got that far, but we talked about a lot of different periods in terms of what would be interesting, where the Borg would go and why, and what we could do there. We realized fairly quickly that there's been a lot of time travel done. Almost any period you go to has been done in one way, shape or form. Then we came up with the idea of doing the near future and to involve what is essentially the birth

of *Star Trek*. Interestingly, the *Star Trek* universe has a continuity that somehow still holds together, and lo and behold, we looked around and found Zefram Cochrane sitting around the same time period. He's the guy who invented the warp drive and in turn made first contact with an alien race. We combined the two adventures and that became our adventure."

At press time, the full scenario of the film goes something like this: Picard awakens in his quarters on the new *Enterprise* E from a nightmare in which he's back aboard a Borg cube ship and is once again Locutus, the Borg he was transformed into in *TNG*'s "The Best of Both Worlds." At that moment, he receives a communiqué from Starfleet Command informing him and his crew that the Borg fleet is approaching from the sector of Deep Space Twelve. Surprisingly, Picard realizes that he was aware of this, that he somehow maintains a connection with the Borg collective. Concerned, Starfleet orders the *Enterprise* to patrol the Neutral Zone while a massive Federation fleet prepares to take on the Borg.

Picard reluctantly follows orders until he learns that a tetragonal Borg ves-

Patrick Stewart (copyright © 1994 by Albert Ortega).

Michael Dorn, who brought Worf from **The Next Generation** *to* **Deep Space Nine**, *returns to the big screen in* **Star Trek: First Contact** *(copyright © 1994 by Albert Ortega).*

• • • •

sel has broken off from the rest and is headed directly toward Earth. He has the *Enterprise* pursue it, and by the time they approach our galaxy, they see the fleet — led by the *Defiant,* under Lieutenant Commander Worf — engaging the enemy and about to be destroyed. Picard has Worf and his crew beamed aboard and, using his strategic knowledge of the Borg, leads the fleet in an attack on a particular area of the Borg ship, destroying it.

A seeming victory turns quickly to defeat when, from the wreckage, a spherical ship shoots out, continuing on its way to Earth. The *Enterprise* is pursuing when a temporal vortex suddenly appears, enveloping the Borg ship. Picard orders his starship to follow. He learns that the Borg have somehow changed history and that his ship was spared from the change due to its being within the "backwash" of the vortex. In an instant, the fleet is gone and Earth becomes a Borg world.

The *Enterprise* finds itself in the mid-twenty-first century the day before Zefram Cochrane (Oscar nominee James Cromwell) is scheduled to make his historic warp flight. The Borg damage

Alfre Woodard portrays a twenty-first-century scientist who helps Captain Picard put history back on track in Star Trek: First Contact *(copyright © 1996 by Albert Ortega).*

A fan takes Lieutenant Commander Worf home (copyright © 1994 by Albert Ortega).

Cochrane's ship but are destroyed by the *Enterprise* before they are able to complete their objective. In an effort to survey the damage to Cochrane's ship, the *Phoenix*, Picard, Data, Troi and Crusher beam down to Resurrection, Montana. There they meet the pilot himself (who turns out to be nothing like they had expected) and his assistant, Lily Sloane (Alfre Woodard), who is injured. Picard gives the order for Riker, LaForge and Troi to help repair the *Phoenix* while he, Crusher and Data beam back to the *Enterprise* with the injured Sloane.

Back on the ship, things continue to grow worse when aberrations in the environmental system lead to the conclusion that the Borg have beamed aboard the *Enterprise* and begun assimilating part of the vessel as well as its crew. It is up to Picard (who has begun seeking revenge for all that the Borg have done to him), Data and Worf, along with Sloane, to combat this threat before complete assimilation by the Borg, who are intent on sending a signal to their contemporaries to lead them to Earth of the twenty-first century for planetwide assimilation. En route, Data is captured in engineering and "seduced" by the Borg queen (Alice Krige),

who offers him the opportunity to truly feel by giving him human skin. In exchange, she wants vital Federation information that will allow the Borg to finally eliminate their toughest adversary.

Picard must stop the onboard threat while Riker does all he can to ensure that Zefram Cochrane isn't late for his date with history.

To put it mildly, *everyone* involved is thrilled with the scenario. "Part of this movie is about the journey of Picard and the ultimate recovery from all he went through with the Borg," says Braga. "But at its core it's a story of vengeance, with Picard dipping down into a twentieth-century kind of mentality. Lily Sloane is making him realize that he's taking too many risks. In many ways he's acting like Captain Ahab with his obsession and quest for vengeance. The Ahab quality is subtle, but it's definitely there and becomes worse and worse as the movie goes on. You'll definitely see a very interesting arc for Picard in this movie. He still harbors a lot of profound anger toward these creatures that he hasn't met with for a while. Patrick has really done some amazing things in this movie."

Stewart reflects on the fact that much of the story development for *First Contact* took place while he was starring as Prospero in *The Tempest* on Broadway, and that there was an intriguing overlap of the two characters. "They were definitely parallel stories," he explains. "Much of *The Tempest* bled into this story — the whole idea of a man who has stored up unexpressed fury, murderous rage, because of a wrong done to him, which was done to both Prospero and Picard. It just happened to bleed across into this script too, but in a way that is filled with action, not with a psychological trauma that incapacitates him. Instead, the crew is largely *restraining* him from action."

Data's arc was a little tougher to crack, with the character having fulfilled his primary quest — to gain human emotions — in *Generations.* "We didn't want to irrevocably change the character again," says Moore. "Giving him the emotion chip was a pretty big deal. We wanted to explore something different with Data but not change the character

In Star Trek: First Contact *Alice Krige portrays the Borg queen who tempts Data with humanity (copyright © 1996 by Albert Ortega).*

permanently. Keep moving him along the spectrum of discovery. What doesn't he have? He's never felt flesh. Flesh and blood is part of the human experience."

Adds Braga, "We didn't want to worry about Data until it came naturally, which happened very late. Once we invented the Borg queen, we realized that Data's being seduced in some way by her would be very interesting. It is the most provocative and strange experience he's ever had, and he does come very close to a physical existence thanks to the Borg. This is actually a romance. It's a sick and perverted romance, but it's perfect because it represents many things, including temptation, seduction and romance, but all filled with Borg perversity."

Brent Spiner, who plays Data, is quite enthusiastic about his role in the film. "I think it's a really cool arc and a logical extension for the character because it's been an ever-evolving process," says the actor. "The last film dealt with him getting emotions and not being able to control them or deal with them because they were new to him. In this film he's much more in control of the emotion chip in terms of how and when he uses it. But I

think the seduction of the flesh is the obvious next step for him. In a way, it's the darkest and most psychologically disturbing part of the story and the film."

Perhaps the most *surprising* part of the film is Berman's choice of director: *Next Generation* cast member Jonathan Frakes, who has helmed numerous episodes of *TNG, Deep Space Nine* and *Voyager.* While this decision was puzzling to a lot of people, Berman sees it as the logical choice. "I believe now, as I did on *Generations,* that it's real important that a person understand *Star Trek* to be able to direct one of these films," he explains. "There are just too many *Star Trek* elements that need to be understood to bring someone else in from the outside. Really, no one has ever been brought in from the outside with the exception of Nick Meyer for the second movie *[The Wrath of Khan],* when it was really pretty much an open field day for someone to come in and write and direct a new movie. Of the people who were available who were directors, who really understood and knew *Star Trek,* Jonathan was one of the best. He's a terrific director, someone who's a close friend and someone who has always had the ambition to direct. His desire to

Brent Spiner (copyright © 1994 by Albert Ortega).

Jonathan Frakes (copyright © 1994 by Albert Ortega).

direct both television and features has been paramount in his mind over the past several years. I knew him well enough to know that he would commit himself to this in a way which is necessary, which is to just be completely absorbed in it for a good six to eight months. With his understanding of *Star Trek* and his relationship with certain crew members and all of the cast members, I knew he was going to be a major plus. And I've been proved right. He's done a great job."

According to Patrick Stewart, Frakes, as a director and star of *TNG,* brings "history" to the film in a way that no one else could. In fact, the first day Frakes walked on the set as a director during the making of the series, everyone knew that he was indeed a bona fide director. "He carries with him a history of the show and an intuitive flair for directing," says Stewart. "And a knowledge of the actors not only in terms of what they can do but what their potential is as well. Given Jonathan's particular personality role in the group — the clown; if something had gotten knocked over, Jonathan had done it; if there was an uproar, Jonathan was at the center of it — it somehow makes him the perfect figure to be taking on this enormous responsibility.

• • • •

The energy he brings to it, the good humor and fellowship, is exemplary. I said to him the other day, 'I cannot think of a situation being better than it is right now.' People are happy and they have good reason not to be, because the hours are brutal and the conditions with smoke and all that are tough. It's thanks to Jonathan that throughout production our spirits were high and positive. In town we had the reputation while doing the show of being the nicest show to guest on, but also the most undisciplined. I think that's a very happy combination."

Frakes is appreciative of such comments, and the general support that was shown to him throughout production. "Obviously I'm familiar with the gestalt of *Star Trek*," he offers. "I also think I have an ease with my comrades which I think allows them as actors to feel comfortable enough to try things that they may not try with a director they don't know as well. We also have a great sense of fun on the stage, and if we can inject some of that into the film, I would be very proud of that as well. Hopefully this movie will never stop. If all goes well, you'll inhale at the beginning and exhale when it's finished."

••••

INDEX

••••